LANGUAGE, LITERACY, *and* POWER *in* SCHOOLING

LANGUAGE, LITERACY, and POWER in SCHOOLING

Edited by

Teresa L. McCarty
Arizona State University

 LAWRENCE ERLBAUM ASSOCIATES, PUBLISHERS
2005   Mahwah, New Jersey   London

KH

Photo Credits:
Cover (clockwise from center) Photograph of young girl at blackboard by Mariana Yampolsky, courtesy of Antonia Candela; Photograph of Noelani Sells, 1992, by Teresa L. McCarty, courtesy of Rough Rock Community School; Photograph of teacher and student sharing books, courtesy of the University of Arizona College of Education; Photograph of teacher with students in a literacy lesson by Carlos Blanco, courtesy of Antonia Candela; Photograph of student writing activity, courtesy of the University of Arizona College of Education.
Page xxviii; Photograph by Carlos Blanco, courtesy of Antonia Candela.
Page 126; Photograph courtesy of the University of Arizona College of Education.
Page 296; Photograph courtesy of the University of Arizona College of Education.

Lawrence Erlbaum Associates, Inc., Publishers
10 Industrial Avenue
Mahwah, New Jersey 07430
www.erlbaum.com

Cover design by Kathryn Houghtaling Lacey

Library of Congress Cataloging-in-Publication Data

Language, literacy, and power in schooling / edited by Teresa L. McCarty.
    p. cm.
Includes bibliographical references and index.
ISBN 0-8058-4646-8 (cloth : alk. paper)
ISBN 0-8058-4647-6 (pbk. : alk. paper)
1. Literacy—Social aspects—United States. 2. Minorities—Education—United States. 3. Limited English-proficient students—Education—United States. 4. Educational equalization—United States. I. McCarty, T. L.
LC151.L27 2005
302.2'244—dc22
                               2004053286
                                        CIP

Books published by Lawrence Erlbaum Associates are printed on acid-free paper, and their bindings are chosen for strength and durability.

Printed in the United States of America
10 9 8 7 6 5 4 3 2 1

4|3|06

To the memory of Galena Sells Dick and David M. Smith—teachers, researchers, and language minority advocates—and to all like them who struggle for educational equity and literacies of empowerment for all.

"Questions of language are basically questions of power."
—Noam Chomsky (*Language and Responsibility*, 1979, p. 191)

Contents

Preface

This volume grows out of a symposium held at the 1999 annual meeting of the American Anthropological Association (AAA), the purpose of which was to bring anthropological perspectives to bear on the negotiation of language, literacy, and power relations in linguistically and culturally diverse educational contexts. The chapters here have benefited from the conversations sparked at the AAA meeting and beyond. Some chapters represent new contributions to those conversations. All are united by the use of critical ethnography to make visible the many literacies and literacy practices inside and outside of schools. Drawing on research in American Indian, Latin American, African American, and urban multiethnic communities, the chapters show how literacy and schooling are negotiated by children, adults, and communities and the ways in which education becomes a key site of struggle surrounding questions of whose knowledge, discourse, and literacy practices "count."

The volume is divided into three parts, each reflecting a distinct focus and unit of analysis. Part I examines the tensions between the local and the general, the margins and the center, and the spaces in between. Borrowing from Kulick and Stroud's (1993) metaphor of "seizing hold" of literacy, the studies in this part of the book examine the ways in which subaltern communities appropriate literacy for local ends. Part II directs attention more specifically to the micro or face-to-face interactions around literacy and literacies in linguistically and ethnically diverse classrooms. In Part III, we widen the ethnographic lens, positioning literacy practices and politics in the larger context of globalization and attendant standardizing regimes.

I preface each part with an introduction to situate the chapters thematically within a larger body of knowledge. Each part concludes with a commentary by a leading scholar in the field. In the afterword, I consider the implications of this work for pedagogy and policy, highlighting the urgent need for critical literacy researchers to engage politically, as current education policies carve out ever-deeper cleavages between those with and without access to literacies of empowerment.

Above all, this is a book oriented toward social action. We write not as an academic exercise, but to bear witness to real, lived experiences of inequality in schools and society. At the same time, the data and analyses presented here illuminate real possibilities for positive social change. We have written for an interdisciplinary audience of scholars, but equally important, for a wider readership of practitioners, policymakers, and citizens. The chapters in this volume have much to teach us about the roots of inequality. More than this, they point the way out of and beyond the policies and practices that produce and legitimate contemporary manifestations of the "Great Divide."

ACKNOWLEDGMENTS

An edited volume is always the product of complex collaborations and timing. I thank those who agreed to participate in the AAA symposium that led to this book: Christine L. Cain, Antonia Candela, Jim Cummins, James Paul Gee, Perry Gilmore, Nancy H. Hornberger, Gloria Ladson-Billings, Ray McDermott, Hugh (Bud) Mehan, Sheilah Nicholas, Elsie Rockwell, and David M. Smith. Ultimately, Bud Mehan was unable to contribute to this volume, but his discussant commentary at the symposium proved to be invaluable in informing chapter revisions. Melisa Cahnmann, Luis C. Moll, Janine T. Remillard, Char Ullan, and Robert Whitman joined the project after the AAA symposium. I thank all of the chapter authors for responding promptly to the many author queries and deadlines along the way, and most of all for contributing such a stellar array of original research.

Tragically, the world lost David Smith just as the volume was being finalized for submission to a prospective publisher. I am proud to have his final scholarly paper in this collection, and am deeply grateful to his wife and writing partner, Perry Gilmore, for so lovingly and painstakingly bringing their joint work to fruition.

It is an unrivaled experience to work with Lawrence Erlbaum Associates Senior Editor Naomi Silverman and the outstanding LEA editorial staff, including Marianna Vertullo and Erica Kica, who worked closely with us on the editing of this book. On behalf of all the volume's contributors, I thank Naomi for the enthusiasm with which she greeted the volume prospectus, her expert help in quickly guiding the prospectus through the LEA approval process, and her and Marianna's unending patience as we worked to turn the prospectus into a finished manuscript. All whose work is featured here benefited tremendously from Naomi's insights and those of Kathryn Au and Patricia Paugh, who provided feedback on an earlier version of this volume.

For providing the time for me to complete this project, I thank Dean Ronald W. Marx of the University of Arizona (UA) College of Education, and Patricia Anders, Head of the Department of Language, Reading and Culture at UA. I also thank Jo Ann Hurley, executive assistant to the dean in the UA's College of Education, for help in compiling the chapters for this volume during my tenure as interim dean there, and Ginny Geib and Anna Sanchez for help with photographs.

To my colleagues at Rough Rock Community School—the late Galena Sells Dick, Ernest W. Dick, Sally Begay, Mary Benally, Fred Bia, Emma Lewis, Susan and Glen Minor, Leroy Morgan, Twylah Morris, Darlene Redhair, Delrey Redhair, Robert and Ruth Roessel, Monty Roessel, Evelyn Sells, Rita Wagner, Treva Yazzie, and Marvin Yellowhair—I extend my everlasting appreciation. You have been my teachers, coresearchers, and friends. I hope you will find on these pages the imprint of your long-term efforts to promote bilingual, bicultural, and biliteracy education for Native American students.

Finally, I thank those who have, over so many years, provided their unconditional intellectual and moral support for my scholarly efforts: my mother and late father, Virginia Doulin and James McCarty; my stepmother, Mildred McCarty; my sisters, Valerie Mussi and Julie Pitchford; my nieces, Amity Roebke and Cathern (Kate) Pitchford; my stepchildren, Jennifer and Stuart Martin and their spouses, Tim Johnson and Stacey Martin; my close colleagues, Perry Gilmore, Tsiania Lomawaima, Mary Eunice Romero, and Ofelia Zepeda; and my dearest friends, Caren Creutzberger, Karyn Gitlis, Jan Kegelman, Diana Pardue, and Diane Zipley. For my husband, John Martin, I reserve a special note of gratitude: I am challenged by your intellect, inspired by your commitment to social justice, and sustained by your loving support.

REFERENCE

Kulick, D., & Stroud, D. (1993). Conceptions and uses of literacy in a Papua New Guinea village. In B. Street (Ed.), *Cross-cultural approaches to literacy* (pp. 30–61). Cambridge, UK: Cambridge University Press.

Introduction: The Continuing Power of the "Great Divide"

Teresa L. McCarty
Arizona State University

> To teach to read and write should not ever be reduced to the reductionistic, inexpressive, insipid task that serves to silence the voices of struggle that try to justify our presence in the world and not our blind accommodation to an unjust and discriminatory world .... Teaching literacy is, above all, a social and political commitment. (Freire, 1993, p. 115)

On the cusp of a new millennium, we also are on the crest of a new language and literacy divide. Globally, the world's linguistic and cultural diversity is imperiled by national and transnational forces that work to homogenize and standardize, even as they stratify and marginalize. In the United States, the forces for standardization have reached new and alarming proportions, with federal and state policies mandating scripted, uniform, remedial reading programs for students identified as "at risk," "limited English proficient," and "deficient in reading skills." The intended targets of these policies are clear. The 2001 federal No Child Left Behind Act, for example, calls specifically for implementing these pedagogies with "underachieving" American Indian, African American, and Hispanic students.[1]

It is not coincidental that these pressures come at a time when the United States is experiencing an unprecedented demographic shift. Much of this

---

[1]See the No Child Left Behind Web site: http://www.ed.gov/nclb/accountability/achieve/edpicks.jhtml?arc=ln).

stems from the new immigration—those who have emigrated to the United States since Congress abolished national origin quotas in 1965. Unlike earlier waves of immigration, which originated in Europe and were largely White, recent immigrants come primarily from Latin America, Southeast Asia, and the Caribbean (Qin-Hilliard, Feinauer, & Quiroz, 2001; Suárez-Orozco, 2001). Difference in the United States is taking on not only new languages, but new colors. People of color now make up 28% of the nation's population, with the numbers expected to grow to 38% in 2024 and 47% in 2050 (Banks, 2001, p. ix). A significant proportion are English language learners who speak more than 150 languages. More than 3.5 million English language learners are presently enrolled in U.S. schools (Suárez-Orozco, 2001).

Most readers are well aware of the disturbing corollaries to these statistics: Students of color and English language learners experience the lowest rates of educational attainment, the lowest family incomes, and the highest rates of depression and teen suicide (Lomawaima & McCarty, 2002; Valdés, 2001). "Among immigrants today," Suárez-Orozco (2001) observes, "the length of residence in the United States seems associated with *declining* health, school achievement, and aspirations" (p. 354). Acculturation and standardization thus appear to lead not to a more equitable distribution of resources and opportunities, but rather to "detrimental health, more ambivalent attitudes toward school, and lower grades" (Suárez-Orozco, 2001, p. 354).

The result is a new form of educational, economic, and sociopolitical segregation—a 21st-century "Great Divide." Great Divide arguments—that is, claims about fundamental differences or divisions between "kinds" of people—have a long history in Western thought (see, e.g., Collins & Blot, 2003, chap. 2). The more recent manifestations of these claims can be traced to a distinction between oral and written language made by Goody and Watt (1963), and subsequently elaborated by Goody (1968, 1977), Olson (1977), and Ong (1982). Briefly stated, the argument is that orality and literacy are fundamentally distinct: As Collins (1995) analyzes the argument, literacy "is essentially abstract, generalizing, and context-free, whereas oral thinking is essentially concrete, particularizing, and context bound" (p. 79; see also Collins & Blot, 2003, pp. 15–22). Literacy not only confers on its users cognitive powers not available in the spoken word; it is autonomous, independent from the social context and from language users, or, as Ong (1982) puts it, "disengaged from everything else." Consider the following statement by Ong (1982), a leading proponent of this view:

[Written] standard English has ... a recorded vocabulary of at least a million and a half words.... A simply oral dialect will ... have resources of only a few thousand words, and its users will have virtually no knowledge of the real semantic history of any of these words. (p. 8)[2]

In this statement we see the manifold dividing lines an autonomous or universalist view of literacy implies:[3]

- Literacy and orality are unitary, bounded, and distinct.
- Literacy is something one either possesses or lacks.
- Literacy empowers; orality limits.
- Literacy is associated with modernity and progress, its absence with "simplicity."
- "Standard" (read Western) language forms are distinct from and more resourceful than (nonstandard, non-Western) "dialects."

One implication of these distinctions is that there are two kinds of people in the world—literates and nonliterates—and a uniform or standard literate form. From this perspective, "becoming literate entails learning how to express and interpret decontextualized meaning, involving the same skills for everyone" (Auerbach, 1992, p. 73). When these understandings of literacy intersect with ideologies of merit and privilege, the result is the naturalization of existing power hierarchies, "whereby deviations from the norm are defined as deficiencies and disabilities" (Collins, 1995, p. 83). We can see this quite clearly in contemporary federal and state education policies and the pedagogies they prescribe.

In contrast to unitary, autonomous views of literacy, the chapters in this volume develop understandings of literacy as socially and historically situated,

---

[2]Interestingly, just a little more than 20 years after the seminal publication in which Ong's quotation appears, the superintendent of public instruction in the U.S. state having the most restrictive English-only policy, Arizona, made a similar pronouncement in his 2004 State of Education address. Citing Edmund Gibbon's 18th-century "Decline and Fall of the Roman Empire," this 21st-century state education official declared, "Without some species of writing, no people has ever preserved the faithful annals of their history, ever made any considerable progress in the abstract sciences or ever possessed ... the useful and agreeable arts of life" (Gassen, 2004, pp. B1–B2). As Collins and Blot (2003) note, statements such as this reflect doomsday projections in which deviations from "normative 'full literacy' ... [are] apt to be viewed as a ... regression to 'barbarism' " and today's children are seen as "our current 'primitives' in need of literacy's 'progress' " (p. 168).

[3]See Street (1993, 2001a, 2001b) for an elaboration of autonomous views of literacy; Collins and Blot (2003) use the term universalist in much the same sense.

fluid, multiple, and power-linked (Barton, Hamilton, & Ivanič, 2000; Gee, 1996; Lankshear, 1997; Pérez, 2004; Street, 2001a, 2001b; Willis, García, Barrera, & Harris, 2003). This theoretical orientation grows out of anthropological and cross-cultural examinations of language and literacy (e.g., Au, 1993; Cazden, 1972; Cazden, John, & Hymes, 1972; Cook-Gumperz & Keller-Cohen, 1993; Delgado-Gaitan, 1990; Edelsky, 1989, 1991; Ferdman, Weber, & Ramírez, 1994; Gumperz, 1982; Heath, 1983; Hornberger, 1996; Michaels, 1981; Schieffelin & Gilmore, 1986; Scribner & Cole, 1981, 2001; Street, 1993), and the New Literacy Studies, discussed more fully in the next section. This orientation does not ignore the psycholinguistic, cognitive, or technical aspects of literacy, but rather embeds them within sociocultural settings and the discursive practices and power relations of everyday life. Here, literacy is understood as inherently political and ideological, where ideology constitutes "the site of tension between authority and power on the one hand and resistance and creativity on the other" (Street, 2001b, p. 434).

This is the theme of this volume. We focus on language, literacy, and schooling as interrelated axes of power in struggles over access to key intellectual, social, economic, and political resources and rights. It is important to point out that power is not a monolithic, concentrated, or unyielding force. Rather, power is constantly negotiated, contested, and (re)constituted in human-built environments and everyday social practice. Thus, although the studies in this volume show the constraints on individuals and communities who are raced, classed, and gendered in schools and society, they also show how individuals and groups can and do challenge, mediate, and transform those marginalizing practices.

Can this research contribute to a larger, concerted action toward social justice and anti-oppressive education? As social scientists, educators, and citizens, we take to heart Freire's statement in the epigraph that begins this introduction, that literacy teaching is, above all, a commitment to social and political action. We understand that commitment as knowledge in practice (Reason, 2004)—a call for critical examination of the multilayered realities and literacies of real people and institutions as a vehicle for positive social-educational change. In this regard this volume challenges the barriers of another "great divide" between theory and practice, knowledge and action. By unpacking the complexity of literacy experiences of those with, about, and for whom we write—their on-the-ground tensions, triumphs, dilemmas, accommodations, and resistances—we seek not only to build new knowledge, but to inform and transform the pedagogies and policies that limit human potentialities. As Williams (1983) wrote so eloquently years ago, once those seeming inevitabilities are exposed and confronted, we can see our way to the practical possibilities for tipping the balance of power, gathering our resources for a "journey of hope" (pp. 268–269).

THEORETICAL AND METHODOLOGICAL UNDERPINNINGS

Understanding Literacy and Literacies

In their synthesizing text, *Literacy and Literacies*, Collins and Blot (2003) describe the field of literacy studies as "large and heterogeneous," the debates "longstanding and contentious" (p. xvii). This volume engages those debates from the perspectives of anthropology, sociolinguistics, and education, working outward from the "social turn" in literacy studies that commenced in the 1970s and 1980s.[4] Szwed (2001) writes of the social turn: It "is not enough to know what a language looks like and to be able to describe and measure it, but one must also know what it means to its users and how it is used by them" (p. 422). Thus, the key question is not whether one reads and writes or does not, but rather the social meaning of languages and literacies—their roles in human social life (see also Graff, 1981). Informed by the work of Vygotsky (1978), Bakhtin (1981), Freire (1970), and various social theorists (e.g., Bourdieu, Foucault, Giddens, Gramsci, Habermas, Marx, Williams), research influenced by the social turn redirected attention from:

- The individual to the social in cognition and learning (Cole, 1996; Lave & Wenger, 1991; Wertsch, Del Rio, & Alvarez, 1995).
- Literacy as a neutral technical skill to literacy as social practice (Gee, 1996; Scribner & Cole, 1981, 2001; Street, 1995).
- Literacy forms to literacy functions and events (Goodman & Wilde, 1992; Heath, 1982, 1983; Smith, 1983).
- Uniform to multiform views of literacy (Cook-Gumperz & Keller-Cohen, 1993; The New London Group, 1996).
- The binary of the oral–literate divide to the plurality of the orality–literacy mix (Heath, 1983; Street, 1995, 2001a, 2001b).

---

[4]For a comprehensive overview of the field of literacy studies, see Cushman, Kintgen, Kroll, and Rose (2001); for an incisive analysis of the claims and counterclaims about "great divides" or universalist versus pluralist accounts of literacy, see Collins (1995) and Collins and Blot (2003); for an extensive review of research on literacy in out-of-school settings, see Hull and Schultz (2001, 2002).

These shifts also redirected attention from "pedagogized" or schooled literacies to situated, everyday, family, and community literacies (see, e.g., Barton
et al., 2000; Cook-Gumperz, 1986; Hornberger, 1996; Knobel, 1999; Majors,
2004; McCarty, 2002; McLaughlin, 1992; Moll, Amanti, Neff, & González,
1992; Searle, 1993; Street & Street, 1991; Taylor, 1997; Taylor &
Dorsey-Gaines, 1988; Varenne & McDermott, 1999).

The broad framework for these more recent investigations has come to be
called the New (or Critical) Literacy Studies. Anthropology has provided particularly fertile conceptual and methodological ground for the New Literacy
Studies. Central to an anthropological approach is the use of cross-cultural
comparison to illuminate the embeddedness of individual activity within cultural systems and wholes. Thus, to test Great Divide theories about the cognitive consequences of literacy, Scribner and Cole (1981, 2001) investigated
literacy practices among the Vai of northwestern Liberia. Scribner and Cole
describe three Vai scripts: an indigenous script, Arabic, and English. Only the
latter two are associated with formal schooling. Disentangling school- and
community-based literacies, Scribner and Cole find no support for the claim
that reading and writing entail fundamental cognitive restructurings, but rather
that different literacies are valued and used in different ways for different purposes and with different consequences. Literacy, Scribner and Cole conclude,
can best be characterized as social practice: purposive, contextualized, and
patterned human activity around print.

Similarly, Street's fieldwork in northeastern Iran in the early 1970s identified three kinds of literacies: *maktab* literacy associated with Islam and the
Qur'anic (or maktab religious) schools, commercial literacy involved in village fruit sales (and based on prior development of maktab literacy), and literacy acquired in state schools (Street, 1984; see also Collins & Blot, 2003, pp.
54–61, for a summary and critique of Street's research). Reflecting on this research more than 30 years later, Street (2001a) notes that there was "actually a
lot of literacy going on," but "there were quite different 'practices' associated
with it" (p. 6).

Embodied in literacy practices are literacy events, action sequences involving one or more persons interacting with print (Goodman & Wilde,
1992; Heath, 1982, 1983). Similar to Hymes's (1974) speech events, literacy
events involve participation rules as well as different structures and uses. In
her classic study of literacy in a Piedmont community of the Carolinas,
Heath (1983) illustrates the variety of literacy events and coexisting relationships among spoken and written language across speech communities

marked by race, ethnicity, and social class. Goodman and her associates document similar, if more school-based processes among young Tohono O'odham writers in southern Arizona (Goodman & Wilde, 1992). The concept of literacy events is helpful, Street (2001a) notes, because it enables researchers to focus on particular situations and engagements around reading and writing. However, the broader concept of literacy practices is still needed, he asserts, to link literacy events to larger social, cultural, and ideological processes. This appears to be the sense in which some researchers have applied the concept of literacy events, as in McLaughlin's (1992) study of Navajo literacy events "consisting of the minutiae of individuals' interactions with print ... and the roles that institutions, ideology, and power play in the distribution of functions for and beliefs about literacy (p. 25).

What all of this work and the burgeoning research growing out of the New/Critical Literacy Studies have in common is a focus on the connection of the psychological and linguistic with the social and cultural, the "mental with the material" (Hull & Schultz, 2001, p. 583). More than something people do with their heads, literacy is understood as "something to do with social, institutional, and cultural relationships" (Gee, Hull, & Lankshear, 1996, p. 1). Like literacies themselves, those relationships are power-laden. Central to current research in Critical Literacy Studies, then, is the coupling of micro and macro analyses of the intersection of literacy and politics, where literacy is seen as both hegemonic and counterhegemonic, and the focus is on relationships among literacy uses, discourses, and power (see, e.g., Cook-Gumperz & Keller-Cohen, 1993; Hull & Schultz, 2001; Willis & Harris, 2003).

Gee, for example, has developed a theory of D/discourses, with uppercase Discourses constituting "ways of being in the world"—"identity kits" that are inhabited and mobilized by socioculturally defined groups of people (Gee, 1996, 2001). Lowercase discourses, on the other hand, are parts of Discourses that are "connected stretches of language that make sense" (Gee, 2001, p. 526). Discourses are inherently ideological and tied to the distribution of power and privilege in society. Any "useful definition of 'literacy,' " Gee (2001, p. 529) writes, "must be couched in terms of the notion of discourse." Drawing on Krashen's (1985) distinction between formal learning and informal, everyday acquisition of a second language, Gee claims that we *acquire* a primary Discourse through our early socialization among family and peers, whereas we can only *learn* secondary Discourses in various non-home-based settings, including schools. Primary Discourses "can never really be liberating literacies;" only by mastering secondary Discourses can we gain access to "powerful" literacies (Gee, 2001, p. 530).

Gee's argument has been challenged as "a dangerous kind of determinism:" "Instead of being locked into 'your place' by your genes," Delpit (1993) states, "you are now locked hopelessly into a lower-class status by your Discourse" (p. 286). Delpit (1993) and Fordham (1999), among others (including the authors in this volume), have shown that dominant Discourses can be appropriated for liberatory purposes without sacrificing one's home-based identity and values. This seems to be in accord with Gee's theory, however; critical, empowering literacies involve the ability to juxtapose primary and secondary Discourses to create a new, humane Discourse oriented toward social justice (Gee, 1997, p. xviii).

In this volume, theoretical and pedagogical understandings growing out of recent critical literacy research are complemented by understandings gained from the fields of bilingualism and bilingual education, multicultural education, and language planning and policy. An overview of all of these fields is beyond the scope of this introduction, but readers are referred especially to the work of Cummins (see, e.g., Baker & Hornberger's [2001] collection of his work), Garcia (2002; see also the reviewers' comments that follow his monograph-length article), and Ovando, Collier, and Combs (2003) on bilingual education; Banks and Banks (2004), Sleeter and McLaren (1995), and Willis et al. (2003) on multicultural education; and Hornberger and Ricento (1996), Ricento and Burnaby (1998), Tollefson (2002), and Tollefson and Tsui (2004) on language planning and policy.

Ethnography as a Way of Seeing, Being, and Acting in the World

Capturing the complexity of literacies and persons within ever-changing social and institutional contexts requires a methodology capable of attending to the fine-grained details of everyday discursive practices and their organization within larger cultural and historical frames. Ethnography, the "field arm" of the discipline of social-cultural anthropology (Spindler & Spindler, 1992), provides a particularly powerful "way of seeing" these micro and macro level processes (Wolcott, 1999, p. 30). The "guts of the ethnographic approach," Spindler and Spindler (1992) remind us, involve direct, prolonged, firsthand observation: "Above all else is the requirement that the ethnographer observe *directly*" (pp. 63–64). The Spindlers define the intellectual purpose of ethnographic research this way: "The object ... is to discover the cultural knowledge that people hold in their minds, how it is employed in social interaction, and the consequences of its employment" (p. 70). In addition to long-term, situated participant observation, ethnographers attempt to do this through structured and semistructured (and sometimes unstructured) interviews, sociological mapping, and document and artifact analysis—all methods aimed at understanding what Geertz (1983) has so famously called local knowledge.

Ethnography enjoys a well-established tradition within the field of language and literacy studies. As early as 1962, Hymes and Gumperz introduced the concept of an ethnography of communication (Hymes & Gumperz, 1964; see also Hornberger, 1995). A decade later, Basso proposed the notion of writing events and called for an ethnography of writing (Basso, 1974). As the emphasis in literacy studies tilted toward the social, ethnography gained wider currency. Szwed (2001), for example, declared that ethnographic methods are "the only means for finding out what literacy really is" (p. 427), and Collins (1988) urged educational anthropologists, whose work has historically focused on achievement inequities, to undertake "close, detailed analyses of the discursive bases of educational practices," contextualizing those investigations within "larger analyses of institutions, language, and society" (p. 320).

At roughly the same time, the field of anthropology was taking a literary turn, as anthropologists began to assume a more critical, self-reflective, and reflexive stance (see, e.g., Hammersley & Atkinson, 1983; Marcus & Fischer, 1986). A "generation of anthropologists emerged," Fabian (1992, p. 84) writes, "which could no longer maintain the illusion of clear distinctions between literate and illiterate societies even if they wanted to." This critical stance is reflected in recent work within the ethnography of reading (Boyarin, 1992), a growing corpus of critical ethnographies (Levinson, Foley, & Holland, 1996), and the newly charted field of the linguistic anthropology of education (Wortham & Rymes, 2003).

The chapters in this volume draw on these bodies of knowledge, adopting a critical ethnographic approach. We are concerned not only with seeing through the lens of ethnography, but with looking and listening critically and with applying ethnographic knowledge toward social justice ends. Scholarship, like language, "is inseparable from both dialogue and domination, and most often contains an admixture of the two" (Boyarin, 1992, p. 8). Like speaking, listening, reading, and writing, scholarship "is a way of being in the world" (Boyarin, 1992, p. 8). This state of being implies responsibility for ensuring that new knowledge is not only produced, but effectively employed. As ethnographers, then, our goal is not only to examine and expose the sites of domination that reinscribe "great divides," but to provoke the dialogic transformations that lead to positive social change.

REFERENCES

Au, K. H. (1993). *Literacy instruction in multicultural settings.* Fort Worth, TX: Harcourt Brace College.

Auerbach, E. (1992). Literacy and ideology. *Annual Review of Applied Linguistics, 12,* 71–85.

Baker, C., & Hornberger, N. H. (2001). *An introductory reader to the writings of Jim Cummins.* Clevedon, UK: Multilingual Matters.

Bakhtin, M. M. (1981). *The dialogic imagination: Four essays by M. M. Bakhtin* (M. Holquist, Ed.). Austin: University of Texas Press.

Banks, J. (2001). Series foreword. In G. Valdés, *Learning and not learning English in school: Latino students in American schools* (pp. ix–xii). New York: Teachers College Press.

Banks, J. A., & Banks, C. A. M. (2004). *Handbook of research on multicultural education* (2nd ed.). San Francisco: Jossey-Bass.

Barton, D., Hamilton, M., & Ivanič, R. (Eds.). (2000). *Situated literacies: Reading and writing in context.* London: Routledge.

Basso, K. (1974). The ethnography of writing. In R. Bauman & J. Sherzer (Eds.), *Explorations in the ethnography of speaking* (pp. 425–432). Cambridge, UK: Cambridge University Press.

Boyarin, J. (1992). Introduction. In J. Boyarin (Ed.), *The ethnography of reading* (pp. 1–9). Berkeley: University of California Press.

Cazden, C. B. (1973). *Child language and education.* New York: Holt, Rinehart & Winston.

Cazden, C., John, V. P., & Hymes, D. (Eds.). (1972). *Functions of language in the classroom.* New York: Teachers College Press.

Collins, J. (1988). Language and class in minority education. *Anthropology & Education Quarterly, 19,* 299–326.

Collins, J. (1995). Literacy and literacies. *Annual Review of Anthropology, 24,* 75–93.

Collins, J., & Blot, R. K. (2003). *Literacy and literacies: Texts, power, and identity.* Cambridge, UK: Cambridge University Press.

Cook-Gumperz, J. (Ed.). (1986). *The social construction of literacy.* Cambridge, UK: Cambridge University Press.

Cook-Gumperz, J., & Keller-Cohen, D. (Eds.). (1993). Alternative literacies: In school and beyond [Special Issue]. *Anthropology & Education Quarterly, 24*(4).

Cushman, E., Kintgen, E. R., Kroll, B. M., & Rose, M. (Eds.). (2001). *Literacy: A critical sourcebook.* Boston: Bedford/St. Martin's.

Delgado-Gaitan, C. (1990). *Literacy for empowerment: The role of parents in children's education.* New York: Falmer.

Delpit, L. D. (1993). The politics of teaching literate discourse. In T. Perry & J. W. Fraser (Eds.), *Freedom's plow: Teaching in the multicultural classroom* (pp. 285–295). New York: Routledge.

Edelsky, C. (1989). *Writing in a bilingual program: Había una vez.* Norwood, NJ: Ablex.

Edelsky, C. (1991). *With literacy and justice for all: Rethinking the social in language and education.* London: Falmer.

Fabian, J. (1992). Keep listening: Ethnography and reading. In J. Boyarin (Ed.), *The ethnography of reading* (pp. 80–97). Berkeley: University of California Press.

Ferdman, B. M., Weber, R-M., & Ramírez, A. G. (Eds.). (1994). *Literacy across languages and cultures.* Albany: State University of New York Press.

Fordham, S. (1999). Dissin' "the standard": Ebonics as guerrilla warfare at Capital High. *Anthropology & Education Quarterly, 30,* 272–293.

Freire, P. (1970). *Pedagogy of the oppressed.* New York: Seabury.

Freire, P. (1993). *Pedagogy of the city.* New York: Continuum.

Garcia, E. E. (2002). Bilingualism and schooling in the United States. *International Journal of the Sociology of Language, 156,* 1–92.

Gassen, S. G. (2004, January 7). Horne speech offends Indians. *Arizona Daily Star,* pp. B1–B2.

Gee, J. P. (1996). *Social linguistics and literacies: Ideology in discourses* (2nd ed.). London: Falmer.

Gee, J. P. (1997). Foreword: A discourse approach to language and literacy. In C. Baker, J. P. Gee, M. Knobel, & C. Searle (Eds.), *Changing literacies* (pp. xiii–xix). Buckingham, UK: Open University Press.

Gee, J. P. (2001). Literacy, discourse, and linguistics: Introduction *and* What is literacy? In E. Cushman, E. R. Kintgen, B. M. Kroll, & M. Rose (Eds.), *Literacy: A critical sourcebook* (pp. 525–544). Boston: Bedford/St. Martin's.

Gee, G. P., Hull, G., & Lankshear, C. (1996). *The new work order: Behind the language of the new capitalism.* Sydney and Boulder, CO: Allen & Unwin and Westview.

Geertz, C. (1983). *Local knowledge: Further essays in interpretive anthropology.* New York: Basic Books.

Goody, J. (Ed.). (1968). *Literacy in traditional societies.* Cambridge, UK: Cambridge University Press.

Goody, J. (1977). *The domestication of the savage mind.* Cambridge, UK: Cambridge University Press.

Goody, J., & Watt, I. P. (1963). The consequences of literacy. *Comparative Studies in History and Society, 5,* 304–305.

Goodman, Y. M., & Wilde, S. (Eds.). (1992). *Literacy events in a community of young writers.* New York: Teachers College Press.

Graff, H. J. (Ed.). (1981). *Literacy and social development in the West: A reader.* Cambridge, UK: Cambridge University Press.

Gumperz, J. J. (Ed). (1982). *Language and social identity.* Cambridge, UK: Cambridge University Press.

Hammersley, M., & Atkinson, P. (1983). *Ethnography: Principles in practice.* London: Routledge.

Heath, S. B. (1982). Protean shapes in literacy events: Ever-shifting oral and literate traditions. In D. Tannen (Ed.), *Spoken and written language: Exploring orality and literacy* (pp. 91–117). Norwood, NJ: Ablex.

Heath, S. B. (1983). *Ways with words.* New York: Cambridge University Press.

Hornberger, N. H. (1995). Ethnography in linguistic perspective: Understanding school processes. *Language and Education, 9,* 233–248.

Hornberger, N. H. (Ed.). (1996). *Indigenous literacies in the Americas: Language planning from the bottom up.* Berlin: Mouton de Gruyter.

Hornberger, N. H., & Ricento, T. K. (Eds.). (1996). Language planning and policy [Special Issue]. *TESOL Quarterly, 30*(3).

Hull, G., & Schultz, K. (2001). Literacy and learning out of school: A review of theory and research. *Review of Educational Research, 71,* 575–611.

Hull, G., & Schultz, K. (Eds.). (2002). *School's out! Bridging out-of-school literacies with classroom practice.* New York: Teachers College Press.

Hymes, D. (1974). *Foundations of sociolinguistics.* Philadelphia: University of Pennsylvania Press.

Hymes, D., & Gumperz, J. (Eds.). (1964). *The ethnography of communication.* Washington, DC: American Anthropological Association.

Knobel, M. (1999). *Everyday literacies: Students, discourse, and social practice.* New York: Peter Lang.

Krashen, S. D. (1985). *Second language acquisition and second language learning.* Oxford, UK: Pergamon Press.

Lankshear, C., with Gee, J. P., Knobel, M., & Searle, C. (1997). *Changing literacies.* Buckingham, UK: Open University Press.

Lave, J., & Wenger, E. (1991). *Situated learning: Legitimate peripheral participation.* Cambridge, UK: Cambridge University Press.

Levinson, B. A., Foley, D. E., & Holland, D. C. (1996). *The cultural production of the educated person: Critical ethnographies of schooling and local practice.* Albany: State University of New York Press.

Lomawaima, K. T., & McCarty, T. L. (2002). When tribal sovereignty challenges democracy: American Indian education and the democratic ideal. *American Educational Research Journal, 39,* 279–305.

Majors, Y. (2004). "I wasn't scared of them, they were scared of me": Constructions of self/other in a Midwestern hair salon. *Anthropology & Education Quarterly, 35,* 167–188.

Marcus, G. E., & Fischer, M. M. J. (1986). *Anthropology as cultural critique: An experimental moment in the human sciences.* Chicago: University of Chicago Press.

McCarty, T. L. (2002). *A place to be Navajo: Rough Rock and the struggle for self-determination in Indigenous schooling.* Mahwah, NJ: Lawrence Erlbaum Associates.

McLaughlin, D. (1992). *When literacy empowers: Navajo language in print.* Albuquerque: University of New Mexico Press.

Michaels, S. (1981). "Sharing time": Children's narrative styles and differential access to literacy. *Language in Society, 10,* 423–442.

Moll, L. C., Amanti, C., Neff, D., & González, N. (1992). Funds of knowledge for teaching: Using a qualitative approach to connect homes and classrooms. *Theory Into Practice, 31,* 132–141.

New London Group. (1996). A pedagogy of multiliteracies: Designing social futures. *Harvard Educational Review, 66,* 60–92.

Olson, D. R. (1977). From utterance to text: The bias of language in speech and writing. *Harvard Educational Review, 47,* 257–281.

Ong, W. J. (1982). *Orality and literacy: The technologizing of the word.* London: Methuen.

Ovando, C. J., Collier, V. P., & Combs, M. C. (2003). *Bilingual and ESL classrooms: Teaching in multicultural contexts* (3rd ed.). Boston: McGraw Hill.

Pérez, B., with McCarty, T. L., Watahomigie, L. J., Torres-Guzmán, M. E., Dien, T., Chang, J., Smith, H. L., & Dávila de Silva, A. (2004). *Sociocultural contexts of language and literacy* (2nd ed.). Mahwah, NJ: Lawrence Erlbaum Associates.

Qin-Hilliard, D. B., Feinauer, E., & Quiroz, B. (2001). Introduction. *Harvard Educational Review, 71,* v–ix.

Reason, P. (2004). Critical design ethnography as action research. *Anthropology & Education Quarterly, 35,* 269–276.

Ricento, T., & Burnaby, B. (Eds.). (1998). *Language and politics in the United States and Canada: Myths and realities.* Mahwah, NJ: Lawrence Erlbaum Associates.

Schieffelin, B., & Gilmore, P. (Eds.). (1986). *The acquisition of literacy: Ethnographic perspectives.* Norwood, NJ: Ablex.

Scribner, S., & Cole, M. (1981). *The psychology of literacy.* Cambridge, MA: Harvard University Press.

Scribner, S., & Cole, M. (2001). Unpackaging literacy. In E. Cushman, E. R. Kintgen, B. M. Kroll, & M. Rose (Eds.), *Literacy: A critical sourcebook* (pp. 123–137). Boston: Bedford/St. Martin's.

Searle, C. (1993). Words to a life-land: Literacy, the imagination and Palestine. In C. Lankshear & P. McLaren (Eds.), *Critical literacy: Politics, praxis and the post-modern* (pp. 167–192). Albany: State University of New York Press.

Sleeter, C. E., & McLaren, P. L. (Eds.). (1995). *Multicultural education, critical pedagogy, and the politics of difference*. Albany: State University of New York Press.

Smith, F. (1983). *Essays into literacy*. Exeter, NH: Heinemann.

Spindler, G., & Spindler, L. (1992). Cultural process and ethnography: An anthropological perspective. In M. D. LeCompte, W. L. Millroy, & J. Preissle (Eds.), *The handbook of qualitative research in education* (pp. 53–92). San Diego, CA: Academic.

Street, B. V. (1984). *Literacy in theory and practice*. New York: Cambridge University Press.

Street, B. V. (Ed.). (1993). *Cross-cultural approaches to literacy*. Cambridge, UK: Cambridge University Press.

Street, B. V. (1995). *Social literacies: Critical approaches to literacy in development, ethnography and education*. London: Longman.

Street, B. V. (Ed.) (2001a). *Literacy and development: Ethnographic perspectives*. London: Routledge.

Street, B. V. (2001b). The New Literacy Studies. In E. Cushman, E. R. Kintgen, B. M. Kroll, & M. Rose (Eds.), *Literacy: A critical sourcebook* (pp. 430–442). Boston: Bedford/St. Martin's.

Street, J. C., & Street, B. V. (1991). The schooling of literacy. In D. Barton & R. Ivanic (Eds.), *Writing in the community* (pp. 106–131). Newbury Park, CA: Sage.

Suárez-Orozco, M. M. (2001). Globalization, immigration, and education: The research agenda. *Harvard Educational Review, 71,* 345–365.

Szwed, J. F. (2001). The ethnography of literacy. In E. Cushman, E. R. Kintgen, B. M. Kroll, & M. Rose (Eds.), *Literacy: A critical sourcebook* (pp. 421–429). Boston: Bedford/St. Martin's.

Taylor, D. (Ed.). (1997). *Many families, many literacies*. Portsmouth, NH: Heinemann.

Taylor, D., & Dorsey-Gaines, C. (1988). *Growing up literate: Learning from inner-city families*. Portsmouth, NH: Heinemann.

Tollefson, J. W. (Ed.). (2002). *Language policies in education: Critical issues*. Mahwah, NJ: Lawrence Erlbaum Associates.

Tollefson, J. W., & Tsui, A. B. M. (Eds.). (2004). *Medium of instruction policies: Which agenda? Whose agenda?* Mahwah, NJ: Lawrence Erlbaum Associates.

Valdés, G. (2001). *Learning and not learning English: Latino students in American schools*. New York: Teachers College Press.

Varenne, H., & McDermott, R., with Goldman, S., Naddeo, M., & Rizzo-Tolk, R. (1999). *Successful failure: The school America builds*. Boulder, CO: Westview.

Vygotsky, L. S. (1978). *Mind in society: The development of higher psychological processes* (M. Cole, V. John-Steiner, S. Scribner, & E. Souberman, Eds.). Cambridge, MA: Harvard University Press.

Wertsch, J. V., Del Rio, P., & Alvarez, A. (1995). *Sociocultural studies of the mind*. New York: Cambridge University Press.

Williams, R. (1983). *The year 2000*. New York: Pantheon.

Willis, A. I., García, G. E., Barrera, R., & Harris, V. J. (Eds.). (2003). *Multicultural issues in literacy research and practice*. Mahwah, NJ: Lawrence Erlbaum Associates.

Willis, A. I., & Harris, V. J. (2003). Afterword. In A. I. Willis, G. E. García, & V. J. Harris (Eds.), *Multicultural issues in literacy research and practice* (pp. 289–296). Mahwah, NJ: Lawrence Erlbaum Associates.

Wolcott, H. F. (1999). *Ethnography: A way of seeing*. Walnut Creek, CA: AltaMira.

Wortham, S., & Rymes, B. (2003). *Linguistic anthropology of education*. Westport, CT: Praeger.

I
"Taking Hold" of Local Literacies

How is literacy appropriated for local ends? In colonial, neocolonial, and diasporic contexts, how are local epistemologies asserted and new norms established for what and whose literacy "counts"?

These questions lie at the heart of the chapters in this part of the volume. Part I's theme is inspired by Kulick and Stroud's (1993) ethnographic study of literacy in Gapun, a rural and then "newly literate" village of about 100 people in Papua New Guinea. "[F]ar from being passively transformed" by English literacy, Kulick and Stroud (1993) state, Gapun villagers "actively and creatively [applied] literacy skills to suit their own purposes and needs," injecting it with functions and communicative strategies used in speech (p. 3). Instead of asking how literacy affects people, Kulick and Stroud found themselves asking how people "seize hold" of those aspects of literacy that have meaning and utility in their everyday lives. (See also McLaughlin's [1992] analysis of English and Navajo literacy, and Street [2001, pp. 8–9].)

This section explores the processes through which local, subaltern communities "take hold" of literacy. What these processes mean for communities, individuals, and the institutions in which they participate is illustrated across a broad range of settings and moments in time. The chapters contribute not only to our understanding of situated, changing, and everyday literacies (see, e.g., Barton, Hamilton, & Ivanic, 2000; Knobel, 1999; Lankshear, 1997), but also to our understanding of the relationship of these literacies to local social organizations and to broader issues of political participation and linguistic human rights.

Elsie Rockwell begins this discussion with a historical analysis of Indigenous literacy in the Chiapas highlands. She argues that literacy, much more than simply alien knowledge to be learned, is a cultural practice forged collectively in particular historical circumstances. Rockwell also demonstrates how oral tradition and literacy intertwine; as she puts it, both writing and speaking are "practices constructed in the context of asymmetrical power relationships," and both are part of the appropriation of literacy for local ends. Rockwell's examination highlights especially the need to recover a historical perspective in our understandings of literacy and literacies.

The next three chapters bring Indigenous experiences to the present moment. Each of these chapters, and Robert Whitman's that follows, present counternarratives—texts and acts that disrupt and disturb "grand stories," challenging the practices that legitimate the status quo (Peters & Lankshear, 1996, p. 2). Sheilah Nicholas explains how both literacy and schooling are being coopted by Hopi people to revitalize their language and culturally valued practices. Here, reading and writing occur "as part of an indigenist effort to represent themselves, their endangered language, their disrupted history" (Collins & Blot, 2003, p. 159). Nicholas's personal narrative embodies this process: Stripped of her native Hopi language by her early socialization and schooling, she "put it aside" for many years. Only in adulthood was she able to reclaim her Hopi language and identity. As Nicholas relates, she continues to fight for this most basic human right. Her story can be seen as an insider's analysis of the way that literacy is shaped by a group's social organization and needs—and as a microcosm of a larger, worldwide struggle for language minority rights (see also Collins, 1998; Fishman, 1991, 2001; Grenoble & Whaley, 1998; May, 2001; McCarty, 2003; Nettle & Romaine, 2000; Phillipson, 2000; Skutnabb-Kangas, 2000).

In the subsequent chapter, I document how the micro processes involved in asserting Indigenous literacies and education rights collide with larger bureaucratic texts. Drawing on my long-term ethnographic work with one Navajo community school, I examine how bilingual teachers quietly but insistently reclaimed their own literacies and pedagogical power—"the power within"—asserting their role as change agents and recentering the community-based mission of their school. This account also problematizes discourses of minority teacher and student empowerment; rather than a final destination or end result, local empowerment in neocolonial contexts is viewed as an ongoing struggle for self-determination and for linguistic, cultural, and education rights.

Perry Gilmore and the late David M. Smith explore self-empowerment struggles among Australian Aboriginal and Native Alaskan adult learners. This chapter, too, narrates counterstories (even "counterplaques") of deliberate resistance by Indigenous students to mainstream academic texts that misrepresent and distort their abilities and experiences. Like the Mayan, Hopi, and Navajo communities described in previous chapters, the Native people with whom Gilmore and Smith worked legitimated subaltern knowledge. Gilmore and Smith introduce the notion of situated freedom, arguing that power is never granted but is rather seized and created in contested social space.

Robert Whitman concludes the empirical chapters with an illuminating student "narration of self." Carefully examining the narrative of a Latina high school student through detailed sociolinguistic microanalysis, he shows how the taken-for-granted discourse of standardized tests indexes powerful negative consequences. Whitman probes deeply into the ways in which ascribed marginalized identities are constructed and resisted across a "moral landscape of peers, teachers, classroom, and community."

In commenting on these chapters, Ray McDermott (re)positions language as a resource (see also Ruiz, 1988). Not unlike Gee's (2001) discussion of primary and secondary discourses, McDermott notes that "nothing is more inhibiting than what a people already know how to say," yet nothing is more liberating than learning new linguistic forms. Why then are minority language speakers so often forced to make either–or choices between the language they know and the language of wider communication? Why are bilingualism, multilingualism, and multiliteracies so often viewed as problematic? As the chapters and McDermott's commentary show, larger social, political, and economic forces make problematic that which is natural and beneficial—thereby limiting what McDermott (quoting the Irish poet Seamus Heaney) calls "further entries into language."

Together, these chapters illustrate the complexity of local literacies, their structuring within local social systems and larger networks of power, and the dynamic interplay of the local and the central (Street, 2001) in real time and real people's lives. The chapters also reveal the dangerous sterility of universalist or autonomous views of literacy and the reductive pedagogies they impose. At the same time, the studies here wedge open new spaces of possibility—alternatives to an either-or, unilingual, and monoculturalist divide. Informed by insiders—those who often are the targets of standardizing regimes—these chapters show the emancipatory potentials that arise when local literacies are claimed and appropriated for local ends.

REFERENCES

Barton, D., Hamilton, M., & Ivanič, R. (Eds.). (2000). *Situated literacies: Reading and writing in context.* London: Routledge.

Collins, J. (1998). *Understanding Tolowa histories: Western hegemonies and Native American responses.* New York: Routledge.

Collins, J., & Blot, R. K. (2003). *Literacy and literacies: Texts, power, and identity.* Cambridge, UK: Cambridge University Press.

Fishman, J. A. (1991). *Reversing language shift.* Clevedon, UK: Multilingual Matters.

Fishman, J. A. (2001). *Can threatened languages be saved? Reversing language shift, revisited: A 21st century perspective.* Clevedon, UK: Multilingual Matters.

Gee, J. P. (2001). Literacy, discourse, and linguistics: Introduction *and* What is literacy? In E. Cushman, E. R. Kintgen, B. M. Kroll, & M. Rose (Eds.), *Literacy: A critical sourcebook* (pp. 525–544). Boston: Bedford/St. Martin's.

Grenoble, L., & Whaley, L. J. (Eds.). (1998). *Endangered languages: Current issues and future prospects.* Cambridge, UK: Cambridge University Press.

Knobel, M. (1999). *Everyday literacies: Students, discourse, and social practice.* New York: Peter Lang.

Kulick, D., & Stroud, C. (1993). Conceptions and uses of literacy in a Papua New Guinean village. In B. Street (Ed.), *Cross-cultural approaches to literacy* (pp. 30–61). Cambridge, UK: Cambridge University Press.

Lankshear, C., with Gee, J. P., Knobel, M., & Searle, C. (1997). *Changing literacies.* Buckingham, UK: Open University Press.

May, S. (2001). *Language and minority rights: Ethnicity, nationalism and the politics of language.* Harlow, UK: Longman/Pearson Education.

McCarty, T. L. (2003). Revitalising Indigenous languages in homogenizing times. *Comparative Education, 39,* 147–163.

McLaughlin, D. (1992). *When literacy empowers: Navajo language in print.* Albuquerque: University of New Mexico Press.

Nettle, D., & Romaine, S. (2000). *Vanishing voices: The extinction of the world's languages.* New York: Oxford University Press.

Peters, M., & Lankshear, C. (1996). Postmodern counternarratives. In H. A. Giroux, C. Lankshear, P. McLaren, & M. Peters (Eds.), *Counternarratives: Cultural studies and critical pedagogy in postmodern spaces* (pp. 1–40). New York: Routledge.

Phillipson, R. (Ed.). (2000). *Rights to language: Equity, power, and education.* Mahwah, NJ: Lawrence Erlbaum Associates.

Ruiz, R. (1988). Orientations in language planning. In S. L. McKay & S. C. Wong (Eds.), *Language diversity: Problem or resource?* (pp. 3–25). Boston: Heinle & Heinle.

Skutnabb-Kangas, T. (2000). *Linguistic genocide in education—Or worldwide diversity and human rights?* Mahwah, NJ: Lawrence Erlbaum Associates.

Street, B. V. (Ed.). (2001). *Literacy and development: Ethnographic perspectives.* London: Routledge.

1

Indigenous Accounts of Dealing With Writing

Elsie Rockwell
Centro de Investigación y Estudios Avanzados, Mexico D.F.

The central assumption of this chapter is that the Maya people of Chiapas, Mexico, as many other groups described in the literature, have had a long history of developing strategies to deal with the dominant uses of literacy. Native accounts of incidents involving writing offer clues to the ways Indigenous communities have perceived, resisted, and appropriated literacy in their ongoing struggle for survival. In this chapter, I interpret accounts taken from texts published by Native writers during the past decade, against the background of the social history of the region. Within municipalities marked by the lowest literacy levels in the country, the significant uses of literacy among the Native people of Chiapas appear linked to religious and political movements and the struggle for land, rather than to the expansion of schooling. I argue that by approaching literacy as a cultural practice forged collectively in particular social processes, rather than as alien knowledge to be learned, we may gain perspective on the apparent resistance to schooling among Native peoples and find novel ways of approaching literacy in ongoing projects.

Rabbit asked his grandmother for some new *huaraches*. In exchange, she asked him for two crocodile's teeth. After wondering how to obtain the teeth, Rabbit decided he would offer to teach the crocodile to read and calculate. When the crocodile was busy with reading and doing sums, he struck him on the very spot of his tail where his soul lies, and thus killed him. Then he pulled out two teeth, and went happily home to get his new sandals.

—*Chiapas Maya folktale*[1]

---

[1]Fragment adapted from "El conejo y su abuela," collected and published, in the original Ch'ol version and in Spanish, by Alejos Garcia (1988, pp. 51–59).

Literacy is undeniably linked to power. As Cook-Gumperz and Keller-Cohen (1993) expressed it, "literacy is a hegemonic and counter-hegemonic instrument, one creating and maintaining power as well as enabling resistance" (p. 285). In tracing the theme of power and writing through the documented history of Chiapas, Mexico, I wish to contribute some thoughts on one aspect that has received little attention: Those in power tend to *both undermine and deny the literacy* of the groups they rule or dominate. The record shows that literacy is not a newcomer to the Chiapas highlands, but has long played a role in shaping collective Indigenous experience. To bring this history into the present, I draw examples from some of the recently published narratives of Native authors that suggest ways in which communities have encountered writing in their everyday life in the context of domination. Finally, I briefly link this historical perspective to current debates on how—and whether—to go about literacy programs in Indigenous communities in Mexico.

My argument does not hinge on the spread of literacy—that is, the number of literate individuals at any given moment. Rather I focus on the collective relationship to literacy, produced through a specific history of appropriation of writing. I understand *appropriation* in this context as a collective cultural process that occurs under conditions of asymmetrical power relationships, as tools or signs of a dominant group are taken up by subordinate groups and incorporated—often with new meanings and uses—into their own cultural history (Bonfil, 1991; Chartier, 1995). Research on literacy has documented many instances of the appropriation of literacy among groups that are not at the center of power (e.g., Bloch, 1998; Collins & Blot, 2003; Fabre, 1993; Hornberger, 1996). In situations of domination, the appropriation of literacy may involve strategic *avoidance of writing*, as well as *strategic uses of written language*. My focus on literacy is not intended to deny the wealth and strength of oral tradition in this region, but rather, to consider it as part of this history of appropriation.[2]

ORAL CULTURES OR MULTIPLE LITERACIES?

The discussion of literacy in Chiapas is often framed by the assumption that Indigenous cultures are inherently "oral." However, an obvious question arises: How did the Maya people of Chiapas, who in the past possessed what is increasingly recognized as a sophisticated writing system,[3] come to be consid-

---

[2]Thus, "illiteracy" may be seen, at this scale too, as an "achievement," as it is in face-to-face interaction. See Varenne and McDermott (1999).

[3]It is now known that ancient Mayan writing had many phonetic elements and syntactic structures, although it has not been completely deciphered.

ered over a period of 400 years members of an oral culture? Scholarly references to Mayan literacy generally concern pre-Hispanic writing systems restricted to a specialized caste in a distant past, seen as irrelevant to present-day debates. In the realm of education, an evolutionary model pervades programs and policies designed to help Indians achieve universal literacy through schooling. In either case, the Indian towns' postconquest experience with alphabetic writing is ignored.

An alternative perspective on present-day concerns, based on the notion of *multiple literacies* that has gained sway in the field, would take into account the long-term history of the Native peoples' experience in dealing with writing. Although Hornberger (1996) and other scholars (Kartunnen, 1998; Richards & Richards, 1996) tend to restrict the notion of Indigenous literacy to writing in the Native language, I include Native uses of written Spanish as part of the history of appropriation of writing. Throughout the colonial and national periods, Indian communities in Mexico encountered and engaged in a variety of literacy practices, particularly in the domains of religion and governance, which had a direct bearing on their destinies. It is only by tracing the history of these practices in particular regions that we may come to understand the present-day configuration and interplay of oral and written language in each community. During the past five centuries, Native groups in Chiapas have appropriated alphabetic writing in diverse manners, and used it for their own ends, at the same time defending themselves against some of the abuses exercised through writing by those in power.

The two models (evolutionary and multiple literacies) come into play in interpretations of the Indigenous experience with literacy. Pitarch Ramón (1996), for example, has claimed that writing is seen as alien in the essentially oral world of the Tzeltal of Cancuc. After noting that the ancient Mayan cultures created a writing system, and that some Tzeltals in past centuries used the alphabet to write their own language, he states, "With these precedents, the written word would seem to be a familiar field for the Tzeltal. However, this is not the case: among the residents of Cancuc it is an attribute of the others" (p. 152, my translation). Among the many dreaded *lab* spirits, bearers of illness that inhabit the Tzeltal religious world, Pitarch Ramón identifies two related to writing: the *lab nombre* (name lab) and the *lab profisol*. He links the first to the fear of being registered on colonial tribute lists. The second spirit, depicted as a small man in black, he sees as representing the teacher (called *profesor* in Spanish), one of the prime mediators between the communities and civilian authorities since around 1800.

Pitarch Ramón (1996) argues that whereas the Tzeltal overtly accepted colonial institutions, they resisted being colonized in their more intimate selves.
In the process, some of them had to "act as though they were Castilian," becoming literate to take on the roles of teachers, scribes, sacristans (*fiscales*),
musicians, party delegates, union leaders, and such. However, most Tzeltal
people, he holds, have traditionally resisted being contaminated by Spanish
(*caxlan*) ways, for example, by sending at most one child to school. Pitarch
Ramón (1996) concludes that the Tzeltal fear harm not so much from
Castilians, as from those among their own people who take on Castilian behavior, such as the elite bilingual caste that has held most government jobs and political posts in the Highland towns. According to Pitarch Ramón, all behaviors
(including writing) associated with "the Castilians," although necessary for
those mediating roles, were felt to lead to a "loss of soul." This position would
seem to offer one possible interpretation of the tale of Rabbit and the crocodile: Learning to read and write leads to loss of soul.

Although intriguing, Pitarch Ramón's (1996) ethnography tends to reproduce the oral–literate divide now largely abandoned in the study of literacy
(Fabre, 1993; Hornberger, 1996; see also the Introduction to this volume). Furthermore, his version runs counter to the growing awareness of the historical
formation of present-day Indigenous communities as a process of invention,
appropriation, and syncretism of diverse cultural elements, as well as of the re-
affirmation of distinct identities (Kartunnen, 1998; Rus, 1994; Ruz, 1998, p.
13). From this perspective, the question should be posed, not as a search for essential traits, but rather as an attempt to recover the appropriation and persecution of Indigenous literacy practices, whether in the Mayan languages of
Chiapas—Tzeltal, Tzotzil, Ch'ol, and Tojolab'al—or in Spanish. These practices should further be placed in the context of relationships of power, as both
rulers and the ruled used strategies involving written language in the ongoing
processes of intensifying or resisting domination. Several well-documented
moments of Chiapas's postconquest history offer evidence of the strategies
wielded by the various agents of power, and of the Natives' response.

THE DESTRUCTION OF WRITING AND THE
STRENGTHENING OF ORAL TRADITIONS

In the initial years of colonial rule (16th century), the first act of the Catholic
missionaries was to destroy all pre-Hispanic books. Highland Mayan religious
and cultural practices were quite suddenly left with no written record. In this

region, the void was not immediately filled with texts in alphabetic writing, as was the case in the Nahua region of central Mexico, where early Franciscans trained Native youth—at times by force—in Spanish literacy and Latin (Cifuentes, 1998). In Chiapas, Ruz (1986) notes, writing skills were scarce even among the early missionaries, who found learning to speak the local languages easier than teaching all the Natives to understand and read Spanish, as the colonial authorities had ordered. However, the Church hierarchy feared the inclusion of heretical notions as Catholic doctrine was translated into the native languages. Control was secured through the official translations—in the form of catechisms, confession manuals, dictionaries, and grammars—that circulated among the friars, generally in handwritten copies. It was explicitly forbidden that these texts reach the Natives; they were intended for the exclusive use of the missionaries (Ruz, 1986, p. 16). To spread official doctrine quickly, missionaries resorted to visual and oral means, including extensive use of religious images and theatrical representation. Thus, in this region, far from imposing an alien writing system, missionaries initially hindered the spread of literacy, in any language or with any writing system. A century later, the Church abandoned its policy favoring the use of the Indigenous languages. The clergy, unable to attend the whole region, began to select and train some Natives to read and write and to take charge of local religious celebrations.

Despite official practice, during the 16th and 17th centuries, the highland Natives, as other Mayan peoples, developed clandestine religious practices (in caves, fields, or homes) involving written scripts, and registered current versions of their beliefs and practices using the alphabetic system taken—or rather stolen—from the conquerors. This covert literary tradition (Kartunnen, 1998) was hidden from strangers and presumably used to reconstruct ritual calendars and interpret ongoing phenomena in the light of ancient Maya history. Nearly two centuries after the conquest, in 1693, ecclesiastical authorities in Chiapas reported the confiscation of 200 texts found in communities, although the languages in which they were written were not specified (Cifuentes, 1998; Ruz 1986). No such books written during the colonial period in Chiapas are known to have survived. It is possible, however, that some were kept hidden by colonial religious authorities (Andrés Aubry, personal communication). If any were comparable to the *Popol Vuh* found in Guatemala, they may have recorded "what readers of the ancient book would say when they gave long performances, telling the full story that lay behind the charts, pictures and plot outlines of the ancient book" (Tedlock, 1996, p. 30). In the religious sphere, the appropriation of alphabetic writing apparently served among other ends to record the oral tradition that accompanied literate knowledge in the pre-Hispanic writing systems. However, the confiscated texts probably served other purposes as well, such as recording local knowledge and ongoing history, or even legitimizing the power of local *caciques* and the colonial structures of domination.

The history of these forbidden texts leads to other questions. Did the experience of persecution and confiscation of writing engender alternative means for preserving and transmitting information? Can the strength of oral tradition be seen as a strategy for cultural transmission developed in the face of these dominant practices of the colonial years? In the Mayan highlands, it may be that the destruction of Native writing was so thorough that it led communities to intensify the use of other means. Thus, they inscribed texts in collective memory through the development of elaborate oral genres, and through ways of "writing without words" (Boone & Mignolo, 1994), such as textile designs.

The official policy did not end with the late colonial reforms nor with Mexican independence. In the civilian sphere, the Mexican Constitution of 1824 further proscribed the use of all Indigenous languages for public, written documents, driving them into the private domain and restricting them to oral use. The use of oral strategies in the past is of course scarcely documented, and one can only begin to imagine what might have happened during the late 18th and 19th centuries in the highlands, a period in which ways of life in the Indian communities underwent fundamental changes. However, it is clear that present-day Indigenous oral narratives are formal texts in their own right, and correspond to elaborate generic and thematic constraints (Montemayor, 1998). Furthermore, they articulate a wide range of information related to nature and communal life and work. Thus, the particular uses of oral language in the highland communities can be regarded as historical constructions rather than essential cultural traits.

Further evidence of these strategies may be gathered from the recent religious history of the Indian communities. In fact, there is presently a relative paucity of any writing in those Catholic churches in Indian towns that follow *la costumbre*, the ritual patterns that originated in the early 19th century after a partial withdrawal of the clergy and the strengthening of civilian authorities (Viqueira, 1998b, p. 233). In the shrines, there is rarely any text associated with the effigies of the saints, nor are written messages (e.g., *ex votos*, letters) placed with them, as is common in other parts of Mexico. The *rezadores*, elders in charge of praying on different occasions, recite long verses from memory. In a few churches, books, pamphlets, or documents are hidden in coffers or chests, and occasionally used in a ritual context, often with little regard for the actual text. The most famous case is a leather-bound volume, the *K'awaltic*, passed down yearly to the incoming traditional religious authorities in Oxchuc. The document is a copy of Royal Ordenances emitted in 1674, containing a number of items concerning obligations and rights as well as instructions for civilian life. It is regarded as a sacred book, although the actual content is of little current value (Esponda Jimeno, 1992). According to one version, the deerskin binding of the book is said to undergo changes that signal a good or poor rainy season for the coming year.[4]

Despite the frequent alliance between followers of *la costumbre* and the official national political powers in these towns (Rus, 1994), religious practice has changed significantly during the past three decades in Chiapas. The later half of the 20th century witnessed a massive conversion of highland Natives by the Summer Institute of Linguistics and various other Protestant missions. The Diocese of San Cristóbal, under Bishop Samuel Ruiz (1960–2000), countered this trend with a renewed missionary effort, designed around liberation theology and the theory of *inculturación*, which selectively incorporated Indigenous beliefs into Catholic doctrine and practice (Leyva Solano, 1998; Viqueira, 1998b). What is significant about both of these religious movements is the production and use of written texts, particularly from the Scriptures, which were being translated into the Indigenous languages by some of the Protestant denominations and Catholic orders. Catholic evangelization involved training hundreds of Native catechists and predeacons to read and write their own languages, as well as Spanish. The effort led to a particularly intensive use of the written word, as the catechists would guide sessions of collective reading and reflection on the Scriptures in ways that constructed shared interpretations linked to contemporary experiences and concerns.[5] These reflections were then set in writing, often in the Native language, and served to orient pastoral programs. It is significant that this literacy practice was again subject to persecution: Some of the religious texts circulated by the Diocese were purportedly "found in caves" and destroyed by the military as "subversive literature."

---

[4]This version was told to me in 1997 by an elderly *rezador* in charge of the temple of Chanal.

[5]During field trips, I observed the constant use of and reference to the written texts during these ceremonies in the Cañada communities.

THE DENIAL OF LITERACY AND OF INDIGENOUS
USES OF WRITING

A second strategy of dominant groups is the denial of autonomous literacy practices. I became aware of the importance of this strategy through Justice's (1994)
account of a peasant rebellion that took place in 1381 in medieval England. The
movement involved the written word, as peasants had been demanding, in writing, that the local bishop produce a copy of a *Charter of Liberties*, which had
been relegated by subsequent documents that deprived them of their ancient
rights. The chronicles of the rebellion were written during the time of the events
from the perspective of those who felt threatened by the uprising. Justice noticed
that some versions contained what appear to be formal letters written by the re-
bel leaders, although the chroniclers presented them as "speeches" delivered
orally, thus concealing the leaders' ability to read and write. He suggests that the
chroniclers justified repression by representing the rebels as "illiterate peasants"
revolting against the literate, civilized world of the clergy and the nobility. According to Justice, "the agencies of power" were able to transform the uprising,
absorb it and use it "for their own ends" (pp. 193–196).

Similar stories surround the uprisings that became part of the official history of Chiapas: the rebellions of 1712 (Viqueira, 1998a) and of 1869 (Rus,
1998). By the 18th century, literacy had spread among local religious leaders
(choirmasters and sacristans) of the Highland townships. Both rebellions were
headed by Natives who had previously held positions in the local civil or religious hierarchy. Writing played an important part in the 1712 uprising, as
proclamations written in Spanish circulated throughout the region, spreading
news of the "Virgin of Cancuc," who had come forth to free them. The messages called on the Indians to cease paying tribute to the king of Spain and the
Church. The leaders set up an autonomous governing system, which mirrored
the colonial model, rejected all attempts at pacification (some were sent in
writing), and were finally defeated by an army sent from the Audiencia of
Guatemala.

In 1869, after the independence of Mexico, state government forces vio-
lently repressed a second uprising led by the literate Chamula *fiscal*, Cuscat.
This movement sought religious and economic independence from both
Church authorities and conservative groups in San Cristóbal, who continued to
impose colonial obligations. Cuscat and his followers were no doubt aware of
the political differences that had been fought out both locally and nationally
between liberals and conservatives. They also had knowledge of the advan-

tages offered by the Liberal Reform laws of the 1850s, which, among other things, guaranteed individual rights and religious freedom.

A decade or two after the uprising, conservative historians of San Cristóbal portrayed the 1869 movement as a violent "caste war" against the regional elite (Rus, 1998). This version claimed that Cuscat had fabricated an idol able to "speak" to his followers, and had thus deceived them into participating in this war of "barbarism against civilization" and "darkness against light" (Pineda, 1986, pp. 72–73). This written version became part of local oral tradition, and spread to Indigenous communities, where it was collected and reproduced as a valid account of the rebellion in early ethnographies, a century after the events (Rus, 1998). Despite these images of "barbarism" and "illiteracy" fabricated by official history, and by early anthropology, it is clear that both movements had taken advantage of written documents in defining their demands and organizing the uprisings.

Casting uprisings as resulting from external manipulation of a mass of ignorant people is a classic form of denial of literacy. Some scholars suggest that literacy was probably more widespread than is often assumed in the Indigenous towns during the late colonial years and the beginning of the 19th century, although it was limited by gender and generation boundaries. From the late 18th century on, colonial authorities assigned male teachers to the larger Indian towns, paying their wages from the communal funds collected from each town (Tanck de Estrada, 1999). After independence, many municipalities continued sustaining local schools for boys. Regardless of the actual number of individuals who learned to read, it seems clear that the import of written documents in political conflicts was evident to those who participated in the uprisings. Both external agencies, such as the Church, and internal social movements account for the significant appropriation of writing in this historical context. However, official accounts tended to deny the presence of writing and of written documents as cultural resources available to highland Natives.

By the 19th century, the tendency to undermine and deny the uses of writing by Natives had succeeded. After the independence of Mexico, many Spaniards or *mestizos* had moved into the Indigenous municipal *cabeceras* (headtowns), setting up commercial or agricultural enterprises. Furthermore, some Indians always contrived to increase their personal wealth and power as intermediaries with the new governing bodies, and were eventually accepted as non-Indians or *ladinos*. This change hinged on the acquisition of Spanish language and literacy and its use for the purposes of control or brokerage (Gosner, 1991; Rus, 1994; Ruz, 1997). Literate members of these groups often held the key position of *secretario* (secretary) in the new municipal civil governments, although the other municipal positions remained in Native hands. Although there were periods when certain townships drove out all non-Indian residents, this general pattern survived well into the 20th century.

When the federal school system entered the region toward the mid-20th century, highland communities that still maintained the use of Indigenous languages could easily be portrayed as oral cultures.[6] The educational programs following the Mexican Revolution (1910–1920) were conceived as "incorporating Indians to civilization through the teaching of Spanish literacy." This "mission" could be fully justified in the public discourse. Nevertheless, public schooling in the highlands always lagged well behind national averages. By itself, schooling cannot account for the recent surge of Indigenous-language publications in Chiapas. We must ponder this recent trend from the perspective of the Native people's long-term experience with literacy.

THE PERSPECTIVE OF NATIVE WRITERS

If the discourses of power tend to deny subaltern uses of literacy, I reflected, perhaps Native voices would testify to the appropriation of literacy.[7] One possibility was to examine some of the testimonies transcribed or written by Native authors in the Indigenous languages of Chiapas and published (with Spanish translations) by the government and by universities or nongovernmental agencies. Although often biased toward the more literate members of the communities, these texts offer insights that are rarely gained from archival sources. The range of genres of this material evidences the breadth of Native uses of writing. Some texts are traditional folktales, related to such themes as the origin and transformation of animals, witchcraft and invisible spirits, heroes, and prodigies (e.g., *Cuentos y relatos indígenas*, 1994–1998). In the folktales, incidents involving writing—such as that of Rabbit and the crocodile—are relatively scarce, although penetrating. This dearth should not be taken as a confirmation of an oral culture, as much the same would be found in similar genres in highly literate societies. Furthermore, the themes and symbols of these narratives have diverse origins, reflecting the multiple strains that are interwoven in culture everywhere (Laughlin, 1992, pp. 15–38; Montemayor, 1998). Other

---

[6]By then, many Indian groups had lost the use of their native languages and progressively melded with the mestizo population.

[7]In another study (Rockwell, 2001), I found local stories that mentioned uses of writing that had become a significant part of a Nahua pueblo's experience.

published sources include community monographs or testimonials recorded or produced by Native writers, often based on accounts given by the elder members of their families. Their content gives valuable clues to the uses of writing in a variety of domains during the 20th century. In what follows, I draw examples related to three themes that appear in the texts: ritual, labor and land, and schooling.

The Mention of Writing in Ritual Texts and Contexts

During the past two decades, a number of Native authors have recorded or transcribed the words spoken during rituals, and passed down as oral tradition among the elders of the communities, a practice that in itself speaks of new uses of literacy. In the majority of these texts, there is little mention of the written word, yet some signs appear. For example, Pérez López (1996) recorded several telling invocations in his monograph on San Pablo Chalchihuitán. One verse (p. 249) asks for protection from the envious: *"Por eso te digo\ que me evites\ la mirada\ la vista\ del envidioso\ del rencoroso\, que no sea lo primero que escriba\ que anote con su lápiz\ que ponga en su libro, señor"* (So I tell you, keep me out of sight of the envious, of the resentful, may I not be the first thing that he writes, that he notes with his pencil, that he puts in his book, Lord). Another solicits the protection of San Pablo, patron saint of the town: *"Que en medio de tu libro\ ... lo cuides todas las mañanas"* (between the pages of your book ... safeguard him every morning; Pérez López, 1996, p. 303). The author mentions that San Pablo has a book so that he might set in writing and keep track of all the petitions they make. In these verses, we again find reference to the recording of names, which marks the accumulated history of literacy in Chiapas, at times as a means of control, at times as a means of protection.

The association of certain saints of the Catholic doctrine with the symbol of a book or scroll led to different interpretations in each town. In the oral tradition of the highlands, the saints acquire a life of their own; they are said to have traveled over long distances, seeking the proper place to establish their homes. One version tells of the apostle, Andrés, who after the destruction of the temple of his native town, found refuge in Chamula, where he began to write the history of his exodus and travels (Díaz Hernández, 1998).

A related theme is the association of writing with certain predestined occupations. Maltil Tulum, a Zinacantan *curandero*, secretary, and musician, reported to Laughlin (1992) that as a boy he had dreamed that the elders had given him certain gifts, including a bunch of lilies and a bunch of pencils. The flowers signaled his curing abilities, and the pencils meant that he would become a scribe. This reference places literacy on a level with other talents revealed to individuals through dreams, such as the case of midwives. In contrast, other tales stress the acquired nature of literacy abilities, as certain persons, whose birth is often associated with such omens, are sent to study and become leaders or priests. In either case, literacy seems integrated through traditional ways of entering communal life.

Narratives of Experience on the *Fincas*[8]

Various folktales recorded by Native writers give clues to the use of writing in the context of relationships between Indian workers and their masters (*patrones*). A recurring incident involves orders to take certain letters or documents to a faraway destination. This is often seen as a ruse to allure the man's wife while he is away, and there follow a number of ways of avoiding the trap, including the intervention of the powerful *nahual* spirits (e.g., Hernández Rodríguez, 1999). These stories point to the association of writing and power that pervades a society where literacy has been restricted to the dominant classes.

A different source comes from the Tojolab'al group in the region of Comitán, and the relation of writing to labor and land, though the experience was similar in all of Chiapas. During the last half of the 19th and well into the 20th century, Tojolab'al people were driven off their land and forced to serve as *baldíos* (indentured servants), tied to the *fincas* through perpetual debt. During the past 60 years, many purchased or obtained (through work or grants) land in the *Cañadas*, the deep gorges that run toward the Lacandon forest. The colonization of these lands became a major theme of oral tradition relayed from the founding generation to the younger family members.

Testimonies of nine survivors of the finca system were recorded and translated by Gómez Hernández and Ruz (1992). Some testimonies convey memories of earlier times, as when visiting bishops would write down their observations in the parochial books. However, the main theme is work on the plantations. A constant element is the existence of the *papeles*, papers or notebooks where individual debts were recorded. Cruz (cited in Gómez Hernández & Ruz, 1992) notes: *"Toda la vida están [los patrones] agarrando el papel, toda la vida"* (The masters are forever holding on to the papers, their whole life; p. 387). Espinoza (cited in Gómez Hernández & Ruz, 1992) exclaims:

---

[8]*Fincas* are the plantations (generally growing coffee, but also other products) in the valleys and lowlands of Chiapas, where the Highland Mayas would migrate for seasonal work.

"Bien oscuro está tu papel, siempre está bien oscuro tu papel, siempre se quedará así todo el tiempo tu papel. Vas a llenar un papel [una hoja] y ya comienzas con [otra] diferente, no terminas de pagar, todo es tu deuda" (Your paper is really dark, it is always really dark, your paper, it will always remain that way, your paper … You fill up one [piece of] paper and you begin with another different one, you don't ever finish paying off, it is all your debt; p. 243). She later adds: *"A veces ahí queda lleno el papel, cuando nos morimos ahí queda, ya los hijos entrarán a pagar"* (Sometimes the paper stays that way, full, when we die, it remains, then the children go into paying; p. 257).

The testimony of Enrique Espinoza (cited in Gómez Hernández & Ruz, 1992, p. 168) tells of what happened when a worker drank the liquor that he was supposed to deliver in town. The *patrón* threatens: " *'Bueno, está bien hijo, va a entrar en tu cuenta en la libreta'—Tres o cuatro pesos va aumentar tu dueda por el garrafón ese … si no sabes leer, eso es lo que le gusta al patrón, que toda la vida estés en yugo, como si fueras novillo. ¡Cuándo va a enseñarte a leer el patrón!"* (" 'OK, it's all right son, it will go into your account in the book.' Three or four pesos added to your debt due to that bottle … if you do not know how to read, that is what the patrón likes, so that all of your life you will be under the yoke, like a calf. When would the patrón ever teach you to read!" p. 168).

According to these accounts, landowners had a number of ways of preventing their workers from seeing their accounts, and never telling them how much they actually owed. Espinoza (cited in Gómez Hernández & Ruz, 1992) continues with an imaginary dialogue with a *patrón*:

"Yo voy a ver mi cuenta." (I'm going to look at my account.)
"No, todavía falta [de pagar], ahí lo vemos luego." (No, you still owe, we will
    look at it later.)
"Pero no, creo que ya a va a dar." (But no, I believe it is almost going to add up.)
"No, falta mucho." (No, it still lacks a lot.)
Al fin, nunca jamás desapareció la deuda. (Finally, the debt never disap-
    peared.)

These fragments suggest that perhaps some plantation workers were able to learn the rudiments of literacy to keep their accounts straight. Whereas some saw writing only as a darkening of pages, others were able to figure their accounts and thus wrest free from bondage. In retrospect, for the elders who tell these histories, such elementary skills seemed to not amount to much, as in the Cañada region being literate came to be equated with knowing "the Word of

God." The following comment of Pablo Cruz (cited in Gómez Hernández & Ruz, 1992) is now echoed by many of the original settlers. *"Ni si quiera había noticia de una biblia, todavía no, ... antes estabamos como un animalito ... pero ahora ya hay catequista, ya hay libro, ya hay biblia, ya escuchamos un poco cuál es la senda, pero antes no se conocía."* (We didn't even know about a Bible, not then, ... before, we were like a little animal ... but now there is a catechist, now there is a book, there is a Bible, now we learn about the right way, but before it was unknown; p. 394). Catholic missionaries and catechists accompanied settlers in the search for what came to be thought of, through biblical analogy, as the Promised Land and forged this discourse that associated literacy with progress and with the Scriptures (Leyva Solano, 1998). The process was somewhat conflictive, as the young catechists displaced the village elders, whose traditional religious knowledge—a historically constructed amalgam of popular Catholicism and Mayan belief—was often considered heretical by the clergy. Nevertheless, many villages and new colonies enthusiastically adopted the renewed Catholic ritual and reflection on everyday life in light of the written word. As suggested earlier, during the late 20th century, evangelization became one of the two most significant domains of appropriation of writing in Chiapas. The other, also reflected in these testimonies, was the struggle for land.

Enrique Espinoza (cited in Gómez Hernández & Ruz, 1992) recalls a time when the baldíos were nominally liberated by the revolutionary armies of Carranza in the late 1910s: *"Ahí juntaron [los papeles] los soldados, les juntaron, los quemaron ... Acabaron los libros, ahí acabó la cuenta, libre quedó la gente."* (The soldiers gathered all the papers, they gathered them and burned them, finished were the books, finished the account, free were the people!; p. 171). Then, he adds, the landowners attempted to hold some workers back, promising them land: *"Pero como mi papá no sabe pues ... si lo supiera diría: 'Bueno patrón, si me la va a regalar deme las escrituras, deme el plano.' [Si se] la hubiera dado con todos los papeles, entonces estaría bien, pero como sólo en balde lo engañaron, para que regresara ... ya no, ya ejido solicitó."* (But because my father didn't know, well ... if he had known he would have said: 'OK, master, if you are going to give it to me, give me the deeds, give me the map.' If he had given him all of the papers, then it would have been fine, but as they were only tricking him in vain, so he would return ... so then, no, then he solicited an *ejido* land grant; p. 171). Although unable to counter the offer with legal arguments, Enrique's father sensed the trap. Indigenous communities had learned, from way back, the importance of written proof of land ownership, for these documents were always stored in the safest hiding places (Villa Rojas, 1990).

The process of purchasing land or petitioning for grants has led, perhaps much more than any other process, to the appropriation of literacy practices among the colonizers of the Lacandon Selva. As with many colonies in the Cañadas, plantation workers soliciting land grants were involved in long and arduous bureaucratic transactions to obtain official documents. As described by one settler (Vos, 1988), it involved many trips over land to the distant state capital, Tuxtla, some taking as long as a month. At the Agrarian office, leaders often found that previous documents had mysteriously disappeared. If the petitioners dared to argue in the terms of the law, they were further mistreated and accused of "having gone to school," as though the condition for obtaining a land grant required total ignorance and dependence on the federal state. As in this case, many of the new communities were forced to renew their petitions time and again, and learned to request from the bureaucracy a written receipt and copies of the ongoing agreements. Indigenous peasants sought help from lettered engineers or lawyers, and resorted to political pressure by establishing unions and other organizations. Many petitions remain unsolved to this day, with the result that land in the Selva region, particularly, has a series of overlapping claims that have made legal solution of conflicts nearly impossible.

The following generations, charged with carrying on this struggle for land, and later for credit to cultivate it, developed skills far beyond those acquired in the rudimentary schooling offered in the region. The organization of the new communities led to a significant increase in the uses of literacy, although official census data place this region far beneath the national norms, as extremely marginal.[9] It is important to note that the process forged a new relationship to the world of writing. It also reconfirmed the fundamental mistrust in the government's deceitful uses of writing that underlies the current resistance in the region. This has been the case, for example, with the unfulfilled San Andrés Accords of 1996, signed by government representatives and the Zapatista leaders.[10] Among other things, the Zapatista movement has actively promoted

---

[9]Over the past century, according to census data, literacy rates in the state of Chiapas rose from 9.1% (in 1895) to 70% (in 1990), although the state still lags behind the 88% national literacy rate, and the total number of illiterates has increased. In the Indigenous regions of the state, official literacy rates are between 30% and 50%.

[10]The national congress passed a law in 2001 which purported to fulfill the Accords, but in fact eliminated the most substantial classes, including autonomy. The law was contested in courts by Zapatista and other Indian organizations but the case was lost.

literacy through its own organizations and schools, rejecting and going beyond what has been offered by the government.

Stories of Experience in School

Several testimonies of Native writers refer to the first time that federal schools were introduced in the Indigenous towns in the 20th century. These versions contain a mixture of voices, reflecting both anecdotes on schooling that abound in village talk and the discourse on the benefits of schooling constructed by the bilingual teachers, many of whom have ceased to live in the villages. For example, some stories mention times when parents would hide their children, especially the girls, or force them to go to the wilderness to keep them out of school. Others report how teachers went from house to house, seeking out the children, while confronting opposition by traditional authorities (Guzmán Méndez, 1994, pp. 299–301). Texts written by bilingual teachers tend to portray schooling in a favorable light, whereas other Native authors have a more critical view of their experience.

Insights on this experience with schooling can be found in two texts published by Aubry (1988), produced by Tzotzil authors involved in the INAREMAC workshops.[11] In his introduction, Aubry notes that the narratives reveal two opposing strategies for dealing with schooling. The first is a testimony reported by Mariano López Méndez (cited in Aubry, 1988, pp. 82–108), taken from an oral account and written as a comic strip. This tale expresses a deliberate resistance to schooling. It tells the story of Domingo, a shepherd boy, whose father first disguised him as a girl and then married him (while still a child) to avoid sending him to school. Villagers burned down the school, and later had to rebuild it. Finally, Domingo's father took him to work on the *fincas* in a deliberate move to take him away from schooling and preserve his Chamula identity. This story has an ironic turn: During his short spells in the classroom, Domingo managed to learn some reading and writing, and life on the finca later taught him Spanish. With these skills, as an adult he was named mayor of his village, although, according to this account, he continued to uphold local custom rather than bowing to government officials, as had the more schooled Chamula leaders of the time.

The other story, an autobiographical narrative written by Antonio López Pérez (cited in Aubry, 1988, pp. 103–112), shows the contrary strategy. Antonio

---

[11]These workshops, organized by Andrés Aubry and Jan Rus, produced transcriptions of oral narratives, collective writing, and alternative forms of writing, and sponsored publications that were distributed within the towns and villages of the Native authors.

tells how his parents had finally decided to send him to school, after being harassed by soldiers bearing papers. After ridiculing the soldiers' bad manners and rude talk (i.e., behavior contrary to what they considered to be well educated), his parents conceded that it would be best "to learn the weapons of the enemy." Antonio recalls insisting: "I want to learn Spanish so that they will respect us, I said, I want to learn to read, and also to write, in order to understand what those papers say." His mother accepted and added, "From now on, you will defend us." With his primary schooling completed, Antonio became a lay teacher, and in 1957, when the town of Zinacantan drove out the non-Indian residents, he was named secretary. He concludes, "I knew nothing about office work, but in the face of necessity, I learned on the job. Doing office work was my schooling."[12]

What is interesting in these cases is the actual appropriation of writing, despite the fear of and resistance to schooling. Other narratives also convey this association of schooling with the value of learning to read and write. For example, versions of the legend of the "bear-man," born in a cave from the union of a woman and a bear, include episodes of the child's passage through school and his fights with schoolmates who molested him because of his strange appearance. In one tale, the boy, Chonman, was expelled from school, and went home crying to his mother. However, they decided that it did not matter much, because he had already learned to read and write (Sántiz Díaz, 1994). Many Indian families use this principle for evaluating a teacher's effectiveness and for deciding whether to send or withdraw their children from school. They have no use for schools that waste a child's time by teaching nothing but disrespect.

As is well known, schooling in the Indigenous towns has not always led to literacy (see Hornberger, 1996). Spending several years in the classroom at times produced a well-developed habit of copying Spanish texts without understanding a word. Several testimonies confirm the experience of children learning to "read" Spanish texts by sounding out the words without knowing their meanings. Native students could thus "learn to read and write" and could even obtain a primary school certificate without having gained much knowledge of the dominant language or other school subjects. This may sound strange to us, yet similar appropriations of writing have occurred in other times and places—for example, the case of Latin literacy in some European monasteries during the Middle Ages.

The ambivalence toward schooling is a constant theme of the testimonies from the Indigenous communities. Opposition is sometimes cast as fleeing

---

[12]Aubry (1988, pp. 106–107, 112). My translation from French.

from the harsh punishments and violence that marked much classroom experience. Furthermore, people in the communities sensed that schooling led above
all to the adoption of the kind of dress, demeanor, and social habits associated
with the *caxlán* (non-Indian) way of life. At the same time, there are testimonies of communities that sought out and even paid the wages of good teachers
so that their children might truly learn basic Spanish literacy.[13]

In Chiapas, the past half-century has witnessed an increase of schooling in
the larger Indigenous towns, although fewer than 20 out of 100 children finish
sixth grade.[14] The rejection of ladino teachers and bilingual teachers who have
taken on caxlán ways is still common in the communities. Grievances expressed
by parents include not only the fact that their children's manners change, but
also, as seen earlier, that they finish elementary schooling without having
learned to "write a letter." Over the past two decades, many Indigenous communities have submitted to the state educational authorities the proceedings of town
meetings in which they decide to expel a state-employed teacher. These documents often specify the grounds for the dismissal, which tend to include not only
failure to teach effectively, but also meddling in local politics, corruption, viola-
tion of local custom, and any other undesirable behavior (e.g., drunkenness, exploitation or sexual harassment of students). In these cases, it is the request for
literacy, and the exercise of collective rights through literacy, that has led Natives
to oppose and resist the government agencies' abuse of power. Many communities have seen through the guise of a system that offers nominal schooling, while
continuing to undermine effective access to the written word.

Returning to Rabbit and the crocodile's teeth, perhaps the story has a different moral: Rather than writing, it is schooling of the sort most commonly offered to the Native communities that leads to a "loss of soul." After all, Rabbit
was literate. Perhaps he has outwitted us again!

REFLECTIONS ON LITERACY AND POWER

Among anthropologists, educators, and missionaries working in Chiapas, Indigenous identity is often related to the survival of an oral culture. Despite the
recent surge of publications by Native writers, scholars of different ideological

---

[13]A novel written by an anthropologist, Castro's (1983) *Los Hombres Verdaderos*, gives a
good idea of this process.

[14]Until very recently, village schools in this region offered scarcely two or three elementary
grades. To complete primary schooling, children had to leave home and attend boarding schools.
Although many schools were formally staffed with bilingual teachers, instruction was usually
conducted in Spanish.

leanings have expressed concern that literacy (in whatever language) may undermine the very conditions of oral tradition and thus of the cultural continuity of the Mayan people. They mention, for example, that many of the Native authors enjoy professional jobs in public institutions, live in cities, and no longer speak the Indigenous languages to their children. Given the scant use of the official bilingual teaching materials in the classrooms, these scholars favor strengthening the oral transmission of the Indigenous languages, and promoting audio and video media that seem closer to the everyday expression of indigenous cultures. Other scholars, on the contrary, view literacy as potentially empowering, and as a valid vehicle for preserving and extending the traditional knowledge of the Mayan people. I believe the jury is still out on the issue. However, I have argued that by recovering a historical perspective on literacy in the region we gain insight into the actual appropriations of writing—in whatever language—that have occurred in the past, and are thus conceivable in the future.

In Chiapas, the history of literacy has been played out within a horizon of conflict and repression. Those in power have used the strategies of destruction and denial of Native writing to prevent the spread of the written word among people at the margins of society. However, the very existence of these strategies is evidence that at different moments, the Indigenous groups appropriated writing and used it for their own purposes. The historical record shows instances of the Mayans' use of written language, as well as use of oral language forms, to resist domination. At different times, highland Mayans attempted to subvert the uses of writing associated with official control, and also struggled to further certain uses of writing for their own ends. By exploring the narratives published in recent years in Chiapas, I have attempted to recover voices that document the experience with writing. The relationship to power has always influenced the way in which literacy was regarded and used in diverse contexts, including those of ritual, the struggle for work and land, and schooling.

In concluding, I recall a few points shared in this field. As is well known, we can no longer examine literacy along a single continuum that goes from orality, understood as the absence of the written language, to literacy, seen as the elaborate use of alphabetic writing. We must account for histories of the particular oral–written matrix of each group (Cook-Gumperz & Keller-Cohen, 1993). In the process of appropriating literacy, some groups may develop alternative strategies—including oral forms—for conserving and transmitting knowledge, in the face of systematic destruction of their own written record.

At the same time, they may resort to uses of writing that are generally denied in official discourse as representing "literacy." These strategies—on both sides—can only be understood if we regard both writing and speaking as practices constructed in the context of asymmetrical power relationships.

Elsie Rockwell is a full professor and researcher at the Departmento de Investigaciones Educativas, Center for Research and Advanced Studies, in Mexico City, where she also holds a doctorate in educational research. She completed a master's degree in history at the University of Chicago, and also studied anthropology at the National University of Mexico. A cofounder of the field of educational ethnography in Latin America, she has contributed articles to *Human Development, Educational Foundations, Anthropology & Education Quarterly*, and *Cultural Dynamics*, as well as chapters to B. A. Levinson et al.'s *The Cultural Production of the Educated Person* (SUNY Press, 1996), and D. Olson and N. Torrance's *The Making of Literate Societies* (Blackwell, 2001). Rockwell currently teaches graduate students and is involved in further research on indigenous experiences with schooling and literacy in Mexico.

ACKNOWLEDGMENTS

I am grateful for comments on this chapter at the session at the 1999 Annual Meeting of the American Anthropological Association, "Language, Literacy, and Power in Schooling," as well as the reviewers of the manuscript. Many of the ideas were developed in close collaboration with my friend and colleague, Dora Pellicer. I thank Dometila Bolom for her careful selection of Native texts.

REFERENCES

Alejos García, J. (1988). *Wajalix bät'an* [The ancient word]. Mexico DF: Universidad Nacional Autónoma de México.
Aubry, A. (1988). *Les Tzotzil par eux-mêmes* [The Tzotzil write about themselves]. Paris: L'Harmattan.
Bloch, M. (1998). *How we think they think*. Boulder, CO: Westview.
Bonfil, G. (1991). Lo propio y lo ajeno: Una aproximación al problema del control cultural [Our own or alien: An approximation to the problem of cultural control]. In G. Bonfil, *Pensar nuestra cultura* [Rethinking our culture] (pp. 49–57). Mexico DF: Alianza.
Boone, E. H., & Mignolo, W. D. (Eds.). (1994). *Writing without words: Alternative literacies in Mesoamerica and the Andes*. Durham, NC: Duke University Press.
Castro, C. A. (1983). *Los hombres verdaderos* [The true men]. Xalapa, Mexico: Universidad Veracruzana.

Chartier, R. (1995). Popular appropriations: The readers and their books. In R. Chartier, *Forms and meanings: Texts, performances and audiences from codex to computer* (pp. 83–97). Philadelphia: University of Pennsylvania Press.

Cifuentes, B. (1998). *Letras sobre voces* [Letters on voices]. Mexico DF: Centro de Investigación y Estudios Superiores en Antropología Social.

Collins, J., & Blot, R. (2003). Literacy and literacies: Texts, power, and identity. Cambridge, UK: Cambridge University Press.

Cook-Gumperz, J., & Keller-Cohen, D. (1993). Alternative literacies in school and beyond: Multiple literacies of speaking and writing. *Anthropology & Education Quarterly 24*, 283–287.

Cuentos y relatos indígenas [Indigenous stories and tales]. (1994–1998). (7 vols.) Mexico *DF: Universidad Nacional Autónoma de México.*

Díaz Hernández, J. (1998). Cuando ampliaron la iglesia de San Andrés [When they enlarged the Saint Andrew Church]. In *Cuentos y relatos indígenas [Indigenous stories and tales]* Vol. 7 (pp. 43–46). Mexico DF: Universidad Nacional Autónoma de México.

Esponda Jimeno, V. (1992). El K'awaltic, las ordenanzas de Oxchuc del Visitador Jacinto Roldán de la Cueva, 1674 [The K'awaltic, the Oxchuc ordinances of the (royal) visitor, Jacinto Robles de la Cueva, 1674]. Tuxtla Gutiérrez, Mexico DF: *Anuario del Instituto Chiapaneco de la Cultura, 1992*, 187–205.

Fabre, D. (1993). Le Berger des signes. [The shepherd of the signs]. In D. Fabre (Ed.), *Ecritures ordinaires* [Ordinary writing] (pp. 269–313). Paris: P.O.L. Georges Pompidou.

Gómez Hernández, A., & Ruz, M. H. (Eds.). (1992). *Memoria baldía: Los Tojolab'ales y las fincas* [Memories of bondage; The Tojolab'al and the plantations]. Mexico DF: Universidad Nacional Autónoma de México.

Gosner, K. (1991). La élites indígenas en los Altos de Chiapas (1524–1714) [Indigenous elites in the Chiapas Highlands (1524–1714)]. In *Los pueblos de indios y las comunidades* [Indian towns and communities] (pp. 80–98). Mexico DF: El Colegio de México.

Guzmán Méndez, J. (1994). Historia de Tenejapa. [History of Tenejapa]. In *Cuentos y relatos Indígenas* [Indigenous stories and tales]. (Vol. 5, pp. 293–302). Mexico DF: Universidad Nacional Autónoma de México.

Hernández Rodríguez, R. (1999). Consejo de Nahual. [Counsel of a Nahual]. In A. Gómez Hernández, M. R. Palazón, & M. H. Ruz (Eds.), *Palabras de nuestro corazón: Mitos, fábulas y cuentos maravillosos de la narrativa Tojolab'al* [Words from our hearts. Myths, fables and marvelous stories of Tojolab'al narrative]. (pp. 259–261). Mexico DF: Universidad Nacional Autónoma de México.

Hornberger, N. (1996). Indigenous literacies in the Americas. In N. Hornberger (Ed.), *Indigenous literacies in the Americas: Language planning from the bottom up* (pp. 3–16). New York: Mouton de Gruyter.

Justice, S. (1994). *Writing and rebellion: England in 1381*. Berkeley: University of California Press.

Kartunnen, F. (1998). Indigenous writing as a vehicle of postconquest continuity and change in Mesoamerica. In E. H. Boone & T. Cummins (Eds.), *Native traditions in the postconquest world* (pp. 421–447). Washington, DC: Dumbarton Oaks Research Library.

Laughlin, R. (1992). *Zinacantan: Canto y sueño* [Zinacantan: Song and dream]. Mexico DF: Instituto Nacional Indigenista.

Leyva Solano, X. (1998). Catequistas, misioneros y tradiciones en Las Cañadas [Catequists, missionaries and traditions in Cañadas]. In J. P. Viqueira & M. H. Ruz (Eds.), *Chiapas: Los rumbos de otra historia* [Chiapas: Orientations for another history] (pp. 375–406). Mexico DF: Centro de Investigación y Estudios Superiores en Antropología Social.

Montemayor, C. (1998). *Arte y trama en el cuento indígena* [Art and plot in the indigenous story]. Mexico DF: Fondo de Cultura Económica.

Pérez López, E. (1996). *Los pableros, dueños del cargo, dueños de la tierra* [The people of San Pablo, owners of a cargo, owners of the land]. Tuxtla Gutiérrez, Mexico DF: Gobierno del Estado de Chiapas, Secretaría para la Atención de los Pueblos Indígenas.

Pineda, V. (1986). *Sublevaciones indígenas en Chiapas* [Indigenous uprisings in Chiapas]. Mexico DF: Instituto Indigenista Nacional.

Pitarch Ramón, P. (1996). *Ch'ulel: Una etnografía de las almas tzeltales* [Ch'ulel: An ethnography of Tzeltal souls]. Mexico DF: Fondo de Cultura Económica.

Richards, J. B., & Richards, M. (1996). Mayan language literacy in Guatemala: A sociohistorical overview. In N. Hornberger (Ed.), *Indigenous literacies in the Americas: Language planning from the bottom up* (pp. 189–211). New York: Mouton de Gruyter.

Rockwell, E. (2001). The uses of orality and literacy in rural Mexico: Tales from Xaltipan. In D. R. Olson & N. Torrance (Eds.), *The making of literate societies* (pp. 225–247). Oxford, UK: Blackwell.

Rus, J. (1994). The "Comunidad Revolucionaria Institucional": The subversion of native government in Highland Chiapas, 1936–1968. In G. Joseph & D. Nugent (Eds.), *Everyday forms of state formation: Revolution and the negotiation of rule in modern Mexico* (pp. 265–300). Durham, NC: Duke University Press.

Rus, J. (1998). ¿Guerra de castas según quién?: Indios y ladinos en los sucesos de 1869 [Caste war according to whom? Indians and ladinos in the 1869 events]. In J. P. Viqueira & M. H. Ruz (Eds.), *Chiapas: Los rumbos de otra historia* [Chiapas: Orientations for another history] (pp. 145–174). Mexico DF: Universidad Nacional Autónoma de México.

Ruz, M. H. (1986). Introducción. In F. D. De Ara, *Vocabulario de lengua tzendal según el orden de Copanabastla* [Vocabulary of the Tzendal language according to the Order of Copanabastla]. (M. H. Ruz, Ed.). Mexico DF: Universidad Nacional Autónoma de México.

Ruz, M. H. (1997). Etnicidad, territorio y trabajo en las fincas decimonónicas de Comitán, Chiapas [Ethnicity, territory and labor on the nineteenth century farms of Comitán]. In L. Reina (Ed.), *La reindianización de América, Siglo XIX* [The reindianization of America, 19th Century] (pp. 267–293). Mexico DF: Siglo Veintiuno.

Ruz, M. H. (1998). Prólogo. [Preface]. In J. P. Viqueira, & M. H. Ruz (Eds.), *Chiapas: Los rumbos de otra historia* [Chiapas: orientations for another history] (pp. 7–17). Mexico DF: Universidad Nacional Autónoma de México.

Sántiz Díaz, M. (1994). Historia del hombre oso [The history of the Bear man]. In *Cuentos y relatos indígenas* [Indigenous stories and tales] (Vol. 1, pp. 15–35). Mexico DF: Universidad Nacional Autónoma de México.

Tanck de Estrada, D. (1999). *Pueblos de Indios y educación en el México colonial, 1750–1821* [Indian pueblos and education in colonial Mexico, 1750–1821]. Mexico DF: El Colegio de México.

Tedlock, D. (1996). Introduction. In *Popol Vuh* (D. Tedlock, Trans.). New York: Simon & Schuster.

Varenne, H., & McDermott, R. (1999). *Successful failure: The school America builds.* Boulder, CO: Westview.

Villa Rojas, A. (1990). *Etnografía Tzeltal de Chiapas* [Tzeltal ethnography of Chiapas]. Mexico DF: Miguel Angel Porrúa, Editor.

Viqueira, J. P. (1998a). Las causas de una rebelión india: Chiapas, 1712 [The causes of an Indian rebellion, 1712]. In J. P. Viqueira & M. H. Ruz (Eds.), *Chiapas: Los rumbos de otra historia* [Chiapas: Orientations for another history] (pp. 103–144). Mexico DF: Universidad Nacional Autónoma de México.

Viqueira, J. P. (1998b). Los Altos de Chiapas: Una introducción general [The Chiapas Highlands: A general introduction]. In J. P. Viqueira & M. H. Ruz (Eds.), *Chiapas: Los rumbos de otra historia* [Chiapas: Orientations for another history] (pp. 219–236). Mexico DF: Universidad Nacional Autónoma de México.

Vos, J. de (1988). *Viajes al desierto de la soledad: Cuando la Selva Lacandona aún era selva* [Journeys to the desert of solitude: When the Lacandon Selva was still a rainforest]. Mexico DF: Secretaría de Educación Pública y Centro de Investigación y Estudios Superiores en Antropología Social.

2

Negotiating for the Hopi Way of Life Through Literacy and Schooling

Sheilah Nicholas
The University of Arizona

Indigenous languages in North America are rapidly being displaced by English. The way of life communicated and embodied in Indigenous languages is therefore in jeopardy as well. This chapter examines an action research project underway in the author's native community of Hopi, in which literacy and schooling are being coopted as vehicles through which the local language and culture can be revitalized and maintained. Utilizing these historically invasive and assimilating institutions requires careful cultural negotiation guided by the understanding that in both its oral and written forms, the Native language communicates the Hopi way of life and Hopi identity. This negotiation also requires a critical, dialogic assessment of past colonizing experiences, and the ways in which individual and collective action can transform present and future possibilities. Finally, cultural negotiation requires that the voices of all stakeholders be heard and included. This chapter explores how the Hopi people have initiated such a process, and the ways in which Indigenous literacies can be vehicles for community empowerment.

> My grandfather used to tell me that us Hopis speak from the heart .... I've come to
> understand what he was talking about. We need to teach our children ourselves.
> —*Participant in a Hopi Language Assessment Project orientation
> meeting, Paaqavi Village, Arizona, January 1997*

I recently addressed a sixth-grade class of Hopi students about why our paths would cross. I told them a personal story about my own educational journey and how my experiences have led me to work toward ensuring that their journeys will be more fulfilling with a firm grounding in their Hopi identity—their personal and collective strength. I recounted my experience as being vastly different from what I envisioned for them. The difference was manifested in pursuing my own life journey disconnected from my Hopi identity. My parents, motivated by what they understood to be in my best interest and informed by their own negative experiences in federal boarding schools, advised me to "put aside" my language and culture while I pursued my formal education. I told these Hopi students that in many ways, because I listened to the message that my language and culture would impede my educational success, I achieved educational "success," but not without sacrifice to my cultural identity and language and not without many struggles (cf. Varenne & McDermott, 1999). I also told the students that a Japanese instructor in my graduate schooling, Dr. Akira Yamamoto, convinced me that I had not lost my language and culture, but that they remained deep within—all that was required was to retrieve them from this depth.

This has been challenging. Today, I am working to fill in the voids created when I "put aside" my language and culture. Through this process I am reaffirming and reclaiming my own Hopi identity and language as well as advocating the same for Hopi youth. In expressing this endeavor to these Hopi students, I also now understand that I was "speaking from the heart," a stance that I bring to this discussion as well.

HOPI SINOM–HOPI TUTSKWA: HOPI PEOPLE–HOPI LANDS

The Hopi reservation is situated on and around the three southernmost fingers of Black Mesa in northeastern Arizona. It is a geographical, linguistic, and cultural enclave within an enclave: The 1.8 million-acre Hopi reservation lies within the larger Navajo reservation, which in turn lies within the boundaries of three southwestern states and the larger U.S. society. About 10,000 Hopis reside in and around 12 Hopi villages, each of which has traditionally been and continues to function as an autonomous, self-governing unit. Throughout the villages, the Hopi language, linguistically linked to the Uto-Aztecan language family, continues to be the medium of interaction during cultural and ceremonial activities and among older Hopi speakers, earning Hopis the distinction of being categorized as a Class A "honor rollee" language in Krauss's (1998) classification of Indigenous languages. As such, Hopi remains a language spoken by all generations, including children, but this is rapidly becoming "Hopi speech interjected with English terms" (Wintermute, 1991, p. 1).

HOPI POTSKWANIAT: THE HOPI WAY OF LIFE

Pay yeesiwni.
Sopkyawat sinom wuyomiqhaqami qatsit naavokyawintiwni. Paypu okiwa.
—*Emory Sekaquaptewa, Hopi elder, anthropologist, and linguist, 1999*

Each Hopi ceremonial dance commences with these words. They are words of fervent prayer for all, embodying the Hopi way of life—that life in the Hopi way will continue to move toward its intended destination. This is a journey toward old age immersed in experiencing spiritually, emotionally, physically, mentally, and materially "the good things of life": health, happiness, family, and sustenance. These values are "rooted in our cornfields," emanating from corn, the basis of Hopi existence; hence, the Hopi have a deep commitment to and faith in corn. The Hopi aspire to experience such a life and pursue it with humbleness and industry. The ultimate goal is to reach self-fulfillment on behalf of the whole (E. Sekaquaptewa, personal communication, April 20, 1999).

This prayer also embodies the Hopi ethic of community, which is the heart of the Hopi way of life. This ethic is recalled in a Hopi woman's utopian memory of a childhood immersed in this way of life. At a Hopi language workshop in 1998, she commented: *"Itam qa suuk pu' tsaqavtat angq noonova oovi itam yanyungwa,"* meaning "We no longer partake of food from a single bowl and therefore are now like this [in a state of language and cultural crisis]. We had no anger toward each other; no one [person] was at the forefront; we put our hearts together to get somewhere."

This community ethic is further exemplified and encapsulated in the Hopi words, *nami'nangwa* and *sumi'nangwa*—to live with mutual love toward one another, and in this mood, united in a common purpose, proceed in this manner of togetherness so that *akw himu pasiwta*—things are made possible. This thought embodies generations of accumulated Hopi life experiences—knowledge and understanding about the environment, the world, and themselves as a people expressed through established language and cultural activities, practices, and rituals. According to Sekaquaptewa, "Words have a 'home' in the context of culture—in the course of daily activities, in social institutions such as naming and marriage activities; they have meaning within these contexts" (personal communication, April 20, 1999).

HOPILAVAYI: HOPI LANGUAGE

When you speak and understand Hopi, then you know what is going on—past, present, future.

Hopi is a way of life ... culture—who we are, who we have been all these centuries passed through the language; so language is very critical. When we begin to lose our language, we begin to lose who we are.

—*Comments from participants attending a Hopi Language Assessment Project (HLAP) orientation meeting, December 1996*

Language is the bridge between the past and present, one that will carry the Hopi people into the future. Maintaining this linguistic bridge is a responsibility for all Hopi people. Today, the Hopi way of life faces a precarious existence and a future jeopardized by language loss, particularly for Hopi children and youth. This crisis has permeated the kivas, key religious sites where the transmission of Hopi cultural knowledge occurs for many youth (see also Kroskrity's [1993] discussion of kiva speech for the Arizona Tewa living within the Hopi reservation). "In the kiva only Hopi should be spoken," stated one individual at a 1991 Hopi language symposium. "[But] it is now necessary to give instructions in English as well because so many younger men do not understand Hopi." Six years later, a new concern was voiced by a Hopi parent at a meeting in the village of Upper Munqapi in January 1997: "These young boys say they don't know what's going on in the kivas; they're just taking part for the fun of it." Accommodating this inability and cultural dislocation further exemplifies the crisis: Most Hopi children and youth are no longer speaking the Hopi language and therefore do not know who they were, who they are, or where they are going. Essentially, their place in and responsibility to their Hopi world is lost to them. At a public meeting, a participant posed this question: "The big question is: Is the Hopi language worth saving? The answer is: Yes. It is our language. We live it day to day" (Hotevilla, Arizona, January 1997).

It is from this perspective that I address the process of negotiating for the Hopi way of life through literacy and schooling. My analysis stems from personal experience as a language learner, and from a participatory action research project at Hotevilla-Bacavi Community School in Hotevilla, Arizona. Specifically, I narrate a movement toward raising consciousness about the Hopi language and culture. Using oral testimony, I first consider the present status of the Hopi language in direct relation to the historical imposition of schools and schooling and their impact on the Hopi way of life. I next consider the legacy of this experience on Hopi attitudes toward language, literacy, and schooling. Finally, I examine the ways in which schools are being coopted as arenas of cultural negotiation and as vehicles for redefining Hopi education through Hopi language literacy. The enormity of the latter challenge cannot be underestimated. Transforming schooling in ways that validate rather than annihilate Hopi identity requires a profound understanding of a long and ongoing struggle, the roots of which lie in the past, and that cannot be untangled from the Hopis' present and future directions.

HOPILAVAYI HAQE' QALAWMA: HOPI LANGUAGE STATUS

No one seems to be speaking the Hopi language anymore. Why aren't we teaching our children the Hopi language at home?
—*Participant at a public meeting, Hotevilla, Arizona, January 1997*

This is an often-asked question among the Hopi today. Supported by a 1997 Administration for Native Americans grant, the Hopi Cultural Preservation Office conducted the Hopi Language Assessment Project (HLAP), quantifying for the first time the current status of Hopi language ability and fluency in village communities. The results noted a significant shift underway from Hopi to English.

The most profound evidence was found in the relationships among Hopi language ability, age, and schooling. Whereas the majority of elders age 60 and up maintained Hopi as a primary language after starting school, the majority of individuals in the 40- to 59-year-old age group spoke English as a primary language from the time they started school. Among children and youth ages 2 to 19, 93% were reported to speak English as their primary language once they began school. Essentially, schools have silenced the Hopi people.

"The school was a foreign influence, something that stood against the Hopi way of life. *Ka Hopi.* Not good" (Qoyawayma, 1964, p. 27). Historically, schools have been viewed by Hopi people as alien institutions established first by missionaries and then the federal government, where Hopi children were forcibly sent to learn the ways and language of the White man. As an 8-year-old child, Helen Sekaquaptewa (1985) recalls:

Very early one morning ... [in] 1906, we awoke to find our camp surrounded by troops who had come during the night .... Eighty-two children ... were now loaded into wagons ... and driven [to school] .... Evenings we would gather in a corner and cry ... "I want my mother. I want to go home." We didn't understand a word of English. (p. 96)

Accustomed to obeying low-voiced instruction, Hopi found little justification for the harsh discipline meted out by non-Indian teachers at the boarding schools. Polingaysi Qoyawayma (1964), a Hopi teacher, recounts:

> Because the girl did not stop talking at once when told to do so, she was placed on top of [an unheated] pot-bellied stove ... and an eraser was shoved into her mouth. She sat there, stiff with fright, head bent in shame and saliva dripping until the teacher's sadistic appetite had been satiated. (p. 27)

Hopi culture and language were prohibited in the schools. The response by the Hopi was to covet these cultural possessions even as they experienced continued dissonance between home and community and school. Although fraught with cruelty and injustice, the Hopi experience also demonstrates a legacy of determination, tenacity, and endurance in the face of great adversity.

At the dawn of the 21st century, the residue of past schooling experiences lives on. An elderly gentleman recalls, "When I was a boy, it was forbidden to speak Hopi at school." As punishment for speaking the native tongue, he had his mouth "washed" with soap. Today, this elder marvels that, "They must not have washed it all out because I still hear a little bit of Hopi language coming out of my mouth sometimes" (Wintermute, 1991, p. 1).

Although the Hopi came to "accept" the White man's school, they continued to teach their children the Hopi way of life through traditional means embodied in the Hopi language. Today, that way of life is wavering under mainstream English-only schooling, social dislocations, intermarriage with non-Hopis, and diffuse social transformations in lifestyle brought on by a wage economy and access to English media and technology. "All of these [factors]," states White Mountain Apache language activist and scholar Bernadette Adley-SantaMaria (1999), "have led to changes in language values and attitudes, and, especially among the young, changes in language practices" (p. 16).

TUTUQAYKI: SCHOOL

> Someone must take the responsibility for [language] preservation, and the logical place today is the *school*.
> —*Emory Sekaquaptewa, in a presentation to Hopi language instructors, 1998*

The Hotevilla-Bacavi Community School (HBCS), funded by a Bureau of Indian Affairs grant, is located on the periphery of Hotevilla Village on Third Mesa. HBCS primarily serves the villages of Hotevilla and Bacavi, although many of its students are residents of other villages. It is one of eight reservation schools. A governing board assists in curriculum development (Hopi Cultural Preservation Office, 1998).

Instruction is provided for kindergarten through Grade 7, with one class for each grade level. In the spring of 1998, the student population totaled 154 students, 99% of whom were Hopi. Twenty-two of the 31 faculty and staff members are Hopi. The faculty included four Hopi teachers and eight Hopi teacher assistants, and the principal, a Navajo, was assisted by a Yaqui educational consultant.

The educational statistics of this school mirror the dismal national statistics of educational achievement among Native American students. The school's 1996 Revised Consolidated Reform Plan outlines goals for improvement in teaching, learning, and evaluation methods.

Initiating language and cultural reclamation in the school poses a tremendous challenge. The challenge is compounded when schooling and literacy continue to be understood as explicitly colonizing practices. The following vignettes, excerpted from my field notes, illustrate the tensions inherent in constructing Hopi-oriented schooling within a historically alien institution.

Scene One. The hallway bulletin boards of Hotevilla-Bacavi Community School display bright, happy colors—Easter egg art and the significance of Easter in this community school on Hopiland is apparent. Students are busily coloring/ dyeing eggs for classroom egg hunts. The traditional Hopi calendar describes this time period as *Kwiyamuya,* "month of the windbreaks." During Kwiyamuya, windbreaks are constructed to keep the topsoil from blowing away by the strong winds that rush across the fields of Hopi farmers, threatening to expose precious moisture lying beneath this top layer of soil. Such protection will ensure that corn seedlings grow to maturity, and more importantly, demonstrates the Hopi farmers' "commitment to corn" even in these changed modernist times. This Hopi curriculum is non-existent at the school.

Scene Two. Language shift is pronounced. English is the medium of communication on the playground, in the cafeteria, classrooms, and hallways among children, children and teachers, children and school staff, and among faculty, staff and administration. A 1983 study conducted in this same village school noted that just 16 years ago Hopi students came to school predominantly speaking Hopi, pursuing projects and school subjects in both Hopi and English, and being introduced to the Hopi writing system (Haussler & Tompkins, 1983). At the time of the present study, Hopi language instruction is allocated 80–120 minutes per week, subject to diminished time if "something else" takes priority.

Scene Three. A beautifully constructed timeline in a fifth-grade classroom depicts significant times and events in the historical evolution of the United States. The importance of these events is evident in the amount of wall space this timeline covers and the large bold letters used to point them out. This is the primary focus of the curriculum that serves to educate Hopi children. The absence of significant times and events of the Hopi within this timeline, albeit "unintentional" on the part of the teacher, presents a strong message that Hopi history is unimportant in the education of Hopi children within the school.

These vignettes illustrate the fact that even in this Hopi community school, the curriculum under which children are educated focuses on English and the standards of most mainstream public schools. However, a recent tribal mandate for reservation-wide educational reform compelled HBCS to hire an outside facilitator to assist the Hopi language committee in inserting Hopi language and culture into the school curriculum. This committee of primarily teacher assistants also constitutes the Hopi language instructors, who bear the responsibility for planning and developing a Hopi language and culture curriculum. Meeting the demands of external mandates while addressing the tribal mandate has created ambivalence among these teacher assistants toward this responsibility. Their varying degrees of Hopi language and literacy proficiencies compound the challenges they face. Thus, the community ethic of "putting our hearts together for a common purpose" is profoundly affected by ongoing colonizing practices. From the preceding vignettes, it would appear that HBCS generally remains an institution in which Hopi children will learn only the White man's language, history, and way of life.

NEGOTIATING FOR THE HOPI WAY OF LIFE: EVOLUTION

We have spoken about these issues for some time throughout the villages. Nothing has been done about it, because of the concerns involved with it.
        —*Participant in a HLAP orientation meeting, December 1996*

This statement reflects awareness by the Hopi people that major upheaval of the Hopi way of life has left them with little alternative but to dialogue about the need to reimagine a way of life that accommodates changes from within the community. "If we want to really see good results of saving our language, we need to change our attitudes," a village elder stated at a HLAP meeting in December 1996. The remainder of this chapter addresses how the Hopi people are negotiating a process, threefold in nature, intended to confront language loss through Hopi literacy and by creating a Hopi cultural community within the schools.

First, beginning in 1983, Emory Sekaquaptewa, Hopi research anthropologist and appellate court judge, began acting on a personal interest in studying the Hopi language. An early database of words on 5" × 7" index cards was compiled from researching ethnographic reports and "lifting" all Hopi words contained in these reports. These words were translated into a standard system. Expanding these word forms significantly increased the number of words originally compiled. Subsequently, a 12,000-word database became the basis of a proposal for funds that would allow Sekaquaptewa to continue this project. His perseverance and determination attracted the interest and help of others, leading to the Hopi Language Dictionary Project. Internal Hopi and external university alliances were essential to the culmination of his efforts with the 1998 publication of the 30,000-word *Hopi Dictionary—Hopìikwa Lavàytutuveni—A Hopi–English Dictionary of the Third Mesa Dialect.* This dictionary now provides Hopi with an orthography and an extensive Hopi lexicographical instrument for Hopi literacy development.

Part two of the process has involved public forums on the history of formal education for Hopi people. Language symposia and village summit meetings spanning more than 15 years have been held for the purpose of addressing the crisis of Hopi language loss.

"Hopi people are a bicultural and bilingual people, and half our education has been neglected by government, public, and private schools" (Eugene Sekaquaptewa, Hopi Cultural Preservation Symposium, 1991). This elder's statement acknowledges that schools have played a major role in the loss of traditional values and language. The fact that formal education has failed them and continues to fail them as a people has been voiced loudly and clearly. The consequences have left Hopi communities "permeated with conflicting values and practices stemming from centuries of struggle and dislocation" (Fettes, 1999, p. 36). Now the Hopi people must confront this situation, embrace the responsibility, and rely on themselves and not others to do something about it—"they must, each as individuals, make the commitment to use and teach the Hopi language" (Eugene Sekaquaptewa, cited in Wintermute, 1991, p. 1).

For some time, Hopis have sought answers and the means to reclaim the Hopi way of life. As the following testimony from village meetings illustrates,

Hopis are looking at and within themselves, while acknowledging the challenges facing them as they struggle to overcome a legacy of colonialism:

> What will future generations be without the Hopi language? How will they call themselves Hopi people?

> A lot of parents who are both verbal in the Hopi language don't even teach their own children.

> [Confronting the issue of language loss] is finally coming about .... It's going to be hard work .... It will happen. I'll help.

These sentiments have attracted the attention of the Hopi Tribal Council. Although it is another externally imposed institution, it is one being reformed and coopted for Hopi purposes. The following excerpts from The Hopi Tribe's (1995) *Hopit Potskwaniat* provide insight into Hopi language dialogue at this level.

The introduction to the Executive Summary announces a call "to preserve the good things of the Hopi life, and to provide a way of organizing to deal with modern problems with the United States Government and the outside world generally" (Hopi Tribe, 1995, p. i). Section II, "Community Values," states that developing a clear vision for the future requires an understanding of "the core community values that must be preserved and built upon ... those principles or standards that the community will not compromise, no matter what ... [those] Hopi values: religion and ceremonies, cultural customs and practices, language ... *Sumi'nangwa, Nami'nangwa* and all the other characteristic traits of Hopi (Hopi Tribe, 1995, p. ii). Additionally, one of a number of "key ingredients" in the Hopi vision addresses the "need to support and enforce Hopi language as the official language of the Tribe" (Hopi Tribe, 1995, p. ii).

Finally, promotion and development of the Hopi language has been delegated to the reservation schools and the education component of the Hopi tribal political structure. These mandates direct "a total Hopi language and cultural immersion program to be incorporated within ... villages, communities, off-reservation Hopi organizations and educational systems on the Hopi Reservation" (Hopi Tribe, 1995, p. 9). Although the effectiveness (and enforcement) of such mandates remains to be seen, the dialogue and action by individual community members and the tribal political structure are an important and necessary part of the process of cultural negotiation and positive change. Such dialogue and action by community members and the tribal political structure are evidence that "negotiation" has entered the cultural preservation and educational arenas.

LITERACY AND SCHOOLING

In the educational arena, the process of cultural negotiation has been twofold. The results of the 1997 HLAP confirmed that the majority (92%) of the Hopi people surveyed wanted the Hopi language to be taught in the homes, villages, and schools. The overriding concern was to maintain Hopi as a conversational language. Strong support was also expressed for literacy development in Hopi. Addressing the results of the survey, the Hopi Language and Education Plan was developed and implemented with the establishment of the Hopilavayi (Hopi Language) Project. The Hopilavayi Project's primary objectives are to provide Hopi language and literacy training to teachers, teacher assistants, village and other Hopi community members involved in the Project's pilot Head Start preschool, village, and school programs (HLAP, 1997).

Second, HBCS, working from its own initiative, requested assistance to incorporate Hopi language and culture into the comprehensive school curriculum addressed earlier in this chapter. The Hopilavayi Project and HBCS invited my involvement as an "inside–outside" participant observer in this process. My role has included assisting Emory Sekaquaptewa in Hopi literacy development training for those involved in the Hopilavayi Project and at HBCS.

It is important to point out that in addition to the pilot programs already identified, individuals and village communities have initiated their own Hopi language maintenance and revitalization efforts at the grassroots level in response to their own assessment of Hopi language and cultural loss. They have included three village youth programs, literacy development in an off-reservation preparatory school, participation in the American Indian Language Development Institute—a summer training program in American Indian linguistics and bilingual and bicultural curriculum development on the University of Arizona campus—and Hopi language instruction through long-distance technology.

Such efforts on the part of Hopi villages, schools, tribal council, and individuals have created many opportunities for discussion as well as heated debate in working toward tribal consensus on confronting language shift and loss. Central to this debate has been the need to consider that (a) each of the 12 Hopi villages has a unique demographic profile, speaks a distinct Native dialect, and faces varying degrees of language loss (thus, a single, undifferentiated program will not suffice); (b) each of the eight reservation schools is diverse in its operation and management; (c) there is the strong belief that only

Hopi people be allowed to learn the Hopi language as it is a Hopi birth and clan-right; and (d) the overriding concern is to maintain the Hopi language as a conversational language (Hopi Cultural Preservation Office, 1998, p. 5).

Compelling questions voiced during village summits held prior to conducting the HLAP included issues surrounding teacher training and certification, resources and funding, possibilities inherent in existing programs, functional use of the language within the Hopi reservation, student graduation requirements, cultural and linguistic content, cultural restrictions, facilities, the role of the schools, dialect, and orthographic standardization. These issues encompass a broad array of language planning processes, including language status, acquisition, and corpus concerns (see, e.g., Adley-SantaMaria, 1999; McCarty, 2001; Ricento & Hornberger, 1996, for recent analyses of these language planning processes).

The focus of my action research, undertaken in 1998, brought Hopi language discussion into the school and community, offering an opportunity for discourse among parents, teachers, teacher assistants, and staff.

> Well, my feeling about doing some work on the Hopi language is that I support any kind of effort that will allow us to pass the language on to our children, because I know that there are lots of adults who don't know the language or they don't speak the language.

This parent also hoped that Hopi language instruction would emphasize oral conversation, which communicates significant life experiences. At the same time, he voiced concern about the potential consequences of Hopi language revitalization efforts—that trying to "bring back" the "old" language would create more conflict within the community. Here, the reference was to the difficult times in Hopi history rooted in Spanish religious and U.S. governmental intrusions into the Hopi way of life, from which deep emotional and social scars remain. "We've never gone through a period of healing," this parent stated. This has "created some of the very strong feelings among our people ... and that is probably one of the more obvious roots of our current problems that we have in our villages." Yet in revitalizing the language, there is hope for change; if the Hopi language were to once again become the primary language in village communities, the parent imagined:

> It would bring back the gentleness, the kindness that was probably Hopi long time ago ... I still hear it today in the old prayers ... [that] talk about life in different forms ... plants and animals, our children, us as human beings and the spiri-

tual beings .... We don't talk about wars ... money ... drought. In fact there's more talk about hope than anything else ... that things are going to be better.

Discussion with school support staff, teacher aides, and teachers also revealed a shared belief that:

The way [the language is] spoken, the words flow. It's like in harmony with everything else ... and it's one of the things that [demonstrates you are] walking the line; that's supposed to be discipline ... dedicated to a certain way of life .... And yes, you ... get that from the language.

For these individuals, the Hopi way of life requires not only that one be dedicated to it, but also that one continuously "demonstrate" adherence and commitment. The Hopi language, in their view, provides the necessary guidance.

Those with whom I worked related the current symptoms of dysfunction, conflict, and all-encompassing imbalance in village and reservation life to language shift and loss. There was marked ambivalence toward village community members—particularly parents, grandparents, and elders—as voiced in these statements:

Who is teaching them [children] at home? Nobody. Even the *so'o*'s [grandmothers] and the *kwa'a*'s [grandfathers] are talking *Pahaana* [English] to them.

And another thing ... if they [children] don't understand [Hopi], why are we initiating kids [into ceremonial societies] that do not understand? It's being explained to them in English ... which shouldn't be.

As a result of the upheavals represented in these statements, children are positioned as the victims of cultural and familial dissonance. They are often characterized by village adults as not having *kyaptsi*—respect—which is taught through the language. They are also described as only "surfing" on the crest of their cultural heritage, denied the opportunity to experience the deep meaning of what it is to be Hopi through understanding and speaking their Native language.

For their part, teachers and teacher assistants have been positioned to bear the responsibility for preparing Hopi youth to participate in both Hopi and mainstream worlds. They also bear the responsibility for making crucial decisions involving more than just the academic needs of their students. This school looks to the community for guidance and support in their language preservation efforts, but as one teacher states, "The community is still stingy [with their knowledge] ... [and are not] coming in to help their own kids ... and [instead] ask, 'Is the Pahaana going to learn it [the Hopi language] too?' "

"Coveting" language and culture is a direct response to historical linguistic and cultural repression; there remains a strong belief that only Hopi people be allowed to learn the language. At the same time, educators describe parents as "uninvolved" with the school—"they're too busy doing their own thing"—a perception reiterated by Emory Sekaquaptewa in a 1998 presentation to Hopi language instructors:

> *The ideal place [to teach the Hopi language] is the home*; but such "ideal" situations in the home have broken down ... Adults today are too busy in other activities ... which then takes time away from interacting with their children. These are the circumstances of modern times.

These statements reveal the tensions inherent in reversing language loss. In spite of the challenges, community educators imagine that:

> If we have it [Hopi language] written in our curriculum, if we just see it on paper saying we need to do this in the school, then there's no objection [from the community].

> The ideal situation would be if we had Hopi teachers and aides ... the things that we have [already in place] to teach the kids for regular White school.

Essentially, these individuals speak of their belief that if we begin to ask ourselves as teachers and students such questions as, "In Hopi [language and culture], what is April? What do we [as Hopis] do in April? And then in May?" "This summer we're having dances—why are we having dances? What is the purpose? What is the meaning?" The motivation generated by this inquiry and interest about who they are would become the catalyst for creating the kind of school community that exists in the imagination of those involved in Hopi language and cultural continuity. In turn, writing and reading the Hopi language becomes an additional tool to facilitate personal learning for students, establishing Hopi literacy as essential in educating youth and adults.

YAN PASIWTINI: THIS IS HOW IT CAN BE POSSIBLE— CONCLUSION

> Someone has to take the responsibility for language preservation, and the logical place today is the school.

This statement turns our focus to how schools might be coopted as arenas of cultural negotiation, and as vehicles for redefining Hopi education through Indigenous literacy development. The oral testimony and discussion of events presented in this chapter suggest that Hopi cultural continuity, embedded in language and culture, must become a significant part of the school's function. Schools are well established, as "new" institutions in today's Hopi society. As such, they are sites of significant cultural activity; much like traditional activities, schools construct meaning within a particular context.

Hopi children spend a tremendous amount of time in these institutions, pursuing their academic, social, and athletic activities and interests. Schools house community and after-school programs that extend the school day and school functions. "Indian Day" activities during which students' families share traditional Hopi dances, songs, food, and cultural knowledge demonstrate not only the continued home and community interest in these activities, but also the shared sense that school is an appropriate—and arguably a necessary—place for such activities as well. Reservation schools have also begun to accommodate community requests for an annual calendar that allows students to participate in significant ceremonial events that previously conflicted with school calendars. Although seemingly small in scope, the cumulative effect of these efforts is to bridge school and community and increasingly, to place the school at the center of the community's cultural negotiation.

Hopi literacy, language, and culture are finding their way into school curricula in varying ways. The Hopi Junior and Senior High School offers Hopi language classes as an elective. HBCS aspires to encourage Hopi children "to truly know who they are so they will become our [Hopi people's] ears, eyes, heart and voice" by learning the "history, traditions, and customs of our people" (HBCS, 1998–1999, p. 11). The primary objective of the Hopilavayi Project is to incorporate Hopi language in Head Start, village, and school pilot programs. These efforts illustrate an active process of cultural negotiation.

The processes underway have raised concern and optimism in two ways. Hopi literacy is a newly emerging phenomenon. Therefore, the distribution of literacy abilities among individuals varies; the lack of Hopi print materials is an additional perceived obstacle to Hopi literacy initiatives. It is equally important to consider, however, that a core of the traditional Hopi lifeway remains integral to contemporary community life: naming, initiations, marriages, and ceremonial gatherings continue to bring the community together in socially significant and meaning-laden activities. These activities offer cultural and linguistic resources that can be incorporated into school curriculum and pedagogy in ways that emphasize the connections between contemporary and "traditional" Hopi life.

Bringing this literary and cultural knowledge to bear on schooling can reverse past patterns of colonial education (see, e.g., McCarty & Watahomigie, 2004). These goals are at the center of our long-term Hopi literacy efforts.

An important step now underway is Hopi literacy training for Hopi teachers and teacher assistants who have been named the "literacy specialists" in the schools (McKay, 1996, p. 431). They are also the disenfranchised individuals —graduates of federal Indian boarding schools—whose schooling convinced them that the language and culture resources they possessed were not only irrelevant in the school setting but were "handicaps" to their achievement (McCarty & Watahomigie, 2004). As Hopi literacy specialists, they face a twofold struggle. First, they must convince themselves that Hopi language and culture are essential to educating Hopi children. Second, they must take responsibility for helping Hopi children acquire the linguistic and cultural resources the educators possess. The following journal reflections by the literacy specialists testify to the emancipating quality of this cultural work:

> My first experience in a formal Hopi language class .... It is really opening up my mind and eyes .... I feel now that I'll be able to write my own ideas in Hopi .... I have learned so much; a whole new area of interest has opened up for me .... I can see that any Hopi speaker has a responsibility for keeping the language alive.

> [Emory Sekaquaptewa] mentioned that children have TV [and] radios at home to listen to them [programs broadcast] in English .... So, teaching Hopi should be done [as well] at school .... I hope someday it will work.

Through Hopi language workshops, these individuals are in fact establishing themselves as "literacy specialists" and partners in collaborative Hopi language ventures. They are developing their Hopi literacy abilities while helping their students to do the same. Interactive games, written and audiotaped books in Hopi, and other Native language activities are now being implemented in classrooms. The literacy specialists also have developed thematic units on such topics as *Tuutuwutsi*, Hopi legends, stories, and narratives; *Hohonaqpi*, Hopi child games; *Navoti*, Hopi history; *Ngyam*, clan histories; *Kiikiqo*, Hopi ruins; and *Hiniwtipu*, significant Hopi events. These activities offer clear evidence that Hopi language and culture offer a wealth of educational content directly relevant to children's academic achievement and literacy learning.

Even before more extensive concrete efforts are undertaken to reverse language loss, engagement in such literacy practices involves "consciousness heightening and reformation" (Fishman, 1991, p. 394). Through their own literacy learning, Hopi educators are reversing their patterns of thought about the education of Hopi children; they are affirming for themselves and their students the value of Hopi literacy. Much work remains to be done. As educators, these literacy specialists are "critical participants within the educational system who have the power to revise and reform that system" (McCarty & Watahomigie, 2004, p. 93).

By attending to the Hopi language, we hope to confirm the belief of the Hopi parent who stated that, "There is more talk [in the Hopi language] about hope than anything else ... that things are going to get better." More important, we hope to position Hopi education and Hopi literacy as vehicles for realizing that vision.

Sheilah Nicholas was born and raised on the Hopi reservation. An educator for 27 years, she is completing a doctoral program in American Indian Studies at the University of Arizona. She has served as Senior Program Coordinator of the American Indian Language Development Institute at the University of Arizona, and as a member of a language survey team for the Indigenous Languages Institute in Santa Fe, New Mexico. As a parent, educator, and student, she is an active advocate for and scholar of American Indian education.

NOTE

American Indian grant schools operate under a contractual agreement with the Bureau of Indian Affairs, whereby locally elected, Indigenous school boards receive federal grant funds to operate community schools. This arrangement grew out of the American Indian self-determination movement begun during the 1960s and 1970s, first codified in the 1975 Indian Self-Determination and Educational Assistance Act, and modified by more recent legislation.

REFERENCES

Adley-SantaMaria, B. (1999). Interrupting White Mountain Apache language shift: An insider's view. *Practicing Anthropology, 21,* 16–19.

Fettes, M. (1999). Indigenous education and the ecology of community. In S. May (Ed.), *Indigenous community-based education* (pp. 20–41). Clevedon, UK: Multilingual Matters.

Fishman, J. A. (1991). *Reversing language shift: Theoretical and empirical foundations of assistance to threatened languages.* Clevedon, UK: Mulitilingual Matters.

Haussler, M., & Tompkins, C. (1983). *Final report. Literacy development in Hopi and English: A descriptive study* (Title VII Research and Development Project). Hotevilla, AZ: Hotevilla-Bacavi Community School.

Hopi Cultural Preservation Office. (1998). *Hopi language education and preservation plan.* Hopi Tribe: Author.

Hopi Language Assessment Project. (1997). *Presentation of Hopi language survey results.* The Hopi Tribe: Hopi Cultural Preservation Office.

Hopi Tribe. (1995). *Hopit Potskwaniat* (Hopi Tribal Consolidated Strategic Plan of 1995). Hopi Tribe: Author.

Hotevilla-Bacavi Community School. (1998–1999). *1998–1999 consolidated school reform plan implementation.* Hotvela Paaqavi, AZ: Hotevilla Bacavi Community School and Sundance Educational Consulting.

Krauss, M. (1998). The condition of Native North American languages: The need for realistic assessment and action. *International Journal of the Sociology of Language, 132,* 9–21.

Kroskrity, P. V. (1993). *Language, history, and identity: Ethnolinguistic studies of the Arizona Tewa.* Tucson: University of Arizona Press.

McCarty, T. L. (2001). Between possibility and constraint: Indigenous language education, planning, and policy in the United States. In J. F. Tollefson (Ed.), *Language policies in education: Critical issues* (pp. 285–307). Mahwah, NJ: Lawrence Erlbaum Associates.

McCarty, T. L., & Watahomigie, L. J. (2004). Language and literacy in American Indian and Alaska Native communities. In B. Pérez (Ed.), *Sociocultural contexts of language and literacy,* 2nd ed. (pp. 79–110). Mahwah, NJ: Lawrence Erlbaum Associates.

McKay, S. L. (1996). Literacy and literacies. In S. McKay & N. Hornberger (Eds.), *Sociolinguistics and language teaching* (pp. 421–435). Cambridge, UK: Cambridge University Press.

Qoyawayma, P. (1964). *No turning back.* Albuquerque: University of New Mexico Press.

Ricento, T. K., & Hornberger, N. H. (1996). Unpeeling the onion: Language planning and policy and the ELT professional. *TESOL Quarterly, 30,* 401–427.

Sekaquaptewa, H. (1985). *Me and mine: The life story of Helen Sekaquaptewa* (as told to Louise Udall). Tucson: University of Arizona Press.

Varenne, H., & McDermott, R. (1999). *Successful failure: The school America builds.* Boulder, CO: Westview.

Wintermute, P. (1991, September 25). Renewal of Hopi language sought. *The Navajo-Hopi Observer, 10,* p. 1.

The Power Within: Indigenous Literacies and Teacher Empowerment

Teresa L. McCarty
Arizona State University

English literacy, often conceived as contextually and ideologically neutral, has served in practice to manage and control Indigenous lives. At the same time, Indigenous literacies, originally developed for the purpose of religious conversion and as part of government literacy campaigns, have been taken by Indigenous communities as a means of opposing dominant discourses and asserting local educational and linguistic rights. Drawing on long-term ethnographic research with one Native American school, this chapter examines Indigenous teachers' efforts to co-construct literacy practices that validate their and their students' language and history. Laced throughout this struggle are teachers' attempts to confront toxic bureaucratic texts, including national standardizing mandates. This analysis problematizes Indigenous/minority teacher empowerment, examining the consequences of taking a pedagogical stance of resistance, and the "power within" Indigenous communities to effect social-educational change.

Teacher 1:[1]	You know, as a teacher, you sometimes feel hesitant to speak up … especially when you don't get any support.
Teacher 2 *(nodding):*	Praise. And then when they [district administrators] come into the classroom, if they could just give you feedback.
Teacher 3:	District administrators need to be here for Parent Night …. They need to be here right by our side, greeting parents …

---

[1] I do not name individuals in the opening vignette to protect their anonymity and privacy. Later in the chapter I use teachers' names, with their consent, as they requested this and it is part of the published record (see, e.g., McCarty, 2002; McCarty & Dick, 2004).

> ***Teacher 4:*** Teachers, parents, administrators—everyone needs to work to-
> gether to make things happen.
> ***T. McCarty:*** So what can we do?
> (… a moment of silence …)
> ***Teacher 2:*** If we want to be powerful, we have to exercise our power.

This conversation took place in the Rough Rock Elementary School teachers' lounge during one of my visits to the school in 1993. I had then been working with the Navajo community of Rough Rock, Arizona, for 13 years, and was engaged with teachers in an action research project on Navajo students' biliteracy development. The conversation at that moment reflected growing unrest among the bilingual program faculty—seven women, all community members—about what they perceived as top-down curricular mandates from White male administrators at the district office. Referring to an outcome-based "mastery learning" curriculum introduced by an administrator relatively new to the district, one teacher observed, "It's forced upon us. It's another thing laid on us from the top."

In this chapter I problematize notions of teacher empowerment a discourse such as this implies. Drawing on my long-term ethnographic work at Rough Rock, I examine Indigenous teachers' attempts to co-construct literacy practices that validate their and their students' literacy histories. The analysis focuses on what Weis (1996) and others call "that space *between* structure and agency" (p. xi), illustrating the ways in which power relations percolate through a system of Indigenous schooling and how teachers struggle against and within that system to (re)claim an Indigenous pedagogy. I conclude by suggesting the broader implications of this work for teacher empowerment and minoritized schooling.[2]

Understanding these issues requires knowing something of "the historical spaces of the past and present" (Popkewitz, 1998, p. 538) within which contemporary cultural and linguistic practices reside. For Indigenous people in the United States, those spaces are saturated with the residue of federally sponsored, English-only schooling, the net effect of which was to reduce the do-

---

[2]Throughout this analysis, I use the term *minoritized* rather than *minority*. As a characterization of a people, minority is stigmatizing and often numerically inaccurate. Navajos living within the Navajo Nation are, in fact, in the numerical majority. Minoritized more accurately conveys the power relations and processes by which certain groups are socially, economically, and politically marginalized within the larger society. This term also connotes human agency to effect change.

mains and registers for Indigenous language use (see also Nicholas, chap. 2, this volume). At the same time, among many Indigenous groups, missionary schooling and later, federally sponsored literacy campaigns and bilingual education programs, introduced the possibility of Indigenous literacies. Although the intent of the former was religious conversion, the effect was often something much different. Listen to one mission school graduate's account of first experiencing her language in print:

> What I remember about the language was that I was so amazed that our *bilagáana* [White, Anglo] teacher could read something out of the Bible and it sounded very familiar. It was in Navajo .... Every day in class we took 30 minutes to go through the Navajo vowel sounds .... And then I thought to myself, "Oh, this is the English letters" ... and she was reading it, but it was coming out as Navajo words. That's what amazed me. And I guess that's how I got interested in it. I thought, "This is *my* language, and this is how *I* can talk."

This individual is Teacher 4. Her words speak of resistance and improvisation (Holland, Lachicotte, Skinner, & Cain, 1998). Appropriating a cultural tool devised by non-Indigenous others, this teacher strategically refashioned it for her own, Indigenous ends. For this teacher, literacy in Navajo fueled a lifetime career as a bilingual educator. Her literacy forms an enduring and critical part of her identity and her sense of agency, autonomy, and control.

In the pages that follow, I sketch a portrait of how Indigenous teachers' agency is both exercised and challenged in the context of school-based language and literacy learning. The setting is Rough Rock, a reservation-interior community of about 1,500 that, in the heady days of federal Great Society reforms, rose to prominence as the first Indigenous community to contract with the U.S. government to run its own school and teach in the Native language. (For more on the school and its development, see Dick & McCarty, 1996; McCarty, 1989, 1993a, 1998, 2002; Roessel, 1977.) However, by the mid-1980s, Rough Rock's bilingual and bicultural program had stalled in the wake of a new federal administration intent on downsizing education programs and a maze of financial and bureaucratic arrangements that, as one school director noted in federal testimony, "would defeat the President of General Motors" (American Indian Policy Review Commission, 1976, p. 259). The K–12 Rough Rock School had nonetheless survived, and Navajo teachers continued to implement a variety of Native language and literacy materials in their classrooms. For the most part, these were individual efforts, with little coordination between teachers or grade levels.

"IT GOT US GOING": THE ROOTS OF CHANGE

In 1983, at the invitation of the elementary principal, personnel from the Hawai'i-based Kamehameha Early Education Program (KEEP) arrived at Rough Rock "for the express purpose of doing our own research" (L. Vogt, personal communication, August 4, 1988). In Hawai'i, KEEP had established a lab school featuring comprehension-based oral language and literacy development and cooperative-interactive participant structures keyed to Native Hawaiian culture (Vogt, Jordan, & Tharp, 1993). KEEP was then beginning to disseminate its approach, and the work at Rough Rock was an extension of those dissemination efforts. The purpose, Vogt and Au (1995) say, was to determine "which [KEEP] features would transfer and which would require adaptations" (p. 113).

KEEP personnel stepped into a tumultuous school environment. Between 1983 and 1986, the elementary principalship had been vacated four times, with one individual holding the position for less than 4 months. With no overall coordination of the bilingual and bicultural program, a phonics-based basic skills program had been installed as the core curriculum. At one point, Vogt and Au (1995) report:

> [T]eachers were required to submit lesson plans once a week to the [non-Indian] principal who monitored the allocated time for each subject written on the plan. The plan was to be on the teacher's desk at all times, and if he [the principal] walked into the room he expected the teacher to be teaching the lesson noted on the plan. (p. 118)

"I felt like a parrot, repeating lines," one teacher recalled of her practice during those times. "We were used to that type of teaching: teachers as technicians," another teacher said.

Although the teachers never spoke to me in these terms, the gender and racial politics of White male authority and Indigenous female subordination were clear. These power relations had marginalized teachers within their own school and classrooms, positioning them as the silenced "other." The inequality carried over to students: How can teachers construct empowering learning environments for children when teachers themselves are devalued within a toxic environment of domination and control?

It was under these conditions that the collaboration with KEEP took root among eight Navajo teachers at the elementary school. As Vogt et al. (1993) describe it:

During the fall semester of 1983, Cathie Jordan, KEEP anthropologist, and Lynn Vogt, KEEP research teacher, lived in the Rough Rock community and worked in a 3rd-grade class at the school. Vogt taught the KEEP reading program, and Jordan organized and ran the research effort. The project involved intensive collaboration with one 3rd-grade teacher, Afton Sells, and her aide, Juanita Estell, and some involvement with the rest of the faculty and staff. All of the faculty except the librarian were Navajo and members of the Rough Rock community. (p. 59)

The work that fall launched a collaboration that would continue for 5 years and provide the foundation for re-establishing a bilingual and bicultural education program at Rough Rock. Afton Sells found that KEEP's approach reinforced literacy practices with which she was familiar and comfortable. Other bilingual teachers joined Sells in piloting KEEP teaching strategies. KEEP teacher-researcher Lynn Vogt continued to make periodic visits to Rough Rock, providing workshops, observing and providing feedback to teachers, and generally working alongside them in their classrooms. In the context of a fluctuating school administration and a school board locked in an ongoing battle with the Bureau of Indian Affairs to keep the school financially afloat, KEEP was the only consistent curricular force in the school. "It was something stable we could rely on," a teacher reflected. "It got us going."

In addition to contextualized and culturally relevant reading instruction, KEEP introduced a crucial process that liberated teachers from their received roles as readers of curriculum scripts: the opportunity to work cooperatively and to critically reflect on their practice. Numerous researchers have identified teacher reflection and collaboration as essential to positive change (see, e.g., Cochran-Smith & Lytle, 1993; Duckworth, 1986; González et al., 1995; Goswami & Stillman, 1987; Hollingsworth, 1994; Kincheloe, 1991; Lipka, 1998; Moll, this volume; Schön, 1983; Short, 1993; Strickland, 1988; Ulichny & Schoener, 1996). At Rough Rock, the opportunity to engage in reflective, collaborative practice enabled teachers to refashion KEEP, which focused on English language development, into a locally responsive bilingual and bicultural program. One teacher explained, "At first, we thought we should follow KEEP strategies strictly. Then we started sorting things out for ourselves. We thought of our own ideas and felt comfortable—we felt confident."

An additional development facilitated the process. In January 1987, after the fourth elementary principal in 4 years resigned, the school board hired Juanita Estell's husband, Dan Estell, as principal. An Anglo teacher who had taught at Rough Rock for several years, Estell held the position of principal for the next 8 years, actively supporting teachers' efforts and lending administrative permanency to the bilingual and bicultural program as it took shape. According to Afton Sells and Lynn Vogt, it was at this time that the Rough Rock English–Navajo Language Arts Program (RRENLAP) "was born."

"I FEEL EMPOWERED"

Just as KEEP ended its formal collaboration with Rough Rock, the elementary school received a 3-year federal bilingual education grant. Supported by this and subsequent federal grants, RRENLAP grew from a K–3 transitional program that moved students out of bilingual instruction at Grade 4, to a K–6 Navajo–English language maintenance program. These changes occurred through a gradual, recursive, and sometimes painful engagement in which teachers observed and provided feedback on each other's practice, critiqued and tried various approaches, and came to embrace a pedagogy grounded in local linguistic and cultural knowledge.

This section details the process of teacher empowerment, using excerpts from my field notes to highlight activity within RRENLAP at different moments in time. I also discuss one particular experience, a teacher study group, that accelerated the transformation of literacy teaching and assessment, and that, in retrospect, seemed to be a defining moment in the transformation of teachers' professional identities and roles.

Thursday, December 5, 1991

RRENLAP coordinator Galena Dick and I begin what has become typical during my bimonthly visits to the school: observing in RRENLAP classrooms, taking notes, talking with teachers and students about their work, and later meeting with teachers as a group, where they share their ideas, questions, and projects, and where Galena and I offer feedback on our observations. We also try to provide feedback in the form of individual memos to teachers, which Galena and I compose together in front of a computer or typewriter. We view this as an opportunity to nudge teacher reflection and critique from points of strength, within a caring and supportive environment.

In the kindergarten class, the teacher tells us that most of her 12 students speak both Navajo and English. Students sit at one of two U-shaped learning center tables, one group with the teacher and one with the teacher assistant. Standing to one side of the teacher's center, we observe students working on a worksheet labeled with the English nursery rhyme, "Little Jack Horner." At the other center, students read this nursery rhyme aloud. All interaction is in English.

On the walls, one bulletin board features commercial pictures of the *Mayflower*, Pilgrims, and Native people; other walls show cutouts of the four sacred mountains that delineate *Dinétah* or Navajo homelands. The teacher shows us students' writing contained in folders labeled "Halloween" and "Thanksgiving." The Halloween writings include stories about goblins, ghosts, and other Halloween characters; the Thanksgiving writings include student-made books on European-American holiday themes. The student writing folders are the beginning of the teacher's plans to implement a system of portfolio assessment (see Tierney, Carter, & Desai, 1991, for definitions of portfolio assessment).

We move to another kindergarten class, where 14 students are working at two learning centers. Activity at one center is conducted in Navajo; at the other center, English is used. We are impressed with the colorful, engaging environment. A *Késhmish* (Christmas) student brainstorming web hangs from the ceiling, along with conventional Christmas decorations, all at child height. The bulletin boards and walls feature students' art and writing projects on the Navajo *hooghan* (a traditional dwelling with sacred as well as practical significance), clowns, and Santa Claus. The teacher shows us student-made storybooks on *Shash* (Bear), a sheepdog, and tells us students are also making an English dictionary book.

In the first-grade class down the hall, 21 students sit at seven tables scattered throughout the room. Construction paper pumpkins and students' writing hang from the ceiling, next to scenes of the *Mayflower* and Pilgrims. A bulletin board features student-made pumpkin books along with worksheets on letter-shape formations. The teacher and teacher assistant work with students on a Christmas art project at separate tables. Galena says that the teacher is emphasizing thematic units, which she plans and shares with the kindergarten teacher whose room we visited first.

Our final visit is to a combination first-/second-grade classroom of 30 students. Bulletin boards are covered with students' writing in Navajo and English, as well as Navajo figures and themes. Students are busy writing in their journals. Studying the journals, we notice that the teacher has corrected students' spelling and grammar in red or blue ink. One student, whose primary language is Navajo, leans over and asks an English-dominant peer how to spell "brother," then looks at her text. The teacher says, "He knows there's an 'r' in there." But he copies "bother" anyway. The teacher asks him to read from his journal. He reads the word "brother" perfectly.

Thursday, February 13, 1992

This is the first meeting of the RRENLAP teacher study group, and teachers have been given release time for the day to meet. Galena Dick, the seven RRENLAP teachers, and I constitute the group; elementary principal Dan Estell also joins us for this first meeting and for several others. Over the past few years, teachers have become increasingly concerned about the limitations of standardized tests and their damaging and demoralizing effects on students and teachers. Not only do the tests label students as deficient, they fail to reveal the rich, multi-layered quality of the literacy processes and performances we regularly observe in RRENLAP classrooms. The teachers decide to form a study group to examine alternative forms of literacy assessment. Like study groups reported elsewhere (e.g., González et al., 1995; Matlin & Short, 1991), our group is voluntary, organized by teachers for their own purposes, and designed to connect a body of professional literature on assessment to our own, action-oriented classroom research (Lipka & McCarty, 1994, p. 271; McCarty, 1993b).

At the group's first meeting, Galena Dick makes it clear that, "This study group is not just a place where we have to listen to one person and have them give us all the answers. We know our kids better than anybody else .... Teachers intuitively know there is more going on than what is represented on standardized tests." Still, teachers seem reluctant to trust their own knowledge. During an initial discussion about educational evaluation, a veteran teacher with 21 years of teaching experience claims she does not know anything about it. Later in the school year, this same teacher will write, "We started off so bare .... It was challenging to develop such a powerful [new] means of assessment."

Gradually, the discourse deepens with words that speak of institutional silencing practices: "We tend to accept what somebody else develops—standardized tests." And then, a breath of possibility: "Why not use our own teacher-developed tests?"

We list the questions we want to have answered through our inquiry in the study group: "How do Navajo children become biliterate?" "How to manage portfolio assessment and have time for other instructional activities?" "How many forms of assessment do we want?"

Later in the day, we break into pairs and read excerpts from Tierney et al.'s (1991) *Portfolio Assessment in the Reading-Writing Classroom.* When we come together as a group to discuss our reactions to the text, we resonate with the book's dual messages that "teachers know their craft," and that conventional, "teacher-proof" assessments subvert both children's and teacher's creative potentials.

March–May, 1992

Over the next several months, the work of the study group continues. We read the book by Tierney et al., along with Hudelson's (1989) *Write On*. We keep and exchange journals with our reflections on the readings, our observations of students' literacy and biliteracy processes, teachers' experiences in trying new forms of assessment, and our questions and concerns. Once a month, the group is released from teaching to meet for a full day; once a week, teachers meet for a few hours after school to discuss what they are reading and their research on students' literacy and biliteracy development.

During each monthly meeting we analyze samples of students' writing, examining writing styles, problems, and questions. We critique the professional texts we are reading and share the literacy assessment strategies teachers are piloting. (For more on this, see Begay et al., 1995; McCarty, 1993b.) We see, as one teacher points out, that regardless of whether students are acquiring English as a second language or have English as their primary language, "They can do it"—they are writers and readers. It also becomes evident that understanding students' English literacy processes and demonstrations requires serious attention to those same processes and demonstrations in Navajo. "Students' writing has taught me a lot," one teacher states. "I need to work at giving my students their responsibilities and control over their learning."

We discuss teachers' experiences in English-only boarding schools, the suppression of their language and literacies, and their desire to "reverse the type of schooling we went through" (Dick, 1998, p. 25). This raises difficult questions of practice, such as how to effectively involve parents in assessment, and how to respond to their own and parents' conditioned beliefs that literacy is a unidimensional skill that can be captured and distilled into a number or letter grade. The kindergarten teacher asserts, "I would tell parents that [students' portfolios are] a rich description of a letter grade."

By the end of the school year, teachers have developed sophisticated bilingual writing checklists geared toward their own classrooms and students. One teacher shares a graphic model of portfolio assessment based on a Navajo ceremonial basket and cornstalk (see McCarty & Dick, 2004, for more on this).

Several teachers are experimenting with some form of portfolio assessment. They write of their accomplishments: "We as a group have learned what a portfolio is all about …. We feel confident enough to use a portfolio for parent conference, open house and parent visitation." They also speak of the changes in their images of themselves and their students: "The role change involves taking a new stance towards the profession. [When students are] invited to be full members of the classroom … they become lifelong learners with … control over things that they're learning."

Finally, teachers speak directly of the value of reflection and collaboration in generating these changes. A teacher who had written simply, "disenfranchised," in one of her first journal entries talks at the end of the school year about her sense of ownership over the process of positive change, her excitement at the possibilities in the year ahead, and the pride she feels toward her students and herself. "In talking and working with the group," she says, "I found out that I actually do some of these things we read and talked about in the classroom." "I feel empowered," another teacher states.

Friday, March 4, 1994

Just 2 years later, Galena Dick and I continue our research in RRENLAP classrooms. Throughout this time, teachers have participated in ongoing collaborative and reflective work with each other; they have attended university institutes and workshops on Indigenous language education, and they have given a number of formal presentations on RRENLAP at national and international conferences. In the course of this work, several have obtained master's degrees. These experiences have increased their pride and ownership over their practice and widened their network of collegial support.

Walking down the hall, we see bulletin boards featuring students' Navajo writing on traditional Navajo topics. The classroom doors are decorated with student- and teacher-made banners featuring various trade books. Galena explains that the banners are part of a school initiative to enable each class to purchase a favorite book for each student.

In the third-grade class taught by the teacher whose kindergarten class we documented in December 1991, 14 students work at tables in three long double rows. Several students are drawing pictures to illustrate number concepts. A few are engaged in a lively discussion, code-switching from Navajo to English, about Olympic ice skaters Tonya Harding and Nancy Kerrigan. The teacher tells us students have been fascinated by the controversy surrounding charges that Harding's bodyguard intentionally injured Kerrigan, Harding's chief rival. Every morning, the teacher says, "We discuss what's in the news."

Students also are studying a thematic unit on Navajo creation stories. As part of their inquiry, they read Yazzie's (1971) *Navajo History*, and Maberry's (1991) *After Sundown—Teaching Stories of the Navajo*, both published by Navajo presses. A bulletin board displays students' English texts on their Navajo forebears. Insects and insect people are central to these stories, and the teacher uses this as an opportunity to connect literature study to science investigations. Another link is to social and political studies: The class is researching and writing stories about the creation of the Navajo Nation. Evaluation of this work includes student portfolios.

In the combination third- and fourth-grade class, the teacher is reading a biography of Martin Luther King to seven students grouped around a U-shaped table. When she finishes, she asks in English, "So, what's a biography?" One student responds, "You write about someone." The discussion continues, in Navajo and English, about how, during the 1960s, people of all races and ethnicities and backgrounds came together for "the poor people's march." While this discussion is underway, two other students work on math at a cluster of desks, two work on an art project, and the school's reading specialist reads a book to a student in the corner of the room.

As we leave, we notice student-made dioramas on one wall from a study of whales. On the other side of the room are student *hooghan* constructions. The teacher explains that these are part of a literature and social studies unit on Navajo kinship.

The last room we visit today is a first grade class where the Navajo language specialist is reading *Na'ahóółailchí'í*, "The Little Red Hen," a favorite of Rough Rock students and teachers.[3] Five boys sit at the front of the class with cutouts of each of the story's animal characters. Ten other students are seated around them on the floor; they read the text aloud in Navajo, as the boys in the front hold up their props and act out various characters' parts. When they finish reading, the Navajo resource teacher leads students in a Navajo song about animals. Other Native songs follow. Students participate excitedly and seem genuinely to enjoy this activity.

---

[3]During a meeting with RRENLAP teachers, I questioned the authenticity of this text because it is a translation of a traditional Anglo-European story. Teachers seemed puzzled by my question; they clearly considered *Na'ahóółailchí'í* to be a Navajo story. In our discussions, I came to understand that the story's familiar animal characters and message of the value of cooperation are, in fact, quintessential Navajo storytelling themes.

As Galena and I walk back down the hallway to her office, we talk about the changes we have observed in Rough Rock classrooms. Virtually all teachers are using authentic Navajo or multicultural children's literature, around which they and their students organize thematic research and writing projects. "You don't see any basal readers on the desk," Galena points out, "and the teachers are making up their own questions to accompany their literature studies." Teachers are using some form of qualitative assessment. Activity in RRENLAP classrooms more closely approximates real-world work environments: Not everyone is doing the same thing at once. Instead, students and teachers come together for activities that require everyone's involvement—storytelling, song, games, and drama, for example—but they also work independently and in small groups, depending on what needs to be accomplished at a given time. Peer assistance is the norm. There is much greater consciousness and use of Navajo by the teachers. Finally, where there had been an emphasis on other peoples' histories and stereotypical representations of Native peoples—as in the Pilgrim and Indian Thanksgiving displays—Galena notes that teachers and students are "studying our own history."

Later in the day, we meet with teachers to reflect on 5 years of RRENLAP and the 10 years that have passed since the initial collaboration with KEEP. "We came a long way," the third-grade teacher begins. "Instead of seeing students as a whole group, each child is working at the student's own rate," the first-grade teacher adds. "Students are more confident of themselves," she continues. Speaking of alternative assessment, the third-grade teacher reiterates, "You know where your students are. This helps you a lot with your teaching."

Teachers also articulate the political dimensions of their work: their increasing confidence and willingness to take risks and to implement approaches that access local knowledge; reclaiming control of their classrooms; and adapting district-level mandates to their own ideas of sound pedagogy. The process, Galena Dick says, "gave us ways of how to develop appropriate materials and assessment …. It gave us that confidence and empowerment."

CHILDREN'S ACHIEVEMENT, BILITERACY, AND SELF-EFFICACY

Beyond these consequences for teachers and their practice, RRENLAP and the study group also had a significant influence on students' biliteracy development and academic achievement. Like other schools, and as part of Rough Rock's contractual obligations to the federal government, students' academic performance is regularly documented on locally developed and standardized tests. Teachers and I analyzed these data as part of our ongoing collaborative research. Using a cohort design, we followed students from kindergarten to sixth grade, comparing their performance on these assessments and teachers' qualitative assessments with that of Rough Rock students who had not participated in RRENLAP.

On locally developed measures of English listening comprehension, RRENLAP kindergartners at the end of the 1989–90 school year posted mean scores of 58%. After 4 years in the program, students' mean scores rose to 91%. On standardized English reading subtests, discriminatory as they are, the same students' scores initially declined, then rose steadily. By the end of third grade, their scores had stabilized, although they were still below national norms. Similar patterns were observed in mathematics (McCarty, 1993b). Although these findings were less dramatic than some school personnel might have hoped, RRENLAP students consistently outperformed a local comparison group who had not participated in RRENLAP. RRENLAP students also were assessed by their teachers as having stronger oral Navajo and Navajo literacy abilities than their nonbilingual education peers. Overall, our data showed that bilingual students who participated in cumulative, uninterrupted initial literacy experiences in Navajo made the greatest gains on local and national measures of achievement (McCarty, 1993b).

THE SOCIAL CONTEXT OF PEDAGOGICAL CHANGE

These changes occurred within a social space of possibility and hope (Weis, 1996, p. xii). Elsewhere we have described this as a zone of safety—a socially constructed space within which teachers moved from a deficit view of their teaching and learners to a stance focused on their and students' agency and strengths (Begay et al., 1995; Lipka & McCarty, 1994; McCarty, 2002). Analyzing a similar process among Yup'ik teachers and elders, Lipka and his colleagues (1998) write, "We believe that a slow, deliberate process of teachers becoming empowered by forming their own groups and by considering questions of teaching, learning, methodology, and school–community relationships becomes an excellent forum for ... school change and reform" (p. 199).

At Rough Rock, those changes began with a fortuitous encounter with KEEP. They were spurred on by an infusion of long-term financial assistance and administrative support from the building principal, and by a fundamental democratization of the teacher–principal relationship. Although it was not a relation of symmetry, teachers' relationship with their building principal was one of mutual concern and support. Within this context, and over a period of nearly 10 years, teachers worked as both apprentices and peer mentors (Lave & Wenger, 1991). In Vygotskian terms, they created and worked within a zone of proximal development—an interactional space in which each individual was able to achieve more through collaboration than alone (Cole, John-Steiner, Scribner, & Souberman, 1978). Importantly, these were the very conditions teachers strove to create with and for their students.

This was explicitly not a "comfort zone;" indeed, this was often a site of pain and discomfort as teachers revisited their own educational histories and challenged the pedagogical assumptions internalized in the course of their schooling (Lipka & McCarty, 1994). The process was equally one of contention and fear, as teachers spoke out against the silencing practices within the higher administration of their community school. The remainder of the dialogue with which this chapter began reveals the tension between institutional constraints and teacher empowerment: "We're just teachers," one person noted, describing shared perceptions of a lack of district-level administrative support for teachers' work. "Peons," another said. "We're just teachers of the kids."

How is it that, in a single dialogue, teachers can imagine themselves as both powerful and "just teachers"—"peons?" This discourse, I believe, must be situated within a conception of schools as contested, contradictory sites. Rough Rock teachers and students did empower themselves through the creative co-construction of new pedagogies based on their language and cultural practices; but sustaining that power required continuous negotiation carried out within a context of historical oppression and bureaucratic coercion. To clarify how Indigenous teachers operated within a context marked by both hope and constraint, it is necessary to examine processes at the macro level of federal Indian policy.

The Quest for Accreditation

On April 28, 1988, just as RRENLAP was taking shape, Congress authorized the Hawkins-Stafford Elementary and Secondary School Improvement Amendments, known as Public Law 100-297. In introducing the Indian education bill that would become part of P.L. 100-297, Senator Dennis DeConcini, a Democrat from Arizona, reaffirmed the federal government's "special duty to the Indian tribes to assure the availability of the best educational opportunities," a duty he insisted "must be fulfilled … in a manner consistent with …

Indian self-determination" (White House Conference on Indian Education, 1992, p. 6).

Among other things, P.L. 100-297 provided a forward-funding system for Indigenous community schools, which for more than a decade had been tied to a highly volatile federal contracting system. For example, at Rough Rock it was typical for funding contracts to be finalized months after the school year began. In the interim, no employee contracts could be signed, no supplies could be ordered, and the school board and administration were in negotiations with the Bureau of Indian Affairs instead of at school when the school year began (Tonigan, Emerson, & Platero, 1975). P.L. 100-297 would enable Indigenous school boards to seek grant status, an arrangement that would provide a lump sum base budget each year, although the final budget would await enrollment counts and any discretionary funding the school might obtain. Schools were free to invest the lump sum, thereby generating additional revenue. Grant status seemed to offer a pathway out of chronic financial insecurity.

Achieving grant status, however, required that schools meet externally imposed standards regulated by national or regional accrediting boards. Thus, Rough Rock began the process of seeking accreditation through the North Central Association (NCA).

At the time the school's accreditation efforts began, NCA accreditation was a three-stage process involving a self-study by school staff, an external assessment by a visiting team of educators, and development and implementation of a "planned program of school improvement" (Commission on Schools, 1983, p. 4). NCA school improvement guidelines directed schools to 12 "quality education principles" addressing such things as school–community relations, staff competencies, curriculum, school climate, and physical facilities (Commission on Schools, 1983, p. 7).

In 1990, the Navajo NCA asked that I chair Rough Rock's NCA evaluation team. Despite deep misgivings about the process, I agreed, knowing the high stakes for the school. From 1990 to 1991, I met regularly with teachers, school officials, and community members to discuss the accreditation procedure. In these meetings, I attempted to demystify NCA's expectations and the accreditation process. At the same time, I emphasized the school's strengths; this seemed an ideal opportunity to direct greater attention to the work within RRENLAP and to encourage similar community-directed change.

It was under these circumstances that Rough Rock's central administration introduced a program called outcome-based education (OBE), intended as a "master plan" for school improvement. OBE's philosophy is stated in seemingly positive terms: "All students can learn and succeed …. Success breeds success." Reading the program documents more closely and critically, however, the underlying message becomes clear: Some students are guaranteed school-defined "success," whereas those constructed as deficient must be drilled and coaxed, and even then, are likely to fall short (see, e.g., Varenne & McDermott, 1999). Neutralized and screened from scrutiny are the efficacy and appropriateness of the OBE program itself.

The OBE *Practitioner's Implementation Handbook* distributed to Rough Rock teachers, for instance, identified "corrective activities" to ameliorate student "deficiencies," including re-teaching and instructing students to re-read their textbooks. In contrast were "enrichment" activities for "fast learners to broaden their horizons" (Danielson, 1989, pp. 82–86). In mandated workshops described by one staff member as brainwashing sessions, Rough Rock teachers were presented with flow charts from the *Handbook* outlining student "role performances" and instructing teachers to fill in boxes with student objectives that would, allegedly, enable students to perform those roles and thereby succeed.

Not surprisingly, RRENLAP teachers viewed OBE as a rejection of their work with alternative assessment and bilingual education curriculum reform. When the district administration linked teacher evaluation to students' performance on standardized tests, tensions mounted. The ironic and troublesome fact was that the NCA evaluation had recommended RRENLAP as a model for districtwide improvement, calling for "meaningful dialogue" about curriculum issues among teachers, district administrators, building principals, the school board, and community members (Navajo North Central Visiting Team, 1990, p. 14). These recommendations appeared to go unheeded at the district level.

Rough Rock succeeded in its bid for NCA accreditation and grant status—a fact that still inspires pride among Navajo and non-Navajo school personnel. The NCA process also succeeded in ensuring the school's survival. However, the process did little to change district-level curriculum and assessment policies. It did not direct greater attention to RRENLAP teachers' attempts to restructure curriculum and pedagogy. Hence, despite Senator DeConcini's call for a policy "consistent with Indian self-determination," the conditions for Indigenous schools authorized by P.L. 100-297 continued to lock these schools in a system of federal constraint and surveillance. Filtered throughout that system, and the daily reality teachers faced, was a web of power relations that buried their voices and privileged the authority of White, mostly male school administrators.

Within this institutional context, RRENLAP teachers continued to negotiate for positive pedagogical change. Eventually, they succeeded in modifying OBE to include Navajo language and literacy, and to accommodate the teaching innovations they had developed over the course of 10 years. To use Weis's (1996) words, the teachers exercised agency and imagination, even as they grappled with the "structures wrapped around their ... lives" (p. xii).

THE ELUSIVENESS OF TEACHER EMPOWERMENT

In an analysis of their researcher–teacher collaboration, university educator Polly Ulichny and English as a Second Language teacher Wendy Schoener (1996) say that teacher empowerment "was the precondition, as well as the outcome, of the transformation process" (p. 520). In reading their account, especially Schoener's words, one is impressed with the way Ulichny and Schoener's collaboration at once affirmed Schoener's pedagogy and encouraged greater scrutiny and risk-taking on her part. Their story is not unlike the experience reported here for bilingual teachers at Rough Rock.

The research and professional literature is liberally sprinkled with similar accounts of teacher empowerment. Yet the words researchers choose to describe this process often fail to do justice to the complicated and treacherous terrain through which the collaborative "we" must walk. The work within RRENLAP suggests that teacher empowerment is neither a precondition nor an outcome, neither a starting point nor a destination. Instead, especially in the context of minoritized schooling, this process is a complex and entangled negotiation at every turn, mediated by coercive relations of power (see also Ruiz, 1991).

The processes glossed by the words "teacher empowerment" are as ephemeral as they are significant. Their importance, Lipka and Yup'ik teacher-researchers point out, "may only be in the 'now' "—the moments of opportunity constructed within a zone of safety that evolve into productive work (Lipka, 1998, p. 203). The transferable lessons within RRENLAP, then, lie in the ways in which such moments of possibility can be created and utilized for Indigenous purposes—that is, in how the "power within" Indigenous communities can be marshaled and strategically deployed. Those lessons also lie in the recognition that, within Indigenous and minoritized schooling, individual and collective empowerment is neither a given nor a final state, but rather an ongoing struggle for self-determination and voice.

ACKNOWLEDGMENT

This chapter is adapted from parts of T. L. McCarty (2002), *A Place to Be Navajo—Rough Rock and the Struggle for Self-Determination in Indigenous Schooling*. Since the initial writing of this chapter, my research partner, Galena Sells Dick, whose work is prominent here, tragically passed away. I offer this account as a tribute to her leadership and vision, and I thank Galena's family for the opportunity to include this account of our work in this volume.

Teresa L. McCarty is the Alice Wiley Snell Professor of Educational Policy Studies at Arizona State University. She has been a bilingual curriculum developer, teacher, and coordinator of American Indian education programs at the local, state, and national levels, and the editor of *Anthropology & Education Quarterly*. She is co-principal investigator on a grant from the U.S. Department of Education Institute of Education Sciences to study the nature and impact of Native language shift and revitalization on American Indian students' academic achievement. Her most recent book is *A Place to Be Navajo—Rough Rock and the Struggle for Self-determination in Indigenous Schooling* (Lawrence Erlbaum Associates, 2002).

REFERENCES

American Indian Policy Review Commission. (1976). *Report on Indian education.* Washington, DC: U.S. Government Printing Office.

Begay, S. M., Clinton-Tullie, V., Estell, D. W., Estell, J., McCarty, T. L., & Sells, A. (1995). Change from the inside out: A story of transformation in a Navajo community school. *The Bilingual Research Journal, 19,* 121–139.

Cochran-Smith, M., & Lytle, S. (1993). *Inside/outside: Teacher research and knowledge.* New York: Teachers College Press.

Cole, M., John-Steiner, V., Scriber, S., & Souberman, S. (1978). *L. S. Vygotsky, Mind in society: The development of higher psychological processes.* Cambridge, MA: Harvard University Press.

Commission on Schools. (1983). *The NCA K–12 guide: An instrument designed to help structure the self-study and team visit of a unit school evaluation.* Boulder, CO: Commission on Schools, North Central Association of Colleges and Schools.

Danielson, C. (1989). *Teaching for mastery* (2nd ed.). Princeton, NJ: Outcomes Associates.

Dick, G. S. (1998). I maintained a strong belief in my language and culture: A Navajo language autobiography. *International Journal of the Sociology of Language, 132,* 23–25.

Dick, G. S., & McCarty, T. L. (1996). Reclaiming Navajo: Language renewal in an American Indian community school. In N. H. Hornberger (Ed.), *Indigenous literacies in the Americas: Language planning from the bottom up* (pp. 69–94). Berlin: Mouton de Gruyter.

3. INDIGENOUS LITERACIES AND TEACHER EMPOWERMENT   65

Duckworth, E. (1986). Teaching as research. *Harvard Educational Review, 56,* 481–495.

González, N., Moll, L. C., Floyd-Tenery, M., Rivera, A., Rendón, P., González, R., et al. (1995). Funds of knowledge for teaching in Latino households. *Urban Education, 29,* 443–470.

Goswami, D., & Stillman, P. (Eds.). (1987). *Reclaiming the classroom: Teacher research as an agency for change.* Upper Montclair, NJ: Boynton/Cook.

Holland, D., Lachicotte, W., Jr., Skinner, D., & Cain, C. (1998). *Identity and agency in cultural worlds.* Cambridge, MA: Harvard University Press.

Hollingsworth, S., with Cody, A., Davis-Smallwood, J., Dybdahl, M., Gallagher, P., Gallego, M., et al. (1994). *Teacher research and urban literacy education: Lessons and conversations in a feminist key.* New York: Teachers College Press.

Hudelson, S. (1989). *Write on: Children writing in ESL.* Englewood Cliffs, NJ: Center for Applied Linguistics and Prentice-Hall Regents.

Kincheloe, J. (1991). *Teachers as researchers: Qualitative inquiry as a path to empowerment.* London: Falmer.

Lave, J., & Wenger, E. (1991). *Situated learning: Legitimate peripheral participation.* Cambridge, UK: Cambridge University Press.

Lipka, J., & McCarty, T. L. (1994). Changing the culture of schooling: Navajo and Yup'ik cases. *Anthropology & Education Quarterly, 25,* 266–284.

Lipka, J., with Mohatt, G., & the Ciulistet Group. (1998). *Transforming the culture of schools: Yup'ik Eskimo examples.* Mahwah, NJ: Lawrence Erlbaum Associates.

Maberry, M. V. (1991). *Right after sundown: Teaching stories of the Navajos.* Tsaile, AZ: Navajo Community College Press.

Matlin, M. L., & Short, K. G. (1991). How our teacher study group sparks change. *Educational Leadership, 49,* 68.

McCarty, T. L. (1989). School as community: The Rough Rock demonstration. *Harvard Educational Review, 59,* 484–503.

McCarty, T. L. (1993a). Federal language policy and American Indian education. *The Bilingual Research Journal, 17,* 13–34.

McCarty, T. L. (1993b). Language, literacy, and the image of the child in American Indian classrooms. *Language Arts, 70,* 182–192.

McCarty, T. L. (1998). Schooling, resistance, and American Indian languages. *International Journal of the Sociology of Language, 132,* 27–41.

McCarty, T. L. (2002). *A place to be Navajo—Rough Rock and the struggle for self-determination in Indigenous schooling.* Mahwah, NJ: Lawrence Erlbaum Associates.

McCarty, T. L., & Dick, G. S. (2004). *Telling The People's stories: Literacy practices and processes in a Navajo community school.* In A. I. Willis, G. E. García, R. B. Barrera, & V. J. Harris (Eds.), *Multicultural issues in literacy research and practice* (pp. 101–122). Mahwah, NJ: Lawrence Erlbaum Associates.

Navajo North Central Visiting Team. (1990). *Report on Rough Rock Community School self-study.* Window Rock, Navajo Nation, AZ: The Navajo North Central Association.

Popkewitz, T. S. (1998). Dewey, Vygotsky, and the social administration of the individual-constructivist pedagogy as systems of ideas in historical spaces. *American Educational Research Journal, 35,* 535–570.

Roessel, R. A., Jr. (1977). *Navajo education in action: The Rough Rock Demonstration School.* Chinle, AZ: Navajo Curriculum Center Press.

Ruiz, R. (1991). The empowerment of language-minority students. In C. Sleeter (Ed.), *Empowerment through multicultural education* (pp. 212–227). Albany: State University of New York Press.

Schön, D. A. (1983). *The reflective practitioner.* New York: Basic Books.

Short, K. G. (1993). Teacher research for teacher educators. In L. Patterson, C. M. Santa, K. G. Short, & K. Smith (Eds.), *Teachers as researchers: Reflection and action* (pp. 155–159). Newark, DE: International Reading Association.

Strickland, D. S. (1988). The teacher as researcher: Toward the extended professional. *Language Arts, 65,* 754–764.

Tierney, R. J., Carter, M. A., & Desai, L. E. (1991). *Portfolio assessment in the reading-writing classroom.* Norwood, MA: Christopher-Gordon.

Tonigan, R. F., Emerson, G., & Platero, P. (1975). *Annual review and evaluation of the Rough Rock Contract School—Second interim report.* Rough Rock, AZ: Rough Rock Community School.

Ulichny, P., & Schoener, W. (1996). Teacher–researcher collaboration from two perspectives. *Harvard Educational Review, 66,* 496–524.

Varenne, H., & McDermott, R. (1999). *Successful failure: The school America builds.* Boulder, CO: Westview.

Vogt, L. A., & Au, K. H. P. (1995). The role of teachers' guided reflection in effecting positive program change. *The Bilingual Research Journal, 19,* 101–120.

Vogt, L. A., Jordan, C., & Tharp, R. G. (1993). Explaining school failure, producing school success: Two cases. In E. Jacob & C. Jordan (Eds.), *Minority education: Anthropological perspectives* (pp. 53–65). Norwood, NJ: Ablex.

Weis, L. (1996). Foreword. In B. A. Levinson, D. E. Foley, & D. C. Holland (Eds.), *The cultural production of the educated person.* Albany: State University of New York Press.

White House Conference on Indian Education (1992). *The final report of the White House Conference on Indian Education* (Vols. 1 & 2). Washington, DC: White House Conference on Indian Education.

Yazzie, E. (Ed.). (1971). *Navajo history.* Rough Rock, AZ: Navajo Curriculum Center Press.

Seizing Academic Power: Indigenous Subaltern Voices, Metaliteracy, and Counternarratives in Higher Education

Perry Gilmore
The University of Arizona and The University of Alaska Fairbanks

David M. Smith

This chapter draws on examples from our mentoring experiences and collaboration with Alaska Native and Australian Aboriginal graduate students in higher education. We describe and analyze efforts to create academic narratives designed to counter the conventional discourse shaping graduate education and characterizing much existing academic literature. We document deliberate resistance to established "grand narratives" and mainstream academic texts that frequently misrepresent, misinterpret, and stereotype Indigenous populations. We explore ways in which students have adopted successful and creative ways to use counternarratives and other forms of expression that (a) more accurately and respectfully present Indigenous knowledge, epistemologies, and worldviews, and (b) reflect presentations of self (both in style and content) more consistent with individual and community identities. The literacy strategies we describe affirm subaltern knowledge, create "free spaces" for authentic voices, and provide access to academic power.

By the Indian Ocean, in the center of a public park in the city of Fremantle, Western Australia, there is a large monument with a weathered plaque that reads:

> This monument was erected by C. J. Brockman as a fellow bushwanderer, tribute to the memories of Panter, Harding and Coldwyer. Earliest explorers of this terra

incognita attacked at night by treacherous natives were murdered at Boola Boola near Le Grange Bay on the 13th of November 1864.

Also as an appreciative token of remembrance of Maitland Brown, one of the pioneer pastoralists and premier politicians of this state. Intrepid leader of the government search and punitive party. This remains together with the sad relics of the ill-fated three recovered at great risk and danger from the lone wilds repose under a public monument in the East Perth Cemetery.

"Lest we forget"

Underneath this plaque is a second much shinier and obviously much newer plaque with the inscription:

This plaque was erected by the people who found the monument before you offensive. The monument describes the events at La Grange from one perspective only: The viewpoint of the white settlers.

No mention was made of the right of Aboriginal people to defend their land, of the history of provocation which led to the explorers' deaths.

The punitive party mentioned here ended in the deaths of somewhere around twenty Aboriginal people. The whites were well armed and equipped and none of their party was killed or wounded.

This plaque is in memory of the Aboriginal people killed at La Grange. It also commemorates all other Aboriginal people who died during the invasion of their country.

"Lest we forget Mapa Jaraiya-Nyalaka"

We happened on this monument near the end of a sabbatical in 1998 spent working with Aboriginal graduate students at the Centre for Aboriginal Studies at Curtin University in Perth. Although we did not know the individuals responsible for voicing the monument's second history, we subsequently heard something of the challenging struggle the authors of the counternarrative account experienced to have the "counter plaque" and its inscription mounted.

Their efforts were not invited. Their retelling of the La Grange story was not solicited. The monument was not originally erected as a site for a contentious historical display but rather as an icon of the dominant discourse, the hegemonic "grand narrative" of postcolonial Australia. The responsible (both in action and in character) activists had to accomplish three things to discursively transform the monument's message. First, they had to deliberately recognize and resist the oppressive historical account. Second, they had to aggressively seize the power to carve an open space (Greene, 1988), or sphere of freedom (Arendt, 1958) to voice their subaltern and subjugated knowledge (Foucault, 1980). And finally, because requests to remove the monument were denied, they had to strategically negotiate with dominant powers to be given the right to publicly transform the monument's offensive message.

This monument could serve as a nearly perfect eponym for the discursive work our Indigenous graduate students at the Centre for Aboriginal Studies were doing in their efforts to write meaningful, relevant, and authentic theses, and to earn legitimate graduate credentials in an Indigenous Research and Development postgraduate university program. Programs such as this one and the students in it struggle to maintain autonomy and integrity within larger Western institutions and knowledge systems that represent well-established epistemological systems "grounded in histories of colonialism, and the subjugation of indigenous knowledges" (Abdullah & Stringer, 2001, p. 1). Strikingly parallel experiences in negotiating academic discourses were shared by our Alaska Native students at the University of Alaska.

Counternarratives have been described as "the means by which groups contest that dominant reality and the framework of assumptions that support it" (Gates, 1997, p. 105). They "dispute the tenets of official culture" (Gates, 1997, p. 106) and hold a set of "hidden transcripts of resistance" (Fine, 1993). Such "counterstories" are viewed as a site for interrupting the dominant script and getting beneath dominant ideologies (see, e.g., Billig, 1995; Harris & Fine, 2001). In counterstories an emerging population of Indigenous scholars around the globe have illustrated Lather's (1991) description of "historical 'others' moving to the foreground, challenging and reshaping what we know of knowledge" (p. xix).

Identities may be chosen or imposed by language use; used to distance and differentiate; or for creating shared identities. In the work we describe in this chapter, Indigenous community counternarrative efforts reassert cultural ties; challenge the dominant culture, language, and ideology; and potentially transform the academic environments where they are implemented. Identity construction and reconstruction in this case are accomplished through a heightened cultural consciousness and "critical discourse awareness" (Fairclough, 1995) in generating academic counternarrative texts. Bucholtz (1999) describes identity reconstruction through language use as "emerg[ing] over time through discursive and other social practices" (p. 12). She suggests that identity is produced in social interaction and through a process of contestation and collaboration. These observations appear to hold true for the discursive experiences we describe in this chapter, where peer and community social and linguistic identities are reinvented, shared, and shaped over time through both oral and written dialogic processes with others.

The examples that follow demonstrate that to be a legitimate participant in academic discourse, like the activists who transformed the monument in Fremantle Park, Indigenous researchers have had to continuously resist ascribed stigmatized status for themselves, their communities, and the linguistic and cultural knowledge they bring. Indigenous researchers also must seize opportunities for academic power, privileging their own marginal positions and legitimizing their own subaltern knowledge. Finally, they must continuously negotiate with dominant culture institutions to reconfigure and scrutinize the range of complex and specific strategies of structure and power they struggle with in everyday local settings (e.g., see Dobkins, 1999, p. 181).

L. T. Smith (1999) argues that Indigenous peoples have been, in many ways, oppressed by theory; she identifies research and theory as significant sites of struggle between the interests and ways of knowing of the West, and the interests and ways of resisting of the "other." She declares that to "resist is to retrench in the margins, retrieve what we were and remake ourselves" (L. T. Smith, 1999, p. 38). As a Maori woman, she writes, "From the vantage point of the colonized, a position from which I write, and choose to privilege, the term research is inextricably linked to European imperialism and colonialism. The word itself, 'research,' is probably one of the dirtiest words in the indigenous world's vocabulary" (p. 1). Kathy Irwin (1992) urges, "We don't need anyone else developing the tools which will help us to come to terms with who we are. We can and will do this work. Real power lies with those who design the tools—it always has. This power is ours" (p. 5).

Thus, although drawing on notions from critical and feminist theory (i.e., critique, resistance, struggle, and emancipation), outsider-conceived theoretical models and methods have largely been seen as "failing" Indigenous and other marginalized peoples. Outsiders' theories are viewed as less than ideal for Indigenous communities where Indigenous researchers are anxious to discover their own ways of naming and carrying out research, informed by and taking into account the legacies of previous research, but not being limited by it (see Gilmore, 2002, for a fuller discussion of this critique).

In our mentoring efforts as professors and graduate advisors with Indigenous students both in Alaska and Australia, our goal—like many of our Native and non-Native peers and colleagues who share these concerns—has always been to encourage and make possible the attainment of legitimate academic credentials without sacrifice of real cultural identity. In this chapter we draw on examples from our mentoring experiences and collaboration with Indigenous students in higher education. We describe and analyze efforts to create academic narratives designed to counter the traditional and conventional discourse shaping research practice and graduate education, and characterizing much existing academic literature. These experiences, we believe, have also changed our own conceptual understandings, ways of knowing, and ways of working within our academic contexts. For this transformation we are profoundly grateful to all the students with whom we have been privileged to work.

In our work in Alaska, which began in 1985, we attempted to become resources to our students as they developed "culturally safe" (L. T. Smith, 1999) and appropriate localized research approaches and methods. (For further discussion of this work, see Gilmore, 2000, 2002; Gilmore & Smith, 1989, 2002; Gilmore, Smith, & Kairaiuak, 1997; D. M. Smith, 2002.) With our students in Alaska and Australia, we have explored deliberate resistance to established mainstream academic texts that have too frequently misrepresented, misinterpreted, and stereotyped Indigenous populations. We have described ways in which students have adopted successful and creative ways to use counternarratives and other forms of expression that more accurately and respectfully present Indigenous knowledge, epistemologies, and worldviews, and that reflect presentations of self (both in style and content) more consistent with individual and community Aboriginal identities. The literacy strategies we describe affirm subaltern knowledge, create spaces for authentic voices, and provide access to academic power. These narratives then attempt to both *rewrite and reright* existing and often damaging academic research.

METALITERACY AND THE TRANSFORMATION
OF ACADEMIC GENRES

By *academic genre* we are not referring simply to the conventional linguistic code used in academic writing—although that in itself embodies a set of necessary skills—but also to the more encompassing issue of the traditional rules for creating and disseminating knowledge. These might recognizably include, among other things, written and unwritten rules of "evidence" to which researchers are expected to adhere, the reliance on existing theoretical frameworks and peer review to establish legitimacy, the kinds of publications counted as appropriate, the decontextualized and impersonal styles expected of authors, and issues of title to ownership and appropriate responses to disputed claims made in writing or oral paper presentations. One could add here the primacy of literature (as opposed to experience) as the only legitimate repository of academic knowledge.

For many Indigenous scholars, for reasons detailed already, becoming a participant in this Western academic discourse has not been a seamless process of socialization, but a challenging balance of resistance and acculturation, often carried out alone, in alien and often unresponsive contexts. In the following examples, we hope to demonstrate the ways in which formal academic literacy has been used to actually reframe and strategically redefine literacy genres. This "metaliteracy" (Gilmore, 1987, 1988) explicitly articulates new paradigms of power in academic discourse. By dealing critically and explicitly with the notion of literacy, Indigenous communities redefine, transform, and privilege a distinct set of culturally appropriate rules for Indigenous peoples' participation in an academic discourse. This metaliteracy thus legitimizes a theoretical framework for counternarratives.

In the following section we describe three counterstory events that illustrate metaliteracy efforts in greater detail. The events provide specific examples of metaliteracy strategies including (a) counternarrative as institutional critique, (b) identification of aboriginal terms of reference, and (c) the specification of Indigenous guidelines, research positions, and documentation and revitalization of Indigenous languages.

Counternarrative as Institutional Critique

At the University of Alaska Fairbanks in 1991, a professor publicly charged that Native students were getting preferential grading treatment. The Native community was shocked and outraged. Students and their families were devastated. The university administration, with near total insensitivity to the way the incident was seen by or its effects on the Native community, treated the incident as a simple "academic" matter that could be cleared up by a rational and impersonal ad hoc committee investigation. This proved to be a serious miscalculation, and as a result the incident escalated to a full-blown media controversy, which was initiated with a bold newspaper headline that read, "Professor alleges UAF graduating unqualified Native students" (1991). The torrent of statewide media attention lasted for an entire year, casting doubt on all Native graduates and generating considerable pain and negative repercussions.

To the Alaska Native students, the year's headlines had read like a catechism of hegemony, a litany of shame, and a pedagogy for the oppressed

(Freire, 1973). Questioning minority credentials and standards is unfortunately not a new or unfamiliar response to minority achievement; nor are these discussions new to academia. Unfortunately these are the common responses to interrupting any "gatekeeping" practices where race, class, and gender lines are crossed. Although remarks such as these must have been uttered many other times, the intensity and persistence of this controversy and its continuous media frenzy seemed to surprise and eventually exhaust everyone. What was it about the moment, the timing, and the context of these remarks that fractured the public discourse? Why was the press so unrelenting, continuous, and unstoppable?

Fed by a frenzy of statewide media coverage, voices were not heard, epistemologies clashed, and misunderstandings magnified. In open forums Alaska Native students expressed their pain and humiliation, sharing personal experiences. Many of these narratives recalled similar experiences of stereotyping, racism, and discrimination in elementary and secondary schools and classrooms. For example, one Yup'ik student recalled her humiliation when, in a second-grade transitional bilingual classroom, her White teacher pulled her hair because she could not pronounce an English word correctly. She explained, using her early school experience as a metaphor, that the accusations about Native student grades being undeserved made her feel as if she was having her hair pulled again. Many of the testimonials at the forum included vivid and violent metaphors to express their pain (e.g., "I felt raped," "I felt like a knife went through me"). These heart-wrenching accounts were viewed as "hysterical" and inappropriate by the university administration, which expected the issues to be dealt with in an objective academic discourse style rather than a personal and passionate one.

One of our graduate students, Apacuar Larry Kairaiuak, no doubt because of his presence and leadership abilities, found himself in the spotlight in the midst of the intense media controversy. In spite of all efforts, a satisfactory or immediate solution could not be achieved at the time in the press or the institutional setting. Transforming our own frustration, outrage, and sense of injustice into academic discourse, we set out to compose a counternarrative to contest the offensive "master narrative" that dominated the media coverage. The three of us—Gilmore, Smith, and Kairaiuak—collected and analyzed the data generated by the incident and eventually published our findings (Gilmore et al., 1997). Although the genre was academic, that discursive context allowed us to give voice to the previously unheard and unrecognized "other" story.

There was some vindication in being able to find a platform from which to speak together to interrupt what we saw as institutional resistance to the increasing successes of a visibly growing minority population on campus. In our analysis we viewed the incident itself as a key communicative event (see, e.g., Gumperz & Hymes, 1972; Hymes, 1964) that captured and illustrated a clash of communication styles and discourse systems. We examined why, at that particular moment in history, the event fractured the public discourse in the interior of Alaska. (See Gilmore et al., 1997, and Gilmore & Smith, 2002, for a fuller discussion of the specific clashes of epistemology, expectation, and style.) We concluded that the incident functioned to maintain hegemonic practices at the university and to obscure the demonstrated and increasing accomplishments of Alaska Native people. By almost exclusively focusing their responses to the incident on issues of academic freedom, standards, and grading practices, the university abdicated its responsibility to provide a safe learning environment for the growing Indigenous population.

In spite of the heavy focus and attention on attrition and remediation of Native students, more and more students were achieving successes. In spite of predictions of failure, students were, in fact, graduating and getting jobs. They held the promise, possibility, and expectation of advanced degrees and they came with the blessing and full support of their communities. Consistent with theories of resistance and reproduction in education (Bourdieu & Passeron, 1977; Freire, 1985; Giroux, 1983), when it could no longer be predicted that Native students would "flunk out" or get "homesick" in their first year at the university, and when graduation statistics included growing percentages of Native students, the discourse shifted to questions of grading and unearned degrees. These were the next logical obstacles in an institutional gatekeeping enterprise. The incident was a painful example of backlash in full display resonating with the new conservative political climate.

To survive in the university environment, the Alaska Native student community learned and demonstrated that it was and is necessary to do certain things. They defined a community of support and established the Alaska Native Education Student Association. They resisted the stigmatized accusations and sought support and guidance from state Native corporations and organizations, drawing strength from their elders and home communities. Although the university had not created a free or safe space, the students were able to maintain their traditional ties and seize a context for themselves. They learned the value of situated freedom, which was not granted but seized and created in the context of many obstacles. That they could so strongly resist the stigma and vulnerability in such a hostile and assaulting environment was a remarkable counterstory of resistance and resilience. In spite of the failure of the university to protect and nurture their educational careers, their spirit was undaunted.

By critically examining and sociolinguistically exploring the institutional responses to this incident with our student, Kairaiuak, we attempted to clear a landscape for possibilities and new directions, taking collective responsibility for social renewal and redesign. This case describes only one small counternarrative, a contested account of a particular moment in history. However, each time we interrupt practices of the suppression or discounting of minority voices and achievements, it is significant. A decade later many dramatic changes, including a new and supportive administration, have increasingly improved the educational environment for Alaska Native students and faculty on the campus.

Aboriginal Terms of Reference

The postgraduate course in Indigenous Research and Development at the Centre for Aboriginal Studies at Curtin University, Perth, Australia, addresses the issue of genre and metaliteracy explicitly as part of the program's philosophy. Built on an action research model developed by Stringer (Abdullah & Stringer, 2001; Stringer, 1999), cohorts of master's and doctoral students are mentored in an approach to action research that produces academically acceptable research that at the same time measures up to Aboriginal terms of reference (ATR). This means "the approach to research is appropriate according to values and principles that are relevant and credible to the Aboriginal contexts in which the we work" (ATR, 1995, p. 1).

The postgraduate program at the Centre worked to balance what they described as two sets of complementary assumptions: ATR, and academic terms of reference (AcTR). ATR "encompasses the cultural knowledge, understanding and experiences that are associated with a commitment to Aboriginal ways of thinking, working and reflecting. ATR incorporates specific and implicit cultural values, beliefs and priorities from which Aboriginal standards are derived validated and practiced" (Kickett, 1992, p. 38).

The following postgraduate program description demonstrates the explicitly articulated philosophical privileging of Indigenous knowledge and worldviews:

> [The] graduate program centers the research process by ensuring that Aboriginal experience and systems of knowledge are at the heart of the research process.

Other systems of knowledge, including those encompassed by Western social and behavioral theory, do not provide the lens through which Aboriginal experience is interpreted. They stand as secondary sources or perspectives emerging in the research process. Primacy is always given to Aboriginal voices, experiences and perspectives. (Abdullah & Stringer, 2001, p. 2)

Students worked to bridge the many conflicts encountered in doing research in a Euro-Australian institution, writing theses that had to meet the demands of Western traditions of scholarship, and at the same time do research that reflected and respected Aboriginal views. The program was new at the time of our participation, which was early in the program's lifetime, but the early positive results were exhilarating to us as visiting professors mentoring their efforts. These were due to the persistence and resilience of the students, the elbow-to-elbow mentoring they received from the program staff, and the encouragement and feedback provided by their cohort of colleagues.

Nancy Gordon is an Australian Aboriginal woman who was a master's student in the Centre for Aboriginal Studies during our stay there. She spent much of her life living on the fringes of Kalgoorlie-Boulder in Western Australia. (*Fringe-dweller* is a term in the mainstream literature given to relatively unassimilated Aboriginal people who live in or on the outskirts of major towns.) Gordon was a member of the "stolen generation," the lighter skinned "half-caste" Aboriginal people who were taken away from their parents by the authorities and raised in institutions. Gordon's experiences as an Indigenous researcher provide insight into the critical language awareness necessary in developing a legitimate and authentic voice while balancing Aboriginal and mainstream academic discourse styles and values.

We had the privilege of working with Gordon as she was finishing her research and thesis on the life of the fringe-dwellers. In a paper in which she reflected on her life and her experience as a graduate student, she writes:

When I began the research project I was aware of the defining principle which was driving the Postgraduate Program at the Centre for Aboriginal Studies: honouring Aboriginal Terms of Reference while combining the requirements of academic research. As my research progressed I could feel a struggle within myself. Initially it was hard for me to go back to the fringe and to look at how and where people lived and try to capture their experiences. Even though I could master the art of code switching from one role to another, this did not alter the childhood feelings of loss, grief and rejection. (Gordon, 1999, p. 2)

In an article entitled, "Ethnography as Narrative," Bruner (1986) argues persuasively that:

> in the 1930s and 1940s the dominant story constructed about Native American culture change saw the present as disorganization, the past as glorious, and the future as assimilation. Now, however, we have a new narrative: the present is viewed as resistance movement, the past as exploitation, and the future as ethnic resurgence. (p. 139)

It is, of course, no accident that during the reign of the earlier dominant narrative we were graduating relatively few Indigenous scholars. It has now, however, become more common for Indigenous people to be taking the lead in and be researching the social issues that confront themselves and their own communities (see, e.g., Abdullah & Stringer, 1999; Cajete, 1994; Kirkness & Barnhardt, 1991; Langton, 1993; Semali & Kincheloe, 1999; L. T. Smith, 1999). In fact, doing such research has become one of the primary means of resistance.

This resistance has many faces. It may be to simply set the record straight, to validate and legitimize Native ways of knowing (Kawagley, 1995), to revitalize Native languages in the face of scholarship that says the task is hopeless (Dementi-Leonard & Gilmore, 1999), or to develop an understanding of the survival needs of fringe-dwellers, so that these needs can be addressed in a way that legitimizes and dignifies their existence (Gordon, 1999). Behind every instance, however, lurks the history of exploitation inevitably affecting the researchers' perception of issues and styles of presentation. Doing the research and putting the results in circulation means coming to terms with the painful exploitation of the past—exploitation that is in no sense a purely academic or distant historical issue. It is a reality that has touched and continues to touch every aspect of Indigenous scholars' lives.

In Australia, many current Aboriginal graduate students are members of the stolen generation, having suffered the unimaginable psychological (and not infrequently physical) pain of being forcibly removed from their families in the name of assimilation, being denied that very assimilation, and then forced to eke out an existence on the fringes. This, of course, is all in addition to the prevailing expectations in institutions of higher education, that Indigenous peoples will either be unsuccessful academics or ungrateful recipients of society's largesse.

Although Indigenous scholars may be willing to pay the painful price of confronting their histories and the indignities of recent colonial exploitation in the interests of creating these counternarratives, this is not the only affront with which they must contend. It has been our experience that research not conforming to the prevailing academic genres still risks being either patronized or denigrated as "not real scholarship." Furthermore, within our universities the "safe places" that have been constructed to encourage and promote Indigenous scholarship must be ever-vigilant in guarding themselves against threats of marginalization or elimination, usually under the guise of making the institutions more cost effective (see D. M. Smith, 1998, for a discussion of this at the University of Alaska). The need to confront the grief and anger at one's past history becomes a major consideration, and a major impetus to create viable counternarratives to the prevailing essentialist views of "Nativeness." It accounts for much of the attrition from many academic programs and the reluctance of Indigenous people to enter certain disciplines, professions, and specific universities and graduate programs.

In spite of these conditions, there continues to be a vibrant and rapidly growing number of Indigenous people who have chosen academic programs carefully, as well as created and negotiated respectful scholarly spaces to become successful and productive scholars, finding the new Indigenous research enterprise rewarding and even healing both individually and for their communities. These efforts are dramatically enriching the knowledge base and ways of knowing in our educational research institutions. In her reflective paper, Gordon (1999) remarked,

> I realise now despite the intentions I had to break the shackles of my "welfare" background, I was still entrenched in this kind of thinking when I started my research. I believe these "shackles" were born from the religious teachings of the Missions and from watching my parents' struggle for social justice. These childhood experiences shaped my perceptions throughout my adult years .... I wanted "to fix" other people's wounds .... On reflection I can see that my research started to flow only when I became my natural self and sat with the people. (p. 14)

Following this she includes a quote from Lila Watson: "If you have come to help me, you are wasting your time, but if you have come because your liberation is bound up with mine we can work together." Gordon goes on to say in discussing this important turning point in her academic life:

> From the beginning I was open to people about the purpose of my research ... [but] I believe I was holding out on them .... I wanted to protect them. I assumed

that these people were helpless .... I became my natural self and sat with the people like I used to. (p. 14)

She concludes,

The shackles had finally broken, and for the first time I felt an inner peace within me as there was a new way of seeing. I was seeing through the eyes of the people, I was hearing what they were saying; that they had a well planned life that they had developed for themselves. (p. 17)

Although Gordon in earlier years had been raised in a village by her father's people, for most of this time she was either under the tutelage of a mission, in training, or serving in a social work position. In seeking her master's credentials, she had unconsciously (although it is often consciously taught and adopted) assumed a stance conditioned by her life in the White world. She saw herself and the people whose lives she was researching as some combination of helper and victim.

As Fanon (1965), Freire (1973), and others have pointed out, one of the legacies of colonialism is often the internalization of the oppression so that the colonizer begins to dictate one's identity. In the university, with its rigid canons of what counts as research, and the unwritten traditions of what privileges one to be a researcher as opposed to a "researchee," both Indigenous scholars and their mentors must be constantly working to make it possible to escape "the shackles" and become free to see and hear through others' eyes and ears, in ways that are not "natural" to non-Indigeneous or Indigenous colleagues in academic settings. Harking back to Bruner's (1986) notion of a dominant research narrative, little will be gained either in successful resistance or successful future resurgence (revitalization) unless we can find ways to privilege new and Indigenous ways of seeing and hearing.

Research Positions, Guidelines, and the Documentation of Indigenous Languages

This final example describes the coauthoring experience of Gilmore and her colleague and graduate student, Beth Dementi-Leonard. The coauthored article described a community-based participatory Athabascan language planning and revitalization effort in the western interior region of Alaska (Dementi-Leonard & Gilmore, 1999). The grassroots language planning project involved a series of regional meetings involving 20 villages in five traditional Athabascan language areas (Deg Hit'an, Holikachuk, Koyukon, Upper Kuskokwim, and Lower Tanana). In these communities there are few remaining Native speakers and many of the speakers are over 50 years old. Dementi-Leonard, an Athabascan linguist at the University of Alaska Fairbanks, was the director of the project, which she wrote up as a part of her master's degree final project. Gilmore was her graduate supervisor and chair at the time and was invited by Dementi-Leonard to be her coauthor in the journal publication. For the purposes of this discussion, we focus on the strategies Dementi-Leonard and Gilmore employed for presenting the study in an academic journal rather than presenting in detail the actual findings of the project.

Resisting Outsider's Theories.   Consistent with Indigenous researchers' values, the authors' first priority was that the publication would contribute positively to community language efforts. As a result, the use of a theoretical framework for the paper initially presented a dilemma. Too often outsiders' research and theories skeptically determine the level of success of language-strengthening efforts. Therefore, the coauthors chose to deliberately resist using the most prominent theories in the language shift literature as a framework through which to interpret the data. For example, the authors decided that using Fishman's (1991) theory as a lens through which to present the data would have presented a dismal and misleading view of the language situation and publicly reinforced the obstacles facing the communities rather than highlighting the focus and determination of the people. They explicitly stated their counterstrategy in the following words:

> This article celebrates the knowledge held in the small villages of western interior Alaska. We have chosen to organize and report our findings in ways that are consistent with that knowledge base and its epistemology. We therefore have chosen a more empirical, descriptive, and less theoretical stance, documenting current practices and providing a public record as a resource. Additionally, we have chosen to rely more heavily on local experts, their knowledge, interpretations, and meanings, and less on scholarly outsiders' analyses and categorizations. As Fishman has recognized, in language and cultural renewal, revivalism, and reversal efforts, community members are in the "process of re-establishing local options, local control and local meaning" (1991, p. 35). Having outside experts determine the level or stage of success of these efforts or label the languages as *dying* and *moribund* can undermine the very notion of local control, local meaning, and certainly local hope. We have tried, therefore, to resist those

categories and instead rely on a posture of possibility in describing events and activities, finding an enabling vocabulary more suitable for capturing the self-determination, resistance, and resilience we found in the communities. (Dementi-Leonard & Gilmore, 1999, p. 39)

Using a more nonconfrontational approach appropriate to local community values, the article did not directly argue the limitations of Fishman's (1991) language shift theories, which would have been more common in conventional academic discourse. Instead, acknowledging his standing in the field, the article cited the views that Fishman held that were consistent with the Indigenous community's language ideologies. Rather than use Fishman's theoretical language use levels to frame the analysis, three major topical themes in the data were identified: critique and resistance, self-determination and activism, and collaboration and leadership. It is worthy of note that Fishman (1999) himself, who not surprisingly was invited to respond to the collection of papers, appeared to have no problem with his model not being the focus of the analysis, making no mention of it in his commentary. He did, however, specifically point out the "powerful sense of community and resistant activism" (p. 122).

Privileging Knowledge.   A second effort was to use conventional literacy strategies to mark and privilege the knowledge of "local experts." Most typically in academic texts elders are acknowledged as helpful "informants," or more recently "consultants" and "collaborators." In this publication the authors instead referenced elders as Indigenous scholars making an effort to cite their work and knowledge in the body of the text, notes, and bibliography, including a range of genres such as translations, dictionaries, traditional narratives, children's stories, school district curriculum materials, public addresses and lectures, letters, and the like. By presenting this knowledge in conventional reference style, the contributions are elevated in the discourse and more parallel to the dominant-culture scholars with whom they are symmetrically cited.

Incorporating Traditional Values and the Imperative of Community Solidarity.   Another metaliteracy strategy enlisted was a blending of academic genre with more traditional Indigenous conventions. For example, consistent with local values, Dementi-Leonard used a traditional description of her lineage, naming her father and identifying her birth place to introduce herself in the text at the outset. Although this is not a common aspect of academic writing, it did not violate any specific conventions and was acceptable to the journal editors and reviewers.

The notion that one should seek knowledge for knowledge's sake is revered in Western traditions of scholarship. Indigenous research seeks to contribute both to academic and local communities. As Dementi-Leonard (2001) has recently pointed out, "Research by indigenous researchers for the benefit of indigenous communities also dovetails with political/post modern movements of self-determination, autonomy and cultural regenesis" (p. 1). In addition, in the mainstream academic community it is conventional to act, whether as student or professional scholar, as individuals. Although mainstream academics may be close to their families and have many ties to their community of residence, there is a conventional expectation that academic and personal lives are to be kept separate. This posture has been somewhat blurred in recent years with growing interest in and legitimacy given to postmodernists, researcher autobiographies, and teacher research. Nonetheless, both of these historic traditions—distinguishing between theoretical and applied, as well as separating personal from professional—are deeply rooted and often clash with Indigenous epistemologies. They involve questions of ownership of data, styles of interaction in the field, relationship of researcher to the data, uses to which the results will be put, obligation of researchers to the community, the right to speak for a community, and so on. For an Indigenous scholar it may be impossible to say, "I am speaking for myself and no one else." This is true first, because of the traditional nature of one's identity, which is not based on what he or she does but on the families or clans of your parents; and second, because the academic community will tend to see the scholar in a marked category, not just a scholar but "a Native researcher" or an "Indigenous writer," and thus a stereotypical representation of the "other." Among other things, in the Western tradition, the attainment of educational credentials entails the authority to speak and act in certain areas of expertise. For Indigenous people the authority to speak for or about others comes from the attainment of particular status in the group.

In writing the article, Gilmore and Dementi-Leonard used several strategies to respect community solidarity and autonomy. Out of respect for privacy, the authors deliberately resisted using extensive direct quotes from the data despite several reviewers' suggestions that it might enhance the effectiveness of the article if they did so. Further, the limited quotes that were included were used only after full review and consent by community participants. All aspects of the project, including data collection, analysis, and write up, were continually reviewed and approved by the community.

This grassroots approach with regard to language planning and documentation was a somewhat new experience for many of the participants in the region who had previously been involved in more "top-down" efforts organized and run by non-Native outsiders. One of the participating community members expressed both her frustration about past experiences with dominant-culture institutions and hope for future Native-controlled possibilities. Her words (which she was willing to have quoted) capture the strong solidarity of community spirit:

> It's been all these years of other people coming and saying how things should be … so how are you supposed to feel about what you've contributed? It doesn't seem very important to some. I know there's good and bad in every culture, but the white culture is one that has come in and it's their way or no way. Now we're trying to get everybody back to where they feel good about themselves and what they can do—trying to undo how many years of the total opposite. (Dementi-Leonard & Gilmore, 1999, p. 44)

As Wideman (1987) has said, "Language is a terrain where differently privileged discourses struggle via confrontation and/or displacement" (p. 8). As the preceding quote suggests, the language planning effort became a community site for contesting the dominant culture as well as a place to reinvent identities through language—not only the Athabascan languages of the region, but also the language of power that marked and privileged the project, and declared community ownership.

CONCLUSION

Heather Kendall-Miller, a prominent Alaska Native attorney who represented the Alaskan village of Venetie in a tribal sovereignty case in the U.S. Supreme Court and has been involved in the English-only legal struggle, addressed the Alaska Federation of Natives Convention in Anchorage on October 23, 1997. Her words capture the collective spirit of resistance, self-determination, activism, and leadership present in Indigenous communities across Alaska: "That flame burns bright today throughout the villages of Alaska, despite the state's best efforts to snuff it out … it does not matter that the state opposes us or the federal government abandoned us. Unity is our strength."

In this united spirit, for example, the Assembly of Alaska Native Educators at their yearly meetings in Anchorage have adopted a set of carefully and collaboratively crafted guidelines including *Guidelines for Respecting Cultural Knowledge* (Assembly of Alaska Native Educators, 2000) and a set of *Guidelines for Strengthening Indigenous Languages* (Assembly of Alaska Native Educators, 2001). These guidelines have been collaboratively crafted and developed by a wide variety of Alaska Native communities and organizations. (For these guidelines and numerous other examples, see The Alaska Native Knowledge Network website at http://www.ankn.uaf.edu). The guidelines can also be viewed as metaliterate texts that embody local cultural epistemologies and language ideologies, and establish Indigenous frameworks for the academic discourse that should surround research, development, and pedagogy in these areas. In one item describing guidelines for researchers, for example, individuals are urged to "utilize the expertise in the communities" and to "use caution in applying external frames of reference in analysis and interpretation;" individuals are described as being "responsible for … accurately representing the cultural perspective and protecting the cultural integrity and rights of all participants."

A strong sense of community values and boundaries echoes through the powerful assertive language of the *Guidelines* in Alaska, in the ATR developed in Australia, and numerous other formal written documents being generated by Indigenous peoples worldwide. Although in many cases these texts protect lifeways and ways of knowing that are a part of an allegedly oral culture, the means for accomplishing the "safe space" for those values is seized through more conventional literate discourse practices. Being literate about literacy sets up new rules and new power. Metaliteracy privileges and theorizes the position from which to carry out the research and writing efforts of the Indigenous communities.

Over the past decade there has been a steadily growing Indigenous presence in the academic community. Newly formed Indigenous conferences, research networks, publications, and associations reflect the strong cultural identity and solidarity among Indigenous international populations. In the face of constant global challenges (e.g., educational, economic, linguistic, and political), Indigenous peoples are transforming the nature of what we count as knowledge and research. The results have been and promise to continue to be enriching not only for the entire academic community, but also for the global community of which we are all part.

Perry Gilmore, an educational anthropologist and sociolinguist, is Professor Emerita of Linguistics, Alaska Native Languages, and Education at the University of Alaska Fairbanks, and Associate Professor of Language, Reading and Culture at the University of Arizona. She has conducted communication, language, and literacy research in a wide variety of urban and rural settings in the United States, Africa, Russia, and Australia. She is the author of numerous ethnographic studies and the coeditor of two major ethnography collections, *Children in and out of School: Ethnography and Education*, and *The Acquisition of Literacy: Ethnographic Perspectives*. Her current research is a six-year collaborative language and identity project that focuses on social aspects of bilingualism and language regenesis in interior Alaska.

David M. Smith (January 23, 1935–December 9, 2000) was Professor Emeritus of Anthropology and Linguistics at the University of Alaska Fairbanks, and Affiliate Senior Researcher at the Bureau of Applied Research in Anthropology (BARA) at the University of Arizona. A visionary and leader in the fields of applied linguistics and anthropology and education, he left a profound legacy of deep commitment to social justice and educational equity through his research, writing, and teaching. In the 1960s he conducted fieldwork for his PhD in anthropology on the Kapsiki language in Cameroon. One of the original cohort of sociolinguists at Georgetown University, he became involved in issues of language minorities and education during the era of desegregation of American schools. This work led him to conduct ethnographic language and literacy research in educational settings across the United States, Russia, and Australia for the next 20 years. While director of the Center for Urban Ethnography at the University of Pennsylvania, he started and for many years directed the University of Pennsylvania Ethnography and Education Forum.

ACKNOWLEDGMENT

This chapter was written with my husband, partner, coauthor, and dearest friend, David Martin Smith, who passed away before the final draft was completed. An anthropologist and linguist, David urged that our challenge as researchers is "not only to surface the narratives of oppression, resistance, and resilience, but for the edification of the academic community it must develop approaches that put these narratives to use in addressing the oppressive equation ... they must become the basis for a radical new pedagogy, one that is based on and privileges these narratives and local knowledge" (D. M. Smith, 2002, p. 181). It is that underlying approach on which this chapter rests and the spirit within which I completed our final chapter together.

REFERENCES

Abdullah, J., & Stringer, E. (1999). Indigenous knowledge, Indigenous learning, Indigenous research. In L. M. Semali & J. L. Kincheloe (Eds.), *What is Indigenous knowledge: Voices from the academy* (pp. 83–98). New York: Falmer.

Abdullah, J., & Stringer, E. (2001, April). *Decolonizing university discourses: Indigenous knowledge and Indigenous experience as core components of a graduate program.* Paper presented at the American Education Research Association, Seattle, WA.

Aboriginal Terms of Reference (ATR). (1995). Centre for Aboriginal Studies, Curtin University of Technology, Perth, Western Australia. (Unpublished document)

Arendt, H. (1958). *The human condition.* Chicago: University of Chicago Press.

Assembly of Alaska Native Educators. (2000). *Guidelines for respecting cultural knowledge.* Anchorage: Alaska Native Knowledge Network.

Assembly of Alaska Native Educators. (2001). *Guidelines for strengthening Indigenous languages.* Anchorage: Alaska Native Knowledge Network.

Billig M. (1995) *Banal nationalism.* Beverly Hills, CA: Sage.

Bourdieu, P., & Passeron, J. C. (1977). *Reproduction in education, society, and culture.* Beverly Hills, CA: Sage.

Bruner, E. (1986). Ethnography as narrative. In V. W. Turner & E. M. Bruner (Eds.), *The anthropology of experience* (pp. 139–155). Chicago: University of Illinois Press.

Bucholtz, M. (1999). Bad examples: Transgression and progress in language and gender studies. In M. Buchhotz, A. C. Liang, & L. A. Sutton (Eds.), *Reinventing identities: The gendered self in discourse* (pp. 3–26). Oxford, UK: Oxford University Press.

Cajete, J. (1994). *Look to the mountain: An ecology of Indigenous education.* Durango, CO: Kivakí Press.

Dementi-Leonard, B. (2001). *Athabascan oral traditions: Deg Hit'an narratives, and Native ways of knowing.* Unpublished interdisciplinary degree proposal, Alaska Native Studies, University of Alaska, Fairbanks, AK.

Dementi-Leonard, B., & Gilmore, P. (1999). Language revitalization and identity in social context: A community-based Athabascan language preservation project in western interior Alaska. *Anthropology & Education Quarterly, 30,* 37–55.

Dobkins, R. (1999). Strong language, strong actions: Native American women writing against the federal authority. In M. Bucholtz, A. C. Liang, & L. A. Sutton (Eds.), *Reinventing identities: The gendered self in discourse* (pp.181–189). Oxford, UK: Oxford University Press.

Fairclough, N. (1995). *Critical discourse analysis.* New York: Longman.

Fanon, F. (1965). *A dying colonialism.* New York: Grove.

Fine, M. (1993, July). *Gender, race, class and culture: The politics of exclusion in schooling.* Lecture given at University of Alaska Fairbanks.

Fishman, J. (1991). *Reversing language shift: Theoretical and empirical foundations of assistance to threatened languages.* Clevedon, UK: Multilingual Matters.

Fishman, J. (1999). Comments and reflections. *Anthropology & Education Quarterly, 30,* 116–124.

Foucault, M. (1980). *Power/knowledge: Selected interviews and other writings, 1972–77.* New York: Pantheon.

Freire, P. (1973). *Pedagogy of the oppressed.* New York: Seabury Press.

Freire, P. (1985). *The politics of education.* South Hadley, MA: Bergin & Garvey.

Gates, H. L. (1997). *Thirteen ways of looking at a Black man.* New York: Random House.

Gilmore, P. (1987, November). *Academic literacy in cultural context: Issues for higher education in Alaska.* Paper presented at the annual meeting of the American Anthropological Association, Chicago.

Gilmore, P. (1988, February). *Metaliteracy: A critical view of ethnography and literacy.* Keynote address for A New Window into the Classroom: Ethnographic Techniques Conference, Hempstead, NY.

Gilmore, P. (2000, November). *Creating culturally responsive schools: An Alaskan case of Indigenous language learning.* Paper presented at the National Council of Teachers of English Conference, Milwaukee, WI.

Gilmore, P. (2002). Methodological challenges of critical ethnography: Insights from collaborations on an Indigenous counter narrative. In H. Trueba & Y. Zhou (Eds.), *The role of educational ethnography in pedagogy: Critical ethnography in a global and interdisciplinary perspective* (pp. 185–194). Oxford, UK: Rowman & Littlefield.

Gilmore, P., & Smith, D. M. (1989). Mario, Gary, Jesse and Joe: Contextualizing dropping out. In H. Trueba, G. Spindler, & L. Spindler (Eds.), *What do anthropologists have to say about dropouts?* (pp. 79–92). New York: Falmer.

Gilmore, P., & Smith, D. M. (2002). Identity, resistance and resilience: Counternarratives and subaltern voices in Alaskan higher education in 1991. In. D. C. S. Li (Ed.), *Discourses in search of members: In honor of Ron Scollon* (pp. 104–134). Lanham, MD: University Press of America.

Gilmore, P., Smith, D. M., & Kairaiuak, A. L. (1997). Resisting diversity: An Alaskan case of institutional struggle. In M. Fine, L. Weis, L. Powell, & L. Mun Wong (Eds.), *Off white: Readings on race, power, and society* (pp. 90–99). New York: Routledge.

Giroux, H. (1983). *Theory and resistance in education.* South Hadley, MA: Bergin & Garvey.

Gordon, N. (1999). *"Thuthibin yah! Martuwonga" ("Josephine talk with the people").* Unpublished manuscript, Centre for Aboriginal Studies, Curtin University of Technology, Perth, Australia.

Greene, M. (1988). *The dialectics of freedom.* New York: Teachers College Press.

Gumperz, J., & Hymes, D. (1972). *Directions in sociolinguistics: The ethnography of communication.* New York: Holt, Rinehart & Winston.

Harris, A., & Fine, M. (2001). Under the covers: Theorizing the politics of counter stories. *International Journal of Critical Psychology, 4,* 6–18.

Hymes, D. (Ed.). (1964). *Language in culture and society.* New York: Harper & Row.

Irwin, K. (1992). Towards theories of Maori feminisms. In R. duPlessis (Ed.), *Feminists' voices: Women's studies texts for Aotearoa New Zealand* (pp. 5–18). Oxford, UK: Oxford University Press.

Kawagley, A. O. (1995). *A Yupiaq worldview: A pathway to ecology and spirit.* Prospect Heights, IL: Waveland.

Kickett, R. (1992). Aboriginal terms of reference: A paradigm for the future. In C. White (Ed.), *Toward 2000: Maintaining the momentum. Proceedings of the National Aboriginal and Torres Strait Islander higher education conference* (pp. 36–45). Toowoomba, Australia: University of Southern Queensland.

Kirkness, V., & Barnhardt, R. (1991). First Nations and higher education: The three R's—Respect, relevance, reciprocity, responsibility. *Journal of American Indian Education, 30*, 1–15.

Langton, M. (1993). *"Well I heard it on the radio and saw it on the television": An essay for the Australian Film Commission on the politics and aesthetics of filmmaking by and about Aboriginal people and things.* North Sydney, Australia: Australian Film Commission.

Lather, P. (1991). *Getting smart: Feminist research and pedagogy with/in the postmodern.* New York: Routledge.

Professor alleges UAF graduating unqualified Native students. (1991, November 1). *Anchorage Times*, p. 1.

Semali, L. M., & Kincheloe, J. L. (1999). *What is Indigenous knowledge? Voices from the academy.* New York: Falmer.

Smith, D. M. (1998). Aspects of the cultural politics of Alaskan education. In Y. Zhou & H. Trueba (Eds.), *Ethnic identity and power: Cultural contexts of political action in school and society* (pp. 369–388). Albany: State University of New York Press.

Smith, D. M. (2002). The challenge of urban ethnography. In H. Trueba & Y. Zhou (Eds.), *The role of educational ethnography in pedagogy: Critical ethnography in a global and interdisciplinary perspective* (pp. 171–184). Oxford, UK: Rowman & Littlefield.

Smith, L. T. (1999). *Decolonizing methodologies: Research and Indigenous peoples.* London: ZED Books.

Stringer, E. (1999). *Action research: A handbook for practitioners.* Thousand Oaks, CA: Sage.

Wideman, J. (1987, December 18). The Black writer and the magic of the word. *New York Times Magazine,* p. 24.

5

Julia's "Story" of Schooling:
A Borderlands Account

Robert Whitman
Eastern Washington University

Drawing on a larger data set on the construction of identities in and through schooling, this analysis focuses on one student's placement of self within a moral landscape of peers, teachers, classroom, and community. Through the organization of places, cycles, voices, and people in this account, one Mexican-American woman presents a strong critique of schooling, and a collectively voiced sense of social injustice in the historical relationship between Anglos and Mexicans in the U.S. Southwest.

1. It's just that I see
2. Like, you can look at the newspaper
3. Uh, we see
4. We take a test
5. Like we take those ( ) or whatever tests

6. And, it's like at the end of the year
7. worst school, Sundown High School
8. Lowest scores, Sundown High School
9. Why? Hispanic kids go there
10. Why? South-side school

These are the opening words of a narrative-like account told to me in the winter of 1997 by a second-generation Mexican-American woman about to graduate from high school in Tucson, Arizona. They remind us that words like *test* and *scores* do not mean just one thing. In the moment of speech and action words are taken up by people to index many different meanings—meanings that have power. In *Marxism and the Philosophy of Language*, Volosinov (1929/1986) outlines a contextualized semiotics where "existence reflected in the sign is not merely reflected but refracted" (p. 23). In the preceding example, the words *test* and *scores* seem to refract as they are spoken. They index multiple meanings. People in the community may not necessarily agree on what particular words like *test* and *score* mean. They often struggle over meaning. Signs carry potential multiple meanings in a given context, what Volosinov (1929/1986) calls "social multi-accentuality" (p. 23).

Multiaccentuality is a perspective and a tool that can be brought to the analysis of speech. This multivocal character of speech has been explored in the analysis of narrative (Briggs, 1996; Hanks, 1996; Hill, 1995). Recent work by scholars such as Wertsch (1998) and Holland, Lachiotte, Cain, & Skinner (1998) brings together concepts of multiple voices within a Vygotskian model of sociohistorical development. In this chapter I examine the multivocal nature of a narrative-like account told entirely in the present tense. The multiple voices and the organization of time and spaces present an unusually critical account as one Mexican-American woman positions herself in relation to peers, community, school, and a historical borderlands divide.

The primary theoretical organizing tool that I use for analysis is the linguistic construction of what Hill (1995) calls a moral geography. A moral geography is a landscape in which people and places are organized in the moment of telling. The geography orients listeners to this complex landscape through which point of view is expressed. Similar to recent work with a focus on cultural models (Holland et al., 1999; Wertsch, 1998), the idea of a moral geography examines the ways in which language is taken in and made a tool that influences our activity and stance toward the world. In addition, the moral geography evokes a landscape in which people take on a moral weight as they inhabit particular spaces. When we use moral geography as a metaphor, the organization of people, places, and the value they take on is the focus of analysis. Using this metaphor I concentrate on three ways geography is created in this particular telling. I first examine the structure of the account that creates places where people act. Second, I examine the creation of persons, the "accents" and voices that populate the narrative, including how others' voices are represented and how those voices represent actions. Finally, I look at the use of the present tense that makes this account not a narrative in the canonical sense. There is no "once upon a time" in this story, and that is also an integral part of this particular moral geography.

These three aspects of the geography serve to orient the hearer toward a particular point of view that is highly ideological in nature. By *ideology* I mean more than a linked system of ideas, although this account certainly meets that criterion. Ideology is meant to suggest that literacy practices and accounts of schooling are "rooted in, reflective of, or responsive to the experience or interests of a particular social position .... Ideology is seen as ideas, discourse, or signifying practices in the service of the struggle to acquire or maintain power" (Woolard, 1998, pp. 6–7). The point of view of the teller in this account is saturated with historical and present-day struggles over how words, actions, and identities will be shaped. The geography is set in a larger processual setting of school, testing, how that is reported in the media, and the effects of this process in the classroom and on the lives of the people involved. Although the story is set in the present, it has accents and voices that evoke a sociohistorical past.

The setting for this study was a community college writing course. In this course it was my job to teach writing to high school students who were bused in from south-side high schools as a part of a school-to-work program involving high schools, the community college, and a high-technology company that made microchips. It was in this classroom on the first day of the semester that Julia, a first-generation Mexican-American woman, wrote a journal entry in response to my prompt, "Why are you here?"

> I chose the ... program because I want to advance my career in technology. First, I enjoy putting thing together, finding out how they work if they do. Second, I like the probabilities of winning a lot of money. I enjoy having money to spend. Third, my teacher during my summer academy got me really interested in semiconductors by the way he taught the class. In conclution, I enjoy technology and thats what I want my career to be developed in, and the ... program was a great opportunity.

> I think that writing and reading are important because you need to know how to write information down. More important you need to know how to read the information given to you. Everythin on this world has somehow something to do with both reading and writing. This technical writing class is going to be important to me because is going to help me understan the meaning of many of the technical words use in technology. I have many problems with writing so this is going to help me improve my vocabulary and specially to find out more information on anything I need to continue with my education. To know how to read and write is one of the most important things you need know in this life.

Julia's journal comment reflects the perspective on the ideological grounding of literacy outlined earlier. Her comments in the first paragraph about "advancing my career," and "having money to spend" could be seen as reflective of ubiquitous ideologies of American culture, what Philips (1998) calls everyday ideologies. Ideology causally links school and literacy with access to better work and greater economic benefit. Julia's comments in the second paragraph include "writing information down," "reading information," "understanding the meaning of technical words," and "improving vocabulary." These could be said to index an ideology of communication and learning, one of decoding and absorbing information, a passive view of learning. However, to draw conclusions about Julia's identity based on this kind of writing would be premature. The discourse of the introduction indexes a very different kind of person, one who is consciously and strongly critical of school. To think about these various presentations of self in schooling I use Bourdieu's (1977a, 1977b) concepts of habitus, field, and capital. In the first instance, and for much of the semester in my writing class, Julia was "doing school." She was presenting a set of enduring dispositions practiced over many years. She was in the "field" of school, and in a social context where she had relatively little capital to draw on. When she gave the oral account below the semester was over, she had a grade, and she was speaking to me in her own home on an early winter afternoon, with her baby daughter on her lap. Julia was 17 at the time of this interview. The account was not a response to any specific question but instead grew out of a conversation between Julia and I about the final writing she had done in class.

DATA

Julia's Story of Schooling

I. Orientation
   1. It's just that I see
   2. Like, you can look at the newspaper
   3. Like, uh, you can say at the end of the year
   4. Umm, we see, we take a test
   5. Like we take those ( ) or whatever tests

   6. And, it's like at the end of the year
   7. worst school, Sundown High School
   8. Lowest scores, Sundown High School
   9. Why? Hispanic kids go there
   10. Why? South-side school

11. It's like they put us down even though we try our best and everything
12. We go into class, even the teachers put us down
13. So it's like …
14. A lot of students we just like
15. "kay Whoaa our teachers put us down,
16. the city's putting us down,"
17. We just … continue with that

IIA. Complication

18. It's just anything, like anything bad
19. it's always on the south side
20. Most of the time it's our school
21. Most of the time either Sundown High School or Pueblo High School
22. *All the time*

23. And there's like umm
24. So our teachers they just don't care
25. Some teachers do
26. Some teachers tell you "you guys there's something we have to prove
27. That we're better"
28. But most of them they're like "well,
29. You guys already have a bad rap, why even worry?"

IIB. Complication

30. Sundown has like really smart students and everything
31. And there's like a lot of us, we try and everything
32. And there's like every-
33. like I'm not a test taking person
34. So I can do like well all through the year
35. But when the test comes up
36. It's like, "I'm out of it"

37. And, it's like
38. They just … umm
39. They criticize us just by the test
40. Just by our looks
41. But they don't criticize us by our mind

IIIA. Complication

42. And it's like how you dress
43. If you don't dress well
44. you're not a good student
45. If you're not wearing Nike shoes

46. If you're not wearing (Fire) shoes
47. If you're not wearing Guess jeans

48. It's like they say
49. "Oh, my God. She's not a good student
50. She doesn't have the money to,
51. To buy her clothes
52. You think she's going to have the money to go to college?"
IIIB. Complication
53. That's how they are with us
54. It's, they don't go to the north side and do that
55. Even though on the north side
56. They don't dress with nice shoes
57. Like umm, jeans, Guess jeans or whatever
58. They don't.
59. But they don't say that about them
60. Cause they live on the north side

61. And even though we try to dress nice or whatever
62. They still like put us down
63. They don't care if we're good or bad
IIIC. Resolution
64. Maybe because they think we're bad people
65. Well, they're the students
66. They're like because most of them on the south side
67. Umm, like you can say Hispanic, Mexican, Black, whatever
68. They live there
69. In the south, uh north side
70. White people live

71. It's like you, cou-
72. it's like maybe … it's just.
73. prejudice, I don't know
74. But they just like treat us different
IV. Coda
75. But if they're gonna give money-
76. the city's gonna give money either to the south side or the north side it's like
77. it goes to the north side
78. even though they have enough money to support themselves

79. To support their school

80. A lotta, a lotta teachers they just tell you
81. "you guys already have a bad rap.
82. People don't care what you guys do, whatever."
83. They just don't care what we do either

84. So if you don't do nothing in the class and you still pass it
85. Well, that's what you did
86. You didn't do nothing in class and that's it.
87. I just try to prove to them that I'm wrong-that they're wrong
88. I just try to do my best

89. Like if I'm gonna pass a class
90. I'm gonna pass it because of the work I did
91. Not just because they want me to graduate
92. Just because they want me to be out of high school

This account was remarkably similar to others spoken in the classroom. In the classroom these kinds of accounts were always more fragmentary and co-constructed by two or more students. Based on data from Julia and others in the class, I treat this account as arising out of a community of practice where it has meaning and power, and constitutes a kind of cultural capital. A focus on her account allows me to explore the possibility that critical perspectives may often emerge from the habitus of particular social communities of practice—from their social practices, discourse forms, and contexts (Bourdieu, 1977a, 1977b; Eckert & McConnell-Ginet, 1992, Lave, 1998). I draw on the concept of habitus from Bourdieu as Abu-Lughod (1986) does. Like her, I ask if legitimate discourse, the discourse of domination, largely structures our unconscious generative linguistic practices. If this is true, then from where does a text like Julia's come? Or, perhaps a better question is this: In what contexts and with whom would this kind of text serve her as legitimate discourse and valuable cultural capital? Theoretically, then, my questions complicate Bourdieu's concept of what constitutes cultural capital and habitus as people decontextualize texts from other places, times, and contexts to represent them in a moment of performance (Bauman & Briggs, 1990).

METHOD

This chapter draws on methods for the analysis of narrative structure (Briggs, 1996; Gee, 1986, 1990; Hill, 1995; Labov & Waletzsky, 1967). Overall narrative structure through sections serves to "orient the listener with respect to person, place, time, and behavioral situation" (Labov & Waletzsky, 1967, p. 32). This includes sections that complicate the actions of a narrative and evaluative sections that reveal the attitude of the narrator toward what he or she is saying by emphasizing relative importance of some units over others. Resolutions may be the last evaluative section and resolve the action. Codas may serve the function of returning the verbal perspective to the present. Although all of these organizational constructs are complicated by the lack of temporality in this account, I use them to show the organization of places as part of the moral geography that Julia wants us to understand.

To organize textual units I draw on arguments about narrative performances that identify units of ideas and organize them in line utterances, thematic units of clustered lines called stanzas, and larger topic or thematic units called sections (Gee, 1986, 1989; Gee, Michaels, & O'Connor, 1992). Idea units were organized into lines containing one piece of information, often in clausal form. I also often separated out clausal units based on a lowering of the pitch at the end of an utterance. Stanzas have a thematic quality and a unitary sense in terms of location and character. They were often separated by pauses as well. Sections, too, were defined in terms of their unitary sense with respect to location or character. They were also signaled by longer pauses (Gee, 1986). This use of narrative analysis brought out the structuring of places. Organization in this account also used a structured deployment of persons as they inhabited places. This organizational analysis comprises a second focus of this chapter.

Hill (1995) discusses people in the moral geography in terms of a voice system that speaks to the quality of morality in the moral geography. Voices are organized through relation to particular geographical locations, people who inhabit them, and how they act. Some of the person deictics have an interesting and multivocalic quality, referencing multiple potential speakers at the same time. These deictics, in connection to particular groups of people and spaces they inhabit, create evaluations of moral worth. Julia's account utilizes the deployment of a voice system through indexical grounding of person and place (Goffman, 1981; Hanks, 1996; Hill, 1995). Through the entire account present tense voice heightens a sense of universality and timelessness.

ANALYSIS

Structure of the Account

One of the greatest difficulties in analyzing an account of this kind is its hybrid nature, but that is also what makes it of such great interest. It is possible to discern in this account aspects of a canonical narrative structure such as the one laid out by Labov & Waletzsky (1967). It also is possible to see evidence of a cyclical structure that is associated with oral storytelling. Finally, there is structure that might come from abstracting and generalizing practices where students go from initial premises, to evidence, to abstract conclusions, a structure associated with essay-based literacy. All of these are present, although none is complete in a canonical sense. All give meaning and power to Julia's point of view.

The account is organized so that the structure of orientation, complications, resolution, and coda stands out. Because of the lack of temporal markers, this structure is carried primarily through the organization of place and through evaluation for each of the four topical sections. The orientation shows this clearly. Section I of the account orients the hearer to all of the places and people that are going to be presented. The order is from largest to smallest, an order that serves as the backbone for the rest of the account. We begin with the largest unit, the citywide taking of tests and the reporting of it in newspapers at the end of the year. This reporting then moves to what is said about specific schools in Stanza 2. We then move to the location of teacher and class, and end up with reported speech of individual students. Overall, we have been oriented toward the account by being introduced to all the places in order, to the people who inhabit them, and to an initial evaluation of the section through the reported speech of the students. This ordered structure of place and evaluation is continued through the other sections, although it reverses as the account moves to the resolution. Organizing the account in this way highlights the movement from largest to smallest spaces except in the complicating section that leads up to the resolution. Each of the sections ends with an evaluative stanza either in the form of evaluative speech or in the form of direct reported speech. This is shown in Fig. 5.1.

In this structure, places and evaluation play a powerful role in organizing the account. We have an orienting section that goes from the largest to smallest places. In Section II, the action is complicated by conflict between

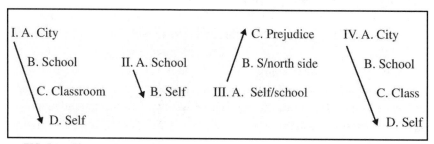

FIG. 5.1.   The organization of place.

the teachers and the students. This complication is further examined in Section III, where the organization of place is reversed to begin with self in conflict with school, teachers, and then on to the larger issues of the south side and the north side. This points to what I am calling the resolution of this account, the naming in terms of prejudice. In the coda, the beginning structure is repeated as we go from largest to smallest places with a second kind of resolution in terms of the self. The evaluative speech plays a key role in organizing the account in that the hearer is oriented both toward the section they have heard and prepared for the section that is to follow. An example can be seen at the end of Section I:

    13. So it's like …
    14. A lot of students we just like
    15. "kay Whoaa our teachers put us down,
    16. the city's putting us down,"
    17. We just … continue with that

This reported speech connects back toward the city and the teachers, but also connects forward to the next section where, "it's just anything, like anything bad" (18), "it's always on the south side" (19). This quality of looking backward and forward is a characteristic of all the evaluative sections in the account. They are part of the glue that holds the account together along with the organization of place. Place organizes people and events. Evaluative speech makes explicit the orientation toward what happens and connects to what comes next.

Another aspect that structures this account is the creation of cycles. This aspect is often associated with oral storytelling, and, mistakenly I believe, with a divide between written and oral cultures. The cyclical nature of this account is carried through cycles of a conflict between Julia, her peers, and her community, with the larger community represented through teachers, school, tests, the papers, and the north side of town.

This cycle of conflict is laid out in all of its complexity in the orientation and then repeated in different locations through the account. This is represented in Table 5.1.

The repeated, cyclical nature of the account is also apparent within stanzas in terms of syntactic parallelism and call and response strategies. So, for example, when Julia talks about the conflict between teachers and students over dress in Section IIIA, she says:

TABLE 5.1

The Organization of Conflict Cycles

    I. The overall cycle—conflict with the city, school, teachers, students
  IIA. The teachers and the school in conflict with the students
  IIB. The students in conflict with the tests
 IIIA. The students in conflict with teachers over dress
 IIIB. Conflict over the north side/south side and evaluations over dress
 IVA. Conflict relating to who lives where (Hispanics/Whites)
 IVB. Giving it a name—prejudice
   V. Repeating the cycle at all levels—ending with a personal response

    45. If you're not wearing Nike shoes
    46. If you're not wearing (Fire) shoes
    47. If you're not wearing Guess jeans

Another kind of parallelism is achieved through the use of call and response as she does in Section I, when test scores come out in the newspaper at the end of the year.

    7. worst school, Sundown High School
    8. Lowest scores, Sundown High School
    9. Why? Hispanic kids go there
  10. Why? South-side school

Although these cyclical structures in the account help in the telling of a "story" in much the way that other cyclical narrative forms do, this account differs significantly from those forms and from canonical temporal forms in its use of evaluative and abstract speech. If we look at the account on those terms it is possible to see yet a third structuring set of characteristics to this account. Those characteristics are ones we usually associate with school-based practices generally, and essay-based literacy in particular.

In essay-based literacy, but also in other activity settings, students practice evaluation and generalization. In essay writing, this kind of discourse can often be found in transitions that point both toward what has been said and what will be said in terms of evaluation. They are connecting statements. In this account Julia uses reported speech and direct evaluative speech to perform this function. Julia uses a mix of the two in the orienting section when she uses her own voice and the voices of "the city" as a way to explain why she and others "continue with that."

Reported and evaluative speech tells the listener how students respond to the overall stance of city, schools, and teachers. In Section IIA, Julia uses reported speech for teachers:

> 28. But most of them they're like "well,
> 29. You guys already have a bad rap, why even worry?"

Then she uses a more direct form of evaluative speech at the end of Section IIB where she talks about criticism in terms of the test:

> 37. And, it's like
> 38. They just ... umm
> 39. They criticize us just by the test
> 40. Just by our looks
> 41. But they don't criticize us by our mind

These evaluative sections lead up to the naming—to what these different evaluations mean in all of these different locations. The naming occurs when Julia gives meaning to all of these cyclical stories of conflict in various settings in terms of an abstraction, a term that lifts the evaluative speech out of the various contexts and generalizes it. The term is *prejudice*.

> 71. It's like you, cou-
> 72. it's like maybe ... it's just ...
> 73. prejudice, I don't know
> 74. But they just like treat us different

The naming of the account uses an abstract term to generalize for the listener what the overall meaning of the various sections is. It also ties together the evaluative speech. By using an abstract term, the account points back to and gives focus to the earlier evaluative speech. This is reminiscent of the kinds of abstracting practices students are asked to demonstrate at the end of written essays. At the end of an essay, paragraphs are tied together in a conclusion where the meaning is formulated in generalizable and abstract ways. The point is that Julia creates structure in a variety of ways to give power to what she is saying.

This structure combines with a voice system and use of tense to help us understand the moral quality of this geography.

The Voices of the Geography

As we have seen in the structure in this account, places are organized from largest to smallest or in reverse order in the sections leading up to the resolution of the account. In this section I look at how deictics create a system of voices. In this system the values and voices of Julia and her community exist in contrast and conflict with those of teachers, school, the north side, citywide institutions of media, and testing.

A voice system orients the hearer toward spaces and the people who inhabit them. Through the creation of distance and intimacy, moral poles are created and Julia links these to place, the people who inhabit them, and what they say. The deictic system heightens the sense of sites of conflict discussed earlier. Finally, the moral geography constructed through deictics and place is also powerfully influenced by a verb system that stays in the present tense. The present tense raises issues of how people universalize, and of protection and responsibility. Julia's voice appears to both protect herself as an individual while establishing a collective or community responsibility in terms of the truth claims in the account. She also directly enters into the speech in terms of "I" at key moments. Distance and intimacy are created through a system of deictics summarized in Table 5.2.

The most intimate voice is when Julia speaks as "I." This happens four times during the account. She begins the account with, "It's just that I see," before shifting to a more ambiguous "you" (1). She situates herself in the center of the text at the end of the first complicating section where she gives herself as

TABLE 5.2
Organization of Intimacy, Distance, Person, and Place

Intimacy	Deictics	Place
Self	I	Classroom
Community	We, us, our	Classroom, school
Multiple	You	Everywhere, teachers speech, description
Other	They, them, (none)	School, city, north side
Distance		

an example of a test taker (30–36). She uses a hedge, "I don't know," immediately after naming the account "prejudice" (73). She also situates herself as someone who tries to do her best at the end of the account, a personal response to the prejudice of tests, school, and teachers. Her personal response is highlighted in lines 87–90 with the deictics of "I' and is contrasted by the next two lines where "they" and "me" are set in opposition to one another. This opposition is constructed between *her* and the *school*.

90. *I'm* gonna pass it because of the work *I* did
91. Not just because *they* want *me* to graduate
92. Just because *they* want *me* to be out of high school

Opposition between what *they* (emphasis added) want and *her* moral stance is reflected in collective deictics that reference her peers. She does not hold this stance by herself. Julia references the community stance of herself and her peers in lines 30–31 when she says, "Sundown has like really smart students and everything, and there's like a lot of *us, we* try and everything." She also uses deictics to clearly signal conflict in this same setting of school, with constructions like (11–12), "It's like *they* put *us* down even though *we* try our best and everything, *We* go into class, even *the* teachers put us down." The deictics signal connection and closeness with her peers through the use of "we," and distance through the use of "they" and "the." Most of this conflict in terms of deictics and people occurs at the site of the school between teachers and students. The greatest opposition always occurs in final stanzas at the end of sections where Julia uses reported or evaluative speech as she does at the end of Section IIB about taking tests.

37. And, it's like
38. They just … umm
39. They criticize us just by the test
40. Just by our looks
41. But they don't criticize us by our mind

In this evaluation, the opposition of "us" and "they" is sharply defined. "They" makes reference back to not only the teachers, but to the publishing of test scores in the paper. It also sharply defines the moral nature of the account where distant people (they) make criticisms based on the test and not on the mind.

The use of the deictic "you" plays at least three roles in this account and in each role the quality of intimacy or distance has a different accent. Julia uses "you" to establish a universal evaluative stance as in "you can look at the newspaper" (2). This introduces the idea that anyone who looks at the newspaper can see the same thing. Another use of "you" is in the direct reported speech (28–29) of the teachers as in "well, *you* guys already have a bad rap why even worry?" Here teachers are directly criticizing the students. A third use of "you" references a generic south side student and how he or she dresses (45–47). "You" references the consequences of not dressing well ("If you don't dress well, you're not a good student"), as well as a description ("If you're not wearing Nike shoes, If you're not wearing [Fire] shoes"). In each case "you" has a different referential quality. In the first instance there is a universal sense to "you" and this helps universalize the whole account. In the second instance the referential character is more direct. Julia uses direct reported speech from teacher to students in the classroom. The third instance is somewhere between the first two with "you" referencing generic students but also who might be criticizing them (teachers, school, north side, media). Overall, "you" has the quality of evaluation, but a more distanced evaluation than deictic constructions of intimacy like "I" and "we." Part of the distancing also serves to displace conflict from the school site to possibly include other people and places. This also serves to universalize the account.

We also see this in a stanza with no pronominal deictics. The effect, as with certain uses of "you," is to blend and universalize who sees what. It could well be that what is seen is the viewpoint of herself and her community. However, the ambiguity leaves open the possibility that anyone could see the implications of these stories if they bothered to look. Moral poles are established as we hear the voices that create an image of scores, schools, and Hispanic kids.

    6. And, it's like at the end of the year
    7. worst school, Sundown High School
    8. Lowest scores, Sundown High School
    9. Why? Hispanic kids go there
  10. Why? South-side school

The use of "they" and "them," as noted before, often sets up conflict and opposition to "we, "our," and "us." It also is used the most when talking about the north side–south side split in the sections leading up to the naming of prejudice. Geographically, these are the largest areas of the account and as Julia describes these areas her more personalized deictics are almost nonexistent. In lines 53–60 when she describes the north side and how teachers do not criticize them for their dress she uses "they" six times with one use of "us." In lines 64–70 where she describes the ethnic and racial makeup of the south side–north side split, she also uses mostly "they" and "them" as deictics. The deictics here establish a position from which "they" speak. This is the other end of a moral geography, the one that exists at the level of larger spaces. Teachers are connected deictically to these spaces as "they" put students down, "they tell you you've gotta bad rap, so why even worry?" This moral pole inhabited by teachers, school, the north side, and the city is a constructed part of the account. This is very clear in the coda where Julia says:

75. But if they're gonna give money-
76. the city's gonna give money either to the south side or the north side it's like
77. it goes to the north side
78. even though they have enough money to support themselves
79. To support their school

80. A lotta, a lotta teachers they just tell you
81. "you guys already have a bad rap.
82. People don't care what you guys do, whatever."
83. They just don't care what we do either

Tense—Creating the Quality of the Action and Responsibility

Present tense is used throughout this account and the first person "I" is rarely used. Julia begins a first person account with *I see* (1) and immediately shifts to a third person *you can look* (2). The shift to this tense and person, together with the adverb modifier *can*, transforms the quality of the account. Both who is speaking and when the action is taking place become diffused. Although scholars have noted that the present tense historical voice gives a sense of immediacy (Hill, 1995; Ochs & Capps, 1996), a purely present tense account has an interesting paradoxical quality. Julia is both speaking directly to me in the present tense and also diffusing that direct speech through people and time. Thus in the second stanza after introducing the action that "we take a test" (4), she presents us with verbs of being. While speaking to me directly in the moment of telling she uses the third person "Hispanic kids" (9) and a verb of being, "it's like" (6) to create a sense of universality for the experience of these kids. The reporting of worst school, lowest scores, and the reasoning behind that (South-side school, Hispanic kids go there) is not anchored to any particular point in time. This process could exist in the past, the present, or the future. It just is.

This sense of being is translated into actions between teachers and students in lines 11–17. The use of "they" in line 11 shows how the use of the third person is starting to already create ambiguity as to who "they" are. It points both backward in the account to the newspaper and forward to the teachers in line 12. This two-sidedness is heightened through syntactic parallelism of these two lines where the media and teachers "put us down." These qualities of person and place are repeated in the following sections where "putting us down" becomes a process engaged in by the city and teachers. The students (a lot of students, we) "continue with that" (17). The verb heightens this processual quality and projects it into action. The overall effect of person and time is to create a sense of immediacy while presenting a processual and historical nature to testing, reporting, teaching, and learning from Julia's point of view.

Because of this diffusive quality, places and the people who inhabit them are difficult to pin down. Yet the actors in this piece are in no way morally ambiguous. There are good people and bad people in this account. They occupy contrasting moral poles. What is difficult to discern is where people are and who is doing the talking. However, if we think of space as oriented on the speaker and her community then we begin to discern how the places of the account are inhabited. The spaces closest to the speaker and her community (I, we, us) are inhabited by the moral people in this account. The somewhat larger spaces inhabited by students and teachers (they) are spaces of conflict. The largest spaces of north side–south side, the media, and the city are the most distant from the speaker in terms of space and those are the places where "putting us down" gets constructed.

For example, in the first six lines, where the action is taking place is unclear. Is it the reading of the newspaper? Is it the taking of the test in a classroom? The use of "I" indicates a personal description. The actions that take place here indicate a space that is in the immediate field of the individual speaker and the members of her community. This is the space inhabited by moral people. In this instance it includes Julia (I) and other members of her community (we). This is set against a space that is distant from her and her peers. This is the place where testing gets constructed and reported. That distance is presented in lines 6–14 and lines 22–26 through an almost complete lack of pronomialization. These spaces are far from her and her peers. A quality of universality and timelessness that characterizes the overall account is made explicit in line 22 with an accented "all the time."

Between the intimate and the distanced is the place where students and teachers come to meet. In lines 11–17, 22–29, and in the coda, the space of the classroom is constructed in terms of struggle. "You guys" in lines 26 and 29 indexes the sense of identity that is being actively contested in the classroom. In this construction who the "Hispanic kids" from the south-side schools (9–10) are and will be is neither an individual matter nor is their sense of who they are wholly determined through the community. Rather, through the construction of space in terms of intimacy and distance we see that all players in this account are actively contesting processes of being "put down" and "having a bad rap," and trying "to do my best."

One of the most interesting characteristics of this account is the simultaneous presence and effacement of a "self." Distributed responsibility allows for a very critical point of view. Julia is an individual who is present, but present through the collective identity of peers in her community. As noted earlier, Julia moves immediately from "I" to "you" in this account. A major shift in terms of taking responsibility for what is being said occurs early in lines 4–5 when Julia invokes "we." This indexical shift from "I" to "you" and "we" remains the primary one of the account. The space of intimacy that Julia experiences is created as both an individual space and a collective one. It is shared across students who inhabit the spaces of the south side high schools. The creation of space as both intimate and shared distributes responsibility of what is said across a range of possible speakers, even to some of the teachers in the school.

Through this artful distribution of person and action Julia often passes out responsibility to the collective "we," protects herself from potential challenges from listeners, and invites complicity and agreement from those like myself who might be willing to listen. However, Julia does present herself very directly at key points in the account. She is clearly present and taking responsibility for what is said. She uses herself as an example of a smart student who is not a test-taking person in lines 33–36. She uses "I" as she names this account in terms of prejudice (71–74), using the hedge "I don't know" immediately after the naming. Thus she is directly present but also diffuses responsibility for this very direct critical assertion. She ends the coda with a statement presenting the same places, actions, and people of the orienting section. She subverts the evaluation of earlier sections where people "just … continue with that" (17) by saying that she will do well in school in spite of the prejudice.

89. Like if I'm gonna pass a class
90. I'm gonna pass it because of the work I did
91. Not just because they want me to graduate
92. Just because they want me to be out of high school

Significantly, at the moment of naming this account "prejudice," Julia looked at her 10-month-old daughter, who she was holding at the time. She then looked to me as she said, "I don't know." She then kept her eyes on me as she spoke the coda. Julia's daughter, as well as myself, were active co-constructors of this speech event (Ochs & Capps, 1996).

DISCUSSION

The organization of space, person, and tense in this account is both structured and has a particular ideological motivation. Julia creates a hybrid structure where evaluative voices often end or begin sections. Space is organized between large and small. A voice system is deployed to orient the hearer toward a particular moral geography where the city, media, and south–north organization are inhabited by critical distant voices. Sites of conflict tend to be in schools. Contestation is highlighted by opposition between personal (I, we, our) and more distant (they, them) constructions. Conflict is also displaced by the present tense voice and use of "you" onto the larger settings mentioned earlier. This displacement is done through the ambiguity inherent to the present tense verbs where "you see" could mean anybody; the self, teachers, the media, the north side, or the city. Places of moral worth are occupied by Julia (I) and her peer community (we, us, our). All of these strategies give power to the truth claims of the account. She creates an ideological stance that refers not just to herself but to a historical relationship between her community and the dominant Anglo society.

At the beginning of this chapter I made reference to the concept of borderlands as a way to make sense of this account. Thinking of where this account comes from, we would have to ask, where does this narration have a chance of being heard? Where does it have power? Where would it act as a form of cultural capital (Bourdieu, 1977a, 1977b)? One could look to her particular borderland community of Tucson and to her peer community. Julia was born in Mexico, went to school there until she was 8, often visits family and friends in Sonora, but unambiguously considers herself to be an American. Her personal stance connects closely to that of her peer community (we, our, us), so the place where this account would have capital might be in her peer community. If this is true, it complicates Bourdieu's habitus, our unconscious and deeply embedded language dispositions. Of habitus, he says, "Strategies originate from the language habitus, a permanent disposition toward language and interactions which is objectively adjusted to a given level of acceptability. The habitus integrates all the dispositions that constitute expanded competence" (Bourdieu, 1977a, p. 655). Bourdieu's habitus tends to be formed through official ideologies, or dominant discourses in a society. These ideologies are granted a "totalitarian role in structuring experience" (Abu-Lughod, 1986, p. 256). Julia's account certainly is constructed in and around official ideologies. It also indexes a self in complex and hybrid opposition to the "official" consciousness of the school, the city, and other institutions of the state. One idea we might consider is that certain cultural situations such as a borderlands context can support the development of critique. Where different cultures have been in contestation for hundreds of years, it is quite possible that the contradictions of dominant ideologies become apparent. Individuals and communities may draw on alternative ideologies as they resist, deconstruct, and comment metapragmatically on those institutions. Rosaldo (1993) identifies these communities as "sites of creative cultural production" (p. 208), where new structures of identity and language ideology are developing in multiple ways. Whereas Julia might display unconscious dominant ideologies in particular settings with respect to work, money, and education, in other settings she might well draw on a different discourse to display alternative forms of consciousness. We can add complexity to our notions of habitus and cultural capital without denying their theoretical explanatory power.

Volosinov's (1929/1986) concept of multiaccentuality, where what words mean is struggled over, is also central to this discussion. Struggle occurs on a number of levels that often overlap as people in the account give various accents to words. The word *you*, for example, as in who *you will be* is struggled over and variously populated with the intentions of the speaker, peers, and teachers. Teachers can take up the word *you* as an expression of solidarity (27) but "most of them, they're like, 'well *you* guys already have a bad rap why even worry.' " Again, there is a distinct feeling of Bourdieu's (1977a) habitus, in the sense of durable dispositions that are brought about through repeated social practices. This sense of habitus is heightened through the use of the present tense to project into the past and the future as when Julia says "we just … continue with that," or when she emphasizes the constant nature of reporting with, *"all the time."*

Julia's presence is both direct and indirect. There is an "I" aspect to this account that I noted earlier. At the same time there is often no explicit pronomialization so who is doing the talking is effaced in a purely linguistic sense. Often, the feeling is of collective speakers telling us this account and they could be telling us about this at any time. It would still be the same. In this way, a very critical point of view is made powerful through collective distribution across speakers and time. Julia also protects herself by doing this.

In conclusion, one can ask why Julia and her peers tell accounts such as this, in this way. One possibility is to consider how audiences co-construct stories. The listener, even when he or she does not speak, is powerfully impacting the telling. Speaking to an Anglo and a teacher, Julia shifts at the beginning to protect herself and distribute responsibility. However, many of the south-side Mexican-American students spoke this way in the classroom, although Julia's story of schooling is the most complete one that I heard. Is this a mode of speech that has grown to be a part of the community of speakers of which she is a member? Julia's daughter also is a member of that community and Julia looked to her as she spoke the word *prejudice*. Is this a form of discourse that has become habitus—a set of durable dispositions that is invoked in certain contexts as a way to deploy ideological positions through linguistic and cultural capital—a form that Julia and her peers bring to schooling every day? A form they pass on to their children? If that is true, then it deserves our attention as a form of constructing knowledge through discourse, as a unique way of presenting collective voice and identity, and as a style for narrating self in multiaccented social and ideological worlds.

Robert Whitman is an assistant professor in the Department of Education at Eastern Washington University. His current research interests include language and capitalism, literacy practices within the context of Indigenous language and culture revitalization, and the ethnography of schooling.

REFERENCES

Abu-Lughod, L. (1986). *Veiled sentiments: Honor and poetry in a Bedouin society.* Berkeley: University of California Press.

Bauman, R., & Briggs, C. L. (1990). Poetics and performance as critical perspectives on language and social life. *Annual Review of Anthropology, 19,* 59–88.

Bourdieu, P. (1977a). The economics of linguistic exchange. *Social Science Information, 16,* 645–668.

Bourdieu, P. (1977b). *Outline of a theory of practice*. Cambridge, UK: Cambridge University Press.

Briggs, C. (1996). Introduction. In C. L. Briggs (Ed.), *Disorderly discourse: Narrative, conflict, and inequality* (pp. 3–41). Oxford, UK: Oxford University Press.

Eckert, P., & McConnell-Ginet, S. (1992). Think practically and look locally: Language and gender as community-based practice. *Annual Review of Anthropology, 21,* 461–490.

Gee, J. P. (1986). Units in the production of narrative discourse. *Discourse Processes, 9,* 391–422.

Gee, J. P. (1989). Two styles of narrative construction and their linguistic and educational implications. *Discourse Processes, 12,* 287–307.

Gee, J. P. (1996). *Social linguistics and literacies: Ideology in discourses.* Bristol, PA: Taylor & Francis. (Original work published 1990)

Gee, J. P., Michaels, S., & O'Connor, R. (1992). Discourse analysis. In M. LeCompte, W. Millroy, & J. Preissle (Eds.), *Handbook of qualitative research in education* (pp. 228–283). New York: Academic.

Goffman, E. (1981). *Forms of talk*. New York: Harper and Row.

Hanks, W. (1996). *Language and communicative practices*. Boulder, CO: Westview.

Hill, J. (1995). The voices of Don Gabriel: Responsibility and self in a modern Mexicano narrative. In D. Tedlock & B. Mannheim (Eds.), *The dialogic emergence of culture* (pp. 97–147). Chicago: University of Chicago Press.

Holland, D., Lachiotte, W., Cain, C., & Skinner, D. (1998). *Identity and agency in cultural worlds.* Cambridge, MA: Harvard University Press.

Lave, J. (1988). *Cognition in practice: Mind, mathematics, and culture in everyday life.* New York: Cambridge University Press.

Labov, W., & Waletzsky, J. (1967). Narrative analysis: Oral versions of persona experience. In J. Helm (Ed.), *Essays on the verbal and visual arts* (pp. 12–44). Seattle: University of Washington Press.

Ochs, E., & Capps, L. (1996). Narrating the self. *Annual Review of Anthropology, 25,* 19–43.

Philips, S. (1998). *Ideology in the language of judges.* New York: Oxford University Press.

Rosaldo, R. (1993). *Creativity/anthropology.* Ithaca, NY: Cornell University Press.

Volosinov, V. N. (1986). *Marxism and the philosophy of language* (L. Matejka & I. Titunik, Eds.). Cambridge, MA: Harvard University Press. (Original work published 1929)

Wertsch, J. (1998). *Mind as action.* New Haven, CT: Yale University Press.

Woolard, K. (1998). Introduction: Language ideology as a field of inquiry. In B. B. Schieffelin, K. A. Woolard, & P. Kroskrity (Eds.), *Language ideologies: Theory and practice* (pp. 3–47). New York: Oxford University Press.

Commentary on Part I
"... An Entry Into Further Language": Contra Mystification by Language Hierarchies

Ray McDermott
Stanford University

I tended to conceive of English and Irish as adversarial tongues, as either/or conditions rather than both/ands, and this was an attitude which for a long time hampered the development of a more confident and creative way of dealing with the
whole vexed question—the question, that is, of the relationship between nationality, language, history, and literary tradition in Ireland .... Luckily, I glimpsed the
possibility of release from this kind of cultural determinism .... I glimpsed an elsewhere of potential which seemed at the same time to be a somewhere being remembered, ... away into some unpartitioned linguistic country, a region where
one's language would not be a simple badge of ethnicity or a matter of cultural
preference or official imposition, but an entry into further language.
—Seamus Heaney (2000, pp. xxiv–xxv)

Ireland entered the 19th century with a population of 8 million, most of them
Irish speakers. Ireland entered the 20th century with about 4 million people,
most of them English speakers. It was not an easy transition. Many starved to
death and many fled for their lives to other countries. It was easy to see Irish
and English as adversarial tongues, and much of Irish politics and literature a
century ago was phrased in terms of warring languages (McDermott, 1988).
Ireland has entered the 21st century with about 5 million people (North and
South), almost every last one of them a native speaker of English. You would

111

think the war is over, and in a way it is. Still, the job of mining the Irish language for connections into Irish culture and its place in the world might just be beginning. The great Irish poets, Seamus Heaney and John Montague, write for our times certainly, but are dedicated to recovering the past to make "an entry to further language." All language, old and new, has something to say, something to be remembered, something to be carried forward. All language, standard and dialect, oral and written, even oppressor and oppressed, can be part of a next moment of language that can be lived in a new way, with new connections, new possibilities. It is not easy work to appropriate language for new purposes, but there is no choice.

Each of the five chapters in this section nicely defines a problematic situation for the relation between language and education. Language—any language at all—should be a great educational resource, and the education of people by people for the greater good of all should be the activity in which any language is most relentlessly engaged. Yet the chapters we have just read report that specific languages, particularly the languages and dialects of disenfranchised (minoritized) voices in various nation states, are a constant source of problems both school personnel and the students in their care. What could be going on? Where is the problem? Is language really the issue? What would a solution to the problem look like, and to whom? Taken one at a time, each chapter develops a sense of the language and education problem as a part of a larger complex of political and economic forces that the authors identify to make a point: Disenfranchised languages, like every disenfranchised person, should be considered more a resource than a hindrance to good education. After restating and celebrating each case, I turn to their collective import. Taken together, they help to define a still larger problem that underlies the dynamics of each of the specific cases, namely, that we have institutionalized crazy ideas about language, education, and their possible relations.

Taken together, the chapters in Part I provide a glimpse of the world Heaney has on call, a world in which two languages (dialects, registers, codes, literacies, etc.) do not have to make an opposition as much as an opportunity, a world in which two or more languages together build "an entry into further language." We need to remind ourselves that better ideas are available. The five chapters before us participate in a long history of people noticing that languages can be better understood as at war with themselves than with other languages. The easy English we have for talking about language, literacy, culture, and education is inadequate to the turbulent cases described in our five chapters—that is why the authors had to write them. Similarly, although the Hopi and Navajo languages 400 years ago were not the kinds of problem English is for Hopi and Navajo people today, they were a problem of a different kind. They harbored no doubt the tensions of Hopi and Navajo life of that moment and made for every new generation a full menu of biases to be discovered, rejected, or accepted. Being forced to give up a native tongue to learn another language is degrading and debilitating, and there is nothing good to be said about the colonizing powers of English, but this situation should not allow us to forget that being limited to one's native language has its own problems. On the way to "further language," nothing is more inhibiting than what a people already knows how to say and, under the right circumstances, nothing is more promising than what can be said in another language. This is an old idea that must be constantly rediscovered, celebrated, and given new place in any transformation of current circumstances. To recover Hopi, Navajo, and the Native Alaskan languages for new generations is a primary goal and a political necessity (too late for the Irish, perhaps, who have invested so heavily in the English of the marketplace), but the task of making further language never goes away, just as the task of educating never goes away. As we rethink the relation between language and education, we must remember to keep both words open. A language is never fixed. Education is never fixed.

The nice chapter by Rockwell on literacy in Chiapas is a great place to start. Thirty years ago, the anthropological literature on Chiapas was excellent but limited to a village-by-village description, as if each village were a world unto itself. Analytic concern for connections across the region was considered news (Aquirre Beltrán, 1979). Literacy was not much a part of the village ethnographies. It was understood as something brought from the outside and instilled into the people in schools as part of the modernization process (Modiano, 1973). If the villagers learned to read quickly it was considered something of a miracle.

Rockwell takes a quite different and much more powerful stand. Literacy, she says, has been a fact of life across centuries in Mexico, first in the form of Mayan writing and then, after that was destroyed by the conquering Spanish, in the form of colonial and state powers. The peasants, as if they were nothing less than ancient Sumerians, knew literacy from land deeds, debt lists, and priestly activities. Words brought from afar had immediate consequences. Analytically, Rockwell, as if by areal photography, has bumped the unit of analysis from the village to region and the wider state, and the literacy that seemed not to be there suddenly appears everywhere. A literacy system exists, and it acquires more and more people as they—in their activities—get closer to centers of power. Those who are not acquired by Mexican literacy, in the sense that they do not read and write much, are nonetheless a systematic part of the literacy system. At the very least, their job in the literacy system is to define its borders, much like failing students define successful students in schools in the United States (Varenne & McDermott, 1998). In more integrated literacy systems at the service of a state educational system—the kinds we see in our other four chapters—the jobs (i.e., the social functions) of those called illiterate can become more complex. For example, they can learn how to read, but not well enough; they can learn how to read well, but not quickly enough for standardized tests; they can learn how to read at the university level, but have their credentials questioned at crucial times. Throughout it all, they might have much more literacy than any official of the system knows, but they use it in ways perpendicular to the purposes of the state. Rockwell says it well: "In situations of domination, the appropriation of literacy may involve strategic *avoidance of writing*, as well as *strategic uses of the written language*." Either way, the people of Chiapas are a working part of a literacy system and have been for a long time.

Rockwell's alternative literacy story pays attention to the same facts about skills and their distribution across a generation of readers and writers, but worries about how the facts might be better considered in their cultural context. By this alternative, literacy is no magic technology of the mind that, however difficult to acquire, transforms people from cognitively simple to complex. Rather, literacy is a tool used in specific ways to do the institutional bidding of the wider culture. Literacy refers less crucially to a set of skills than to a medium of participation. It is not particularly difficult to acquire, although it does take constant practice and use for a full mastery to be developed and maintained. If there is a differential in reading and writing competencies across subgroups in a population, this is better understood as an index of how much people have had access to the institutions requiring literacy than as an index of their mental skills. If differential access leads to a reification of persons into literate and illiterate camps over generations, then it is best understood that this is what the culture in question does: It divides people into classes and uses literacy as one of the dividing lines. This is not a bad description of what many early empires, both East and West, did with literacy. Nor, unfortunately, is it a bad description of what our culture does with various measures of educational success; we seem ever ready to divide ourselves into increasingly many ways of being measurably competent and incompetent. Literacy is not one thing, but many things depending on the cultural and political environments in which it is embedded.

By this alternative account of literacy and its relations to contemporary problems, we do not so much need more literates in the sense of more people with more skills as we need more institutions ready to make good use of people in ways that will encourage, require, and nurture their work lives and, incidentally but significantly, their literacy. We need to worry less about how people acquire literacy and more about how literacy is institutionally glued to our lives in ways that acquire people differentially.

This reformulation brings us to the excellent chapter by Gilmore and Smith. In fact, one point of origin for the reformulation of illiteracy as social fault to illiteracy as a category used by those in power to degrade those without power is work done by Smith, Gilmore, and others in and around Philadelphia in the early 1980s (Smith, 1987; see also Schieffelin & Gilmore, 1986; Shuman, 1986). In their chapter in this volume, they leave Philadelphia off the map and give instead an account from centers for Native education in Alaska and Australia. Remember their account of the Native Alaskan students being called into question by a professor who claimed that her colleagues gave out easy grades to Native Alaskan students. Interestingly enough, decades before, the professor initiated research on the limitations of Native environments for cognitive growth, a popular game that dominated education research in the late 1960s and early 1970s. How could it be, then, that Native Alaskans could go to a university and do well? Someone, goes the accusation, must be making it easier for them.

> The incident itself functioned to maintain hegemonic practices at the university and to obscure the demonstrated and increasing accomplishments of the Alaska Native population. The university, by almost exclusively focusing their responses to the incident on issues of academic freedom, standards, and grading practices, abdicated their responsibility to provide a safe learning environment for the growing Indigenous population.

The conservative Alaskan press loved the controversy, and it stayed alive in the papers for over a year. The students were mortified—well, at first. Then they were angry. Then they organized in protest. Eventually the storm passed. The students went back to work, but with a new story to tell about themselves, complete with websites. The story, their new story, includes an account of what they are up against. Not only do they have to learn a new language and culture at the university, they have to do so in the context of people apparently waiting for them to fail, perhaps even looking forward to them failing.

The normal literacy story has it that it is difficult to acquire for people who are not surrounded by a print culture. Maybe, although there are startling cases of high rates of literacy among tribal peoples—for example, among the Hanunóo in the Philippines (Conklin, 1949; Kuipers & McDermott, 1996). Once people do become literate, however, good things should happen, both mentally and culturally. That would be nice. So everyone is in favor of literacy; the more the better.

The Alaskan case points in a different direction (Gilmore & Smith, 2002). Why should people be invested in finding out what others cannot do, or cannot do as well as perhaps others? That is a good question to put to American education overall. Why do we as a people love failure? Or better, why do we love the failure of others? A harsh view is that we do not really care about literacy. We only care that some can always be shown to be more literate than others, and, if the wrong people are showing up on the wrong side of the scale, we can claim that someone is making it easier for them. The rhetoric of literacy is the rhetoric of those who own both literacy and ways of discounting the literacy of others. If we can make up kinds of people (Frake, 1980, 1998), we can make up kinds of skills. Gilmore and Smith show us that there is no end to the political mischief that can be done with a word like *literacy*.

If literacy is not the problem people face when they seem not to have enough of it, and if establishment accounts and measures of literacy are a problem even when people have more than enough of it, then we can imagine how any effort to enrich the literacy of any disenfranchised people must run into constant confrontations with mainstream powers. We can imagine also how much work it might take to run a successful Native language and literacy program in a regular school with the dual problems of getting everyone to learn as much as possible and as measurably as possible while protecting them from the biases in the very measures used by the mainstream system. Actually, we do not have to imagine any more. We can read the poignant chapter by Nicholas and the relentless account by McCarty of language programs for Hopi and Navajo, respectively.

Nicholas has few illusions of what she is up against: As of 1997, of the people over 60 years old, 60% had kept Hopi as their primary language; of those under 19, only 7% have been able to old on. The stakes are high, for the language carries with it the most essential values of Hopi culture:

> Children have become the victims of this cultural and familial dissonance. They have become beneficiaries of such characterizations of them by village

adults as not having *"kyaptsi"*—respect—which is taught through the language. They are described as only "surfing" along the crest of their cultural heritage....

To make matters even more difficult, given various pressures on family life, the institutional site for renewal has moved to the school: "The enormity of the challenge cannot be underestimated. Transforming schooling in ways that validate rather than annihilate Hopi identity requires a profound understanding of the long struggle—past, present, and future." In 1906, Hopi children were carted off at gunpoint to boarding schools, and, for a long time since, to the person caring about Hopi language and traditional values, it must feel like the same phenomenon gets played out every day that Hopi children go off to school. What is the possibility that the school can be made the nexus for new generations of Hopi children and their past? It has not worked well in many places, but steps are being taken. "Hopi literacy is newly emerging." Some people are excited. There is hope.

I called McCarty's chapter relentless, and so it is that she documents the relentless efforts required—one meeting after another—to hold onto Navajo language and culture through the schools. Style and content are joined across a documentation of more than a decade of innovations at the Rough Rock School: early experimentation with KEEP (a pedagogical program for initial reading), implementation of portfolio assessments and home-grown bilingual writing checklists, increasing use of Navajo or multicultural literature for children in the school, and (mostly) increasing test scores with both local evaluation tools and even, although less so, standardized ones. To keep such a focus on change for so long requires a relentless determination and a dream—and yes, just as important, "an infusion of long-term financial assistance and administrative support" and a teacher–principal relationship of "mutual concern and support." Even all these pieces were not enough. Something more, something terribly intangible, something we do not hear enough about was required. The school was "not a 'comfort zone.' " I am so tired of the required comfort zones in teacher education and professional development. Change does not happen in comfort zones. Bad things happen while people are attending to their comfort zones. Change happens when people are putting comfort to risk. The teacher meetings that McCarty dutifully attended and documented over a decade were less a comfort zone, and more "often a site of pain and discomfort as teachers revisited their own educational histories and challenged the pedagogical assumptions internalized in the course of their schooling."

There is a basic rule of planned social change to which Rough Rock's teachers report for duty. I was once party to a group that stated it (Greeno et al., 1999), but I assume many others have stated it as well, for example, Horton (1990) or Gramsci (1971). The rule: Planned change is only possible if the group planning the change is prepared to have their relations reorganized as well. If the planning group opts for comfort, no other change will take place; not in the classrooms, not in the school, and not in the community. Ethnography is always difficult work; ethnography of a long-term program of social change is that much harder; and ethnography of a long-term program of social change in which one is also a participant is the hardest of all, but important enough that the difficulty of doing the work should give way to the exhilaration: Relentlessness first, then exhilaration. This is the right order for important work.

Whitman's chapter is different from the other four. If Rockwell gives a real photography, chapters by Gilmore and Smith, Nicholas, and McCarty give us an analysis from an on-the-ground telescope; that is, each starts with an event or two and then widens the lens to include quotes from various others in the community until we get a sense of the wider terrain. Whitman is more a pointillist. He gives us one speech turn (interlocutor activities are not included) from a young woman, Julia, in an interview about life and school, and he stays with it. Whereas the first four chapters offer intrinsically interesting research strategies, Whitman's approach requires some defense. By looking at some of the linguistic detail in how the young woman handles space, person, and tense, Whitman gets to point to much of the same world of constraints—the prejudices of the school system, the built-in putdowns, the systematic inattention—that faces the protagonists in the other chapters, and, by looking closely, he can deliver them, possibly, with a little more rigor or, just as important, with a little more attention to what is systematically not delivered. This would be too much to ask for a small chapter, but I will say here what he did not: When he sticks close to the discourse, for example, using the categories of Labov and Waletzsky (1967), he is able to speak with much more certainty than when he uses categories from Bourdieu (1977). Grammar allows for a precision of analysis that society does not, just as conclusions about grammar are not easy conclusions about society. A next step in the analysis would be to try a handful of analytic types for an account of their respective powers in producing, first, a rigorous description and, second, an image of the wider world that invited and makes use of Julia's talk. An even better next step would be to limit the analysis to categories developed not by Labov or Bourdieu, but by Julia and Whitman in the course of a more extended ethnographic engagement. By proceeding carefully, Whitman's chapter has invited calls for even more rigor and responsibility. He is to be thanked for keeping these procedural questions front and center. We will not make enough progress against the established categories of language, literacy, and educational policy without more of his deep empiricism.

When we add up the five chapters, we get a sense of good things happening. In each chapter, there are people delivering efforts to make change in the tight ties between language performance and the system that delivers educational curricula, forms of pedagogy, and institutionalized evaluations, and, in the midst of all that, someone has taken the time to write a chapter to tell us how to rethink the categories we use to talk about language and education. Hooray for everyone! Hooray, but only until the morning. Then we will have to start up again, resisting constraints, making change, revising ideas, and then again, and again. Along the way, it might be nice to know that we are not the first to have our concerns. In fact, they are old concerns. One point of origin remains wonderfully exciting.

To close these comments, I remind us of some writings from the early 1840s by Marx, a then-young and now long-dead White man who worried in advance about the world we have made. I use Marx to redefine how we might better think about and confront the institutions that have brought us the current and ridiculous situation that pits various language competencies against children learning in school.

In 1844, Marx warned us that the language of political economy has two problems: First, it is inadequate to the full complexity of its object, and second, it is systematically distorting. Later by 84 years, Volosinov (1928/1973) and Bakhtin (1981) developed a theory of language with the same claim: All language faces the dual problem of being "resisted" by, first, the complexity of the objects it seeks to name and describe and, second, by its own political history. Because all language activity, down to its very last speaker and its very last word, is filled with a history of compromises over what dimensions of various objects and events are to be highlighted and articulated or submerged and ignored, every utterance must be understood as descriptively inadequate and illocutionally distorting. In the language of Marx, every utterance, like every other productive activity, is alienated, taken from its maker and used to fulfill the ambitions of others. As disappointing as this sometimes is, it is not a reason for silence (silence being no less of an activity in its own right), but a reason for constant confrontation with our talk and with those using it for unbecoming ends.

Make it another 76 years, and we can bring the same concern to the language of learning, to the theory of learning, and their systematic use in institutions designed specifically, however unproductively, for the enhancement of learning. Twentieth-century psychology has been relentless (and virtuous) in showing us that it is difficult to talk carefully about learning. The complexity of learning activities seems to resist all efforts to make learning an object visible at work in the real world. Psychologists retreated adaptively (and in this way not so virtuously) to limiting their inquiries to the small range of learning phenomena that can be theorized and methodically operationalized—make that distorted—in laboratory experiments or psychometric mock-ups of experimental control. Precision, and a wobbly precision at that, was exchanged for relevance, and the learning of real people in the real world was narrowed down to their performance on tests that separated the supposed best from the rest. Whatever a person learns takes its value from what others can make of it; whatever a person learns is taken from its maker and used to fulfill the intentions of others. It is estranged learning that counts, that is accountable, that is the bottom line, that requires tuition, that pays a return, that is the key to success, and that makes the alumni proud. Institutions of learning have adopted—and in this way so without virtue as to appear at best invidious, at worst evil—the language of tests, competition, natural ability, and skill without an attendant account of what such a language leaves out or systematically distorts.

It is enough to encourage a reading of "learning" through the critical lens of Marx on political economy as if they were the same phenomenon wrapped up in different representations 160 years later. In 2004, we can complain that the language used to talk about learning and education has two problems: First, it is inadequate to the full complexity of its object, and second, it is systematically distorting.

There is a fit between Marx's account of the struggles of estranged workers in the industrial capitalism of 1844 and young children competing their way through schools in the information democracy of the new millennium.[1] If

---

[1]Quotations from Marx (1867/1967), rewritten for topics of relevance for a book on language, literacy, and power in school (for a more extended effort, see Lave & McDermott [2002] using Marx's essay on "Estranged Labor" [1844]; rewritten words shown in italics):

I.

"Money, like every other commodity, cannot express the magnitude of its value except relatively in other commodities."

Fluency, "like every other commodity, cannot express the magnitude of its value except relatively in other commodities."

Expertise, "like every other commodity, cannot express the magnitude of its value except relatively in other commodities." (*continued*)

Marx's unit of concern in 1844 was the sweating laborer working in a mill in exchange for having his products taken away and sent to market, then Marx's unit of concern 160 years later might be the young child sweating through an exam in exchange for others making of it what they have to given the competition for access.

After writing the foundational essay on "Estranged Labor" in 1844, Marx gave his remaining 39 years to detailing how the capitalist system was organized and how it could be confronted. In our remaining few pages, I proceed similarly, although in a way attuned to the new unit of concern. We are not going to call for a takeover of the factory system by the state, and we certainly are not going to call for a nationalization of the educational system by the state. Instead we want to ask these questions directly of the educational system: How does the learning system work that it so conveniently winds up generation after generation producing the same problems and the same nasty results? How might it be confronted? The answers will ultimately involve a critique of the political economy, of course, but the contributions of the educational system to various inequalities—by class, race, language, and gender—could now run on its own, without direct feedback from economic constraints. My sense is that if the American population dwindles down to two adults and two children, the adults will set up a school to see which child is doing better than the other. Is it possible that the industrial capitalism of estranged labor has grown so familiar to us that we do not even notice that we are the oppressors of our own children? Is it possible that the very language of teaching and learning with which we interpret the lives of our children has been so loaded by its place within the political economy that we do not know how descriptively inadequate and illocutionarily invidious it is?

---

[1](*continued*)

II.

"All commodities are non-use values for their owners, and use-values for their non-owners."

"All *words* are non-use values for their speakers, and use-values for their interpreters."

Knowledge has "non-use values for its owners, and use-values for its non-owners."

III.

"Coins are, so to speak, made responsible for each other."

Words, in the dictionary, as in life, "are, so to speak, made responsible for each other."

Minds, in the university as in life, "are, so to speak, made responsible for each other."

IV.

"Price is the money name of the labor objectified in a commodity."

The dictionary *definition* is the accountable "name of the labor objectified" in a word.

An *SAT score* is the accountable "name of the labor objectified" in a student.

"We are nothing but falsehood, duplicity, contradiction; we both conceal and disguise ourselves from ourselves," warned Pascal (1960, p. 68), and it would be nice to confront ourselves about whether our biases on language and learning should really organize the way we live. We could use better biases. Does learning have to be thought of as owned, from inside the head, dependent on individual aptitude, or is this simply the way we have learned to lie to ourselves given our place in a fiercely competitive, capitalist society in which everyone, in school as much as the marketplace, has to do better than everyone else?

Margaret Mead, the champion of making "Us/Not Us" cultural differences for the edification of stay-at-home Westerners (Geertz, 1987), once noted an important cultural difference in the organization of learning in the Pacific societies she had lived with:

> Miscarriages in the smooth working of the transmission of available skills and knowledge did occur, but they were not sufficient to focus the attention of the group upon the desirability of teaching over against the desirability of learning. Even with considerable division of labor and with a custom by which young men learned a special skill not from a father or other specified relative but merely from a master of the art, the master did not go seeking pupils. (Mead, 1943, p. 634)

This sounds right to me. We have made teaching into a fetish. Whatever people do not know, for whatever reason, we think we should put them into classrooms where one person will teach and others learn. We have given the desirability of teaching sway over the desirability of learning. We have given the desirability of learning, particularly measurable and taught learning, documentable and credentialed learning, over the desirability of participation. We have made learning, or at least that narrow strand of learning that can be taught and measured, into a fetish. Most societies have done well without any theory of learning, and we might do better without one ourselves (Lave, 1996). Children come into the world and learn. That is the way it is, unless strange tasks are put aside to locate some children—the percentage depending on how many those in charge need to keep out—learning more or faster than others. That is what we have done, and with the opposite effect than we would seem to want. Or is it exactly what we want? Is it exactly the case that half the people of the United States wake up in the morning anxious to show others how they have learned more, whereas the other half wake up cowering in the shadow of those who might know more, or at least who are good at claiming that they know more. If you are reading this page, you are likely from the top half and worrying about making policy for the other half. Back off. You, me, we are part of the problem. Literacy is a great thing, and damn the society that has made it available to us only as we stand on the faces of others. Language, literacy, and learning are about being in the world. They do not have to be about a rush to teaching, and teaching does not have to be about a rush to hierarchy.

We have gone from Marx, through Mead, to us. Now we can return to our chapters on literacy. It sounds like such a good idea. Everyone should have literacy, of course. By virtue of everyone needing it, in a society that commodifies everything into a market price, it becomes not just a problem for those who do not have enough, but an opportunity for those who would seem to have a surplus, a stock at hand—in short, a capital. Literacy is a big business. Learning disabilities are a big business. Degrees are a large chunk of our Gross Domestic Product. Without illiterates, without learning disabilities, and without school failure, what would happen to education? What would happen to schools of education? What would happen to the Gross Domestic Product? Locked in the service of a capitalist political economy, our literacy system is as good at acquiring illiterates as literates, as good at acquiring dunces as geniuses (McDermott, 1993, 2004a, 2004b; Varenne & McDermott, 1998). The term *illiteracy* is less than 200 years old (Donald, 1983). The term has been acquiring people at an alarming rate, and this likely without regard for the extent of literacy throughout the population. The activities of reading and writing, the activities of getting and giving information, conceptual clarification, and even revolutionary ideas, all good activities on their own, should help any society to do better whatever it does. Literacy, on the other hand, as the thing people in the know have and test for in others, may have been designed with a different purpose in a class- and race-divided society. This is the literacy that, regardless of the reading and writing people are doing, divides people into classes with differential access to the rewards of the system. Yes, literacy helps a society do its jobs, and in the United States, this means that literacy helps to keep people in their respective places.

REFERENCES

Aquirre Beltrán, G. (1979). *Regions of refuge.* Washington, DC: Society for Applied Anthropology.

Bakhtin, M. (1981). *Dialogic imagination.* Austin: University of Texas Press.

Bourdieu, P. (1977). *Outline of a theory of practice.* New York: Cambridge University Press.

Conklin, H. (1949). Bamboo literacy in Mindoro. *Pacific Discovery, 2,* 3–11.

Donald, J. (1983). How illiteracy became a problem. *Journal of Education, 165,* 35–51.

Frake, C. (1980). Genesis of kinds of people in the Sulu Sea. In A. Dil (Ed.), *Language and cultural description* (pp. 311–332). Stanford, CA: Stanford University Press.

Frake, C. (1988). Abu sayyuf: Displays of violence and the proliferation of contested identities among Philippine Muslims. *American Anthropologist, 100,* 41–54.

Geertz, C. (1987). *Works and lives.* Stanford, CA: Stanford University Press.

Gilmore, P., & Smith, D. (2002). Identity, resistance, and resilience: Counter narratives and subaltern voices in Alaskan higher education in 1991. In D. C. Li (Ed.), *Discourses in search of members* (pp. 103–134). Washington, DC: University Press of America.

Gramsci, A. (1971). *Selections from the prison notebooks.* New York: International.

Greeno, J., McDermott, R. P., Cole, K., Engle, R., Goldman, S., Knudsen, J., et al. (1999). Research, reform, and the aims of education. In E. Lagemann & L. Shulman (Eds.), *Issues in education research* (pp. 299–335). San Francisco: Jossey-Bass.

Heaney, S. (2000). *Beowulf.* New York: Farrar, Straus, & Giroux.

Horton, M. (1990). *The long haul.* New York: Doubleday.

Kuipers, J., & McDermott, R. P. (1996). Insular Southeast Asian scripts. In P. Daniels & W. Bright (Eds.), *The world's writing systems* (pp. 474–484). London: Oxford University Press.

Labov, W., & Waletzsky, J. (1967). Narrative analysis. In J. Helm (Ed.), *Essays on the verbal and visual arts* (pp. 12–44). Seattle: University of Washington Press.

Lave, J. (1996). Teaching as learning in practice. *Mind, Culture, and Activity, 3,* 149–164.

Lave, J., & McDermott, R. P. (2002). Estranged labor learning. *Outlines, 4,* 19–48.

Marx, K. (1964). *Economic and philosophic manuscripts of 1844.* New York: International. (Original work written 1844, not published until 1932)

Marx, K. (1967). *Capital* (Vol. 1). New York: Penguin. (Original work published 1867)

McDermott, R. P. (1988) Inarticulateness. In D. Tannen (Ed.), *Linguistics in context* (pp. 37–68). Norwood, NJ: Ablex.

McDermott, R. P. (1993). The acquisition of a child by a learning disability. In S. Chaiklin & J. Lave (Eds.), *Understanding practice* (pp. 269–305). New York: Cambridge University Press.

McDermott, R. P. (2004a). Materials for a confrontation with genius as a personal identity. *Ethos, 32,* 278–288.

McDermott, R. P. (2004b). Putting literacy in its place. *Journal of Education, 184,* 11–30.

Mead, M. (1943). Our educational emphases in primitive perspective. *American Journal of Sociology, 48,* 633–639.

Modiano, N. (1973). *Indian education in the Chiapas highlands.* New York: Holt, Rinehart & Winston.

Pascal, B. (1966). *Pensées.* London: J. M. Dent & Sons. (Original work published 1670)

Schieffelin, B., & Gilmore, P. (Eds.). (1986). *The acquisition of literacy.* Norwood, NJ: Ablex.

Shuman, A. (1986). *Storytelling rights.* Philadelphia: University of Pennsylvania Press.

Smith, D. (1987). Illiteracy as a social fault. In D. Bloome (Ed.), *Literacy and schooling* (pp. 55–64). Norwood, NJ: Ablex.

Varenne, H., & McDermott, R. P. (1998). *Successful failure: The school America builds.* Boulder, CO: Westview.

Volosinov, V. N. (1973). *Marxism and the philosophy of language.* New York: Academic. (Original work published 1928)

II
Literacy Practices in Diverse Classroom Contexts

In Part II, we shift the focus from the interplay between the "local and the central" (Street, 2001, pp. 14–15) to a closer look at the local, analyzing literacy practices in multiethnic and multilingual classrooms. The concept of literacy practices has its genealogy in the social turn (see this volume's Introduction), particularly the work of Scribner and Cole (1981), Heath (1982, 1983), Barton and his associates (Barton, 1994; Barton & Ivanič, 1991), Gee (1996), and Street (1984, 1993, 1995). This section also investigates the related concept of literacy events—situations and interactions involving reading and writing that are socially and culturally meaningful (see, e.g., Goodman & Wilde, 1992; Heath, 1982).[1] The notion of literacy practices is generally construed as more encompassing, linking "the events and patterns around literacy" to "something broader of a social and cultural kind" (Street, 2001, p. 11).[2]

In the past two decades, a considerable body of research has emerged on the relationships among home-, community-, and school-based literacy practices in

---

[1] As noted in the Introduction to this volume, the concept of literacy events derives from Hymes's (1974) seminal work with the ethnography of communication and his formulation of the concept of speech events.

[2] In actuality, researchers have tended to merge the concepts of literacy practices and literacy events. See, for example, McLaughlin's (1992) study of written language in a Navajo community, in which literacy events are defined as both "interactional minutiae" and the "roles of institutions, ideology, and power" (p. 19). See also Grillo's (1989) even broader concept of communicative practices, defined as the social activities, institutional contexts, and ideologies that "guide processes of communicative production" (p. 15). In Grillo's framework, literacy constitutes one type of communicative practice.

bilingual and multicultural environments (see, e.g., Au, 1993; Cook-Gumperz & Keller-Cohen, 1993; Delgado-Gaitan, 1990; Edelsky, 1989; Hornberger, 1996; Hull & Schultz, 2001; McCarty & Zepeda, 1995; Michaels, 1981; Moll, Amanti, Neff, & González, 1992; Pérez, 2004; Willis, García, Barrera, & Harris, 2003). The chapters in this part of the volume expand on this literature, using ethnographic methods to probe the character and meaning of literacy practices in culturally and linguistically diverse classrooms in the United States and Mexico. Through complex and iterative processes, the minute-by-minute, day-by-day interactions in these classrooms reflect, contest, and produce larger institutional and ideological forces.

Gloria Ladson-Billings begins with a chronicle from a 3-year ethnographic study of early literacy among students in an urban multiethnic school in the United States, examining the relationship of literacy to unspoken ideologies surrounding constructions of race.[3] In this setting, teachers' literacy practices are deeply coupled with ideologies about race, even as they erase race from the language of schooling. We can "predict with high accuracy which students will not become accomplished readers," Ladson-Billings notes, yet the relationship of this fact to race remains veiled and unacknowledged (see also Pollock, 2001). Informed by critical race theory, Ladson-Billings's study instantiates the lingering and racialized power of the Great Divide. Literacy is "deeply embedded in our conceptions of humanity and citizenship," she states. For those barred from emancipatory literacies—such as the African-American students in the school she describes—that access is further restricted by racist ideologies that construct some students as less than human and therefore unworthy of or unable to benefit from high-level literacy engagements.

The chapters by Nancy Hornberger and Janine Remillard and Melisa Cahnmann illustrate alternatives to the either–or, literate–nonliterate dichotomies Ladson-Billings documents. Reflecting on her long-term ethnographic work in bilingual and multilingual schools in Philadelphia and elsewhere, and building on her continua of biliteracy, Hornberger argues for the coexistence of "standard" and "nonstandard" language varieties in bilingual and multilingual classrooms. The important question, she maintains, is not whether schools should develop one variety or another, but rather which literacies to develop for what purposes. In Hornberger's analysis (and consistent with

---

[3]For a broad ethnographic treatment of race as a social construction and its implications for urban schooling in the United States, see the March 2004 (Vol. 35, No. 1) theme issue of *Anthropology & Education Quarterly*, entitled *Race, Power, and the Ethnography of Urban Schools*.

Gee), literacies are social practices through which one participates in "ways of being in the world."

Janine Remillard and Melisa Cahnmann extend this analysis to the relationship between literacy learning and mathematics. Asking "what it means to teach meaningful and empowering mathematics to linguistically and culturally diverse students," they examine teachers' literacy and numeracy practices in 14 classrooms of Latino, African American, and White students in Philadelphia. More than presenting a picture of "polished" teaching practices, Remillard and Cahnmann are concerned with illuminating the challenges and struggles teachers face in developing these practices in urban schools.

Antonia Candela further interrogates classroom-based literacy practices through an analysis of discourse in a Mexican school serving socially and economically marginalized students. Her microexamination of talk within fifth-grade science lessons shows that even within conventional initiation–response–evaluation routines, students construct themselves as subjects who actively and creatively probe academic content, challenging the teacher for control over turn-taking, questioning, and legitimatization of whose knowledge counts. Reminiscent of Delpit's (1988, 1995) critique of power and pedagogy in educating other people's children, Candela concludes that "a school that exclusively utilizes family learning and teaching practices" may not be "as rich as ones that open new forms of learning …. It is rather a question of how the connection between these different practices is made."

In his commentary, Luis Moll emphasizes the increasing diversity in U.S. schools, adding social class to race and ethnicity as critical factors in understanding literacy teaching and learning in these contexts. Moll connects the research in this section to national pedagogical and policy debates, including English-only initiatives and scripted reading programs, the vehemence for which seems to override concerns for students' learning and teachers' professional development. Drawing on his and his associates' funds of knowledge research (e.g., González, 1995; Moll et al., 1992), Moll also stresses the importance of teachers developing personal relationships with students and their families as a pathway to empowering literacies.

What each of these chapters and Moll's commentary share is a commitment to transforming the possibilities in school-based language and literacy practices. Changing reductionist and discriminatory literacy practices requires structural and institutional changes that, on the surface at least, seem beyond the reach of individual educators. Yet educators are critical participants within the educational system who have the power to change it. How teachers interact with students; teachers' attitudes, expectations, and sense of responsibility for student learning; and the overt and symbolic messages they convey, all profoundly influence literacy practices and potentials in the classroom and beyond. The microanalyses in this section illuminate the ways in which literacy practices constrain or make possible the development and expression of liberatory literacies. As Ladson-Billings points out, those possibilities are shaped by educators' constructions of students themselves: The task is "not so much how we teach students, but how we construct them as students."

REFERENCES

Au, K. H. (1993). *Literacy instruction in multicultural settings.* Fort Worth, TX: Harcourt Brace.

Barton, D. (1994). *Literacy: An introduction to the ecology of written language.* Oxford, UK: Blackwell.

Barton, D., & Ivanič, R. (Eds.). (1991). *Writing in community.* London: Sage.

Cook-Gumperz, J., & Keller-Cohen, D. (Eds.). (1993). Alternative literacies: In school and beyond [Special issue]. *Anthropology & Education Quarterly, 24*(4).

Delgado-Gaitan, C. (1990). *Literacy for empowerment: The role of parents in children's education.* New York: Falmer.

Delpit, L. (1988). The silenced dialogue: Power and pedagogy in educating other people's children. *Harvard Educational Review, 54,* 280–298.

Delpit, L. (1995). *Other people's children: Cultural conflict in the classroom.* New York: New Press.

Edelsky, C. (1989). *Writing in a bilingual program: Había una vez.* Norwood, NJ: Ablex.

Gee, J. P. (1996). *Social linguistics and literacies: Ideology in discourses* (2nd ed.). London: Falmer.

González, N. (Ed.). (1995). Educational innovation: Learning from households [Special issue]. *Practicing Anthropology, 17,* 3–25.

Goodman, Y. M., & Wilde, S. (Eds.). (1992). *Literacy events in a community of young writers.* New York: Teachers College Press.

Grillo, R. (1989). *Social anthropology and the politics of language.* Cambridge, UK: Cambridge University Press.

Heath, S. B. (1982). Protean shapes in literacy events: Ever-shifting oral and literate traditions. In D. Tannen (Ed.), *Spoken and written language: Exploring orality and literacy* (pp. 91–117). Norwood, NJ: Ablex.

Heath, S. B. (1983). *Ways with words.* New York: Cambridge University Press.

Hornberger, N. H. (Ed.). (1996). *Indigenous literacies in the Americas: Language planning from the bottom up.* Berlin: Mouton de Gruyter.

Hull, G., & Schultz, K. (2001). Literacy and learning out of school: A review of theory and research. *Review of Educational Research, 71,* 575–611.

Hymes, D. (1974). *Foundations in sociolinguistics: An ethnographic approach.* Philadelphia: University of Pennsylvania Press.

McCarty, T. L., & Zepeda, O. (Eds.). (1995). Indigenous language education and literacy [Special issue]. *Bilingual Research Journal, 19*(1 & 2).

McLaughlin, D. (1992). *When literacy empowers: Navajo language in print.* Albuquerque: University of New Mexico Press.

Michaels, S. (1981). "Sharing time": Children's narrative styles and differential access to literacy. *Language in Society, 10,* 432–442.

Moll, L. C., Amanti, C., Neff, D., & González, N. (1992). Funds of knowledge for teaching: Using a qualitative approach to connect homes and classrooms. *Theory Into Practice, 31,* 132–141.

Pérez, B., with McCarty, T. L., Watahomigie, L. J., Torres-Guzmán, M., Dien, T. T., Chang, J.-M., Smith, H. L., et al. (2004). *Sociocultural contexts of language and literacy* (2nd ed.). Mahwah, NJ: Lawrence Erlbaum Associates.

Pollock, M. (2001). How the question we ask most about race in education is the very question we most suppress. *Educational Researcher, 30,* 2–12.

Scribner, S., & Cole, H. (1981). *The psychology of literacy.* Cambridge, MA: Harvard University Press.

Street, B. V. (1984). *Literacy in theory and practice.* Cambridge, UK: Cambridge University Press.

Street, B. V. (Ed.). (1993). *Cross-cultural approaches to literacy.* Cambridge, UK: Cambridge University Press.

Street, B. V. (1995). *Social literacies: Critical approaches to literacy development, ethnography and education.* London: Longman.

Street, B. V. (2001). Introduction. In B. V. Street (Ed.), *Literacy and development: Ethnographic perspectives* (pp. 1–17). London: Routledge.

Willis, A. I., García, G. E., Barrera, R., & Harris, V. J. (Eds.). (2003). *Multicultural issues in literacy research and practice.* Mahwah, NJ: Lawrence Erlbaum Associates.

Reading, Writing, and Race: Literacy Practices of Teachers in Diverse Classrooms

Gloria Ladson-Billings
University of Wisconsin-Madison

In the early 1900s, W.E.B. Dubois argued that the color line would be the problem of the 20th century. His proclamation proved to be prophetic. This chapter examines the ways in which race continues to color the perceptions of teachers working with children struggling to become literate. Drawing on a 3-year ethnographic study of early literacy, I examine how teachers talk "around" race even when race is at the center of the educational problem. A careful look at teacher discourse both inside and outside the classroom indicates that teachers avoid talking about race, even as it bears on student achievement. This chapter explores the practices of teachers who have learned the language of schooling, devoid of race talk, while being submerged in a racial ecology. The chapter concludes with an examination of researcher behaviors that provide an opportunity for teachers to approach the subject of race or the racial subject.

> The denial of race in these "color-blind" perspectives about the modern past or the postmodern present is the intellectual counterpart of the denial of the legacy of white supremacy in our society and world. As long as race is simply added to the central dynamics of modernity or glibly marginal to the emergence of sustenance of American society, this lethal denial persists.
>
> —West (1998, pp. 301–302)

The U.S. and Western penchant for measuring and calibrating has brought us to a moment in our educational history where finer and finer gradations are conceived of to determine our children's academic achievement. Currently, we have a language of literacy achievement that describes students on a continuum from emergent to accomplished reader. Teachers spend endless hours conducting "running records" and organizing portfolios documenting students' literacy accomplishments. The National Research Council's (1998) report on early literacy states that the majority of reading problems faced by today's adolescents and adults could have been avoided or resolved in the early years of childhood. However, this report is noticeably silent on the fact that we can predict with a fairly high degree of accuracy which students will not become accomplished readers.

It is no surprise that children of color, particularly African Americans, Native Americans, and Latinos, routinely and regularly fail to become proficient and accomplished readers. What may be surprising is the fact that talk of race is rarely combined with discussions of student academic performance even when congruence exists between the two. For example, at a high school I recently visited, none of the school's 400 African-American students was in the National Honor Society. Honors and advanced placement courses routinely had no African-American students. Remedial and basic courses had African-American enrollment of better than 40% (despite the fact that African-American students comprised only 20% of the total school population). There appeared to be a clear relationship between race and student achievement, but there was no space in the school where the two could be mentioned in the same breath.

Like Morrison's (1991, p. 17) "unspeakable things yet unspoken," schools have developed a comfortable and familiar discourse about students' achievement that is simultaneously devoid of and replete with the issue of race. This chapter describes an ongoing research project with experienced teachers who have learned the language of schooling, devoid of race talk. The paradox with which the teachers live is that they are submerged in a racial ecology where White, middle-income parents maintain enough power and influence to quell any talk of race but use their own racial positions to leverage the school system on behalf of their children.

THE NATURE OF THE PROBLEM

At no other time in history has the process of "becoming literate" been more complex. Today's students are challenged to read within and across a variety of media (Mahiri, 1998). Traditional texts (i.e., books) are but one form of literacy "event" for students. Computer programs, music videos, rap songs, and video games also are part of students' literate environment. How do teachers connect students, many of whom come to school with differential access to American edited English, with traditional forms of literacy such as textbooks, trade books, workbooks, and other written forms?

The relationship between literacy and power is well established in U.S. history. The early experiences of Africans in the Americas underscores this relationship. It was illegal to teach an enslaved African to read because White slave owners knew that literate slaves would be difficult to oppress. V. J. Harris (1992) asserts that a theme in the early literary works of African-American authors is the belief that literacy can serve both emancipatory and oppressive functions: "Literacy serves emancipatory functions when appropriated to reconstruct society and/or provide individuals with the options needed to participate in all sociocultural institutions" (p. 277). Conversely,

> Literacy functions in an oppressive manner ... when curricular materials, educational philosophy, and pedagogical techniques combine to inculcate an ideology that denigrates a group, omits or misrepresents the history and status of a group, or limits access to knowledge that would enable the individual or group to participate in all cultural institutions. (V. J. Harris, 1992, p. 277)

Today, many African-American students continue to struggle to acquire the kind of literacy that leads to liberation. In an earlier article (Ladson-Billings, 1992) I described a teacher whose pedagogical philosophy and practice supported students' literacy and liberation. The teacher's literacy practices stand in stark contrast to many urban classrooms I have visited where African-American students sit disengaged and bored with mindless tasks of school-based "reading."

Researchers in the field of reading suggest the reasons students fail to become skilled readers include a "failure to understand or use the alphabetic principle ..., failure to acquire and use comprehension skills and strategies to get meaning from text, and a lack of fluency" (National Research Council, 1999, p. 127). However, I would argue that these "technical" reasons for reading failure mask the more powerful social structural and symbolic ones that are a part of the wider U.S. culture.

In this chapter I argue that literacy is deeply embedded in our conceptions of humanity and citizenship; that is, one must be human to be literate and one must be literate to be a citizen. In the days of U.S. slavery, the failure of enslaved Africans to read signaled to slave holders that the Africans were not human. This positioning of African Americans as "beings" lacking humanity justified the brutal treatment of enslaved human beings and reinforced notions of racial superiority.

Even in those instances where enslaved Africans were able to acquire literacy, their literate behaviors were considered "tricks" similar to those showcased with house pets. Phillis Wheatley, the first African American to publish a book, was considered an oddity and the veracity of her work was challenged (Gates & McKay, 1997). Acknowledging the intellectual capabilities of Africans in the 18th century meant acknowledging their humanity. Acknowledging their humanity called into question the humanity of the Europeans. How could a civilized human being knowingly enslave another human being?

It is important to remember that from its colonial beginnings, the United States was a socially stratified society. The magnificent words of the Declaration of Independence and the U.S. Constitution only extended citizenship rights to property-holding White men. Enslaved Africans were the lowest on the social hierarchy. Without the designation of "human" it was impossible for enslaved Africans to be considered citizens. Perhaps more important is the way Whiteness was seamlessly mapped onto humanness and then how that humanness and Whiteness was mapped onto citizenship. This philosophical and political sleight of hand allowed the Europeans to continue their overt commitment to freedom, justice, liberty, and Christianity while engaging in the most heinous crime against humanity—chattel slavery.

My analysis of the relationship between literacy and race is grounded in critical race theory (CRT), a form of scholarly legal critique that argues "racism is normal, not aberrant, in American society" (Delgado, 1995, p. xiv). Critical race theorists employ narrative or story to contextualize the sterile legal treatise of American jurisprudence. According to Delgado (1995), "Many Critical writers are postmoderns, who believe that form and substance are closely connected. Accordingly, they have been using biography and autobiography, stories and counter-stories to expose the false necessity and unintentional irony of much current civil rights law and scholarship" (p. xv).

In this chapter, I examine the relationship of literacy and race through the practices of elementary teachers by constructing a brief narrative from 2.5 years of qualitative data collected from 1997 to 1998. First I provide a brief background of the research site and the participants. Next, I share the narrative (or perhaps, counternarrative) of teachers avoiding race talk in a racially infused environment. Finally, I provide an analysis of the narrative that addresses why the relationship between literacy and race must be explored before African Americans and other children of color can acquire sufficient literacy for social advancement and liberation.

THE RESEARCH COMMUNITY

Bret Hart Elementary[1] is a large school (approximately 500 students) serving low-income and working-class families in a midsize, midwestern U.S. city. Approximately 25% to 30% of the student population is African American. For many years, Bret Hart posted the lowest standardized reading and mathematics scores in the school district. I worked with a colleague, Mary Louise Gomez, to gain entrée at Bret Hart. We began by negotiating with the school superintendent to locate an elementary school where teachers would be willing to allow researchers to observe in their classrooms and agree to participate in a professional community to share ideas about literacy teaching.

Our research questions were, "How can teachers use small, local professional communities to improve the literacy of struggling early readers?" and "What literacy strategies do teachers attempt to improve the literacy of struggling readers?" Our research design called for the use of mixed methods. Qualitative data were collected via participant observation (Spradley, 1971), interviews, and the group conversation method (DuBois & Li, 1974). Quantitative data were gathered from the students' test scores on the district writing sample and the Primary Language Arts Assessment.

Seven primary grade teachers (Grades K–2) volunteered to participate in our project. All were White women. Each teacher was asked to identify those children about whose literacy they were most concerned. We did not ask the teachers to specify criteria for determining the students they selected. We were content to accept the teachers' concerns as legitimate and worthy of investigation. We secured informed consent from both the teachers and the parents of the students in their classes.

We used observations and interviews to draw richly textured portraits of each classroom—the students, the teachers, and the interactions between and among them. While we observed in classrooms two to three times per week, we met with teachers as a group once a month. The monthly meetings were structured around questions and dilemmas of literacy teaching. Because the teachers were asked to share openly with each other, we expected that some of their shared teaching strategies and ideas would find their way back into the classrooms. Subsequent observations after each monthly meeting demon-

---

[1]School and teacher names are pseudonyms.

strated that collegial input did have an impact on classroom practice. However, these pedagogical changes did not signal changes in teachers' willingness to engage in more candid talk about race.

All classroom observations were recorded in field notes, transcribed, and coded. All monthly teacher meetings were audiotaped (supplemented by notes), transcribed, and coded. Classroom observation transcripts were shared with individual teachers for further comment and reflection. What follows is a narrative of our experiences at Bret Hart School.

ONE OF THE BRET HART CHRONICLES

Each time I walk into Bret Hart Elementary School I ask myself, "What committee designed this building?" There is little rhyme or reason to the layout of this sprawling, old edifice. The building contains an old and "new" section but the room numbers follow a curious sequence, fathomable only to the experienced visitor. More than many of the school buildings in this city, Bret Hart reminds me of the school buildings I grew up in (and later taught in) in Philadelphia. Every inch of wall space in the corridors of Bret Hart is covered with examples of student work. I am particularly fond of the chocolate chip and toothpick people constructed by the kindergarten class on the first floor.

Our first meeting with the school principal caused my colleague and I to doubt whether or not we would be able to conduct meaningful research in the building. The principal was a longtime school district employee and we were talking to him about an "innovative, teacher-centered research project" 6 months before he planned to retire. I do not think he cared what we did, as long as it did not bring any unflattering attention to him and his school.

Despite the principal's lukewarm support, we were able to convince seven primary grade teachers to participate in the project. The group consisted of five classroom teachers and two reading specialists. We asked them each to identify children about whose literacy they were most concerned. As we listened to the names we recognized that almost all of the identified children were African Americans. "I'm worried about Marquis and Terrell," one teacher said. "And I'm concerned about Jamal and LeShon," said another. When my colleague and I went over the names back in our offices we found that about 80% of the names offered were those of African Americans. More than 90% were children of color. None of the teachers mentioned the preponderance of African-American students on the list. This was my first inkling that race would be submerged in this research relationship.

During our visits to the classrooms we observed multiple instances where African-American students were set apart from the mainstream of literacy instruction. Sometimes that separation was a result of compensatory programs such as Title I or Reading Recovery. Other times they were separated to participate in some sort of one-on-one interaction with a volunteer tutor or parent. During our visits we were "assigned" children of color to work with. These were additional instances where race was present in our experiences but absent in the discourse.

For almost 6 months the routine rarely changed. We observed in classrooms. We assisted students who were struggling. We facilitated meetings and listened to the teachers talk about their struggles to teach. At one meeting we asked the teachers to discuss what they had taught in reading the previous week. One by one the teachers shared what they were doing in their classrooms. We heard stories of fun "activities" but little in the way of reading instruction. Finally, the one teacher in the group, Paulette, who had been somewhat socially marginal to her colleagues, provided a detailed explanation of the decoding, vocabulary development, and comprehension work she was doing with her students. Somewhat embarrassed, one of the other teachers said, "Well, I guess I haven't really been teaching any reading." Several of the other teachers nodded in agreement. My colleague and I stole sly glances at each other. We had discussed what we saw as the lack of instruction that was occurring in the classrooms. The teachers were nice and kind to children but much of their time seemed to be taken up with entertaining or amusing the children.

In fairness to the teachers, they were working in a district that had exercised almost no instructional leadership. Although ostensibly a "whole language" district, what that actually meant in practice was a far cry from what scholars such as Goodman (1998) and Edelsky (1998) advocate. Many teachers merely passed out trade books to the children, asked them to read them (or read them aloud), and came up with some activity (e.g., draw a picture, make a bookmark) related to the text. Teachers could only talk in vague generalizations about what their children knew or were able to do. They could identify good, average, and emergent readers, but they could not identify any substantive strengths or weaknesses the children demonstrated in reading.

The notable exception was Paulette. Paulette knew exactly what every student in her class was reading and all of her students were reading. Listening to Paulette and watching her colleagues' responses to her reminded me of Delpit's (1986) discussion of the skills versus process dilemma she faced as an elementary teacher. During our classroom observations of Paulette we were struck by the amount of time she spent focused on instruction. In her first-grade classroom the students were regularly called to the chalkboard to identify sounds, word parts, and the number of syllables. Paulette's students also did a lot of writing. Paulette made certain that she stopped at each student's desk to discuss his or her work and ask questions about the student's understanding of particular words and concepts. When we observed in Paulette's classroom we left exhausted. She recruited us to check students' journals and to reinforce the concepts she taught. The work went at a rapid pace but Paulette circulated throughout the room, paying particular attention to the students she had identified on her list of concerns.

At one of our monthly meetings we asked the teachers to bring examples of their students' work to share with colleagues. Paulette brought a pile of neatly written thank-you letters her students had written in response to a field trip they had taken. "Did you have your kids copy these from the board?" asked one of the other teachers. "No," replied Paulette. "Each student wrote their own paper. That's an expectation in my room." My colleague and I exchanged glances once again and we could see that Paulette's stock was starting to rise in the group. Although most of her colleagues thought her approach to literacy was "old-fashioned" and "too skills driven," it was apparent that they were impressed with her results.

At the end of one of our monthly meetings Paulette told me that she had taught in Gary, Indiana, before coming to this community. "I never had trouble teaching the Afro-American [sic] children. Their parents want them to learn to read just like anybody else does. I push them just as hard as I possibly can." Why was Paulette telling me this after the group meeting? Did she recognize that conversations about race were out of bounds for the group? Did she want me to know that although race, as a topic, was not on the table, she was aware that race and coded notions of race were circulating around the entire project? Paulette's "confession" reminded me of the Christian notion of being "in the world, but not of it." Was Paulette in the Bret Hart group, but not of it?

Another set of our observations documents the way teachers granted African-American students "permission to fail" (Ladson-Billings, 1999). In one of the combination kindergarten and first-grade classrooms, a little African-American girl, Shannon, regularly refused to participate in the literacy activities. Daily the students were required to come up with one sentence about some question or activity that was the result of the opening morning exercises. The teachers called the children together on the carpet and discussed various things—what they did over the weekend, what they were planning for Halloween, what their favorite meal was. After the discussion the students were instructed to talk with the children at their tables to select one sentence they would all attempt to write. Many children could not accurately write the sentences they chose, but most could put down a beginning sound or a beginning and ending sound. Indeed, students were encouraged to use invented spellings so that teachers could see how close their writing paralleled what they heard and knew. Shannon could not write because she could make no sense of the sound–symbol relationship. Shannon did not know how to match sounds with letters and rather than be embarrassed about her inadequacies, she became defiant. "I ain't writin' nuthin' " was a familiar refrain from her. Each day, the response of the teacher was to say, "All right, Shannon, maybe you will feel like writing tomorrow." Were we witnessing an act of racism that teachers would be unable to discuss?

At our last meeting for the school year, we invited the teachers to a working lunch at the university. We also invited one of the school district's testing coordinators to share the test score data from the school with the group. Prior to this, we relied on the teachers to tell us how they thought students were performing in literacy. It was clear from both the teachers' conversations and the public discourse that an antagonistic relationship existed between the district's new assessment policy and the teachers. A hallmark of the district had been the independence of teachers to determine the kinds of assessments they would use to determine student progress. Increasing public demands for accountability and some standard measures of performance prompted the district to require more tests.

The test data indicated that Bret Hart students were among the lowest performing students in the district. Eighty-five percent of the students in the district performed above standard on the state's third-grade reading test. At Bret Hart, only 62.5% of the students performed above standard—the lowest rate in the district. The testing coordinator also organized the data to show how Bret Hart compared with some of its neighboring schools that served similar student populations. The teachers were discouraged to learn that even among schools that looked at lot like their own, Bret Hart remained the lowest performing school.

The test data were also organized by race and gender. The most striking statistics were the degrees to which African-American boys differed from the rest of the cohort. An eerie silence hung over the room as the teachers examined the data. Later, various teachers talked about the need to do a better job monitoring student performance and providing parents with more accurate feedback. My colleague and I sat impassively. Finally, out of the blue, one of the teachers blurted out, "We're doing a terrible job with the Black boys! Don't you think race has something to do with this?" There, it was out on the table. Someone (White) had named it and for the first time we could talk about "unspeakable things yet unspoken" (Morrison, 1991, p. 17).

In a "good" story, I would be able to report that this first spoken-aloud statement about race propelled the group to examine it carefully and meaningfully throughout the life of the project. However, this is not a "good" story. It is a real story and as such, we are continuing to tread lightly around issues of race. There are no teachers of color in our Bret Hart cohort. Issues of race and ethnicity typically are introduced by my colleague and me, who sometimes feel as if we are Detectives Muldar and Scully of television's *The X Files*—seeing and experiencing things that no one else sees or believes.

THE RACIALIZATION OF LITERACY TEACHING
AND LEARNING

One might ask how it is possible to configure the Bret Hart Chronicles as a story of race merely because it took the teachers 6 months to "recognize" the racial dynamic that was occurring with the lack of reading success for African-American male children. However, a CRT analysis of the chronicle looks at the tale the way Morrison (1991) explores literary texts that seem to have omitted an Africanist presence. By examining the "impact of racial hierarchy, racial exclusion, and racial vulnerability and availability" in fiction on non-Black readers and writers, she demonstrates how readers almost always are positioned as "White" by using "serviceable" representations of "the Black" (Morrison, 1991, p. 11). Morrison's (1991) analysis of literary texts reveals how the sycophancy of White identity functions hegemonically in these relations of representations. According to King (1995):

> Because hegemony legitimates the social framework's White normative cultural model of being and identity, Morrison's analysis suggests that Black people's humanity can only be affirmed and valued—and everyone else freed from the conceptual belief structure of race—if society is reinvented and reorganized around a different cultural model of the human. (p. 279)

Thus, Morrison (1991) argues that, "the world does not become raceless or will not become unracialized by assertion" (p. 46).

The racial valence that was applied to the Bret Hart situation was one that consistently rendered African-American children one down in the literacy equation. Almost none of the Bret Hart teachers had been in a personal relationship with an African-American adult or child who was of equal or greater social status than she. The notable exception was Paulette, who had spent part of her teaching career in Gary, Indiana, where she had taught successfully in classrooms that were 100% African American. She knew and had associated with a variety of African Americans.

In a district where African-American students were the worst performers (at all levels), their reading failure did not come as a surprise to teachers. Failure seemed to be a place reserved for African-American students. Each of the compensatory programs (e.g., Reading Recovery, Title I) had a majority of African-American students, whereas the gifted and talented and instrumental music programs had almost no African-American students.

The teachers in our study are not unlike teachers throughout the United States. They are well meaning and practice a kind of "racial etiquette" (Haney Lopez, 1995, p. 193) that requires that race be ignored at every turn. Indeed, the teachers cannot notice race because such noticing will require that they examine their own pedagogical practice in relationship to race. As long as the children's reading failure was about their poverty and the deficiencies of their parents, the teachers could absolve themselves of any responsibility for the reading failure.

However, the teachers were mapping the students' illiteracy onto their humanity (or lack thereof). When teachers conducted a simple survey we asked of them, some surprising information emerged. We asked the teachers to ask the "focus children"[2] three questions:

- What does it mean to be a good reader in this classroom?
- Who are the good readers in this class?
- Are you a good reader?

What we learned was that children were equating being a good reader with being a good person. The moral superiority of the good reader was being transmitted to children via the differential way teachers responded to students according to their reading abilities. Good readers rarely were sanctioned for misbehavior. Poor readers received regular reprimands. Granted, poor readers

---

[2]Focus children were those two or three children whom teachers initially identified as unlikely to show adequate progress in literacy.

probably were off task more often and invited more teacher attention for mis-behavior. However, teachers took no responsibility for uncoupling reading ability and morality in the children's minds.

Although the teachers themselves were shocked to hear how the children were conflating literacy and "goodness," they seemed unaware that the way they were conflating race and humanity led to differential access to learning and dif-ferential achievement. Like C. Harris's (1993) notion of "Whiteness as prop-erty," the teachers enjoyed a series of rights from which the African-American students were excluded. Those rights include the rights of disposition, rights to use and enjoyment, reputation and status property, and the absolute right to ex-clude. In earlier writing, William Tate and I (Ladson-Billings & Tate, 1995) ex-plain how this notion of Whiteness as property functions in education.

Because property rights are described as fully alienable (i.e., transferable) it is difficult to see how Whiteness can be construed as property. However, alien-ability of certain property is limited (e.g., entitlements, government licenses, professional degrees or licenses held by one party and financed by the labor of another in the context of a divorce). Thus, Whiteness when conferred on cer-tain student performances is alienable. When students are rewarded only for conformity to perceived "White norms" or sanctioned for cultural practices (dress, speech patterns, unauthorized conceptions of knowledge), White prop-erty is being rendered alienable. In the context of our project, students who were learning to read were having Whiteness conferred on them and those who struggled to read were receiving no such property rights. Indeed, one might ar-gue, those White children who struggled to read risked being made Black.

Legally, Whites can use and enjoy the privilege of Whiteness. As McIntosh (1990) has explicitly demonstrated, Whiteness allows for specific social, cul-tural, and economic privileges. At Bret Hart, the large number of African-Amer-ican children participating in compensatory education programs meant that they did not get to enjoy other aspects of the curriculum as readily as their White classmates. For instance, teachers chose to do activities and projects involving the arts or science when the "Chapter kids" (those in remedial programs) were out of the room. We cannot infer that the teachers were deliberate in denying Af-rican-American students these curriculum opportunities. Rather, the question for us as researchers was why so much silence persisted about the way Afri-can-American children's experience with the curriculum was more scripted and regimented, whereas White children got to enjoy aspects of learning that al-lowed them to use their literacy skills in more creative and authentic ways.

Reputation and status property is represented in legal cases of libel and slander. Thus, to damage someone's reputation is to damage some aspect of his or her personal property. In schools, reputation and status property become associated with race. For example, a White student who is experiencing academic difficulties in schools is just that—a (read, "individual") White student with problems. African-American children who experience academic problems, on the other hand, often serve as a proxy for all other African-American children. So strong is the reputation and status property in schools that certain programs and courses of study already have racial valences attached. For instance, English as a Second Language (ESL) or Chapter I programs are automatically assumed to be programs for the "other." Conversely, advanced placement and honors courses are assumed to be programs for White children. Notable exceptions are those of Asian American students who have been able to successfully negotiate the school system. Liu (1998) argues that some Asian Americans have been viewed as the "new Jews" based on their ability to assimilate and appropriate White, middle-class culture. Of course Liu's observation is based on a monolithic reading of American Jewish culture and economic success and he runs a dangerous risk of essentializing in setting up Jews as a template of success. However, in both cases—African American school failure and Asian American school success—we have examples of how reputation and status property are deployed based on race.

Once while visiting a California high school I wandered into a laboratory science classroom. One of the few White students in the class remarked to me, "Yeah, this is Asian physics, if that's what you're looking for." The class was not a physics class for ESL students but because the majority of the students were of Asian descent, the speaker had used the reputation and status property of the Asian students as a descriptor for the course. I presume I was supposed to view the White student more favorably because he was willing to compete in the rigorous "Asian physics" class.

Conversely, African American students have been heard to say things like, "Black people don't do math" or "Black people don't play in the orchestra," because schools (and society) have helped to create a reputation and status property of Whiteness that is to be associated with such activities. Thus, the "acting White" phenomenon, described by Fordham and Ogbu (1986), is not a creation of African-American students; rather, it is a result of their astute observations of the way White and Black children are assigned to social roles and cultural spaces in the school.

Students do not acquire an academic identity in high school. Such a sense of self begins developing in the early school years. African-American students who regularly have been placed in remedial classes, assigned to special pull-out programs, and assigned to low groups are aware enough to notice which of the other children join them in these groups. When the groups are regularly constituted of other African-American children it is not surprising that when they see African-American children in "new" groups (e.g., gifted and talented education, orchestra, advanced placement classes), they question that placement.

Finally, the Whiteness as property argument deals with the absolute right to exclude. The ability to say who is or who is not in a category is ceded to Whites. Indeed, the very notion that "one drop of Black blood" (whatever that means) constructs one as Black speaks to the presumption that "Blackness" is somehow contaminating. This exclusion power is important because it could have been just as easy for Whites to argue that "one drop of White blood" means that one is White. However, doing so would have opened up the category of Whiteness in ways that would undercut the ability to exclude. Almost every African American could lay some claim to Whiteness under those conditions. However, the right to exclude permits a policing and monitoring of the category "White" that limits who might lay claim to it and enjoy its benefits.[3]

In school, the absolute right to exclude is demonstrated in a variety of ways—school segregation, resegregation in magnet or demonstration schools, tracking, access to advanced courses, and other benefits. The African-American children in our study were excluded from particular aspects of the curriculum because their "need for remediation" required that they leave the classroom at key times in the school day.

A more subtle and perhaps more pernicious example of this right of exclusion occurred when I learned of a White high school freshman girl who had joined the swim team at her school. Very quickly, her upper class team members supplied her with copies of papers, tests, projects, essays, and other assignments she might encounter that year. All other students were "excluded" from access to inside knowledge about ninth grade. Clearly, many other students, regardless of race, are excluded from inside knowledge in this instance, but the example is used not so much for its intrinsic worth as for its symbolic worth.

Many White middle-class students have access to particular sets of "networks" that provide them with social and academic advantages in schools.

---

[3]A fascinating discussion of racial categorization is found in the work of S. Lee (1993), who examines the U.S. Census Department's use of Question 4, "What is your race?"

These networks may form as a result of sports activities (soccer, Little League, swim club) or arts activities (dance lessons, music lessons, drama), where parents are involved and invested. The parental network creates a buffer against failure for such children. Even when the students themselves show little or no interest in school tasks, the network that surrounds them keeps them from falling too far. No such network typically exists for African-American students. In a few cases, social organizations such as Jack and Jill, which cater to middle-class African Americans, serve a similar function. However, no such organizational scaffold exists for the vast majority of African-American children.

HOW TEACHERS MIGHT BEGIN TO THINK
OF LITERACY AND RACE

Regardless of the CRT analysis of literacy in schools, we are still left with the dilemma of helping teachers think about teaching African-American students successfully. Merely making surface-level changes—curriculum selection and teaching techniques—is unlikely to result in improved literacy performance for African-American students. Instead, a more deliberate approach toward race and culture is warranted. C. D. Lee (1992, 1993) has demonstrated the need for "cultural modeling" to support students' literacy learning. Her work describes the way the literacy skills that students already possess can be deployed to acquire the language and discourse of school literacy. For example, the students' understanding of popular culture forms such as rap and music video can be used to demonstrate rather conventional literary and literacy skills, including detecting symbolism, unreliable narrators, and authors' attempts at situating the reader and audience.

However, as excited as I am about work such as that of Lee, I continue to have serious concerns about teachers' willingness to unlearn racial codes and symbols and learn new ways of constructing and conceptualizing Blackness in general and African Americans in particular. Thus, the task is not so much how we teach students, but rather in how we construct them as students. Literacy remains an important social marker in this world. Those who are "literate" have access to certain advantages—social, economic, political, and cultural. However, more than these external advantages, they have the ability to confer civilization on themselves. Their access to identities as "civilized" beings reinscribes their humanity. They (and their offspring) are entitled to be literate, but there are the masses of people who are rendered uncivilized and inhuman. Conferring literacy on such people would force us to humanize them, and in a social order obsessed with binaries (Black–White, male–female, liberal–conservative, civilized–uncivilized), that conferring would place all identities—including our own—in flux.

Willis's (1995) description of the frustration her son faced as a young African-American boy in a third-grade class is a classic example of the "dailyness" of the struggle for human agency African Americans confront. Early on, Willis's son, "Jake," began to remove himself from the academic tasks of the classroom because of the additional burden of having to prove his humanity and civility. In Jake's class the students were competing in a national essay assignment on the topic, "What it means to be an American." How is it possible for African-American students to seriously grapple with such an assignment without the pain of admitting that one really does not know because American citizenship is so tentatively held by African Americans?

Perhaps one glimmer of hope exists for the race-literacy conundrum in the annals of our history. Beginning as far back as 1661, Africans in the Americas understood the political power of and need for literacy. Cornelius (1991) points out that literate slaves petitioned colonial courts for their liberty and by the 18th century, Ottabah Cugoano published a powerful antislavery treatise entitled *Thoughts and sentiments on the evil and wicked traffic of the slavery and commerce of the human species.* It is interesting to note that Cugoano asserts his humanity, not his African-ness, here. Similarly, Olaudah Equiano (in Carretta, 1998) wrote powerfully of his travails as an enslaved man. Somewhere in the horror of slavery, African people found literacy as an emancipatory tool.

By the time of the modern civil rights movement[4] it was clear that literacy would play an important role in liberating African Americans from the shackles of Jim Crow segregation and abject poverty. Federal government attempts at adult literacy failed miserably because once again, African Americans were denied their basic humanity to participate in such programs. Morris (1984) details the work of Myles Horton, Septima Clark, and Esau Jenkins as they worked with African-American community members to improve their literacy skills in what they termed Citizenship Schools. Instead of treating the mature adults like children (as the federal literacy programs did), Horton and Clark designed a program to meet the people's human needs. In Horton's words (cited in Morris, 1984):

---

[4]I argue that African Americans have been engaged in a civil rights movement since their arrival in the Americas. However, I designate the time between post-World War II and the early 1970s as the "modern" civil rights movement.

We decided we'd pitch it on a basis of them becoming full citizens and taking their place in society and demanding their rights and being real men and women in their own right. Putting into practice all these religious things they talked about, and the humanitarian things they talked about and doing something about it. (p. 151)

The success of Horton's, Clark's, and Jenkins's work created a huge demand for Citizenship Schools among African Americans throughout the South. African Americans understood literacy to be a key component of liberation and pursued it with vigor. The Citizenship Schools became the prototype for organizing against racism and oppression and their graduates became "teachers" in subsequent Citizenship Schools.

The purpose for reciting this history is to prompt us to ponder what has transpired to interrupt this quest for literacy in the African-American community and to ask what can be done to reinvigorate it. The relationship that exists between literacy and race in the United States is complex and deep. Race is always already in our midst, yet teachers insist on ignoring it. We cannot understand school failure merely by making technical adjustments to teaching and learning. We cannot understand the power of race and racism by pretending they are not there. Our challenge is to grapple with them together in an effort to conquer them simultaneously.

Gloria Ladson-Billings is the Kellner Family Professor in Urban Education in the Department of Curriculum and Instruction at the University of Wisconsin–Madison. Her work focuses on culturally relevant pedagogy and CRT in education.

REFERENCES

Carretta, V. (Ed.). (1998). *The interesting life of Oladauh Equiano*. New York: Penguin.

Cornelius, J. D. (1991). *When I can read my title clear: Literacy, slavery and religion in the antebellum South*. Columbia: University of South Carolina Press.

Delgado, R. (Ed.). (1995). *Critical race theory: The cutting edge*. Philadelphia: Temple University Press.

Delpit, L. (1986). Skills and other dilemmas of a progressive Black educator. *Harvard Educational Review, 56,* 379–385.

DuBois, R., & Li, R. (1974). *Reducing social tensions and conflict: The group conversation method*. New York: Association Press.

Edelsky, C. (1998). It's a long story—and it's not done yet. In K. Goodman (Ed.), *In defense of good teaching* (pp. 39–55). York, ME: Stenhouse.

Fordham, S., & Ogbu, J. (1986). Black students' school success: Coping with the burden of "acting White." *The Urban Review, 18,* 1–31.

Gates, H. L., & McKay, N. Y. (Eds.). (1997). *The Norton anthology of African American literature.* New York: Norton.

Goodman, K. (1998). Who's afraid of whole language? Politics, paradigms, pedagogy, and the press. In K. Goodman (Ed.), *In defense of good teaching* (pp. 3–37). York, ME: Stenhouse.

Haney Lopez, I. (1995). The social construction of race. In R. Delgado (Ed.), *Critical race theory: The cutting edge* (pp. 191–203). Philadelphia: Temple University Press.

Harris, C. (1993). Whiteness as property. *Harvard Law Review, 106,* 1709–1791.

Harris, V. J. (1992). African American conceptions of literacy: A historical perspective. *Theory Into Practice, 31,* 276–286.

King, J. E. (1995). Culture-centered knowledge: Black studies, curriculum transformation, and social action. In J. A. Banks & C. M. Banks (Eds.), *Handbook of research on multicultural education* (pp. 265–290). New York: Macmillan.

Ladson-Billings, G. (1992). Liberatory consequences of literacy: A case of culturally relevant instruction for African American students. *The Journal of Negro Education, 61,* 378–391.

Ladson-Billings, G. (1999, May). *"I ain't writin' nuthin' ": Permission to fail versus demands for success in urban classrooms.* Paper presented at the Language Colloquium, Minneapolis, MN.

Ladson-Billings, G., & Tate, W. F. (1995). Toward a critical race theory of education. *Teachers College Record, 97,* 47–68.

Lee, C. D. (1992). Literacy, cultural diversity and instruction. *Education and Urban Society, 24,* 279–291.

Lee, C. D. (1993). *Signifying as a scaffold for literary interpretation: The pedagogical implications of an African American discourse genre.* Urbana, IL: National Council of Teachers of English.

Lee, S. (1993). Racial classification in the U.S. census: 1890–1990. *Ethnic and Race Studies, 16,* 75–94.

Liu, E. (1998). *The accidental Asian: Notes of a native speaker.* New York: Vintage.

Mahiri, J. (1998). *Shooting for excellence: African American and youth culture in new century schools.* New York: Teachers College Press and National Council of Teachers of English.

McIntosh, P. (1990). White privilege: Unpacking the invisible knapsack. *Independent School, 49,* 31–36.

Morris, A. D. (1984). *The origins of the civil rights movement: Black communities organizing for change.* New York: Free Press.

Morrison, T. (1991). *Playing in the dark: Whiteness and the literary imagination.* Cambridge, MA: Harvard University Press.

National Research Council. (1998). *Preventing reading difficulties in young children.* Washington, DC: Author.

National Research Council. (1999). *Starting out right: A guide to promoting children's reading success.* Washington, DC: Author.

Spradley, J. (1971). *Participant observation.* New York: Holt, Rinehart & Winston.

West, C. (1998). Afterword. In W. Lubiano (Ed.), *The house that race built* (pp. 301–303). New York: Vintage.

Willis, A. I. (1995). Reading the world of school literacy: Contextualizing the experience of a young African American male. *Harvard Educational Review, 65,* 30–49.

Student Voice and the Media of Biliteracy in Bi(multi)lingual/ Multicultural Classrooms

Nancy H. Hornberger
University of Pennsylvania

Beginning from an ideological premise that takes linguistic diversity as resource, and from conceptual principles for ethical human discourse that posit that human beings should seek to avoid harming or taking advantage of others in their social practices, this chapter argues that making space in classroom literacy practices for dissimilar and divergent language varieties and orthographies and for bi(multi)lingual learners' simultaneous, criss-crossed language and literacy acquisition promotes inclusion of students' voices and, concomitantly, their active participation in their own identity and knowledge construction. My goal is to pose the question, not so much "How to develop bi(multi)literacy?" but rather, "Which bi(multi)literacies to develop for what purposes?" Reflecting on my own and others' long-term ethnographic studies in bi(multi)lingual and multicultural classrooms and schools in Philadelphia's Puerto Rican community and elsewhere, and taking my continua model of biliteracy as heuristic, I propose three dimensions of diversity related to what I have called the media of biliteracy, which deserve educators' attention in the interests of promoting student voice. Specifically, I take up the coexistence of multiple standard and nonstandard language varieties in bilingual classroom contexts, the varying mixes of language expertise and allegiance among bilingual students, and bilingual discourse (code-switching) practices in and out of classrooms. I argue that inclusion of student voice via these medium-related dimensions allows for the organization of curriculum, pedagogy, and social relations in ways that promote students' identity and knowledge construction.

In sociolinguistically and socioculturally informed educational research, Ruiz's (1984) notion of a language-as-resource orientation, as a promising ideological alternative to more prevalent language-as-problem and language-as-right orientations, is by now well diffused and indeed taken for granted. Originally formulated with respect to language planning, the language-as-resource orientation is one under which individuals, institutions, and societies plan and implement language policies that accept, value, and seek to develop diverse language and literacy practices as resources for all. Such inclusive language ideologies and policies are highly appealing to educators (myself included) who seek to improve educational chances for historically marginalized and oppressed social groups. Yet, the inclusion of diverse, and, in particular, discriminated languages in meaningful ways is by no means unproblematic. Recently, Ruiz (1997) has warned against "language planning in which the 'inclusion' of the language of a group [might] coincide with the exclusion of their voice" (p. 320).

Similarly well accepted among sociolinguistically and socioculturally informed educators is Gee's (1996) notion of Discourses as "socially accepted association[s] among ways of using language, other symbolic expressions, and 'artifacts,' of thinking, feeling, believing, valuing, and acting that can be used to identify oneself as a member of a socially meaningful group or 'social network' " (p. 131), and of literacies as masteries of those Discourses. In this view, literacies are understood first and foremost as social practices, through which one participates in "ways of being in the world" (Gee, 1996, p. 127). Elsewhere, Gee (1993) has suggested that because education is "always and everywhere the initiation of students as apprentices into ... social practices" (p. 291), it should be a matter of moral concern that some children's literacy practices are advantaged whereas others' are disadvantaged in schools. He proposes two conceptual principles that he believes would be acceptable to any human being and that might serve as the basis of ethical human discourse, namely: (1) "that something would harm someone else ... is always a good reason ... not to do it;" and (2) "one always has the ethical obligation to try to explicate ... any social practice that there is reason to believe advantages oneself or one's group over other people or other groups" (Gee, 1993, pp. 292–293).

Taking these premises, definitions, caveats, and principles as givens, this chapter argues that making space in classroom literacy practices for dissimilar and divergent language varieties and orthographies and for bi(multi)lingual learners' simultaneous, criss-crossed biliteracy acquisition—that is, for what I have called the media of biliteracy—promotes inclusion of students' voices and, concomitantly, their active participation in their own identity and knowledge construction. My goal is to pose the question, not so much "How to develop bi(multi)literacy?" but rather "Which bi(multi)literacies to develop for what purposes?" (see also Hornberger, 1994, p. 76).

Reflecting on my own and others' long-term ethnographic study in bi(multi)lingual and multicultural classrooms and schools, and taking my continua model of biliteracy as heuristic, I propose a series of language and literacy medium-related dimensions of diversity present in classrooms that deserve educators' attention in the interests of promoting student voice. These are the coexistence of multiple standard and nonstandard language varieties, the varying mixes of language expertise and allegiance among bilingual students, and bilingual discourse (code-switching) practices.

Martin-Jones (1995, p. 103) has recently reminded us that Fishman early on challenged researchers in bilingual classrooms to take account of the social dimensions of the teaching and learning process, namely curriculum organization, pedagogy, and social relations (Fishman, 1977). I argue here that inclusion of student voice via the medium-related dimensions previously mentioned allows for the organization of curriculum, pedagogy, and social relations in ways that promote students' identity and knowledge construction.

THE MEDIA OF BILITERACY
WITHIN THE CONTINUA MODEL

The continua model of biliteracy offers a heuristic not only for research, but also for educational policy and practice in multilingual settings (Hornberger, 1989, 2003; Hornberger & Skilton-Sylvester, 2000). In the model, biliteracy refers to "any and all instances in which communication occurs in two (or more) languages in or around writing" (Hornberger, 1990, p. 213), where an instance might be, for example, an individual biliterate actor, interaction, practice, program, situation, or society. The notion of continuum is intended to problematize the many dichotomies that seem to crop up so easily in work on language and literacy, and to convey that although one can identify and name endpoints and other points on the continuum, "those points are not finite, static, or discrete. There are infinitely many points on the continuum; [and] any single point is inevitably and inextricably related to all other points" (Hornberger, 1989, pp. 274–275). In other words, what is in between the endpoints is as important as, or more important than, the endpoints themselves. Arguing from the model, and citing examples of Cambodian and Puerto Rican students in Philadelphia's public schools as illustrative of the challenge facing American educators, I have suggested that the more their learning contexts allow learners to draw on all points of the continua, the greater are the chances for their full biliterate development (Hornberger, 1989, p. 289).

As a heuristic, the continua model provides a comprehensive account of the dimensions of any particular instance of biliteracy, while allowing a focus on one or selected continua for pedagogical, analytical, activist, or policy purposes. The model as a whole comprises 12 continua, grouped into four sets of three, representing the development, contexts, content, and media of biliteracy. The 12 continua are conceptualized as both nested and interlocking, to demonstrate the multiple and complex interrelationships among them (Figs. 7.1 and 7.2). Specifically, the model depicts the development of biliteracy along intersecting first language–second language, receptive–productive, and oral–written language skills continua; in contexts that encompass micro to macro levels and are characterized by varying mixes along the monolingual–bilingual and oral–literate continua; with content that ranges from majority to minority perspectives and experiences, literary to vernacular styles and genres, and decontextualized to contextualized language texts; and importantly

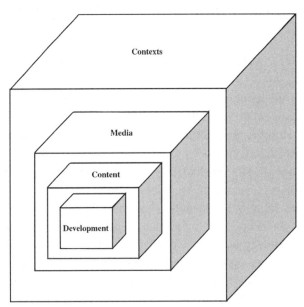

FIG. 7.1.   Nested relationships among the continua of biliteracy. From "Revisiting the Continua of Biliteracy: International and Critical Perspectives," by N. H. Hornberger and E. Skilton-Sylvester, 2000, *Language and Education: An International Journal, 14,* p. 97. Copyright 2000 by Multilingual Matters Publishers. Reprinted with permission.

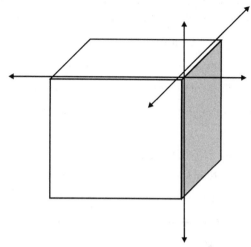

FIG. 7.2.   Intersecting relationships among the continua of biliteracy. From "Revisiting the Continua of Biliteracy: International and Critical Perspectives," by N. H. Hornberger and E. Skilton-Sylvester, 2000, *Language and Education: An International Journal, 14,* p. 97. Copyright 2000 by Multilingual Matters Publishers. Reprinted with permission.

for our purposes here, through the media of two (or more) languages and literacies whose linguistic structures vary from similar to dissimilar, whose scripts range from convergent to divergent, and in patterns of acquisition and exposure ranging from simultaneous to successive (Hornberger, 1989; Hornberger & Skilton-Sylvester, 2000).

Skilton-Sylvester and I have argued from the continua model that in educational policy and practice regarding biliteracy, there tends to be an implicit privileging such that one end of each continuum is associated with more power than the other (e.g., with respect to media of biliteracy, the privileging of standard over nonstandard orthographies), and we argue for a contestation and transformation of that privileging (Fig. 7.3). This is not to suggest that particular biliterate actors and practices at the traditionally powerful ends of the continua are immutably fixed points of power to be accessed or resisted, but rather that although those actors and practices may currently be privileged, they need not be. Indeed, the very nature and definition of what is powerful biliteracy is open to transformation through what actors—educators, learners, researchers, community members, and policymakers—do in their everyday practices (Hornberger & Skilton-Sylvester, 2000, p. 99).

My focus in this chapter is on the media of biliteracy. The term *media* is used here, not in its popular sense of mass media, but rather as the plural of *me-*

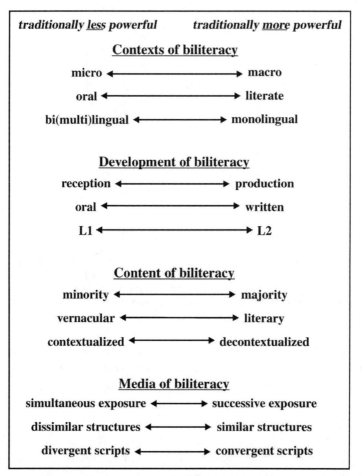

FIG. 7.3.   Power relations in the continua of biliteracy. From "Revisiting the Continua of Biliteracy: International and Critical Perspectives," by N. H. Hornberger & E. Skilton-Sylvester, 2000, *Language and Education: An International Journal, 14*, p. 99. Copyright 2000 by Multilingual Matters Publishers. Reprinted with permission.

dium, referring to the means, or vehicles, through which biliteracy develops. My usage corresponds to such notions as "medium of expression" or "medium of instruction;" it is akin to what Hymes (1997) designated "instrumentalities" in his SPEAKING heuristic and, like instrumentalities, encompasses the whole range of codes and channels through which humans communicate. That is, media of biliteracy include both verbal and nonverbal codes—languages, dialects, styles, registers, as well as paralinguistic and prosodic features; and vocal and nonvocal channels—spoken and written language, telegraphic, kinesic, and proxemic signals, as well as gesture, gaze, and silence (see also Saville-Troike, 1989, p. 145). Media of biliteracy may also extend to news media, media of communication, or electronic media, as means of communication through which bi(multi)lingual language and literacy are expressed; the primary focus is, however, the combinations of language structures and orthographic scripts that make up biliterate expression.

THE MEDIA OF BILITERACY AND STUDENT VOICE IN BI(MULTI)LINGUAL AND MULTICULTURAL CLASSROOMS

In the sections that follow I propose three medium-related dimensions of diversity in classrooms that deserve educators' attention in the interests of promoting student voice. My reflections are prompted primarily by my own and others' long-term ethnographic studies in bi(multi)lingual and multicultural educational settings in Philadelphia's Puerto Rican community; in particular, in two North Philadelphia schools that seek to provide enrichment, two-way bilingual education to their students. The Potter Thomas School in Philadelphia has been a two-way bilingual school since 1968, when Eleanor Sandstrom[1] and the School District of Philadelphia first established it under a Title VII grant (Cahnmann, 1998). Throughout that period, this K–5 school has sought to provide an enrichment, or developmental, bilingual education for its students, such that all students graduate bilingual and biliterate in Spanish and English (Hornberger, 1991). Throughout that period, too, the school has struggled to adapt its program structure to meet the diverse and constantly fluctuating academic and linguistic needs of its student population, which has gradually become more African American and Latino over time, due to changing neighborhood demographics and economics. The Julia de Burgos Bilingual Middle School, in the same neighborhood, also has sought to provide exemplary two-way bilingual education to a segment of its population since its founding in the early 1990s (see Hornberger & Micheau, 1993, on an effort beginning in 1992; and Freeman, 2000, on the sequel, beginning in 1995). In what follows, I also make occasional reference to ethnographic work in other bi(multi)lingual and multicultural settings.

---

[1]Dr. Eleanor Sandstrom, Director of the Office of Foreign Languages of the School District of Philadelphia, "authored what would become a million dollar Title VII grant that would support the first six years of bilingual education planning and implementation in Philadelphia, of which the Potter Thomas model program was a key piece" (Cahnmann, 1998, p. 70).

Coexistence of Multiple Standard and Nonstandard Language Varieties

Two of the continua of the media of biliteracy relate, respectively, to similarities or dissimilarities across the structures of the language varieties involved, and to convergence or divergence across their writing systems (Fig. 7.3). Researchers in bilingualism and literacy have asked whether greater convergence of scripts or similarity of structure across a biliterate's two languages might facilitate learning (see also Hornberger, 1989, pp. 287–288). Skilton-Sylvester and I have argued that similarity and convergence have been privileged in educational settings and that what is needed is more space for dissimilarity (difference) and divergence, not only in terms of different languages, but also different dialects of the same language, or even different forms and meanings across discourse communities speaking "the same" language (Hornberger & Skilton-Sylvester, 2000, pp. 116–117). The relevance of this for our purposes here is that the increasing linguistic and cultural diversity of many classrooms in Philadelphia, the United States, and elsewhere juxtaposes multiple standard and nonstandard varieties of languages, and the privileging of one or another has consequences for learners whose own varieties may be closer or farther from the privileged variety.

To pose a few (partially hypothetical) examples relevant to the Philadelphia Puerto Rican case, a school with a two-way program decides, after many years of English-language standardized testing, to inaugurate Spanish-language standardized testing as well, in an effort to obtain a more representative picture of their students' biliterate accomplishments. The only trouble is that the only standardized testing materials available reflect Mexican, not Puerto Rican language varieties and identities, and thus hardly promise to render a truer picture of the Puerto Rican students' expertise. Similarly, another school elects to develop portfolio assessment in Spanish and calls in an English-language expert on the subject, who is in turn stymied by the discovery that the teachers in the school, who speak varieties of Puerto Rican, Cuban, and other Latin American Spanishes, cannot agree on the "correct" form of Spanish to use.

Although the existence and relative statuses of standard and nonstandard varieties of English have received a lot of attention in U.S. public and educational discourse for some time (e.g., Baratz & Shuy, 1969; Burling, 1973; Lippi-Green, 1997; Mufwene, Bailey, Rickford, & Baugh, 1999; Smitherman, 1998; Wolfram, 1991), the existence of multiple varieties of

Spanish and accompanying attitudes and prejudices has received considerably less public or educational attention, although it is increasingly documented in research. Zentella's (1997) ethnographic study of bilingualism in New York City's *el bloque* documents the multiple varieties of Spanish and English spoken there: Popular Puerto Rican Spanish, Standard Puerto Rican Spanish, English-dominant Spanish, Puerto Rican English, African-American Vernacular English, Hispanicized English, and Standard NYC English (p. 41). Based on research in another Puerto Rican community, Urciuoli (1996) explores the social meanings of such cultural constructions as "good English" and "mixed" or "broken" language, as they reflect deep-seated language and racial prejudices.

Among the first to draw attention to the need for educators to pay attention to the existence of multiple varieties of Spanish were Keller and Valdés. In a 1983 article, Keller posed the question: Which variety of Spanish to use in the classroom? He pointed out that the answer has often been made in the form of one of two extremes—either the local vernacular or world standard Spanish—although sociolinguists chart a middle course that fosters bidialectalism. He argued that the debate was being worked out in classrooms and programs across the country, but that resolution of this corpus planning issue would be extremely difficult to achieve without the conferral of power and authority on a group of corpus planners (Keller, 1983, pp. 257–264).

Valdés (1983) also made an early plea for language planning on this issue. Her article, entitled "Planning for Biliteracy," called for *linguistas comprometidos*—"committed linguists"—to be involved, among other things, in teaching Spanish as a subject in high school and college to Hispanic bilinguals, with a "focus on the written language and not on eradicating the students' home dialect" (p. 259). In her 1981 coedited book, she reported on a series of studies on Spanish language classes designed for Hispanic students in which the disturbing picture that emerged was one of language classes "designed to show speakers of that language that theirs is not really that language—perhaps is not really *any* language" (Ruiz, 1997, p. 320, commenting on Valdés, 1981). Ruiz cites this as an example in which inclusion of a group's language coincides with exclusion of their voice.

For those voices to be included requires attention to divergence and dissimilarity across varieties of the language, and not an unreflexive legitimizing of only the standard variety. Further, such inclusion must encompass not only different languages, but also different dialects and discourses. Recent examples from Creole and Aboriginal contexts illustrate how this might be so.

Lankshear (1997) cites the case of West Indian Creole-speaking students at the University of the Virgin Islands, as described by Anderson and Irvine (1993): "These students channeled their anger at being assigned to a non-credit remedial English class into a critical investigation of language and dialects" that ultimately had an impact on their language practices in and out of class. They began to write "consciously in a variety of genres: using standard English for research papers, letters to editors, etc.; Creole for fictional stories addressed to other West Indians on themes of shared interest; and Creole for letters of thanks to guest speakers from the community, etc." (Lankshear, 1997, pp. 36–38). What is interesting about this example is that it is not just about the use of different dialects, but also of the orders of discourse and ways of being that those dialects entail; hence, the idea of not just bidialectal, but also multidiscoursal, education.

A teacher development project taking a two-way bidialectal and multidiscoursal approach to the education of Aboriginal students in Western Australia provides another example (Malcolm, 1997). This project involves a "team of Aboriginal and non-Aboriginal linguists and educators at the University ... working with Aboriginal education workers from schools across the state and the teacher-partners they have nominated" (Malcolm, 1997, p. 6). One bicultural team is carrying out research on the varieties of Aboriginal English spoken (and in particular the cultural imagery, or discourses, it represents); another makes use of material from the accumulating semantic and pragmatic database, as they prepare curriculum that both meets the state curricular requirements and reflects the underlying discourses (dialects, genres, styles, and voices) of Aboriginal English. The material is then trialed by the teams in the schools. The project operates under the basic premise that most Aboriginal people today are functioning in complex bicultural contexts, employing different varieties of English that represent different and sometimes competing discourses, identities, and cultural schemas for behaving and interpreting behavior, and that it is the job of education to recognize and allow learners to build on those resources.

These two examples illustrate how curriculum, pedagogy, and social relations can be redirected toward inclusion of more divergent and dissimilar languages and literacies in classrooms, thereby enabling students' active participation in identity and knowledge construction. We turn now to the third of the three continua of the media of biliteracy, where the privileging has been on the side of successive exposure to and acquisition of the languages and literacies involved, although in reality this is far from many learners' experience. Two medium-related dimensions of diversity fall under this third continuum: the mixes of language expertise and allegiance among bilingual students and classroom bilingual discourse (code-switching) practices.

Varying Mixes of Language Expertise and Allegiance Among Bilingual Students

As a result of circular migration patterns between the island and the mainland (Zentella, 1988, 1990), Puerto Rican students arrive (and rearrive) at schools at all times of the school year and with widely different constellations of Spanish and English language and literacy skills. This poses a complex challenge to schools, even to those schools that seek to develop a two-way bilingual program that builds on both languages for all students.

When Julia de Burgos Middle School sought to implement a targeted two-way program for an initial cohort of 60 gifted students assigned to Spanish-dominant and English-dominant sections, a problem arose:

in that the Spanish language proficiencies of the English-dominant section encompass a great range, from [non-Puerto Rican] African-American students who have never had any Spanish instruction at all to Latino students who are fluently bilingual and in some cases biliterate in Spanish and English. The English language proficiencies of the Spanish-dominant section likewise span a range from the recent arrivals from Puerto Rico who are beginners in English to fluently bilingual and, in some cases, biliterate students. (Hornberger & Micheau, 1993, pp. 44–45)

Potter Thomas Elementary School has encountered similar diversity of language proficiencies throughout its 30-year bilingual program. At one time, educators there sought to address this diversity through a complex stream and cycle structure, where students regularly cycled through heterogeneously grouped homeroom classes in the Anglo and Latino streams where bilingual language use was the norm, and homogeneously grouped reading classes where language separation was expected, and back again. Interestingly, assignment to Anglo and Latino streams was not a clear-cut process:

When students first arrive at Potter Thomas, they are assigned to the Anglo or Latino stream according to their home language, that is, the dominant language in the home, as reported by the parents. Parental preference also plays a role in children's placement; parents may choose, for linguistic or cultural reasons, to place their child in the Anglo stream, even if the child is Spanish-dominant; or vice versa. Thus Anglo and Latino are neither clear cultural nor monolingual language categories, but reflect two clusters along a continuum of language use, as well as a range of attitudes toward Spanish language maintenance and assimilation to U.S. culture. (Hornberger, 1991, p. 230)

The fact is that assignment of students to so-called English-dominant and Spanish-dominant streams for two-way bilingual education just does not work in Philadelphia's Puerto Rican community, given the myriad constellations of language use, ability, and exposure present in a community where ongoing circular migration is a fact of life for nearly everyone to one degree or another. Most Puerto Rican children do not grow up with just one (dominant or only) mother tongue and then acquire the second language in school, but rather they are constantly crossing back and forth between both languages and the meanings and identities they convey. Rampton (1995) has suggested that *mother tongue* and *native speaker* are in any case problematic terms in many multilingual settings worldwide; he proposes instead that we think in terms of expertise, affiliation, and inheritance when characterizing individuals' language proficiencies and allegiances. In his terms, expertise has to do with a speaker's skill, proficiency, and ability to operate with a language; and affiliation and inheritance are two different, socially negotiated routes to a sense of allegiance to a language; that is, identification with the values, meanings, and identities the language stands for (Rampton, 1995, pp. 336–344).

My study of one fourth- and fifth-grade homeroom teacher at Potter Thomas School showed how she found ways to build on the mix of biliterate affiliations, inheritances, and expertise that her students brought with them to school, making a strength rather than a weakness out of students' crisscrossed, simultaneous (rather than successive) acquisition of two languages and literacies, through such practices as allowing "small-group peer interaction to occur spontaneously and a-systematically as a natural outgrowth of shared cultural values, emphasiz[ing] her students' community-based prior knowledge, and seek[ing] to help her students to "connect and transfer" strategies across languages" (Hornberger, 1990, p. 227). In other words, she structured social relations, curriculum, and pedagogy in the classroom in ways that promoted student voice and, concomitantly, their active participation in identity and knowledge construction.

Bilingual Discourse (Code-Switching) Practices

Bilingual code-switching has long been recognized as a community discourse practice in U.S. Latino communities and in multilingual communities around the world. There is also increasing recognition of its ubiquity in educational settings (e.g., Martin-Jones & Heller, 1996). At the same time, there is a continuing and deep-seated ideology that a bilingual learner's two languages should be kept separate to avoid confusion (of languages and of mind). A number of researchers have argued that, given that code-switching is a natural communicative practice in Chicano and Puerto Rican communities of the United States, it only makes sense to incorporate it in classroom settings as well (Jacobson, 1979; Jacobson & Faltis, 1990; Zentella, 1981); yet the belief that this is somehow damaging to students' cognitive development is a persistent one (see Irujo, 1998, pp. 94–100 for a very clear summary of the debate over separate or concurrent language use in bilingual classrooms). Recently, researchers have begun to look closely at the ways curriculum, pedagogy, and social relations are structured through bilingual classroom discourse (Heller & Martin-Jones, 2001; Martin-Jones, 1995; Martin-Jones & Heller, 1996), yielding significant insights into the advantages of bilingual classroom discourse practices for students' active participation in identity and knowledge construction.

Two examples from U.S. Latino bilingual classrooms illustrate the productive and effective use of code-switching in structuring curriculum, pedagogy, and social relations in ways that promote student voice. During the 1997–1998 school year at Julia de Burgos Bilingual Middle School, students worked with Ms. Muñoz, the director of the TV/Communications Lab at the school, in producing a *telenovela* (Spanish soap opera), which they titled *Amor Imposible* (Impossible Love) and which eventually achieved such popularity that it was broadcast in every classroom at the beginning of every day and (incidentally and noticeably) began to serve as motivation for students to arrive at school on time. Freeman (2004) shows how Muñoz's ideological stance is reflected in her bilingual classroom discourse practices in this *telenovela* project. Muñoz pursues the project as a way of refuting language prejudice in the school, explicitly seeking to link bilingualism with technology to "challenge the local assumption that students in the bilingual program were monolingual Spanish-speaking 'hicks' … [and] instead … to position students as bilingual and technologically sophisticated individuals who could work through two languages in the high-tech, high-profile field of TV/Communications" (Freeman, 2004, p. 205). Muñoz's ideology is reflected in the use of code-switching in her

classes. Freeman's close microethnographic analysis of an interaction between one working group and their teacher as the students write and story-
board upcoming scenes for the *telenovela* shows

> how the students worked with Muñoz to negotiate their understanding of their
> participant roles relative to each other ... [and] how the group's switch from
> English to Spanish functioned to position [a "Spanish-dominant"] student as a
> legitimate participant and Spanish as a legitimate language in this classroom.
> (Freeman, 2004, p. 207)

In a second- and third-grade two-way Spanish immersion classroom in Los
Angeles, Gutiérrez, Baquedano-López, and Tejeda (1999) show how the
teacher's and students' acceptance encouragement of "hybrid language practices" (including multiple languages and registers, unauthorized side-talk,
movement, spontaneous interaction, and collaboration) promote children's
learning. Using Lave's activity theory (in Engeström, 1999), and Vygotsky's
(1978) zones of proximal development as frames for closely analyzing one
6-week learning event, the authors identify "third spaces in which alternative
and competing discourses and positionings transform conflict and difference
into rich zones of collaboration and learning" (Gutiérrez et al., 1999; pp.
286–287). Similarly to Freeman's study, the authors highlight ways in which
these hybrid language practices allow for reorganizing the activity and
incorporating local knowledge.

CONCLUSION

Following Fishman (1977) and Martin-Jones (1995), I have argued that making space in classroom literacy practices for dissimilar and divergent language
varieties and orthographies and for bi(multi)lingual learners' simultaneous,
criss-crossed language and literacy acquisition (i.e., for an inclusive view of
the media of biliteracy) allows for the organization of curriculum, pedagogy,
and social relations in ways that promote inclusion of students' voices and,
concomitantly, their active participation in their own identity and knowledge
construction. Examples from bi/(multi)lingual and multicultural classrooms
in Philadelphia's Puerto Rican community and elsewhere offer some evidence
that inclusion of students' diverse language practices, as defined along the
whole of the media of biliteracy, moves bi(multi)lingual education beyond
simply using students' languages to promoting student voice (see also Ruiz,
1997). If we take seriously Gee's (1993) admonitions about avoiding harm to

others and explicating social practices that advantage one group over another, it seems particularly important for educators to be alert to the full range of the media of biliteracy in our discourse practices as we seek to include and promote student voice in bi(multi)lingual and multicultural classrooms.

Nancy H. Hornberger is Professor of Education and Director of Educational Linguistics at the University of Pennsylvania Graduate School of Education, where she also convenes the annual Ethnography in Education Research Forum. She specializes in sociolinguistics, language planning, bilingualism, biliteracy, and educational policy and practice for Indigenous and immigrant language minorities in the United States, Latin America, and internationally. Her recent books include *Continua of Biliteracy: An Ecological Framework for Educational Policy, Research, and Practice in Multilingual Settings* (Multilingual Matters, 2003), *Indigenous Literacies in the Americas: Language Planning From the Bottom up* (Mouton, 1996), *Sociolinguistics and Language Teaching* (Cambridge, 1996, with S. McKay), and *Research Methods in Language and Education* (Kluwer, 1997, coedited with D. Corson). She serves on numerous editorial boards and coedits, with Colin Baker, a book series titled *Bilingualism and Bilingual Education* for Multilingual Matters.

REFERENCES

Anderson, G., & Irvine, P. (1993). Informing critical literacy with ethnography. In C. Lankshear & P. McLaren (Eds.), *Critical literacy: Politics, praxis and the postmodern* (pp. 81–104). Albany: State University of New York Press.

Baratz, J., & Shuy, R. (1969). *Teaching Black children to read*. Washington, DC: Center for Applied Linguistics.

Burling, R. (1973). *English in black and white*. New York: Holt, Rinehart & Winston.

Cahnmann, M. (1998). Over 30 years of language-in-education policy and planning: Potter Thomas Bilingual School in Philadelphia. *Bilingual Research Journal, 22,* 65–81.

Engeström, Y. (1999). Activity theory and individual and social transformation. In Y. Engeström, R. Miettinen, & R. Punamaki (Eds.), *Perspectives on activity theory* (pp. 19–38). Cambridge, UK: Cambridge University Press.

Fishman, J. A. (1977). The social science perspective. *Bilingual education: Current perspectives* (pp. 1–49). Washington, DC: Center for Applied Linguistics.

Freeman, R. D. (2000). Contextual challenges to dual-language education: A case study of a developing middle school program. *Anthropology & Education Quarterly, 31,* 202–229.

Freeman, R. D. (2004). *Building on community bilingualism*. Philadelphia: Caslon.

Gee, J. (1993). Postmodernism and literacies. In C. Lankshear & P. L. McLaren (Eds.), *Critical literacy: Politics, praxis, and the postmodern* (pp. 271–295). Albany: State University of New York Press.

Gee, J. P. (1996). *Social linguistics and literacies: Ideology in discourses*. London: Falmer.

Gutiérrez, K. D., Baquedano-López, P., & Tejeda, C. (1999). Rethinking diversity: Hybridity and hybrid language practices in the third space. *Mind, Culture, and Activity: An International Journal, 6*, 286–303.

Heller, M., & Martin-Jones, M. (Eds.). (2001). *Voices of authority: Education and linguistic difference*. Norwood, NJ: Ablex.

Hornberger, N. H. (1989). Continua of biliteracy. *Review of Educational Research, 59*, 271–296.

Hornberger, N. H. (1990). Creating successful learning contexts for bilingual literacy. *Teachers College Record, 92*, 212–229.

Hornberger, N. H. (1991). Extending enrichment bilingual education: Revisiting typologies and redirecting policy. In O. Garcia (Ed.), *Bilingual education: Focusschrift in honor of Joshua A. Fishman on the occasion of his 65th birthday* (pp. 215–234). Philadelphia: John Benjamins.

Hornberger, N. H. (1994). Literacy and language planning. *Language and Education, 8*, 75–86.

Hornberger, N. H. (Ed.). (2003). *Continua of biliteracy: An ecological framework for educational policy research and practice in multilingual settings*. Clevedon, UK: Multilingual Matters.

Hornberger, N. H., & Micheau, C. (1993). "Getting far enough to like it": Biliteracy in the middle school. *Peabody Journal of Education, 69*, 30–53.

Hornberger, N. H., & Skilton-Sylvester, E. (2000). Revisiting the continua of biliteracy: International and critical perspectives. *Language and Education: An International Journal, 14*, 96–122.

Hymes, D. (1974). *Foundations in sociolinguistics: An ethnographic approach*. Philadelphia: University of Pennsylvania Press.

Irujo, S. (1998). *Teaching bilingual children: Beliefs and behaviors*. Pacific Grove, CA: Heinle & Heinle.

Jacobson, R. (1979). Can bilingual teaching techniques reflect bilingual community behaviors? In R. V. Padilla (Ed.), *Bilingual education and public policy in the United States* (pp. 483–497). Ypsilanti: Eastern Michigan University, Department of Foreign Languages and Bilingual Studies.

Jacobson, R., & Faltis, C. (Eds.). (1990). *Language distribution issues in bilingual schooling*. Clevedon, UK: Multilingual Matters.

Keller, G. D. (1983). What can language planners learn from the Hispanic experience with corpus planning in the United States? In J. Cobarrubias & J. A. Fishman (Eds.), *Progress in language planning: International perspectives* (pp. 253–265). Berlin: Mouton.

Lankshear, C. (1997). *Changing literacies*. Philadelphia: Open University Press.

Lippi-Green, R. (1997). *English with an accent: Language, ideology, and discrimination in the United States*. New York: Routledge.

Malcolm, I. (1997). *Two-way bidialectal education*. Unpublished manuscript.

Martin-Jones, M. (1995). Code-switching in the classroom: Two decades of research. In L. Milroy & P. Muysken (Eds.), *One speaker, two languages: Cross-disciplinary perspectives on code-switching* (pp. 90–111). Cambridge, UK: Cambridge University Press.

Martin-Jones, M., & Heller, M. (1996). Education in multilingual settings: Discourse, identities, and power. *Linguistics and Education, 8*(1, 2).

Mufwene, S. S., Bailey, G., Rickford, J., & Baugh, J. (Eds.). (1999). *African-American English: Structure, history and use*. London: Routledge.

Rampton, B. (1995). *Crossing: Language and ethnicity among adolescents*. London: Longman.

Ruiz, R. (1984). Orientations in language planning. *NABE Journal, 8*, 15–34.

Ruiz, R. (1997). The empowerment of language-minority students. In A. Darder, R. Torres, & H. Gutierrez (Eds.), *Latinos and education: A critical reader* (pp. 319–328). New York: Routledge.

Saville-Troike, M. (1989). *The ethnography of communication: An introduction* (2nd ed.). New York: Basil Blackwell.

Smitherman, G. (1998). *Talkin' that talk: Language, culture and education in African America.* London: Routledge.

Urciuoli, B. (1996). *Exposing prejudice: Puerto Rican experiences of language, race, and class.* Boulder, CO: Westview.

Valdés, G. (1981). Pedagogical implications of teaching Spanish to the Spanish-speaking in the United States. In G. Valdés, A. G. Lozano, & R. Garcia-Moya (Eds.), *Teaching Spanish to the Hispanic bilingual: Issues, aims, and methods* (pp. 3–29). New York: Teachers College Press.

Valdés, G. (1983). Planning for biliteracy. In L. Elías-Olivares (Ed.), *Spanish in the U.S. setting: Beyond the Southwest* (pp. 259–262). Washington, DC: National Clearinghouse for Bilingual Education.

Vygotsky, L. S. (1978). *Mind in society: The development of higher psychological processes* (M. Cole, V. John-Steiner, S. Scribner, & E. Souberman, Eds.). Cambridge, MA: Harvard University Press.

Wolfram, W. (1991). *Dialects and American English.* Englewood Cliffs, NJ: Prentice Hall.

Zentella, A. C. (1981). Tá bien, you could answer me en cualquier idioma: Puerto Rican codeswitching in bilingual classrooms. In R. Durán (Ed.), *Latino language and communicative behavior* (pp. 109–131). Norwood, NJ: Ablex.

Zentella, A. C. (1988). The language situation of Puerto Ricans. In S. L. McKay & S. L. C. Wong (Eds.), *Language diversity: Problem or resource?* (pp. 140–165). Cambridge, MA: Newbury House.

Zentella, A. C. (1990). Returned migration, language and identity: Puerto Rican bilinguals in dos worlds (two mundos). *International Journal of the Sociology of Language, 84,* 81–100.

Zentella, A. C. (1997). *Growing up bilingual: Puerto Rican children in New York.* Malden, MA: Blackwell.

8
Researching Mathematics Teaching in Bilingual–Bicultural Classrooms

Janine T. Remillard
University of Pennsylvania

Melisa Cahnmann
University of Georgia

Current wisdom in bilingual education calls for the teaching of language in ways that are authentically connected to content. However, few examples in the literature provide images of what it means to teach meaningful mathematics content in ways that build on diverse students' cultural and linguistic knowledge. The authors of this chapter, a mathematics educator and a bilingual educator, are engaged in research examining the challenges faced by teachers in bilingual and bicultural classrooms in urban schools. This chapter offers an analysis of fundamental issues involved in studying mathematics teaching in culturally and linguistically diverse, urban settings. We discuss and critique a framework that presents a view of teaching practices that integrates concerns about cultural contextualization and meaningful mathematics. We raise questions about research that depicts teaching as either successful or not according to idealized models of practice, arguing that teaching is best understood as existing along multiple, intersecting continua. Finally, we make recommendations for the focus and stance taken by researchers pursuing similar questions.

Educators are under increasing pressure to attend to issues of language and culture in all areas of the curriculum. Although there are many examples in the literature of how to integrate multicultural themes within social studies and literature, there are relatively few examples of what it means to teach meaningful mathematics in ways that build on diverse students' cultural and linguistic knowledge. This chapter explores fundamental issues involved in research that examines this question. The authors of this chapter, a mathematics educator and a bilingual educator, have been engaged in research on mathematics teaching in bilingual and bicultural classrooms in urban schools. Janine Remillard is a teacher educator with interests in mathematics teaching and learning; Melisa Cahnmann is a teacher educator whose research interests are in literacy and bilingual and bicultural education.

The story of this chapter began in 1997 when a group of bilingual educators from an elementary school in North Philadelphia consulted with Cahnmann about developing equitable assessment practices for their largely bilingual, Puerto Rican student population.[1] Several teachers decided to focus on mathematics during their initial exploration because they believed "numbers were numbers" and thus assessing mathematics knowledge would involve relatively few language or cultural issues (Cahnmann & Hornberger, 2000). Cahnmann then learned there were two primary reasons why this logic was flawed. First, if numbers are really language-free, how might educators explain the well-documented history of Latino and African-American students' poor performance on mathematics assessments relative to their majority counterparts (Cahnmann & Hornberger, 2000; Khisty, 1995; Silver, Smith, & Nelson, 1995)? Second, the new mathematics curriculum adopted by the school appeared more language-rich than any traditional mathematics textbooks in previous years. No longer were students to copy and complete pages of computational exercises; the new mathematics reforms emphasized communication and problems embedded in everyday contexts. Therefore, more questions needed to be asked regarding the relationship among language, culture, and mathematics education.

Cahnmann began consulting with Remillard to understand the goals of these language-rich mathematics reforms from the perspective of a mathematics educator. At that time Remillard was in the initial stage of a multiyear research project on mathematics teaching and learning in an urban elementary school in West Philadelphia. The school served mostly African-American and White students from low-income and middle-class families. She was supporting teachers' efforts to teach mathematics in ways that were accessible to all students in the school, not just higher income, White students who had traditionally been successful. Thus began our collaboration that mirrors a concern

---

[1]From 1997 to 1999, Cahnmann carried out ethnographic research at this school site. Her original research questions were largely about reading and writing practices among bilingual youth. These questions changed in response to teachers' interests in mathematics and bilingual education.

in current educational research: how to attend to language, culture, and content learning all at the same time (August & Hakuta, 1997; Chamot & O'Malley, 1996; Sleeter, 1997). Likewise, both of us were concerned about prevailing, albeit false notions, that mathematics was acultural and a universal language, and therefore those teaching mathematics were somehow absolved of responsibility for attending to cultural and linguistic differences.

As a result of our work together, we have learned that our two respective fields—mathematics education and bilingual and bicultural education—have only begun to examine what it means to teach meaningful and empowering mathematics in ways that take into account the needs and experiences of culturally and linguistically diverse students. Our current research aims to clarify what is involved in negotiating the terrain between these two fields. We believe that doing this involves moving beyond locating ourselves in one field and extending our hand to the other; rather, this work involves framing contexts where the two are integrated. Our aim in this chapter is to discuss our efforts to do this work as researchers.

We begin with a review of existing research and theory, the myths we view as crucial to dispel, and the gaps in theoretical understanding we aim to fill. We then introduce a framework we have developed to focus on the movement involved along two intersecting continua of mathematics and bilingual and bicultural concerns. Lastly, we raise questions about research and practice that idealize successful teaching or demoralize failure, without a focus on the large area of process and struggle that is more likely to occur between these two extremes (Cahnmann, 2001). We conclude by making recommendations for the focus and stance taken by researchers pursuing similar questions.

EXISTING WORK ON MATHEMATICS AND BILINGUAL AND BICULTURAL EDUCATION

Throughout our collaboration we have found a small number of researchers who, like ourselves, aim to understand the relationship between mathematics and bilingual and bicultural education. For example, Moschkovich (2000) and Khisty (1995) have uncovered some of the linguistic difficulties involved in teaching and learning mathematics in Spanish and English. Moschkovich (2000) described the confusion that can arise for bilingual students between everyday talk and the mathematics register across two different languages. For instance, a single mathematical term such as *menos* in Spanish may have multiple English terms associated with it such as *minus* in "treinta *menos* diez [thirty *minus* ten]" and *less* as in "diez *menos* que treinta [ten is *less* than thirty]" (p. 87). In addition, second language learners may be challenged by English words such as *table* and *set* that have unique everyday and mathematics meanings (e.g., "set the table" vs. "a set of objects" or "a table of data"). Khisty (1995) found bilingual teachers also struggle when teaching mathematics. Teachers fluent in two languages do not necessarily have command of the mathematics registers of both languages, and often make translation errors in one language or the other. Khisty also found that bilingual teachers, like many elementary teachers (Ball, 1988; Remillard, 1993), tend to be uncomfortable about mathematics in general, regardless of the language of instruction. Teachers' limited bilingual fluency compounded by discomfort with mathematics content exacerbates the difficulties of successful instruction with bilingual and bicultural students.

These concerns over language fluency and mathematical knowledge have been heightened by current reforms that aim to embed students' mathematical learning in everyday situations and emphasize mathematical talk. As mathematics education moves away from rote procedures and rules and toward conceptual thinking, teachers in bilingual and bicultural settings find themselves negotiating unfamiliar mathematical terrain across languages and cultures. Much of the initial reform-focused research concentrated on suburban, middle-class schools, leaving urban and rural schools with little guidance on how to bridge cultural and linguistic gaps. Only a relatively small number of research-producing efforts to improve mathematics curriculum and pedagogy have focused specifically on ethnic minority and low-income communities (e.g., the QUASAR project by Silver et al., 1995; and Project IMPACT by Campbell & White, 1997). Findings from these initial studies suggest that it is possible for urban teachers to offer challenging mathematics to their students. Nevertheless, these studies indicate that progress among teachers and students proceeds slowly and is often hampered by policies and conditions outside the control of teachers such as class size, institutional bureaucracy, and limited resources.

Furthermore, some scholars warn that uncritically embraced reforms that are carelessly implemented may have detrimental effects on students of color (Delpit, 1988) and students from low socioeconomic conditions (Lubienski, 1996, 2000). In other words, reform-initiated practices may do more harm than good if they are not implemented in culturally appropriate ways that are also true to the deep conceptual goals of mathematics instruction. Even when reform-initiated curriculum materials and professional support do make their way to urban schools they may not improve diverse students' mathematics expertise. The cultural and linguistic biases inherent in many mathematics reform materials can implicitly privilege White, middle-class experience, background knowledge, and assumptions. There is evidence that these biases actually widen rather than reduce the gap between groups (Tate, 1997).

A growing body of research looks at the role of the teacher's cultural and linguistic identity in bridging the gap between students' home experiences and academic curricula that assume White or middle-class experience. Several studies identify the advantages of shared attributes between teacher and learner. For example, Cazden (1988) found that the use of *cariño*, a nurturing communicative style, appeared to contribute to the strong and positive sense of community she found among Mexican-descent teachers and students in a Chicago elementary school. Similarly, Foster's (1989) study described the forms and functions of shared speech style between an African-American teacher and her African-American students and analyzed how such features contributed to her success in the classroom. Other studies illuminate the possible ways teachers and other school personnel can actively build solidarity and rich learning experiences with students who are culturally, linguistically, and socioeconomically different from them (Erickson & Shultz, 1982; Hornberger, 1990).

The studies described above are not specific to mathematics instruction. Rather, they illuminate ways teachers, regardless of cultural or linguistic background, might use culturally contextualized teaching practices, materials, and assessments to educate youth, in all content areas. Studies by Gutstein, Lipman, Hernandez, and de los Reyes (1997) and Gutiérrez (1999) represent the small, but growing number of studies that address such culturally contextualized practices as they pertain to teaching mathematics. Gutstein et al. (1997) present a model for culturally relevant mathematics teaching that developed out of studies of successful middle school math teachers in a Mexican-American community. Gutiérrez (1999) examines the practices of a high school mathematics department that is successful in advancing large numbers of Latino students.

Studies such as those described here offer portraits of idealized mathematics or bilingual and bicultural practice. We believe these studies provide a critical first step in imagining pedagogical possibilities appropriate for bilingual and bicultural settings. However, depictions of polished practice offer few insights into the struggles and challenges involved in developing such practices in urban schools. We see this lack of attention to the process of developing practices that integrate these two fields to be a critical gap in the literature. Our research with teachers working at the intersection of mathematics and bilingual and bicultural education suggests that success is not an either–or proposition and that a great deal of hard work and partial success lie between the ideal presented in much of the literature and the impoverished pedagogies that both fields seek to eliminate. This terrain is not well understood or studied. We believe that understanding it is critical to improving mathematics learning opportunities for all students, especially low-income students of color who have traditionally had less success in mathematics education (Tate, 1997).

The framework we discuss in this chapter represents our efforts to illuminate the work involved in integrating sound mathematics and bicultural and bilingual pedagogies in the classroom. This framework emerged from our studies of elementary teachers in two urban schools, one largely Latino and African American, the other largely African American and White. We spent 2 years conducting ethnographic fieldwork, including participant observation in 14 mathematics classrooms and formal and informal interviews with teachers and students. A central goal of our research was to examine the challenges and opportunities of teaching in low-income, ethnically diverse settings.

A FRAMEWORK FOR EXAMINING CLASSROOM PRACTICES

In our efforts to conceptualize the relationships among language, culture, and mathematical content in teaching, we draw on a framework designed to examine classroom practices with these dimensions in mind (Cahnmann & Remillard, 2002). The framework, which grew out of our analysis of mathematics teaching in urban classrooms, contains two intersecting continua (see Fig. 8.1). The horizontal axis represents mathematics, and has, at one end, mathematical learning that is built on deep, conceptual understanding and critical thinking. At the other end is mathematics that is built on procedural knowledge and memorization of discrete facts. The vertical axis represents what we call a "contextualized continuum." At one end are lessons that are authentically contextualized within a dynamic view of students' cultural and community experiences (Gutstein et al., 1997). At the other end are lessons that do not attempt to build on students' cultural and experiential knowledge or do so in superficial ways. We choose "culturally contextualized" rather than other terms used in the literature, such as culturally relevant or congruent, to emphasize the critical role that accessible contexts play in supporting students'

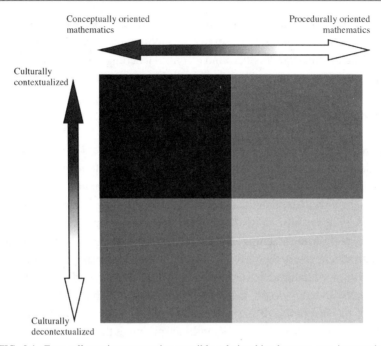

FIG. 8.1. Four-cell matrix representing possible relationships between two intersecting continua.

mathematical learning. Whereas the latter might assume that all mathematical tasks or representations draw on elements of students' home cultures, the former assumes that mathematical learning needs to be embedded in classroom contexts that are accessible to students. We believe it is possible and desirable for teachers to create meaningful contexts in the classroom through shared experiences, rather than explicitly link every math lesson to students' cultural knowledge.

It is our view that accomplishing genuine change in urban classrooms requires teachers to push their practices along each continuum, which involves integrating sound mathematics teaching with practices that are culturally contextualized. Nevertheless, doing so is remarkably difficult because neither continuum is a simple line on which teachers simply reposition themselves by employing a new strategy or textbook. Both the mathematics and the contextualized continua are complex and multifaceted. The following examples focus on the work of two teachers, one from each school, who illustrate the complexities faced by practitioners as they struggle with both continua. We chose the two teachers, Zoey Kitcher and Linda Arieto,[2] because they were typical of the kinds of partial successes we observed throughout the urban classrooms in the study. The examples revolve around a central teaching instance that is typical of the activities and interactions we observed in their classrooms.

Zoey Kitcher

Zoey Kitcher, who during our study taught third grade at Carter Elementary, provides an example of a teacher whose strength was in the area of mathematics. She wanted students to understand the conceptual underpinnings of mathematics, be able to explain their ideas and understandings, enjoy mathematics and appreciate its relevance to their lives. These commitments were evident in her conversation and teaching. As she put it: "One of the goals is for children to see math as relevant to their life. I'd like them to enjoy math, you know. I'd like them to think of math as something that's fun, that, um that's something that they can do and they do do, that they do it in lots of different ways."

Since the beginning of her teaching career, Kitcher considered herself a progressive educator and tended to embrace practices that involved students in reasoning, solving problems, and exploring conceptual ideas. Thus, the current reforms in mathematics education were a welcome fit. She used curriculum resources that focused on concepts rather than rote procedures and designed lessons that would build mathematical concepts from students' informal experience. When teaching multiplication, she used students' experiences with things that come in groups—such as a six-pack of soda—to help them understand the fundamental idea of grouping. The students brainstormed lists of grouped items, and then considered what they would get if they had more than one group. For example, if one six-pack of cola contains six cans, then three six-packs contain 18 cans or three groups of six ($3 \times 6 = 18$). She extended this focus with a homework assignment, asking students to draw a picture of something they found at home that came in groups. The next day in class she asked them to write three sentences describing their groups along with a number sentence. The example she provided was:

There are four flowers.
There are five petals on each flower.
There are 20 petals altogether.
$4 \times 5 = 20$

---

[2]We have used pseudonyms throughout this chapter.

When working with students on these activities, she focused on the relationship between addition and multiplication and number sense by encouraging students to count their total items in multiple ways—by ones, using repeated addition, and multiplication. As students shared their drawing, Kitcher used pedagogical approaches that reflected recent reform efforts (National Council of Teachers of Mathematics, 2000). She pushed them to explain their thinking and how they figured out how many in all.

Kitcher was less strong in her ability to make cultural connections with her students. As a White, middle-class teacher, she did not see cultural identity (hers or her students') as relevant to her teaching. Rather, she avoided making specific references to race and class and was disinclined to examine overlaps between race and successful school performance. For example, when asked whether she saw differences in students' involvement according to race, she said that she did. However, she was quick to point out that she attributed these differences to ability, not race. "I have a handful of White kids and they tend to be strong academically. So, you know, do they participate because they're strong or do they participate because they're White?" Because Kitcher viewed the differential participation in her class as a product of ability variation, she was not inclined to question the overlap between race and ability.

This tendency to adopt a color-blind perspective on her teaching allowed Kitcher to overlook ways that her practice may have been culturally biased. Even though she had students draw on their home experiences to find multiplicative situations for homework, she struggled to maintain this connection during the second phase of this lesson. After soliciting students' multiplication sentences, she wanted students to reframe them as a question, which she referred to as a riddle. Rather than stating, for instance, "There are five petals on each flower," she wanted them to pretend they did not know this information and ask, "How many petals are on each flower?" These questions were to be answerable, given what they know from the other two sentences (in this case, the number of flowers and the total number of petals).

Kitcher's mostly African-American students were unable to offer questions when she asked them for their riddles. Instead, they were inclined to restate the information they had. Kitcher made multiple attempts to get the students to ask a question, repeatedly asking, "If I cover this sentence up, what do I not know?" Eventually, one of the few White students in the class produced the "question" she was looking for. Trying again, Kitcher covered a different sentence and asked for a riddle. Again, one of the White students in the class was able to answer after several attempts.

It seemed that Kitcher was not aware that using the riddle in this context may have been an unfamiliar genre for her students. Moreover, her request for a question rather than an answer upset typical classroom norms. Furthermore, when trying to help students understand how to change their statements to a question, Kitcher repeatedly used her own example of petals and flowers, rather than any of the contextualized examples the students had brought from home, such as wheels on a truck, fingers on a hand, or packs of yogurt.

Linda Arieto

Linda Arieto was a third-grade teacher at Peter Towns Elementary. In contrast to Kitcher, Linda Arieto provides an example of a teacher whose strength lies in the domain of cultural contextualization. Arieto, who was Puerto Rican and grew up in a low-income community in the Bronx, shared a great deal in terms of language, culture, race, and class background with her students. She was committed to creating a bridge between her students' home experiences and the academic expectations of school. For example, Arieto used her first language, Spanish, to instruct students in difficult content matter that they might have had trouble understanding in English. She was also skillful using and responding to multiple varieties of language familiar to her students such as Puerto Rican Spanish, Puerto Rican English, Black English vernacular, and standard English. In the area of mathematics, Arieto consistently found and used lessons in the text that made links to her students' cultural backgrounds and urban experiences. She highlighted activities from the curriculum that made the strongest links to students' home experiences. For example, she frequently used number sense manipulatives such as dominoes because they corresponded to a game that is popular in Caribbean culture.

Unlike Kitcher, Arieto was not shy about issues of language, culture, race, and class. She was explicit with her students about the inequities that exist. She frequently taught students explicit lessons about how to avoid the dangerous traps of poverty. For example, she modeled the importance of patience and delayed gratification, linking these practices to skills her students needed on the streets. She hoped to offer a positive example of a Puerto Rican woman who made it out of poverty and into a professional career. As she put it:

> I see my children and I know some of them will be selling drugs on the corner. I know that. Some of them will not reach adulthood. I know that. And it makes me very sad because it's all around them. But you hope that a lot of them will make it. And I keep telling them, I was raised like this. I lived in a terrible neighbor-

hood, I had horrible parents. And I made it. You could do it too, and education is the key.

Arieto was less at ease in the mathematics domain. Where her bilingual fluency allowed her to create connections and establish trust with her students, it was less useful in mathematics teaching. She struggled with the translation of the specialized language used in mathematics and, in particular, those terms and ideas emphasized in the reforms. The school had adopted an all-English curriculum for her third-grade transition class. Arieto's own experience in mathematics was entirely in English in New York City schools. Her Spanish–English dictionary was not always helpful, especially when translating the mathematics language that is particular to the new mathematics series. For instance, she struggled to translate newly coined terms such as "frames and arrows" used by the new math series to describe relationships between operations. Arieto also found that cultural references, such as a discussion of height and velocity through kite-flying in a grassy park, did not make sense to her students. She struggled with lessons that made assumptions about knowledge that students did not have.

Arieto's own discomfort with mathematics also limited the extent to which she was able to implement the reform ideas in her practice. Several lessons we observed showed evidence of good intentions—cultural connections, high levels of student involvement, and invitations to communicate about mathematics—that were never fully realized. For example, during one lesson Arieto had students work in pairs using *topitos* (dice) to fill out a chart indicating numbers of pennies, nickels, dimes, quarters, and dollars and their corresponding values. Two nickels and a dime, for example, summed to 20 cents. Each student was to roll the die five times per turn and decide where to place each of the numbers to have the highest total at the end of the game. If a student rolled a 2 she would have to decide whether to place that 2 in the dollars, quarters, dimes, nickels, or pennies column, aiming to get a higher score than her opponents (see Table 8.1).

TABLE 8.1
Model of the "Making Change" Activity Sheet, Player 1

	P	N	D	Q	$1	Total
Turn 1	2	5	3	6	4	$ 6.07
Turn 2	1	3	3	2	6	$ 6.96
Final score						$13.03

As the students worked on the activity, many became confused about the directions. Some students wrote down the coin values (e.g., $.25, $.10, etc.) rather than the value rolled on the die. Others were adding the sum of the rolled dice numbers, rather than the value of the coins (see Table 8.2).

TABLE 8.2

Two Examples of Student Errors in "Making Change" Activity Sheet

	P	N	D	Q	$1	Total
Turn 1	2	5	3	6	4	20 (2 + 5 + 3 + 6 + 4)
Turn 2	.01	.05	.10	.25	1.00	$ 1.41

Arieto tried several times to revise the lesson to make it easier for students to understand, but this ended up making the instructions even more complicated and unclear. Eventually, she became confused and frustrated. Convinced that students were not ready for such a lesson, she announced, "I'm gonna have to drill the coins every minute!" She spent the remainder of the class time leading the students in counting together by fives.

In another lesson we observed, Arieto brought in her personal collection of Matchbox cars for students to use in a graphing lesson. As students began counting and graphing the cars, there was no indication that accuracy in counting was important. When confusion began about how to graph cars with more than one color, Arieto first stressed each student's responsibility for making these decisions. However, as students' talk about these decisions became loud and chaotic, Arieto revoked her earlier decision and told students which color to assign to particular cars. When a boy held up a burgundy car, for example, and asked, "*Es púrpura maestra?* (Is it purple, teacher?)," Arieto shook her head and told the boy to count that car as red.

THE COMPLEXITIES OF EACH CONTINUUM

These two teachers' experiences with reform-oriented mathematics in bicultural and bilingual settings illuminate the complexities of the mathematics and cultural continua. They illustrate different yet complementary challenges teachers face when trying to move their practices toward conceptual understanding and critical thinking in ways that validate students' diverse cultural and linguistic experiences. As we look across the struggles faced by these teachers, as well as those from data not described here, we see three types of challenges involved in this work. The first is related to the knowledge required of teachers to work within both domains. The second is related to how teachers use this knowledge to find or develop tasks that are both mathematically sound and culturally appropriate. The third is the ongoing challenge of upholding the intent of the task through the "in-flight" (Jackson, 1968; Ulichny, 1996) bumps that emerge while students work on it.

New and More Knowledge

As the framework suggests, it is not enough for a teacher to have strong cultural or mathematical knowledge alone. Working in these complex areas requires that teachers develop knowledge of both culture and mathematics. Moreover, this knowledge needs to be deep and substantive rather superficial. For most teachers, this degree of understanding in both areas is unfamiliar.

In the area of mathematics, pushing one's teaching along the mathematics continuum toward meaningful mathematics requires conceptual understanding and willingness to explore new mathematical ideas with one's students. Arieto's "Making Change" lesson is a reminder that reforms in mathematics education often require much more mathematical knowledge than is common among most elementary school teachers. When using conceptually based mathematical tasks, teachers frequently confront uncertainty about how to guide students. As teachers enhance their understandings of mathematics, they are more likely to use this new knowledge as a guide in making pedagogical decisions.

In the contextualized continuum, teachers need to develop knowledge about their students—how they identify themselves culturally, their language, their experiences at home and in the world. They also need to learn to analyze their own cultural identity and language use as a way of reflecting critically on their practices. The difficulties Kitcher had in reaching her mostly African-American students illustrate challenges teachers, particularly those from White, middle-class backgrounds, face along the contextualized continuum. Although the tasks she gave were designed to develop an understanding of multiplication as it occurred in students' daily lives, she had difficulty recognizing ways that the task and the example she used were inaccessible to students.

Challenging and Meaningful Tasks

The second challenge presented by the two intersecting continua involves using one's knowledge to select, develop, or adapt tasks that have mathematical integrity and are accessible and engaging to one's particular students. As both teachers illustrate, it is possible for mathematical tasks to be superficial from either a mathematical or a cultural perspective. Arieto, for example, frequently used tasks that involved dice, dominoes, or Matchbox cars because they had meaning to her and she believed her students would be enticed by them. Nevertheless, as the graphing and making-change activities described earlier suggest, the tasks were underdeveloped in terms of mathematical learning goals. Kitcher, on the other hand, was able to develop tasks that focused on meaningful mathematical ideas, but struggled with how to make them accessible to her predominantly African-American students. Students who were familiar with giving answers had difficulty changing their answers into questions or riddles. It is not surprising that the task of making riddles was suggested by the curriculum she was using, because pedagogical styles and curriculum that are most common in American schools assume that certain forms of communication are universal rather than particular to the dominant culture (Delpit, 1988).

Through our interactions with teachers, we have observed a tendency to equate cultural congruence and accessibility with "fun." In other words, tasks that are fun for students to do are assumed to be mathematically and culturally accessible. We have found that tasks that lead to high degrees of student involvement or enjoyment are not necessarily indicators that students are involved in meaningful mathematical learning. One challenge that teachers in urban settings face is to find tasks that are engaging and enjoyable to students and that make important mathematical ideas accessible.

Managing Tasks In-Flight

A final challenge illustrated by both teachers on numerous occasions involves upholding the intent of the mathematical task in the midst of one's teaching. In the process of implementing mathematical tasks, teachers find themselves making impromptu decisions in response to students' actions, questions, struggles, and confusion. Although some of these instances might be anticipated, they cannot be planned. Teachers rarely know precisely which questions will emerge and exactly how they will manifest themselves among a particular group of students. Such improvisational moments are an inherent part of teaching; however, they are more common in classrooms where teachers are trying to cross cultural and linguistic boundaries and when they are trying to engage students in mathematical thinking and problem solving.

One of the dilemmas that teachers frequently face when engaging students in exploring mathematical ideas involves balancing classroom control with students' intellectual autonomy. Although these two goals are not necessarily mutually exclusive, many teachers accustomed to controlling and directing students' learning struggle with sharing intellectual autonomy and decision making with students, even when they believe that helping students develop as mathematical thinkers involves relinquishing some degree of intellectual control. In the graphing lesson, described earlier, Arieto wanted students to think for themselves and make their own decisions about how to count the irregular cars. However, as soon as the noise rose above her level of comfort, she decided to revoke that freedom and replace it with a more controlled approach.

The emergence of student confusion also requires teachers to make on-the-spot decisions about how to respond. As both Arieto and Kitcher illustrate, student and teacher confusion is more likely when teachers are negotiating unfamiliar, complex terrain, whether it be mathematical, cultural, or both. In many cases, spontaneous mathematical interactions have the potential to lead to significant learning (Remillard, 1996, 2000; Remillard & Geist, 2002). Nevertheless, because they require action in the moment, these interactions place extraordinary demands on teachers. When these demands get beyond a teacher's grasp, he or she is likely to reign in and simplify the task, limiting its potential richness (Stein, Grover, & Henningsen, 1996). We saw Arieto reduce and simplify the task at hand when she and students became confused during the making-change and graphing lesson.

For teachers like Arieto and Kitcher, who are negotiating multilayered, unfamiliar terrain, the particular cause of the confusion may be unclear. For example, Kitcher attributed her students' difficulties coming up with a riddle to limited mathematical understanding. From the observer's perspective, the confusion appeared to grow out of a cultural mismatch. Heath (1983) argues that most critical cultural mismatches occur within the context of routine classroom interactions. Ironically, Kitcher's inclination in addressing the students' confusion was to return to the same mathematical explanation. The challenge for teachers is to develop both mathematical and cultural knowledge that they can draw on during these improvisational moments.

CONCLUSION

Our aim in examining challenges faced by teachers in urban schools is to focus analysis on the bumps and barriers teachers face when trying to integrate sound mathematics teaching in bilingual and bicultural settings. Much of the research available in this area offers either images of teachers who have successfully overcome these challenges or images of teachers who have failed. Research from either genre—studies that focus on successful practices or those that describe and critique unsuccessful and undesirable practices—have brought to light many of the subtle, and not so subtle, biases inherent in mainstream teaching practices and identified the consequences of teaching practices and curriculum that exclude non-White, non-middle-class students. Research in both these areas has provided a critical first step in articulating problems in current practices and offering possibilities and alternatives. At the same time, looking at teaching as either successful or failing oversimplifies the demands of helping all students learn meaningful mathematics and ignores the process of movement along each continuum.

Our analysis of the challenges inherent in the work of teachers bringing together both domains leads us to offer a second step in this research that highlights the struggles teachers confront as they seek to improve their teaching. We believe *portraits of struggle*, that is narrative and interpretive accounts of lived moments of practice, can move the field beyond identifying appropriate or inappropriate practices to understanding the work involved in improving practice (Cahnmann, 2001). In using the term portraits of struggle, we are referring to research that seeks to understand and explain the struggles faced by practitioners as they grapple with the complex demands of teaching meaningful mathematics in urban schools. Our aim in using the framework to examine teaching practices is to emphasize the struggle teachers engage in as they seek to improve their teaching.

We believe that the understanding of teaching offered by research that focuses on struggle is critical to improving the field of bilingual and bicultural education for two reasons. First, research that seriously examines and makes explicit the struggles that teachers face acknowledges and makes visible the real, multidimensional work of teaching. A clearer understanding of teachers' struggles can stimulate changes in the supports and resources available to teachers. This knowledge can also guide the design of professional learning opportunities specifically for teachers in bilingual and bicultural settings. Second, a focus on the struggles inherent in the work depicts teaching as a dynamic process, rather than a finished product. A view of teaching as dynamic assumes that change is possible and natural. Polished images of practice, on the other hand, contribute to mainstream views of teachers as either masters or inadequate. In light of the extraordinary pressure on teachers, we argue for conceptualizing the profession as an ongoing learning process. Thus, teachers and the researchers, administrators, and public with whom they work will be better prepared to support and encourage teachers' growth rather than condemn less-than-perfect practice. For these reasons, we urge scholars of teaching in bilingual and bicultural settings to engage in analyses that complicate notions of success and failure that have dominated the research landscape and to theorize the nature of struggle.

Janine T. Remillard is an assistant professor at the Graduate School of Education at the University of Pennsylvania. Her research interests include mathematics teaching and learning, urban education, and teacher learning. Her research on teacher learning and pedagogical change in urban schools was funded by a National Science Foundation Early Career grant. Currently, she is co-P. I. of Metro Math: The Center for Mathematics in America's cities, a Center for Learning and Teaching funded by the National Science Foundation. Her research has been published in *Curriculum Inquiry, Elementary School Journal, Urban Review, Journal of Mathematics Teacher Education, and Journal for Research in Mathematics Education.*

Melisa Cahnmann is an assistant professor in the Graduate School of Education at the University of Georgia. Her research interests include biliteracy, bilingualism, multicultural education, and enhancing qualitative inquiry through poetic and arts-based approaches. She is P. I. of the F.U.N.D. (Finding Unity in Diversity) project, funded by Teacher Quality Programs. Her work has been published in *Educational Researcher, Urban Review, The Bilingual Research Journal, Educators for Urban Minorities,* and several literary publications.

ACKNOWLEDGMENT

Research described in this chapter was funded in part by the National Science Foundation (grant no. REC-9875739). The views expressed in the paper are the authors' and are not necessarily shared by the grantors.

REFERENCES

August, D., & Hakuta, K. (1997). *Improving schooling for language-minority children: A research agenda.* Washington, DC: National Academy Press.

Ball, D. L. (1988). *Knowledge and reasoning in mathematical pedagogy: Examining what prospective teachers bring to teacher education.* Unpublished doctoral dissertation, Michigan State University, East Lansing, MI.

Cahnmann, M. (2001). *Shifting metaphors: Of war and reimagination in the bilingual classroom.* Unpublished doctoral dissertation, Language in Education Division, University of Pennsylvania, Philadelphia.

Cahnmann, M., & Hornberger, N. (2000). Understanding what counts: Issues in language, culture, and power in mathematics instruction and assessment. *Educators for Urban Minorities, 1,* 39–52.

Cahnmann, M., & Remillard, J. T. (2002). What counts and how: Mathematics teaching in culturally, linguistically, and socioeconomically diverse urban settings. *Urban Review, 34,* 179–205.

Campbell, P. F., & White, D. Y. (1997). Project IMPACT: Influencing and supporting teacher change in predominantly minority schools. In E. Fennema & B. S. Nelson (Eds.), *Mathematics teachers in transition* (pp. 309–355). Mahwah, NJ: Lawrence Erlbaum Associates.

Cazden, C. (1988). *Classroom discourse: The language of teaching and learning.* Portsmouth, NH: Heinemann.

Chamot, A. U., & O'Malley, J. M. (1996). The cognitive academic language learning approach: A model for linguistically diverse classrooms. *The Elementary School Journal, 96,* 259–273.

Delpit, L. (1988). The silenced dialogue: Power and pedagogy in educating other people's children. *Harvard Educational Review, 58,* 280–298.

Erickson, F., & Shultz, J. (1982). *The counselor as gatekeeper.* New York: Academic.

Foster, M. (1989). Talking that talk: The language of control, curriculum, and critique. *Linguistics and Education, 7,* 129–150.

Gutiérrez, R. (1999). Advancing urban, Latino youth in mathematics: Lessons from an effective high school mathematics department. *Urban Review, 31,* 263–281.

Gutstein, E., Lipman, P., Hernandez, P., & de los Reyes, R. (1997). Culturally relevant mathematics teaching in a Mexican American context. *Journal for Research in Mathematics Education, 28,* 709–737.

Heath, S. (1983). *Ways with words.* Cambridge, UK: Cambridge University Press.

Hornberger, N. H. (1990). Creating successful learning contexts for bilingual literacy. *Teachers College Record, 92,* 212–229.

Jackson, P. W. (1968). *Life in classrooms.* New York: Holt, Rinehart & Winston.

Khisty, L. L. (1995). Making inequality: Issues of language and meanings in mathematics teaching with Hispanic students. In W. G. Secada, E. Fennema, & L. B. Adajian (Eds.), *New directions for equity in mathematics education* (pp. 279–297). Cambridge, UK: Cambridge University Press.

Lubienski, S. T. (1996). *Mathematics for all? Examining issues of class in mathematics teaching and learning.* Unpublished doctoral dissertation, Department of Teacher Education, Michigan State University, East Lansing, MI.

Lubienski, S. T. (2000). Problem solving as a means toward mathematics for all: An exploratory look through a class lens. *Journal for Research in Mathematics Education, 31,* 454–482.

Moschkovich, J. (2000). Learning mathematics in two languages: Moving from obstacles to resources. In W. G. Secada (Ed.), *Changing the faces of mathematics: Perspectives on multiculturalism and gender equity* (pp. 5–12). Reston, VA: National Council of Teachers of Mathematics.

National Council of Teachers of Mathematics. (2000). *Principles and standards for school mathematics.* Reston, VA: Author.

Remillard, J. (1993, April). *Using experience to break from experience: An elementary mathematics methods course.* Paper presented at the Annual Meeting of the American Educational Research Association, Atlanta, GA.

Remillard, J. T. (1996). *Changing texts, teachers, and teaching: The role of curriculum materials in mathematics education reform.* Unpublished doctoral dissertation, Department of Teacher Education, Michigan State University, East Lansing, MI.

Remillard, J. T. (2000). Can curriculum materials support teachers' learning? *Elementary School Journal, 100,* 331–350.

Remillard, J. T., & Geist, P. (2002). Supporting teachers' professional learning through navigating openings in the curriculum. *Journal of Mathematics Teacher Education, 5,* 7–34.

Silver, E. A., Smith, M. S., & Nelson, B. S. (1995). The QUASAR project: Equity concerns meet mathematics education reform in the middle school. In W. G. Secada, E. Fennema, & L. B. Adajian (Eds.), *New directions for equity in mathematics education* (pp. 9–56). Cambridge, UK: Cambridge University Press.

Sleeter, C. E. (1997). Mathematics, multicultural education, and professional development. *Journal for Research in Mathematics Education, 28,* 680–696.

Stein, M. K., Grover, B. W., & Henningsen, M. (1996). Building student capacity for mathematical thinking and reasoning: An analysis of mathematical tasks used in reform classrooms. *American Educational Research Journal, 33,* 455–488.

Tate, W. F. (1997). Race-ethnicity, SES, gender, and language proficiency trends in mathematics achievement: An update. *Journal for Research in Mathematics Education, 28,* 652–679.

Ulichny, P. (1996). What's in a methodology? In D. Freeman & J. C. Richards (Eds.), *Teacher learning in language teaching* (pp. 178–196). New York: Cambridge University Press.

Local Power Construction in a School of Socially Marginalized Students

Antonia Candela
Centro de Investigación y Estudios Avanzados, México D.F.

This chapter presents a discourse analysis of classroom interactions, focusing on local power as a feature of discourse. The primary aim is to demonstrate that discursive resources through which the teacher exercises power in the classroom also are available to students, who appropriate and use them for defending alternative versions to those proposed by the teacher. The specialized tools of conversation analysis within an ethnographic perspective are applied to teacher–student interaction in science classes in an elementary school within a marginalized community in Mexico City. This analysis shows students managing to contradict the teacher's orientations and even evaluating peers and the teacher's assertions. Through these interventions, the children reverse the interactional roles, change the situational power asymmetry, and wield power to locally control the discursive interaction. The study shows that, even in this marginalized environment, students construct themselves as subjects who discursively establish their roles as knowledgeable and competent communicators who are able to influence classroom social interaction.

To illustrate how economic and social structures can be seen in face-to-face classroom interactions, Mehan (1998) describes several practices in which teachers display differential treatment toward students, and in which working-class children display forms of resistance toward academic tasks that lead to their academic failure. The examples and analysis in this chapter show how discourse interaction can be viewed as a situation in which social relations in Mexican classrooms are constructed—especially local power relations between teacher and students of low-income families—in a negotiation between teachers and students without resistance behavior.

Erickson (1986) postulated that only teachers have "legitimate" power in the classroom because of their institutional position and greater knowledge of the topic. However, he explains that students have the power to resist teacher-directed learning. Resistance, Erickson states, can become a form of power when it changes the interactional dynamics. In this first approach, students' power is defined as resistance to learning (Alpert, 1991; Willis, 1976). This resistance has been studied as one of the causes of children's exclusion from paths that lead to academic achievement.

Yet more work needs to be undertaken not only to examine the local manifestation of institutional, political, or economic power as a constraint on classroom talk, but also to analyze the local reconstruction of power that participants perform within discursive interactions, which can change the dominant features of institutional power. This chapter examines students' responses to the teacher's demands to interrogate teachers' power over students' discourse, and whether children's refusal to follow the teacher's orientations necessarily implies resistance to learning. My aim is to show how power relations between teachers and students are constructed through a discursive negotiation of social roles and academic content.

Power, as an interactional construction, is analyzed in terms of the way in which participants in discourse deal with it. Differentiated use of discursive resources in specific talk contexts displays and constitutes the asymmetries of power among the participants. This participant orientation feature of the analysis allows us to appreciate the influence of pupils in classroom talk.

From the conversation analysis used in this chapter, asymmetry is not given by institutional roles prior to interaction, but is one of the interactional features revealed in discourse. Recent ethnographic, dialogic, and classroom discourse studies emphasize a reflexive interpretation of discourse, whereby asymmetrical aspects of local interactions are not considered a preestablished reality, but rather features of the relationships displayed and oriented to by the participants (Drew & Heritage, 1992; Gutiérrez, Rymes, & Larson, 1995; Marková & Foppa, 1991; Schegloff, 1992).

Diamond (1996) defines two different types of power relations: institutional and local. Institutional rank is based on gender, age, nationality, race, family relations, occupation, institutional position, economics, marital status, education, and other factors that are more or less fixed. However, institutional status alone does not account for the relative power and political effectiveness of members. There is also a local rank constituted by those social variables with meaning that is internal to a particular community. This differentiation of rank has implications for power in discourse. When people bid for the floor, compete, negotiate rules, interrupt each other, or overlap, they are vying for local rank. Although institutional rank permeates and affects roles in discourse, the actual institutional rank of each member cannot be contested through discourse. Within the local community, the battle for equality and power is waged at the level of local rank. Although hierarchies are created and enforced by social norms and institutional status, microanalysis shows that individuals contest power and compete for leadership roles in every verbal interaction (Diamond, 1996, p. 11). Diamond further argues that local power is consensual because there are no permanent power assignations. Local power requires acknowledgment and ratification; hence, as Erickson (1986) anticipates, the participants who ratify local power hold power themselves. With Diamond, I share an interest in microanalysis of power as a discourse feature accessible to all participants.

By local power I mean the differentiated use of discursive resources or actions that influence the discourse of other participants. These discursive resources or actions are manifest in the control of turn-taking, adjacency pairs, or discursive patterns, and in the ability to influence knowledge construction within the interaction. Local power may indicate what the participants take to be differences in knowledge, as seen in the ability to win an argument, introduce a new topic, gain popularity, modify local relationships, change roles, or use special resources to deal with the links within discourse.

Gutiérrez et al. (1995) have analyzed power construction between teachers and students in terms of scripts and counterscripts. Scripts are normative patterns with particular social, spatial, and language structures that represent an orientation that members come to expect after repeated interactions in contexts constructed both locally and over time (Gutiérrez, 1993). If a rigid monologic teacher script dominates classroom interaction, students may not follow it, constructing their own counterscript. True communication in the classroom can only occur in a "third space" in which a Bakhtinian social heteroglossia is possible.

To study this interactional construction of power relations, I analyze conflict settings within classroom interactions. Mehan (1998) notes the importance of the study of conflict and resistance, not only of "guided participation" (Rogoff, Kistry, Göncü, & Mosier, 1993), to understand the tensions present in teaching–learning settings (see also Grimshaw, 1990). If shared knowledge is basic for communication, nonshared knowledge or conflict talk is an excellent place to look for new knowledge production. Conflict settings show how students and teachers actively participate and confront their versions, usually through an argumentative organization of discourse. These conflict settings provide important insights into students' ideas, their versions of educational topics, the discursive resources used to state and defend a position, and their subjectively constituted roles in the discursive interaction. I therefore focus on misunderstandings, disagreements, confrontations, and challenges as sites where knowledge and social relations are constructed and negotiated.

In this chapter, I analyze those discursive structures that follow the initiation–response–evaluation (IRE) sequence as an extreme case in which the teacher's power is asserted. Traditional work on classroom discourse establishes that the teacher-directed interactional sequence or IRE allows teachers to control classroom discourse, as they are the ones who ask the questions, orient students' responses, and evaluate their answers (Cazden, 1986; Leith & Myerson, 1989; Mehan, 1979; Sinclair & Coulthard, 1975; Wells, 1993). Teacher control has been frequently mentioned as an inhibitor of students' ideas (Edwards & Furlong, 1978; Edwards & Mercer, 1987). It has been suggested that this control is a mechanism that causes students to develop competence in giving the "correct" answer, rather than looking for an explanation (Holt, 1969). The IRE sequence also deadens discussion and induces student passivity (Mehan, 1998). My goal is to investigate whether the IRE structure always entails teacher control, or whether students (in this case, in an elementary science classroom) can seize local power and wield it to defend their versions of educational topics, even within this discourse format.

The analysis focuses on the discursive context in which the interaction takes place, paying attention to the control of both turn-taking and participation defined as scripts, counterscripts, and "third spaces." The setting is a school of low-income students in a marginalized district on the periphery of Mexico City, whose population has recently migrated from the countryside, in some cases from Indigenous regions. They maintain some of their traditions— for example, food preferences and certain festivities. Most of these students' families work in the informal sector of the national economy. Teachers in this school are young, with few years of teaching experience but a strong interest in improving their teaching practice. My concern is to see if within "traditional" lessons with these socially marginalized children, the teacher always maintains power, or whether pupils, even under these conditions, can manipulate the local construction of discourse to construct their own representation of curricular topics. The study of the IRE structure in classroom discursive interaction among low-income children is especially noteworthy because this discursive sequence has been characterized as a middle-class interactional pattern and thus one of the features that contributes to home–school cultural discontinuities. For this analysis, I focus on the students' perspectives, taking into account the fact that the discursive structure is constructed among all classroom participants.

METHODOLOGY

To analyze relationships of power, it is necessary to examine not only the grammatical form but the content of discourse. I analyze several transcriptions of science classes in an elementary school, focusing on how power relations are constructed and become relevant as part of the discursive interaction between teachers and students. Science classes further permit an examination of whether and how scientific language affects power relations.

The data collected include ethnographic notes, video recordings, and audio recordings of daily lessons in several fifth-grade classes at a public elementary school. At the time of the study (1993), the students were 10 to 11 years old. Most classrooms had between 35 and 40 students; approximately half were girls and half were boys. The topics under study included gravity, relative densities, and carbon dioxide production during combustion. These topics were taken from the science textbooks that are part of the official curriculum in Mexico.

I use conversation analysis tools such as preference patterns to examine how students' participation influenced the turns of classroom talk, interactional dynamics, and the construction of knowledge in science classes (Candela, 1995, 1997a, 1997b, 1998, 1999). The analysis is based on transcriptions of the audiotape recordings, with special notation (Edwards & Potter, 1992),[1] complemented by ethnographic notes and visual data from the videotape. I translated the original Spanish-language data into English, adapting the special notation to the differences in semantics. An overall ethnographic approach

---

[1]The transcript notations are as follows:

T: Teacher.
B: Boy.
G: Girl.
Ch: Several children at the same time.
↑   Marks rising shifts in intonation.
↓   Marks falling shifts in intonation.
=>   Indicates significant utterance for the analysis.
° °   Indicates a passage of talk quieter than the surrounding talk.
CAPS Indicates a passage of talk louder than the surrounding talk.
*   Indicates background noise of children murmuring or talking to each other.
**   Indicates higher background noise.   *(continued)*

provided helpful information on classroom contexts. Conversation analysis permitted a detailed study of turn sequences to describe the work at each turn in the discursive construction of everyday interactions (Pomerantz, 1984; Sacks, 1973, 1992; Sacks, Schegloff, & Jefferson, 1974).

In analyzing discourse in these classrooms, the study of the preference structure proved to be very helpful. Preference characterizes conversational events in which participants choose between several alternative and nonequivalent actions (depending on the lexical choice, design of the phrase, or sequence of action; Sacks, 1973). Pomerantz (1984), analyzing the ways second turns of talk agree or disagree with prior turns, finds normative rules that relate first and second assessments. I understand these rules to indicate that if the second assessment does not act as an immediate acceptance (no hesitation) of the previous turn, its function is that of denying it.

RESISTANCE TO LEARNING?

The following dialogue excerpt was part of a fifth-grade class sequence following a textbook lesson on combustion. Before this sequence, the group had discussed the importance of fire in the history of humankind. Later, the teacher commented on the role of friction in the production of heat. A few activities proposed in the text were carried out, including an experiment to see what fire produces, besides light and heat. The children observed a glass covering a lit candle and followed the teacher's questions, which attempted to guide them to the conclusion that water is produced during combustion. The dominant structure of this part of classroom discourse was that of IRE, following the teacher's script.

The last part of the lesson was another experiment in which the teacher asked the children to determine the difference between lime water put in a glass with recently burnt cotton, and lime water in another glass with an un-

---

[1](*continued*)

> <	Indicates a passage of talk quicker than the surrounding talk.
< >	Indicates a passage of talk slower than the surrounding talk.
(0.3)	Indicates a silent pause of more or less than 3 seconds.
(.)	Indicates a short untimed silence.
[	Indicates the beginning of overlapping talk.
::	Indicates elongated syllable.
=	Equal signs are latching symbols.
__	Underlining shows vocal stress or syllable emphasis.
((it))	Double parentheses enclose transcriber comments.
,?.	Indicates pitch level rather than sentence type.

burnt piece of cotton. The teacher not only suggested an answer by various implicit discursive mechanisms, but also directly stated that the students should see the difference between water that is more or less transparent. He was requesting confirmation of this "fact" from the students. Throughout a sequence of 73 lines, only five students responded and all denied that they could see what the teacher suggested they should see.

918 *		*((The teacher is preparing the two glasses with lime water, one*
919 *		*with a piece of burnt cotton and the other with an unburnt*
920 *		*one. Lots of pupils are joking among themselves.))*
921 *	T:	oka::y (0.2) now, let's see the difference between
922		these <u>two</u> lime waters (.) oka:y? (0.3) THIS IS SO THAT
923		you do not say that the cotton has faded (.)
924		that the cotton (.) made (.) the lime water ge::t
925		milky but that it was only a consequence of the combustion
926		(0.2) ↑on this pla::ce (0.5)
927	=> Bj:	IT CAN'T BE SEEN::::
928	Ch:	he:: he::
929	T:	on this side² (.) the lime water is almost
930		transparent (0.2) isn't it Javier?
931	=> Bj:	no[:::
932	T:	[and on this other side it looks whiter (0.2)
933		in spite of having [pieces of burnt paper (0.2)
934		and let's=
935 *	=> B:	[I cannot see it teacher
936 *		*((there are several incomprehensible comments but*
937 *		*the teacher doesn't stop talking))*
938 *	T:	=pass by your places so you can see it (0.2) can you?
939 *		let's put here (0.2) a bit more lime water (0.4)
940 *		tha::t's it (.) let's pass by here (0.2) <u>Have</u> you
941 **		seen it? (.) here it looks a little
942 **		>whiter< (.) the water that is here still
943 **		looks transparent (0.5)
944 **		*((lots of children's comments in low voices))*
945 **	T:	both of you look at it (.) have you both seen it?

---

²Each time the teacher said "on this side," he was showing one glass; later he showed the other glass, trying to demonstrate the differences visible between the lime water in the two glasses.

946 ** => B: no
947 **   T: ye::s look here it looks whi::ter and here it
948 **   still looks almost transparent (.) as we prepared it from
949 **   the beginning (.) isn't it Maricela? (0.2) ↑SIMON
950 **   (.) KEEP QUIET (.) WILL YOU? (.) please (.) have
951 **   you seen (.) on this side (.) it looks whi::ter
952 **   the water is more like milk than in this other
953 **   one, in this one it is completely transparent as
954 **   when we began (0.3) can you see? (0.5) this one
955 **   is clearer isn't it?
956 ** => G: °no° ((lots of pupils speaking quietly))
957 **   T   °'scuse me (0.3) I'll drop it°
958 **   ((the teacher has been lowering his tone))
959 *   T: °more transparent° have you seen in this side ((glass))? (0.6)
960 * => B: °oh:: how ugly°
961 *   T: °can you see it?° ((he is saying the same in
962 *   turn to each boy and girl around the classroom but
963 *   they only look at it without saying anything))
964   T: °this water looks more transparent than the one on
965   this other side ((glass)), on this side it looks more
966   transparent° (0.2) ↑can you now see that on
967   this side it looks more transparent than on this
968   other one? (.) ↑well it is because it has carbon
969   dioxide that has been mixed (.) on this glass it
970   i::s more transparent than on this other and on
971   this one it has more gases ↓isn't it? Do we all
972   agree? (.) look this one's more transparent (.)
973   isn't it? without color and this one i::s whiter
974   ↑can you see it now? (0.4) are you loo::king at
975   it? (0.2) Ta:nia? (0.2) on this side it is whiter
976   and on this side it has less color it is more
977   transparent (0.2) isn't it? (0.2) ↓we::ll(.)↑WELL
978   just a moment before on page number one hundred
979   and thirteen of your textbook (.) it clearly says
980   tha:t (0.2) this solution is called lime water
981   ↑pay attention! (.) Maricela! (0.5) on page one
982   hundred and thirteen it says that this solution is

983   called lime water and it turns mi::lky (0.2) when
984   it mixes with carbon dioxide ↑that is an
985   in<u>vi::sib</u>le gas (.) carbon dioxide cannot be seen

Throughout this sequence there is a constant confrontation between two versions of "what can be seen" in the experiment. The teacher's script consists of a demonstration of an alleged experimental fact by manipulating the experimental tools and then showing the difference in the transparency of the lime water in two glasses. He asks questions from the beginning to the end of the sequence, requesting that children confirm his statement: "On this side *((glass))* the lime water is more transparent." A student begins to intervene, saying that, "IT CAN'T BE SEEN::::", provoking laughter within the group. The teacher ignores that assertion, continuing with the script, describing differences in the lime water of the two glasses, and asking for confirmation. The children's responses become lower in tone, but they continue to insist that they cannot see a difference: (no[::::; [I cannot see it teacher; no; °no°; °oh:: how ugly°). From turns 934 to 958, the students give a few public answers but increase their private comments. A rising murmur dominates the classroom. Finally, in lines 961 to 983, the students cease talking among themselves, but they also stop responding to the teacher's insistent, direct, indirect, personal, or group questions. There are several pauses (from 1 to 5 seconds) after the teacher raises questions that function as demands for a response, but the children refuse to respond.

The students' participation can be seen as a counterscript in two senses: First, all of them followed their observations, which were different from the teacher's demands. Second, they did not follow the teacher's participation structure, failing to answer most of the teacher's questions even when a question was directed to a particular student. The script of the teacher and the counterscript of the students were parallel but disengaged from one another.

In this sequence, the students produced three types of answers to the teacher's questions: (a) verbal denial of the requested answer in 3 cases, gradually lowering their voices; (b) whispering as a form of resistance and refusal to participate in the public space; and (c) silence as a response to direct requests for participation in 13 cases. In the first response type, the IRE structure was maintained but the teacher did not control the content of students' answers. In the other two response types the teacher was the only participant in public interaction, even though he asked students to confirm his assertions. As a form of discursive disengagement, the children directed their comments to the private space of peer communication, excluding the teacher.

In this example, the teacher appeared to have the floor but was far from controlling the students' discourse. If we attend to the entire sequence, we see that students' responses, murmuring, and silence were not a refusal to learn or misbehavior, but rather a counterscript consisting of a different version of what was seen. By refusing to follow the teacher's orientations and resisting the appeal to participate, students exercised power, as the teacher needed their collaboration to carry out the activity and maintain communication (Mercado, 2002). Refusal to participate (Erickson, 1986; Rockwell, 1987) modifies the asymmetrical power relations that allow the teacher to determine the orientation of students' discursive interventions.

DIFFERENT RESPONSES TO TEACHERS' QUESTIONS

Sacks (1992) states that questions have an interactive format that entails certain normative rules: (a) the questioner has the right to speak after the answer; (b) the questioner controls the conversation because he or she defines the relevance of the next turn and decides or orients the topic; (c) there is a general tendency to be in the position of questioner; and (d) there are many ways to elude an answer in a debate for control, including responding with another question. The next sequence illustrates several student responses when faced with a question from the teacher within an IRE structure.

This excerpt derives from a fifth-grade lesson about relative densities. The students had weighed the same volume of different materials in a balance to analyze the concept of density. After the activity, the teacher asked every child to make a list of 10 materials in descending order of density. This excerpt is part of the debate that ensued to reach a collective decision about the first place on a common list. The students discussed which material should be first on the list—wood, iron, or stone—and then the teacher intervened:

30	T:	Who has wood?, let's see (0.2) which one is denser,
31		iron or ::: (0.2) stone?
32	Sts:	ir [on
33	B:	[iron
34	B:	stone=
35	T:	=here:: only e:::: Jorge, Armando and Juan Carlos
36		have said that it is stone
37	G:	AND ALSO WOOD

```
38          B:   teacher I also said that it is [wood
39          T:                              [↑IS IT ALSO
40               wood dense::r (0.2) than iron? (.)
41               is it heavier?
42          B:   No:::
43          B:   teacher, it looks like a piece of wood is missing
44          T:   well, let's see now which one::: is next (0.2)
45          ((a child raises his hand insistently))
46          T:   OK MY SON (.) TELL ME
47          B:   that >some times< (0.2) wood is heavier than
48               i:::ron
49          T:   are you sure?
50          Sts: yes::::: ((chorus answer))
51          B:   yes because (.) try to carry a tree to see if
52 **            it is not heavy
53 **       ((a lot of children make comments among themselves; the
54 **       teacher smiles))
55 *        T:   okay (0.2) let's put iron (.) based on the
56               majority's opinion, we'll later continue the list=
57 =>       B:   =how can we know if it's:: right now?
58          T:   Let's see (0.2) can you come up Ruben (.) to put
59               the second one?
```

In this sequence the teacher presents an apparently open activity in which each student can state which material is denser to construct a consensual list "based on the majority's opinion." However, the teacher's real script is to orient the construction of the list by evaluating each child's answer, accepting only those responses that agree with his opinion about the order of the materials. The students appear to follow the script, responding when the teacher asks, but they do not accept the teacher's ordering of the materials. To see what is happening, it is necessary to analyze turn by turn.

From the teacher's first intervention, it is noticeable that he is trying to remove wood from the discussion, as he mentions it in an interrogative way and immediately states the options as only iron and stone. Some of the children (lines 32, 33, and 34) seem to attend to that orientation but the girl in line 37 and the boy in line 38 do not accept ruling out wood. Without allowing the boy, in line 38, to finish his intervention, the teacher responds in a loud voice, questioning that wood is denser than iron. The repetition of an utterance in interrogative tone functions as a refusal of the previous turns (Pomerantz, 1984). The next intervention by a boy denying that wood is denser than iron shows an understanding and acceptance of what the teacher wants. However, even with two utterances by the teacher disqualifying wood, when he tries to continue with the list, another child, insistently raising his hand, forces the teacher pay attention to him and reasserts the possibility of wood being heavier than iron, softening his position with a "sometimes" (lines 46–47).

In line 49, the teacher attempts to deny the previous turn and the option of wood once more, showing doubt (are you sure?). This time the boy, instead of being corrected, receives collective support for the option of wood and produces an argument based on an empirical example. The teacher smiles but does not incorporate the point into his discourse. He drops the subject by saying "okay," and by stating explicitly his decision on iron. Even as he expresses this decision, he demonstrates that his word is not convincing enough by supporting his option with the majority opinion. Then he continues with the rest of the list (lines 55–56).

Without any pause, in line 57, a boy asks a question that rejects the teacher's statement (Pomerantz, 1984), showing his appropriation of the teacher's devices to reject an utterance and openly expressing doubt about the correctness of the teacher's statement. The student asks for a criterion to validate or refuse the teacher's version, implicitly questioning the teacher's position as the "knower" and therefore the one in control of the lesson. Indirectly the student is also questioning the criterion of majority opinion, which the teacher has used to legitimate his version. With this question, the boy constructs a counterscript in which he is positioned to request accounts—a position generally reserved for the teacher. By not accepting the teacher's version, students present themselves as knowledgeable and as having the right to defend a different position.

The teacher seems reluctant to give the student control over the next turn and does not respond to this intervention, constructing it as inconvenient or inadequate. However, the students do not accept his rejection; in the next turns they propose wood as second place on the list. The children construct a counterscript—another version of the correct order—but do not change the activity content. With some exceptions (the child's intervention in line 57), they follow the participation structure the teacher poses.

In this and the previous example, we see that a sequence following the teacher-posed activity with an IRE discourse structure does not guarantee that the teacher controls the discourse, because the children's responses (whether verbal or nonverbal) may not correspond to what the teacher is evidently trying to achieve. We also see that the IRE structure can be broken by students' questions. In this case the teacher continued with his script. Yet even following the teacher's IRE-structured script, it is not a given that children's ideas will be inhibited or that the teacher controls the construction of knowledge.

STUDENTS EVALUATING TEACHER AND PEER INTERVENTIONS

In the classes observed, students did not simply express and defend their versions and judgments; they also provided evaluations of other contributions, including those made by the teacher. On some occasions these evaluative interventions were individual, but in other cases classroom discourse was conducted within a constant background of group comments that served as a social evaluation of the ongoing interventions. Line 57 of the previous sequence, (=how can we know if it's:: right now?), is a good example of an evaluation of the teacher's version by a student.

The following example, taken from a lesson on gravity in another fifth-grade group, illustrates the relevance of the collective evaluative participation of students in classroom discourse, and the importance they assign to peer opinion. This sequence begins with the teacher's questions and the students' answers, and then proceeds to reading the textbook.

1	T:	OKAY (.) do you know who investigated all this
2		about gra::vity? or who gave us all
3		this about what gravity is?
4	B:	[no::
5	G:	[when Christopher [Columbu:::s traveled
6	Ch:	[Bu:::::
7		*((lots of children shout, making fun of her))*
8	T:	Let's see, tell us, we are going to see if it
9		is right (0.2) when Christopher Columbus
10		traveled (.) what else ? (0.7)
11		*((the girl doesn't say anything))*
12	T:	gravity, or the term gravity (.) was proposed by
13		(0.4) *((she takes the textbook and reads it*

14	*silently for some seconds))*
15	T: He was an Englishman ca:lle:d (0.4)
16	*((she writes Isaac on the blackboard))*
17	G: Isaa::::c *((reading from the blackboard))*
18	T: Isaac Newton (0.2) they say (0.2) who knows if
19	it's true (.) that mister Newton was in the
20	countryside (0.3) *((children at the back of the*
21	*room can be heard talking))*
22	T: Do you know the story already?
23	G$_{11}$: he said that the Earth [was round
24	=> Ch: [Bu:::::: *(making fun))*
25	=> B: [Norma knows the sto::ry
26	G: [Norma
27	T: Norma (.) tell us
28	*((Norma doesn't say anything))*
29	Ch: she says that an apple fell down on him
30	*((children adjacent to Norma))*
31	T: while in the countryside Newton saw an apple
32	fall down from a tree (0.3) he asked himself
33	why when the apple separates from the tree it
34	falls down to the ground instead of flying off?
35	*((children laugh))*
36	T: (0.2) he found in his research, that it was
37	because a force acting at a distance, that is called
38	gravity, attracts everything to the earth's center

In this excerpt the teacher states the script as a review of some already known information about the gravity. The children follow this orientation but negotiate every turn to insert their content. The teacher's first question (lines 1, 2, and 3) has two overlapping answers. One is a "no" and the other is a comment from a girl about the voyage of Christopher Columbus (line 5). However, in line 6, several students interrupt the girl with a joking chorus of "Bu::::::." This gibe, clearly evaluative of the girl's answer, stops her from saying what she was going to say. The students' chorus functions interactionally as a negative evaluation—as a refusal.

Nonetheless, the teacher's following turn is a positive evaluation, revoicing the girl's intervention, trying to encourage her to continue and even making it clear that she will be evaluated when she finishes her version (Let's see, tell us, we are going to see if it is right (0.2) when Christopher Columbus traveled (.) what else? (0.7)). This intervention by the teacher also rejects the rest of the group's comments, which forced the girl to end her response. That is, the teacher also takes the children's joking as a denial, and counteracts it with a positive evaluation and encouragement. In this case, there are two competing evaluations of the girl's intervention.

Despite the teacher's encouragement and a long 7-second pause, the girl refuses to continue. Silence seems to be the way in which the girl rejects the teacher's insistence for her to continue participating; she acts discursively by giving more power to her peers. There is a power asymmetry in favor of the social consensus among pupils.

In line 24 the students again collectively evaluate the intervention of another girl by mocking her. This interactionally negative evaluation also leads this girl to interrupt her response. Also, at this point, the students not only refuse the intervention of G_{11}, but immediately after, in line 25, they propose a different girl's (Norma's) answer as adequate.

As a group, children may reject (interactionally) an answer and propose another, without intervention from the teacher. In this case, the students ask for Norma's private comment to be socially and publicly legitimized. Faced with Norma's refusal to participate, the children socially revoice the girl's private comment, saying out loud what she whispers. The teacher also picks up on the students' orientation and invites Norma to openly participate.

These child interventions in lines 25, 26, and 29 correspond to a discursive phenomenon studied by Shiffrin (1993): "speaking for another." Shiffrin finds that this interactive move may have a negative meaning, as occurs in "butting in" or denying someone his or her proper place. However, it also may have a positive influence as reinforcement for the other person by indicating that his or her position is shared. In this case, in addition to sharing Norma's position, the students keep Norma in the primary interactional slot, respecting her rights as the original source of the idea by mentioning her in each intervention. Shiffrin finds that this move of "speaking for another" produces realignments in the way participants relate to one another. In this case it seems that by promoting Norma's private comment to the public arena, the students jointly endorse that version, as though saying that they know "the stories" as well.

This is also an excerpt in which children's interventions followed the teacher's script. Students participate by evaluating their peers and the teacher's versions, displaying approvals as well as denials. Repeated negative evaluations by the students can force the teacher to justify his or her idea, or to develop more convincing arguments. This situation places the students in control of turn-taking. However, the children also evaluate themselves and their peers, sometimes even in opposition to the teacher's evaluations. Also, in this analysis, it can be seen that these interventions sometimes have even more influence on the next turn than the teacher's implicit orientation. When we examine the fine details of recorded interaction, we find that students can influence the discourse content and the person who might participate in the next turn. Thus, they gain power over the process of classroom talk even when they follow the teacher's script.

DISCUSSION

Among these socially marginalized students, participation in classroom discourse was active and complex and did not always follow the teacher's attempts to control discourse content. Students' interventions influenced classroom discursive dynamics; even within IRE-structured discourse, students broke free of the teacher's control. In several cases they followed the teacher's script in the sense of doing the activity but they constructed a counterscript about the activity's content. They did this by denying the teacher's orientations, refusing to participate, or defending alternative versions of particular topics. In their responses, the children made use of their relative autonomy to decide whether or not to follow the teacher's orientation, depending on the academic task and their opinion of the lesson content.

These data also illustrate situations in which the IRE form was maintained, but students assumed the role of asking evaluative questions and evaluating others' turns, thus reversing interactive roles. In the process, they appropriated the functions through which the teacher developed her or his power to influence the discourse of others. Individually and collectively, children evaluated previous turns of the teacher and peers, individual versions, and collective positions. With these interventions, they were able to confront institutional authority, creating new conditions of relevance for the following turns. When their evaluations took the form of collective utterances presented as a social consensus, they had an even greater influence than the teacher on next turns. In these cases, power shifted to the students, as they managed to alter communicative roles and relationships.

Children in this Mexican school did not try to change the proposed activities or resist learning. Rather, they expressed their autonomy by asserting a different version of school knowledge than the teacher's. In doing this they constructed counterscripts about the activity's content. Without changing the lesson format, they argued for their versions. In doing this they sometimes reversed the IRE structure, positioning themselves as questioners and evaluators, and defining who could intervene in the next turn.

Students from low-income backgrounds who are typically assigned to a subordinate role in these instances used discursive strategies to contest, dispute, and resist that role. They positioned themselves as active and competent communicators, using available discursive resources, including arguing for their viewpoints, appropriating the teacher's arguments to reject nonshared options, using preference structure mechanisms to indirectly reject versions they did not share, making audible nonpublic comments, directly expressing content differently from what was asked for, and evaluating others' versions or speaking for others. With their interventions, the students influenced and often controlled the dynamics of classroom interaction, even within the IRE structure and teacher's script.

It appears, then, that the educational relevance of the IRE structure has been exaggerated. This structure does not automatically relate to forms of exclusion of marginalized students. Cultural discontinuity does not necessarily exist between the discourse of children from socially marginalized backgrounds and the classroom discourse structure of IRE. The fifth grade students in these examples learned how to manage this discourse structure; their home culture did not inhibit them from expressing their views within a structure consistent with middle-class norms. It is also important to point out that the examples here are from classes in which all children came from economically and socially disadvantaged families; that is, within the classroom, they were not a "minority." This may suggest different implications than those derived from discourse studies in multicultural classrooms.

These findings lead me to agree with Paradise's (1998) comments on Mehan's work regarding the differences between school and family learning and teaching practices. However, I am not convinced that a school that exclusively utilizes family learning and teaching practices is as rich as ones that open new forms of learning and talking for the children. It is rather a question of *how* the connection between these different practices is made and not to delete them.

A comment about the importance of conflict settings is also pertinent. Conflict settings can prove to be rich in learning conditions because they are open spaces for intellectual negotiation of academic content. The examples here show that resistance to learning is not the only or the dominant consequence of conflict situations, as there are also challenges and alternative content constructions that may be debated.

This study shows that the discursive orientation of culturally and socially marginalized children is not necessarily resistance to learning, as has been frequently described (Alpert, 1991; Erickson, 1986; Mehan, 1998; Willis, 1976). This suggests that the patterns of school failure among these children should be reanalyzed, taking into account the complexity of the discursive processes involved. In all the excerpts analyzed, children were engaged in discussions with strong viewpoints about the academic content, expressing their interest even while holding opinions different than others'. When students become engaged with the academic task, their participation in knowledge construction is active and complex, with empowering learning consequences.

It is clear that power asymmetries exist, however. These are partially derived from the institutional and political order. For example, the teacher states the classroom script and attempts to maintain its continuity. However, this asymmetry is reconstructed, negotiated, manipulated, and even inverted rather than being merely imposed or denied. Power relations are not only a matter of vertical display of institutional asymmetry and its reproduction, but also a local construction that depends not only on the teacher's actions, and that can transform dominant local relations. There is a dialectic relation between institutional and local power construction; even when the teacher guides classroom discourse, children are not necessarily subordinated by him or her. Power is not only coercive, but also involves the ability to persuade others to one's version and to orient discourse dynamics.

Asymmetry in classroom power relations appears on two levels. On the one hand there is predefined institutional asymmetry because the teacher has, in principle, "legitimate" knowledge to transmit. This institutional power places teachers in the role of guiding, organizing, and orienting school tasks. This power is attended to by the students, who may in fact insist on it when teachers depart from their institutionalized roles (Candela, 1995). However, institutional power does not explain the dynamic features of the interaction that influence social relations in the classroom. Asymmetry is built and defined in the turn-by-turn details of classroom talk, in which the power to influence next turns is an endemic feature, such that both discourse dynamics and context are modified and negotiated between teacher and students. In discursive interaction, local power dynamics are constantly re-created and participants' roles are reconstructed.

With these discursive actions, students negotiate their social roles. They indexically display themselves as having knowledge of the academic content and as competent communicators, appropriating alternative discursive devices to defend their points of view in their interactions with teachers. They can even perform the pedagogic functions of rejecting some versions and reinforcing others by speaking for others.

This suggests the dependence of the social participation structure on the relevance of the academic task for the participants. Social participation dynamics depend not only on different interactional signals (e.g., discourse timing, rhythm, intensity, tone, emphasis, or sequential positioning), but also on the various contextualizing cues (Gumpertz, 1982) that follow teachers' demands. This analysis shows the important influence that content significance has on participants, and the relevance of the academic tasks on the social structure of participation, a relationship that has not been well studied.

With these complex actions, the social structure is reconstructed by the unique way in which each participant deals with the dominant structure, and with every contribution participants make to classroom discourse. Here I assume that each social group's history provides specific cultural strategies and resources to deal with the dominant culture (Rockwell, 1992). Thus, the cultural and social dimensions of teacher–student relationships should not necessarily be taken as constraints on the performance of educational tasks. These relationships are also matters of construction in face-to-face interactions that do not simply reproduce dominant structures, and that are much more versatile and complex in their constructions.

As Diamond (1996, p. 12) has noted, studies that focus on the "dominated" participants in interaction carry both ethical and sociopolitical significance, because they reveal these participants' communicative competence, discursive creativity, and ability to influence interactions. Just as Labov (1972) documented the richness and creativity of African-American English, careful discourse analysis from the child's perspective can show that so-called subordinated students are communicatively competent to defend their own versions, influence interventions, and even determine their own roles against the teacher's position in the discursive dynamics of the classroom.

Antonia Candela is a Mexican physicist who completed her doctorate in sciences in educational research. She specializes in ethnography and discourse analysis in science classes. She has written *Ciencia en el Aula: Los Alumnos Entre la Argumentación y el Consenso* (Science in the Classroom: Students Amid Argumentation and Consensus Construction), *La Necesidad de Entender, Explicar y Argumentar: Los Alumnos de Primaria en la Actividad Experimental* (The Necessity to Understand, Explain and Argue: Elementary School Students and the Experimental Activity) and 26 official science textbooks.

REFERENCES

Alpert, B. (1991). Students' resistance in the classroom. *Anthropology & Education Quarterly, 22,* 350–366.

Candela, A. (1995). Consensus construction as a collective task in Mexican science classes. *Anthropology & Education Quarterly, 26,* 1–17.

Candela, A. (1997a). Demonstrations and problem-solving exercises in school science: Their transformation within the Mexican elementary school classroom. *Science Education, 81,* 497–515.

Candela, A. (1997b). The discursive construction of argumentative context in science classes. In C. Coll & D. Edwards (Eds.), *Teaching, learning and classroom discourse: Approaches to the study of educational discourse* (pp. 89–105). Madrid, Spain: Fundación Infancia y Aprendizaje.

Candela, A. (1998). Students' power in classroom discourse. *Linguistics and Education, 10,* 139–164.

Candela, A. (1999). *Ciencia en el aula: Los alumnos entre la argumentación y el consenso* [Science in the classroom: Students amid argumentation and consensus construction]. Mexico City: Paidos.

Cazden, C. (1986). Classroom discourse. In M. E. Wittrock (Ed.), *Handbook of research on teaching* (pp. 432–463). New York: Macmillan.

Diamond, J. (1996). *Status and power in verbal interaction.* Amsterdam: John Benjamins.

Drew, P., & Heritage, J. (Eds.). (1992). *Talk at work: Interaction in institutional settings.* Cambridge, UK: Cambridge University Press.

Edwards, A. D., & Furlong, V. J. (1978). *The language of teaching.* London: Heinemann.

Edwards, D., & Mercer, N. (1987). *Common knowledge: The development of understanding in the classroom.* London: Methuen.

Edwards, D., & Potter, J. (1992). *Discursive psychology.* London: Sage.

Erickson, F. (1986). Qualitative methods of educational research. In M. Wittrock (Ed), *Handbook of research on teaching* (pp. 119–161). New York: Macmillan.

Grimshaw, A. (Ed). (1990). *Conflict talk: Sociolinguistic investigations of arguments in conversations.* Cambridge, UK: Cambridge University Press.

Gumperz, J. (Ed.). (1977). *Language and social identity.* Cambridge, UK: Cambridge University Press.

Gutiérrez, K. (1993). How talk, context and script shape contexts for learning: A cross-case comparison of journal sharing. *Linguistics and Education, 5,* 335–365.

Gutiérrez, K., Rymes, B., & Larson, J. (1995). Script, counterscript, and underlife in the classroom: James Brown versus Brown v. Board of Education. *Harvard Educational Review, 65,* 445–471.

Holt, J. (1969). *Why children fail.* Harmondsworth, UK: Penguin.

Labov, W. (1972). *Language in the inner city: Studies in Black English Vernacular.* Philadelphia: University of Pennsylvania Press.

Leith, D., & Myerson, G. (1989). *The power of address: Explorations on rhetoric.* London: Routledge.

Marková, I., & Foppa, K. (Eds.). (1991). *Asymmetries in dialogue.* Hemel Hempstead: Harvester Wheatsheaf.

Mehan, H. (1979). *Learning lessons: Social organization in the classroom.* London: Harvard University Press.

Mehan, H. (1998). The study of social interaction in educational settings: Accomplishments and unresolved issues. *Human Development, 41,* 245–269.

Mercado, R. (2002). *Los sabres docentes como construcción social* [Teacher's knowledge as a social construction]. Mexico, DF: Fondo de Cultura Económica.

Paradise, R. (1998). What's different about learning in schools as compared to family and community settings? *Human Development, 41,* 270–278.

Pomerantz, A. (1984). Agreeing and disagreeing with assessments: Some features of preferred/dispreferred turn shapes. In J. M. Atkinson & J. Heritage (Eds.), *Structures of social action* (pp. 57–101). Cambridge, UK: Cambridge University Press.

Rockwell, E. (1987, October). *Reproducción y resistencia en el aula: La interpretación de la evidencia sociolingüística* [Reproduction and resistance in the classroom: The interpretation of sociolinguistic evidence]. Paper presented in the I Coloquio Mauricio Swadesh, Instituto de Investigaciones Antropológicas, Universidad Nacional Autónoma de México.

Rockwell, E. (1992). La dinámica cultural en la escuela [Cultural dynamics in school]. In E. Gigante (Ed.), *Cultura y escuela: La reflexión actual en México* (pp. 21–38). Mexico, DF: Conaculta.

Rogoff, B., Kistry, J., Göncü, A., & Mosier, C. (1993). Guided participation in cultural activities by toddlers and caregivers. *Monographs of the Society for Research in Child Development, 58,* 1–174.

Sacks, H. (1973). *The preference for agreement in natural conversation.* Paper presented at the Linguistic Institute, Ann Arbor, MI.

Sacks, H. (1992). On questions. In G. Jefferson (Ed.), *Lectures on conversation* (Vol. I, pp. 49–56). Oxford, UK: Blackwell.

Sacks, H., Schegloff, E. A., & Jefferson, G. (1974). A simplest systematics for the organization of turn-taking in conversation. *Language, 50,* 596–735.

Schegloff, E. (1992). On talk and its institutional occasions. In P. Drew & J. Heritage (Eds.), *Talk at work: Interaction in institutional settings* (pp. 101–134). Cambridge, UK: Cambridge University Press.

Shiffrin, D. (1993). "Speaking for another" in sociolinguistic interviews: Alignments, identities and frames. In D. Tannen (Ed.), *Framing in discourse* (pp. 231–263). New York: Oxford University Press.

Sinclair, J. M., & Coulthard, R. M. (1975). *Towards an analysis of discourse: The English used by teachers and pupils.* London: Oxford University Press.

Wells, G. (1993). Reevaluating the IRF sequence: A proposal for the articulation of theories of activity and discourse for the analysis of teaching and learning in the classroom. *Linguistics and Education, 5,* 1–37.

Willis, P. (1976). The class significance of school counter culture. In M. Hammersley & P. Woods (Eds.), *The process of schooling* (pp. 188–200). London: Open University Press.

Commentary on Part II
Language and a
Changing Social Context

Luis C. Moll
University of Arizona

It is a pleasure to comment on chapters written by colleagues whose work I have followed and admired for several years. These are very interesting times in education, especially given the rapidly changing demographics that have increased dramatically the social and cultural diversity of students attending public schools in the United States. These are also very disturbing times, with the legislation of mandated, highly restrictive reading programs, the onset of mass testing as a reform strategy in lieu of teacher involvement and professional development, and the expanding prohibition of bilingual education—all measures that severely curtail what teachers can do to help children learn, especially if they are English-language learners, poor, or of the working class (Moll & Ruiz, 2002).

The presence of diversity in schools is being treated with alarm, suppression, and desperate attempts at imposing uniformity on teaching and learning. The message is clear about who is in charge in the schools, and it is not Latinos, African Americans, or working-class families, the majority population in virtually all major urban school districts in the United States. On the contrary, their interests are hardly addressed in policy initiatives, and reforms have tended to silence and obviate their participation. It is equally clear that issues of equity in education are not a priority, to state the obvious, in the conservative political agenda that has achieved prominence within education (Orfield, 2000).

It is with this context in mind that I want to address some of the important points made in the chapters in this part of the volume. It is perhaps Ladson-Billings's chapter that most clearly raises issues of literacy and power that are so central to any discussion of equity or reform. She points out how the dynamics of race are missing from the teachers' discourse within the school that she studied. That is, race is treated as a "taboo" topic, even when (or, perhaps, especially because) African-American children are the students having the most academic difficulties. The point, however, is not only the lack of rigor in the schooling that African-American children receive, thus granting them "permission to fail," as she calls it, even at the hands of well-intentioned teachers. This academic neglect is, after all, systemic, a perennial characteristic of working-class schooling, regardless of the students' race or ethnicity. The point is that any discussion of race (or class, I would add) might bring into consciousness how African-American children remain "marked" within the system, and how White privilege—and most teachers are White—remains "unmarked" and, as Ladson-Billings asserts, unspoken.

I remain struck, however, by the multiple ways through which the status quo, and systematic inequality, are maintained. Consider how teachers had, inadvertently, established a model of the moral worthiness of the good readers and, conversely, of the "immorality" of the poor readers, mostly children of color. These attributions contribute to the "construction" of African-American identity as problematic for academic learning, where school failure is considered as something the children do (or fail to do), not something done to them. It is also important to understand how such schooling practices are linked to broader ideologies. Bialostok (1999), for example, has recently analyzed middle-class ideologies about reading, and the "moral worthiness" attached to certain forms of reading associated with middle-class status, most notably book reading. Any deviations from such models of what counts as worthwhile literacy are considered morally reprehensible, such as the case of mothers who do not read books to their children. Such broader cultural models, linking literacy practices, morality, and social class, seem to be reproducible in classrooms, especially by middle-class teachers working with working-class children, and especially with language minority children having difficulty reading.

However, this reproduction need not necessarily be the case, as Ladson-Billings also suggests. Creating special settings for teachers to reflect on their work, the values and resources found in local communities, and the ideologies underlying their teaching can certainly contribute to a reconceptualization and change of schooling practices. I found it noteworthy that the one exception among the teachers in the study, the only teacher emphasizing the academic preparation of the students, was the one who had a history of personal relationships with African-American adults and children. This point reminds me of our work with teachers in documenting the "funds of knowledge" of local households and, in the process, developing more personal relationships with the children and their families. A consequence of these ethnographic home visits, in which the teachers approach local households as learners, is in altering positively the perceptions teachers and families have of each other (see, e.g., Moll & González, 1997). The importance of such personalized relationships between teachers and families also reminds me of Siddle Walker's (1996) historical analysis of the centrality of a school presence, enhanced through regular home visitations and other forms of parent–teacher interactions, in the African-American community she studied in segregated North Carolina.

Hornberger's chapter also addresses the social and linguistic dynamics involved in schooling practices, in this case centered on the teaching and learning of biliteracy. Her interest is in exploring forms of "additive" bilingual schooling for working-class children that promote students' identity and knowledge construction. The challenge, as she points out—and it is considerable—is how to accommodate or facilitate the beneficial coexistence, in terms of children's literacy development, of what she terms "the media-related dimensions of diversity." These are the great range of language varieties, allegiances, and discourse practices, few of them ever formally privileged in schools, that characterize much of the urban school experience. Her analysis builds on her "continua of biliteracy" model, which I do not elaborate here, except to mention that the "media" of biliteracy, and the language diversity it represents, are key aspects of her model.

According to Hornberger, the very definition of what counts as powerful forms of biliteracy (and for what purposes) is always open to transformation through the particular agency of educators, students, community members, and others, and through their arrangements of everyday practices. Her call is for serious attention to and inclusion of different language varieties as valuable resources for both students and teachers in developing "multidiscoursal" forms of education. However, such inclusion is always constrained by the institutional limits of schooling that, although never absolute, narrow the possibilities for human action. What are teachers to accomplish when their actions are predetermined by the decision of others distant from their classrooms, and under threat of litigation or dismissal if they do not comply, as is currently the case in California and Arizona under repressive antibilingual education measures, or as imposed by rigid, legislatively mandated reading programs? This is not to say that the proposals by Hornberger are not desirable—they are indeed—but current barriers to positive action are quite formidable, especially actions intended to acknowledge and include working-class students' "voices" and facilitate their participation in knowledge construction (or meaning making), as part of their developing subjectivities or identities. The process of student identity formation, therefore, is always "situated," for it interacts with the particular (and heterogeneous) characteristics of the institutional context of schooling. Hence the value of Hornberger's continua model is that it provides a way of conceptualizing important dynamics that shape schooling contexts, especially in relation to biliteracy development.

Candela's is the only chapter in this part on research conducted outside the United States, thus presenting a very interesting contrast to the other chapters. Her analysis acknowledges the ubiquity of certain interactive routines, especially the much-researched initiation–response–evaluation (IRE) sequence that represents the dominant participation structure of schooling, apparently in Mexico as well as in the United States. However, she claims that even within such a structure, widely assumed to limit progressive instructional innovations, teachers and students can create the necessary "discursive space" to challenge limiting forms schooling. Her claim is based on her analysis of what she calls the "local reconstruction of power," accomplished by modifying the dominant interactive features of instruction. Her point is to remind us that participation structures such as the IRE sequence are always interactional accomplishments. Even within such "teacher-dominated" structures, one can never be sure if the teacher is in control, as intended, of the children's knowledge, appearances to the contrary notwithstanding.

Candela's examples underscore the influence of students on the discursive dynamics of classrooms. Either through verbal participation or though their silence or off-task interactions with peers, students have many ways of shaping the teacher's role and talk. As Candela points out, the power asymmetry of lessons can even shift to the students' side, reversing the interactive roles of the IRE participation structures. Her analysis also suggests the importance of content, and the display of alternative content knowledge by students, in motivating the negotiation of social roles within the classroom.

However, it seems to me that what does not change, even in the examples provided by Candela, is the overall "transmission" conception of instruction that adherence to an IRE participation structure entails. There is alteration of the IRE structure in her examples, but little evidence of any alternative dialogic structures emerging from these changes that would challenge the transmission model of schooling. That the IRE structure can be expanded and is always challenged by student discursive influences and interests seems clear. I am not ready, however, to dismiss the educational relevance of the IRE structure in constraining the intellectual participation of students, especially those working-class or poor students often assigned to low-track classrooms (Nystrand & Gamoran, 1997).

Remillard and Cahnmann's contribution seeks to bridge classroom research in bilingual and mathematics education, especially in relation to connections among language, culture, and mathematics teaching and learning. Through two contrasting case examples, these authors depict the need for teachers, especially those working with language minority students, to be both mathematically adept and culturally knowledgeable. The challenge is to engage the students, and this often requires making ideas or tasks culturally meaningful, in mathematical activities that are academically worthwhile. Interestingly, one of their examples is of a teacher who, reminiscent of a point made in Ladson-Billing's chapter, did not consider issues of race or culture of relevance pedagogically. Thus, she ignored the social and cultural embeddedness of the mathematics she practiced and taught. In contrast, the second example is of a teacher who shared certain background experiences with students, but was less than successful in using this commonality to mediate the teaching and learning of mathematics in her classroom.

Both issues—the first teacher's weak knowledge of her students' backgrounds and resources, and the second teacher's weak knowledge of mathematics—represent considerable theoretical and practical challenges in mathematics education, especially in light of the growing student diversity in schools (cf. González, Andrade, Civil, & Moll, 2001). The authors propose the need to conceptualize teachers as ongoing learners, and the necessity of creating conditions for teacher inquiry on the difficult dynamics of practice. I would add at least two points to their discussion. One is that what is at issue are the teachers' ways of conceptualizing students as learners. However, any possibilities for change in the ways teachers talk and think about students are seriously constrained by working as isolated practitioners. A second point to consider is that any serious attempts at reconceptualizing students have consequences for the identity of teachers, just as any substantive change in pedagogy has implications for the identity of students, involving, as it does, changes in roles, relationships, and expectations (see Civil & Planas, 2004; Engeström, Engeström, & Suntio, 2002).

So it seems that an initial, necessary step in the teachers' "struggles," as the authors call them, to improve their teaching, is to create a social setting for them to think together about their work with other teachers. In such a setting teachers can become resources for each other, and exchange funds of knowledge not only about students but about their teaching, in this instance about teaching mathematics with minority students. Equally important is for teachers to develop the theoretical tools to address the pedagogical challenges they each face, including, as mentioned, changes in their identity as teachers as a consequence of their attempts at improving their practices.

In addition, positive changes in the bilingual schooling of Latino children or African-American children are unlikely to occur unless race and class (and language) ideologies are addressed explicitly by the pedagogy (Hubbard & Mehan, 1999). Therefore, developing a sophisticated theoretical understanding of these and other issues, such as the restrictive political mandates that shape practice, requires strategic alliances and the efforts of many different people, especially given the changing social contexts of schooling.

Luis C. Moll is professor of Language, Reading, and Culture and associate dean for academic affairs in the College of Education at the University of Arizona. He is a member of the National Academy of Education, and serves on its Board of Directors and Committee on Teacher Education. In 1999, he received the National Association for Multicultural Education Outstanding Researcher Award. He has published extensively on biliteracy, cognition, and Latino and language minority education. His books include *Vygotsky and Education* (Cambridge, 1990), and *Funds of Knowledge: Theorizing Practices in Households, Communities, and Classrooms* (with N. González & C. Amanti; Lawrence Erlbaum Associates, in press).

REFERENCES

Bialostok, S. (1999). *Discourses of literacy: Cultural models of White, urban, middle-class parents of kindergarten children.* Unpublished doctoral dissertation, Department of Language, Reading and Culture, University of Arizona, Tucson.

Civíl, M., & Planas, N. (2004). Participation in the mathematics classroom: Does every student have a voice? *For the Learning of Mathematics, 24,* 7–12.

Engeström, Y., Engeström, R., & Suntio, A. (2002). Can a school community learn to master its own future? An activity-theoretical study of expansive learning among middle school teachers. In G. Wells & G. Claxton (Eds.), *Learning for life in the 21st century:*

Sociocultural perspectives on the future of education (pp. 211–224). London: Blackwell.

González, N., Andrade, R., Civíl, M., & Moll, L. C. (2001). Bridging funds of distributed knowledge: Creating zones of practice in mathematics. *Journal of Education for Students Placed at Risk, 6,* 115–132.

Hubbard, L., & Mehan, H. (1999). Race and reform: Educational niche picking in a hostile environment. *Journal of Negro Education, 68,* 213–226.

Moll, L. C., & González, N. (1997). Teachers as social scientists: Learning about culture from household research. In P. M. Hall (Ed.), *Race, ethnicity and multiculturalism* (pp. 89–114). New York: Garland.

Moll, L. C., & Ruiz, R. (2002). The schooling of Latino students. In M. Suárez-Orozco & M. Páez (Eds.), *Latinos: Remaking America* (pp. 362–374). Berkeley: University of California Press.

Nystrand, M., & Gamoran, A. (1997). The big picture: Language and learning in hundreds of English lessons. In M. Nystrand (Ed.), *Opening dialogue* (pp. 30–74). New York: Teachers College Press.

Orfield, G. (2000). Policy and equity: Lessons of a third of a century of educational reforms in the United States. In F. Reimers (Ed.), *Unequal schools, unequal chances: The challenges to equal opportunity in the Americas* (pp. 401–426). Cambridge, MA: Harvard University Press/David Rockefeller Center for Latin American Studies.

Siddle Walker, V. (1996). *Their highest potential: An African-American school community in the segregated south.* Chapel Hill: University of North Carolina Press.

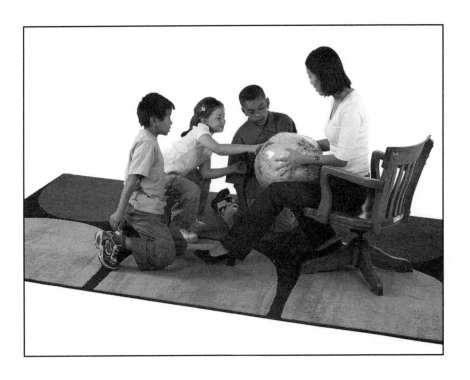

III
Literacies and Knowledges in a Changing World Order

We are living in a time of "hyper-modernity," Heller (1999) writes—an era in which control over the relations of production is shifting from the local and the state to the corporate and the global. The corporatization and internationalization of the access to and distribution of wealth, technology, and information threaten to create an even deeper and more far-reaching divide between rich and poor, both within nation-states and internationally. Globalization, Fairclough (2001) observes starkly, "benefits some people and hurts others" (p. 207). However, globalization is not only an economic process; as Fairclough (2001) also points out, language and power are central to "the academic analysis of the new world order and political struggles over it" (p. 204). Literacy education sits at the nexus of those struggles.

Part III widens the analytic lens to investigate these broader social, political, and economic forces and their interweaving with literacy education for children and adults. Gee and his colleagues describe the context for these investigations as the "new work order"—a social and economic landscape characterized by the global provision of goods and services to groups of people (markets), who in turn identify themselves by the goods and services they consume (Gee & Lankshear, 1997, p. 85; see also Gee et al., 1996; Street, 2001, pp. 2–6). Collaboration and team projects, "knowledge in use," and situated expertise take precedence over hierarchical, assembly-line organization, propositional knowledge, and singular expertise. Meeting the demands of this new, transformed capitalism requires critical language awareness, higher order

219

thinking skills, and the ability "to solve problems at the 'edge of [one's] expertise' " (Gee & Lankshear, 1997, pp. 84, 86).

How are educational systems responding to these shifts in economic relations? Who has access to the knowledges and communicative abilities required by the new capitalism? How do language education policies and programs cultivate, sort, and distribute those knowledges and abilities?

The chapters that follow take up these questions, using ethnographic methods to examine the interface between larger economic forces, literacy learning, and education in the United States and along the U.S.–Mexico border. James Paul Gee begins, observing that U.S. schools continue to be structured to produce workers for the "old" capitalism, skilling and deskilling students according to race or ethnicity and social class. Examining the moment-by-moment interactions between teachers and students in a culturally diverse, "liberal-thinking" school, Gee shows how teachers construct students as right or wrong, good or poor readers. A new divide is being produced, Gee warns, between the wealthy elite—the symbolic analysts at the top of an hourglass-shaped economic structure—and the service and manual workers at the bottom.

Char Ullman analyzes parallel processes in the economy impacted by the North American Free Trade Agreement (NAFTA) along the U.S.–Mexico border, where the loss of manufacturing jobs has displaced some 26,000 workers, mostly middle-aged Mexican-American women who speak little English. When school systems interact with the economic and social needs of capitalism, Ullman states, the result is often the reproduction of distinctions along gender, race, age, and social class lines. Many of the women Ullman interviewed were being retrained in English literacy programs "to perform a new incarnation of the same jobs they and their ancestors have done ... for more than 100 years—domestic work." Yet the border is fluid, changing, a "place of possibility," Ullman maintains. At one adult learning center, counterdiscourses challenge the reproductive model of adult education and illustrate the "political struggle of people who have refused to let globalization determine the course of their lives."

Christine Cain returns the discussion to literacy reforms for poor, working-class, English-language learners in California, documenting a recent literacy crisis initiative there in which English was iconically bonded to academic success. Analyzing teacher, school administrator, and journalist discourse, Cain shows how these complex and textured narratives connect to public uses of language, legitimating language crisis and language-as-a-problem orientations (see also McQuillan, 1998; Ruiz, 1988). The issue in such literacy campaigns, Cain asserts, is "what kind of meaning is being made, by whom, directed to whom, and to what ends."

Together, these three chapters investigate the lingering question of what and whose literacies and knowledges will predominate in an era of global capitalism. In his commentary, Jim Cummins asks whether—and how—schools can challenge the coercive power relations within these evolving new forms of social-economic organization. It is incumbent on critical literacy researchers, Cummins maintains, to document in clear and credible ways the impacts of "back to basics" pedagogies and the conditions under which certain achievement patterns arise. Teachers should not have to choose between social justice and standards, Cummins insists: "Instruction that challenges coercive power relations is the best way ... to boost students' academic achievement."

REFERENCES

Fairclough, N. (2001). *Language and power* (2nd ed.). Harlow, UK: Pearson Education/ Longman.

Gee, J. P., & Lankshear, C. (1997). Language, literacy and the new work order. In C. Lankshear, J. P. Gee, M. Knobel, & C. Searle (Eds.), *Changing literacies* (pp. 83–102). Buckingham, UK: Open University Press.

Gee, J. P., Hull, G., & Lankshear, C. (1996). *The new work order: Behind the language of the new capitalism.* Sydney: Allen & Unwin and Westview.

Heller, M., with Campbell, M., Dalley, P., & Patrick, D. (1999). *Linguistic minorities and modernity: A sociolinguistic ethnography.* London: Longman.

McQuillan, J. (1998). *The literacy crisis: False claims, real solutions.* Portsmouth, NH: Heinemann.

Ruiz, R. (1988). Orientations in language planning. In S. L. McKay & S. C. Wong (Eds.), *Language diversity: Problem or resource?* (pp. 3–25). Boston: Heinle & Heinle.

Street, B. V. (Ed.). (2001). *Literacy and development: Ethnographic perspectives.* London: Routledge.

10

Literacies, Schools, and Kinds of People in the New Capitalism

James Paul Gee
University of Wisconsin-Madison

In this chapter, I first develop a perspective on our new high-tech and global capitalism, a capitalism that is producing a tripart employment hierarchy with "symbol analysts" at the top, service and temporary workers at the bottom, and technical workers in the middle. This changing employment structure holds a number of important implications for schools and society. It demands, for example, the production of "new kinds of people"—new kinds of students and workers—a demand that has important implications for issues of equity and justice in society. Next I develop specific examples, using discourse analysis as a research tool, that are meant to help us think about some of the issues discussed earlier as they play out in schools and in the lives of teenagers from different socioeconomic classes. My focus throughout is on the ways in which different sorts of socially situated identities are called forth by the new capitalism and played out in schools and society.

This chapter has three sections. The first develops a perspective on the "new capitalism" (Drucker, 1993; Gee, Hull, & Lankshear, 1996; Greider, 1997; Rifkin, 2000) and its implications for schools, societies, and the production of "new kinds of people" (e.g., new kinds of students and workers). The second and third sections develop specific examples that are meant to help us think about some of the issues discussed in the first section as they play out in schools (the second section) and in the lives of teenagers from different socioeconomic classes (the third section). My focus throughout is on the ways in which different sorts of socially situated identities are called forth by the new capitalism and played out in schools and society.

SCHOOLS AND WORK IN THE NEW CAPITALISM

Throughout most of the 20th century, schools in the United States did an impressive job of producing workers "fit" for the sort of industrial capitalism now fast disappearing in the United States. This meant, in part, producing large numbers of students suited for industrial jobs. These jobs required relatively low-level skills and the ability to follow instructions (and, often, the ability to cope with a good deal of boredom), yet they often led to good wages, good benefits, and middle-class standing. Such jobs are rare today—and will be rarer yet tomorrow (Greider, 1997; Rifkin, 1995; Thurow, 1999)

The schools produced, as well, a much smaller number of students suited for "careers," that is, a management or professional job seen as a stable trajectory where one rose through the ranks toward the top of the hierarchy. These jobs, too, are scarce in the new capitalism, where hierarchies are flatter, people are as liable to go up as down, and people are expected to change jobs and fields several times in a lifetime. Indeed, both low- and high-level workers are now, in the new capitalism, supposed to see themselves as independent entrepreneurs, working for themselves and not for a business or institution. The business or institution now owes them no secure job. While on the job, they must be eager to stay (totally committed), but, once their project is over or times have changed, they must be ready to leave (Drucker, 1993, 1999; Gee et al., 1996; Rifkin, 2000)

Although the way in which U.S. schools managed to reproduce the class structure of industrial capitalism has been rightly bemoaned by a great many research studies, nonetheless, U.S. schools produced the most productive workers (in economic terms) in the world (Thurow, 1999). Of course, schools have always done more than produce "fit" workers and there have always been those who argued that the goals of schooling should not be defined primarily, or even at all, in economic terms. Nonetheless, it is obvious that a school system that produced unproductive workers would eventually lead to an economic system that would be unlikely to sustain schools for any higher purposes. Of course, the problem is how to produce productive workers without, at the same time, ensuring that the same sorts of people end up at the bottom and top of society (and schools have, of course, been quite poor at disentangling these two objectives).

Today we face the interesting situation that the economic system has changed. The so-called new capitalism (a global capitalism driven by scientific and technological advances) is giving rise to new categories of workers (Drucker, 1999; Gee et al., 1996; Reich, 1992). At the same time, it is rendering both traditional industrial jobs (with their relatively decent wages and benefits) and secure middle-management white-collar jobs (another source of the middle class) rarer and much less rewarding economically. The traditional middle class, largely composed of these two groups, is shrinking, whereas a group of very wealthy elites at the top (largely entrepreneurially focused) and poor (largely in service jobs) at the bottom are growing apace (Greider, 1997; Rifkin, 2000).

Brutally and oversimply, but shortly put, the new capitalism looks to be producing three sorts of jobs or work positions. At the top of the economic hourglass (remember we have a big top and a big bottom, but a smaller middle) are what Reich (1992) calls *symbol analysts*. These are the people who create, adapt, and transform knowledge and symbols, largely for entrepreneurial purposes. I have argued elsewhere (Gee, 1996) that the highest (and most rewarded) form of knowledge these people leverage is "socioctechnical design knowledge." This is knowledge that allows one to design new products, services, delivery systems, symbols, workplaces, technologies, identities, and social relationships. Such people will make up, perhaps, one fifth of a new capitalist economy.

At the bottom of the economic pyramid are the multitude of service workers, temporary workers, contract workers, manual workers, and the remaining, now often unionless, industrial workers (Drucker, 1993). I will call these people simply *service workers*, because this is what most of them are or will be. In the last several decades, the United States has been a virtual job creation machine. Unfortunately, almost all these jobs have been service jobs (Thurow, 1999).

Service workers have little sociotechnical design knowledge to sell in a knowledge economy, beyond "people skills." Because the new capitalism will only pay (well) for sociotechnical design knowledge that "adds value," service workers are poorly rewarded, unless there is nearly full employment in an economy. In the case of full employment, new capitalist leaders call for "slowing down the economy" (i.e., engaging in policies that will increase unemployment at the bottom, thereby keeping wages for service jobs low). Service workers (and others who will not get paid for value-added knowledge work) will make up something like three fifths of the new capitalist workers. Drucker (1993)—the most insightful management figure of the 20th century—has said that the fate of civil society in the United States will depend on how well we mitigate the "plight" of the hoards of poorly paid service workers the society will contain.

The middle of this new capitalist hourglass is quite strange. It is much smaller and riskier than the middle of the old capitalist pyramid. It is composed of the remaining middle managers, always at risk of being downsized or replaced by new empowered work teams supervising themselves, and white-collar workers who often now make rather poor wages. The middle—really the top of the bottom—is composed, as well, by a new category of worker that we might call *low-level technical workers* (what, elsewhere, I have referred to as "enchanted workers;" see Gee et al., 1996). These workers, working in industry and other sites, must leverage quite sophisticated technical skills—for instance, using computers and statistics in a quality control setting, and designing and redesigning their own work practices in collaborative teams. Such workers sometimes gain adequate wages, but more often they do not; instead they work for low wages and bonuses paid for greater and greater productivity (e.g., consider the workers at an electronic assembly plant described in Gee et al., 1996).

Low-level technical workers are often at risk of having their jobs disappear when technology or the state of the economy changes. Such workers have to think for themselves, be able to work collaboratively, and be able to learn to deal with technology and technical information quickly and well. At the same time, paradoxically, though they are meant to think for themselves and even leverage critical capacities to redesign their work practices, they are not supposed to challenge the basic values and ideologies of their workplaces or of the new capitalist society itself (e.g., criticize how small their pay is in comparison to the rewards flowing to stockholders).

We are all aware of the "crisis" in our schools today, spurred on by, and, in part, created by standards and testing movements in every state and by heated academic and political controversies like the current "Reading Wars" (Gee, 1999b). These crises are, as far as I am concerned, a reflection of the fact that U.S. schools are structured to produce workers, managers, and professionals for the old capitalism, when the society and the economy have changed and are demanding workers for the new capitalism. That is, to the extent that schools are today reproducing class structure, they are often reproducing the old one and not the new one. At the same time, waves of contradictory reforms are transforming schools, often leaving them unevenly caught between the old capitalism and (competing visions of) the new.

EXAMPLE: A CULTURALLY DIVERSE ELEMENTARY SCHOOL

Thus, what one sees in classrooms today is strange, transitional, and often chaotic. Nonetheless, there are indications, I think, of where we might be headed.

Let me provide an example, more to engage meditation on what might be going on than to offer any definitive analysis.

Before I develop my example, let me be quite explicit about what its point is. Schools today, under the current standards and testing regime, are engaged in sophisticated reform-driven sociotechnical designing (engineering) of environments, relationships, and people. However, schools have always been about producing different "kinds of people" (Hacking, 1986) for the larger society within which schools exist (e.g., gifted learners, good citizens, diligent workers, critical thinkers, learning-disabled students, at-risk, etc.). These kinds, of course, change over time as schools and society change. Thus, I want simply to consider an extended example from a contemporary reforming school and think about what sorts of socially situated identities or "kinds of people" (coupled with particular models of what constitutes learning) might be being produced.

Schools, as always, still engage a great deal in pedagogical practices meant largely to produce quiescent students who have basic skills and can follow orders. These pedagogies are often primarily directed at minority and poor students, although today they are often the result of standards and testing regimes. These regimes are placing forms of teacher-proof, scripted "direct instruction" (Engelmann, 1980)—originally designed for and formerly exclusively reserved for the poor—into classrooms with claims (made by people like George W. Bush and his "scientific" fellow travelers; for discussion, see Coles, 2000) that such pedagogies are for "all children." Of course, these pedagogies are often, even when intended for all, evaded by those children in private schools, magnet schools, charter schools, and wealthy suburbs (as well as by those "gifted" children who are "downstairs" in my later example).

Partly as a result of the Reading Wars and related controversies that have attempted to establish the hegemony of a certain narrow body of largely psychological-driven "scientific" research, it is common today to see in schools quite technically sophisticated and reform-driven practices used to accomplish the age-old purpose of enforcing the hidden curriculum of subjugating poor and minority children. That is, to put the matter bluntly, we are getting better and better, in a technical sense, at simultaneously skilling and deskilling poor children (i.e., they pass basic reading tests and still go on to fail in school and end up at the bottom of the society).

For example, consider the following episodes from a culturally diverse second-grade classroom in a "liberal" city with nationally ranked schools and "well-trained" teachers. This school, like many others, is strongly caught up with the current standards and testing regime. It is also a professional development school for a local university and attempts to discover and implement current best practices, especially in literacy. I choose an example that, based on my observations at the school, is typical of many interactions in the school, although of course there are exceptions.

Furthermore, it should be kept in mind that this school prides itself on its "liberal" attitude toward race and cultural diversity. However, what we are going to look at here are some moment-by-moment interactions between teacher and students, not anyone's "theories" or espoused viewpoints (which might, indeed, be quite different). This is because what I want to think about is how such moment-by-moment interactions create spaces that encourage children to become different "kinds of people"—that is, different kinds of learners.

The teacher, a White American veteran educator, is sitting at a desk with four children, while other children are working by themselves or in pairs around the room. This is a common classroom configuration today in "literacy blocks," sometimes loosely called "guided reading" (Fountas & Pinnell, 1996). The teacher dictates a sentence with the word love in it and the students write the sentence down. She then dictates a set of words, each of which the children attempt to spell. An African-American girl sitting next to the teacher spells each word as follows:

      _____*dove*_____
      _____*sume*_____*[some]*
      _____*glove*_____
      _____*one*_____
      _____*shuve*_____*[shove]*
      _____*come*_____
      _____*none*_____

The teacher then has the children correct the original sentence and then each word in the list one by one, eliciting the correct spelling of each item from the group of children. When she gets to *some*, the second word on the list, the African-American girl next to her corrects it, then notices what the pattern is and goes ahead and corrects *shuve* further down the list. The teacher stops her and sharply reprimands her, saying that they have to go "one at a time" and she should not "go ahead."

Of course, the irony here is that the whole (cognitive) point of this exercise is for the child to notice that "ove" makes up a spelling *pattern* (one that, in fact, violates a larger pattern that vowel + consonant + e usually contains a so-called "long vowel," as in *made, code,* and *tile*). Nonetheless, the teacher has clearly communicated to the student that following instructions, routines, and procedures is actually more central than the ostensible cognitive goal of the activity. Far from being praised for seeing the underlying conceptual point of the exercise, the girl is castigated.

The teacher moves on to have the small group of children engage in a "picture walk" of a book. This is an activity where children read the pictures in a book, using each picture in turn to predict what the story in the book might contain. The African-American girl bounces in her chair repeatedly, enthusiastically volunteering for each picture. The teacher tells her to calm down. The girl says, "I'm sorry, but I'm so happy!" The teacher responds, "Well, just calm down." Of course, we can note that the teacher here fails to respond to the little girl civilly in terms of the values of their shared "life world" (she would, then, have said something like, "But, oh, what happened to make you so happy?"), and responds to the girl only in terms of their formal roles as manager and controllee. The teacher also communicates to the girl that the body, happiness, and enthusiasm, as well as personal relationships between teacher and student, are not part of—and not to be recruited into or integrated with—literacy in school.

When the African-American girl takes her turns, she sometimes predicts what might be in the book by drawing inferences that go beyond the literal information given in the picture (based, e.g., on her knowledge of the title of the book, what had occurred in previous pictures, or what she thought would be in subsequent pictures). The teacher tells her to stop this, that she is only to base her predictions on what was literally in shown in the picture on the given page. At the same time, a White middle-class girl in the group several times used the words on the page to make her prediction, rather than the picture. The teacher never reprimanded her. Furthermore, even though the White girl's responses were often wrong and the African-American girl's never were, at the end of the session, the teacher turned to me and said how smart the White girl was.

As we will see further later, the ways in which this teacher produces different children as "right" or "wrong" or "smart" and "not smart" (or, as we will see, "good readers" and "not good readers") has little to do with what the children actually do from any cognitive point of view. This is despite the fact that this teacher is using curricular materials and pedagogical practices that are cognitively inspired; that is, they stem from a research-based analysis of how thinking works in spelling and reading.

The teacher then calls the next group up to the table—a "better" group of readers. This group contains four children as well. They are reading a book that says "fifth-grade level" on the spine (remember, this is a second-grade class). The book was written as if a child had written it, so some of its sentences are awkward or too short or too long. The teacher has each student in the group read a piece of the book out loud and then, orally and on the spot, "rewrite" the piece into a more adult-like form. One African-American boy, whom the teacher had told me would not talk to her except in direct response to her instructions, takes his turn and, speaking in fairly heavy African-American vernacular phonology, deftly reads a very long sentence and shortens it into three separate sentences. (There may be some connection to why this boy did not like to talk to the teacher and the fact that she had told me earlier that her "African-American students come to me with no names for things").

After being in this teacher's class, I attended the end of a class in the basement of the school. This class occurred during the same "literacy block" time I had been attending in the other classroom. Thanks to a grant, this school took from all its second grades the "best readers" and put them downstairs with a "gifted and talented" teacher during literacy block. When I entered the room, it was deadly silent, as each child worked on his or her own activity, reading a new book, writing in a journal, writing an essay comparing and contrasting two books, or writing a review of a chosen book. The teacher sat at her desk, engaged in her own writing, although children could come up to her for guidance and help. All the children were White, save one child of foreign parents, and in designer clothes and with designer haircuts. In this school, these were close to all (probably all, in fact) the White upper and middle-class children in the second grades.

The teacher, toward the end of the period, called all the children together and read them a story that she later told me was at the "fifth-grade level." It was a story about a White middle-class manager who gets downsized and loses his job (the children moan—the first noise I have heard in this classroom), but later comes into a large sum of money, in part thanks to his wife and family (the children softly cheer). This is clearly a room where the children are agents under their own steam and personally involved in the literacy practices at several different levels. These children are quite literally "sheltered" and "hidden" from the standards- and testing-driven pedagogies going on upstairs (and, thus, politicians can proudly claim these pedagogies were for "all" children in this school).

Having seen this classroom, I returned to the teacher in whose room I had been previously, struck by the fact that the last group I had seen in her room was composed of minority children reading a book that was also at the "fifth-grade level." I was particularly wondering about the African-American boy who had so deftly decomposed the sentence from a book that seemed to me much harder, in fact, than the one being read downstairs. I asked the teacher why the children in the last group were not "good readers," why they were not allowed downstairs. She said to me, "They're just *my* good readers, the ones left when they take the *real* good readers out."

So here we see that people with the same skill levels, reading equally difficult material, are constructed as different people. The African-American boy is being primed to pass the basic reading test at a high level. He is set, perhaps, to end up a technical worker at the top of the bottom of the society. The elite children downstairs are exempted from the whole standards and testing regime (so confident are the school and their parents that they will ace the test) and allowed to experience literacy as an arena of their own agency and control, integrated with their own emerging identities as members of their social class, a social class facing a risky world where only agency, self-governance, and entrepreneurial skills will keep one at the top. Their class downstairs is all about ego and identity development—the literacy and literature skills in and of themselves hardly matter. That brings me to my last example.

Of course, one can readily say (and it is true): There's nothing new here—this is just the old "hidden curriculum" game in which instructional goals are really at the service of control and domination. However, what I want to point out is that this teacher is, in fact, using practices that, from a technical point of view, are considered in current educational reform to be best practices. She is not teaching spelling as disconnected word lists; rather, she is teaching patterns that ensure children will learn to link underlying principles of decoding (going from print to sound) and spelling (going from sound to print). She is not engaged in round-robin reading; rather she is using the pictures to create the background knowledge by virtue of which both decoding and comprehension can be facilitated when the children read for meaning. She is ensuring that decoding and spelling and reading for meaning are all in the curriculum. She is, with her more advanced students, integrating oral and written skills, as well as facilitating meta-reflection on grammar and style.

This is not old-fashioned decontextualized "drill and skill." This teacher is quite sophisticated and knows very well what she is doing, at least from the point of view of current reform standards as these are driven by the current testing regime. Indeed, in this school, the teachers are hyperaware that they and their school will be judged by how well their students later do on the state's third-grade basic reading test (for which they are preparing even in second grade). So here we see quite sophisticated techniques being used to enforce the old-style hidden curriculum, but in a way that will, in fact, produce students with better basic skills, fit for service jobs or, if the child is a bit more advanced, technical jobs. However, these children (who will, indeed, pass the third-grade basic reading test) may very well not end up with a sense of agency and identity linked to and fully integrated with higher order academic (semiotic) thinking, language, and literacy skills—that is, the sorts of "skills" connected to becoming a symbol analyst.

I cannot leave this example without pointing out, as well, that when we talk about the school failure of many poor and minority children, we often talk about their lack of early school-based preparation at home or dearth of school-related experiences outside of school. However, this example shows certain forms of creativity being suppressed and certain forms of success being defined as less than fully successful. There is nothing about the "insides" (i.e., minds) of these children that is making them into students who do not belong downstairs. They are produced as such from the outside in by the systems in which they participate and the moment-by-moment interactions that (re-)produce those systems.

EXAMPLE: WORKING-CLASS AND ELITE MIDDLE SCHOOL STUDENTS

I want now to take up these sorts of issues from a different angle, by looking briefly at interviews we have conducted with middle school teenagers (13 years old, or near it on either side). Some of the teens come from working-class families in a postindustrial urban area in Massachusetts where, in fact, traditional working-class jobs are fast disappearing (and have disappeared already for many of the parents of these teens). Some come from upper middle-class families, attend elite public schools in Massachusetts suburban communities, and have parents one or both of whom are doctors, lawyers, or university professors. Our interviews ask teenagers questions about their lives, homes, communities, interests, and schools, as well as their views on issues like racism and sexism.

I briefly discuss three findings from our interviews (Gee, 1999b, 2000; Gee, Allen, & Clinton, 2001; Gee & Crawford, 1998). First, a variety of discourse analytic techniques showed us that the working-class teens fashion themselves in language in our interviews as immersed in a social, affective, dialogic world of interaction, whereas the upper middle-class teens fashion themselves as immersed in a world of knowledge, argumentation, and achievements. The working-class teens talk directly about acting and speaking in the material and social world. The upper middle-class teens, on the other hand, talk about material things and social events largely in terms of what they have to do with their own claims to knowledge, accomplishments, and achievements. Strikingly, the upper middle-class teens never mention high school (which they have not yet attended). They do, however, talk a good deal about college, in terms of where they want to go to college, what it takes to get into elite colleges, and the visits they have made to such colleges.

Let me give just one example of what I mean by saying the working-class teens were dialogically oriented, whereas the upper middle-class teens were more oriented to their trajectories through what we might call achievement space toward "success." When Sandra, a working-class girl, says things like, "I think it is good [her relationship with her boyfriend]" or "I think I should move out [of the house]," she makes clear elsewhere in her interview that other people have said they do not like her boyfriend and that there is a debate about who should move out of the house. Or, when Maria, another working-class girl, says, "I think I'm so much like a grown up," she has made it completely clear that this is a response to an ongoing struggle with her parents who will not give her the independence she wants.

On the other hand, when Emily, an upper middle-class girl, says, "I think it's okay for now [living in her current town]," nothing in her interview suggests that this is in reaction to anything anyone else has said or thought. Her interview makes clear that this is simply her assessment of where she is, at the present time, in her trajectory toward her goals for success. When Karin, another upper middle-class girl, says, "I think they [her parents] want me to be successful," nothing in her interview suggests that this is in response to any doubts or debates about the matter—far from it, because Karin, in fact, repeatedly says how supported and well understood she is by her parents.

Because I cannot here discuss much of our data, let me simply note a minor but perhaps emblematic example. An upper middle-class girl, Karin, says things like, "I *do* soccer and gymnastics and tennis" or "I *do* tennis in Holiston." Our working-class teens never use this way of talking. They use the verb *do* for jobs or work (e.g., "I do dishes"), not for play (e.g., "I play football"). In fact, our upper middle-class teens regularly talk about everything they do (traveling, playing musical instruments, camping, playing sports, engaging in hobbies, etc.) as if it was on a résumé, part of a list of achievements that will ensure admission into an elite college and success later in life.

A second finding of our interview studies is that the teens use different social languages. The working-class teens often use narrative language and, even when they do not, they often personalize their responses. On the other hand, the upper middle-class teens narrativize very little. They tend to use a less personalized language and engage more in talk that involves arguments, viewpoints, and exposition. However, it seemed to us that the upper middle-class teens often used their more expository language to distance themselves from very real personal fears and to cloak their quite personal self-interest in the social issues we were discussing with them.

For example, consider Jeremy, a working-class teen, answering a fairly abstract question. He answers in a quite personalized way. On the other hand, consider how abstractly two upper middle-class teens, Brian and Karin, answer questions about society:

Interviewer: *Is there racism [in society]?*

Jeremy: Like colored people I don't, I don't like. I don't like Spanish people most of 'em, but I like, I like some of 'em. Because like if you, it seems with them, like they get all the welfare and stuff. Well, well White people get it too and everything but, I just- And then they think they're bad and they're like- They should speak English too, just like stuff like that.

Interviewer: *Why do you think there are relatively few Hispanic and African-American doctors?*

Brian: Well, they're probably discriminated against, but, but it's not really as bad as—as people think it is, or that it once was. Because, uh, I was watching this thing on TV about this guy that's trying to- How colleges and and some schools have made a limit on how many White students they can have there, and a limit- and they've increased the limits on how many Black and Hispanic students they have to have. So, a bunch of White people (rising intonation) are getting- even if they have better grades than the Black or Hispanic student, the Black or Hispanic student gets in because they're Black or Hispanic so. So, I think that that kinda plays an effect into it.

Interviewer: *Just say that it's a really really poor neighborhood um or a ghetto school, and, um, do you feel like somebody who goes to school there would have a chance, um, to succeed or become what they want to become?*

   Karin: Not as good as they would in a good school system. It depends on- I know that they probably don't. If they don't have enough money, they might not have enough to put into the school system and not- may not be able to pay the teachers and, um, the good supplies and the textbooks and everything. So maybe they wouldn't- they probably wouldn't have the same chance. But, I believe that every person has equal chances, um, to become what they want to be.

Jeremy personalizes his response and subordinates his argumentative facts to his by no means distanced viewpoint on minorities. Brian does not, at first, seem to personalize his response in the same way. However, in an interview replete with worries about "making it" in terms of going to a top college and having a successful career, there is little doubt that Brian's response is quite personal nonetheless (note also the rising emphatic intonation on "a bunch of White people"). Although he most certainly could have stated his concerns as directly related to his own fears of affirmative action negatively impacting on his plans and desires, he chose not to.

Karin (upper middle-class), after having spent a good deal of time discussing how good her school is and how important this fact is to her future, is then asked about the connection between poor schools and success. She first offers an argument, consistent with her views on her own school and future, that such schools will lower children's chances of success. However, she then contradicts her own argument when she says that she believes that every person has equal chances to become what they want to be. Given the fact that Karin spends a great deal of her interview talking about her hopes and fears for a successful future, it is easy to interpret her remark "they probably wouldn't have the same chance" as meaning the "the same chance as *me.*" Karin's "distanced" argument has come too close to rendering the grounds of "worth" and "distinction" (of the sort she seeks) a matter of "chance," or, worse yet, injustice.

What these first two findings seem to tell us is this (and this is supported by a good deal more of our data): The upper middle-class teens use school and the activities in their out-of-school lives, as well as the school-based forms of language they are acquiring, to produce themselves as a certain kind of person. I have elsewhere called this kind of person a "portfolio person." Portfolio people are, in fact, the types of people that the new capitalism seems to demand at the top of its hourglass structure. Portfolio people view all their experiences, in and out of school (or jobs), as sources of attributes and achievements that they can place in their portfolio. In turn, they can flexibly arrange and rearrange these attributes and achievements to shape-shift themselves into ever new identities for ever new opportunities and demands as things change and they must enter new institutions, new projects, or new jobs.

Our upper middle-class teens certainly seem to view themselves as the repository of ever more achievements and accomplishments that compose their risky trajectory through achievement space. At the same time, they appear to use school-based language to render their "right" to success, and the risks they face, an impersonal and objective matter, not one rooted in social relations between the rich and poor in society.

This leads to the third finding I want to discuss. Although our upper middle-class teens show a strong belief that whatever they learn in school will someday and somewhere pay off, they appear to consume school not primarily for the information and skills they are gaining there, but to give them specific attributes they need for their "portfolios." Let me give one example of what I mean.

Five of our upper middle-class teens had the same social studies teacher, a man who taught an overtly politicized antiracist curriculum. For each of these teens, this was their favorite teacher. As Karin said, "We have learned so much and my parents always tell me how we have to learn that not everyone is just like [our town], cause it's [a] pretty sheltered town." Karin liked this teacher because "he's pretty worldly, because he lived in, um, a village in Africa for a couple of years, and then he taught in the Canary Islands for a couple years." What she values in this social studies class, it seems, is how it offers her access to "worldliness." Indeed, several of our upper middle-class teens worry about how and whether they are "worldly" enough given the "sheltered" nature of their towns (the teens use just these terms).

Another upper middle-class teenager says that in this teacher's class, "stereotypes" were "kind of a big thing that we learned about a lot this year." This teen goes on to say that he has learned that "people just have an oversimplified point of view, and judge people usually in a negative way that they shouldn't … that's what society does to certain groups of people, and which isn't fair I don't think." The social studies teacher has made it "very clear" that the students should not stereotype people, "and now, we can't call things 'weird,' we can't call them 'odd,' the word we use, have to use is 'different.' " "Different" becomes the "worldly" way to say "weird" or "odd."

Despite what this student has to say about his social studies class, much later in his interview, when he is asked about racism, he says, "There's not a lot of racism around here, but some places around the world I think there's racism." When he recalls an instance of a fellow student using a racial epithet, he says, "I mean, it's just one of those things that you don't mean to say that just happens, it's not like he's really a racist person at all." He concludes the racism topic by saying, "Particularly now, I mean, racism, it's not *that* big of a problem anymore, it's not like it's *real* big ... I think [African Americans] have a fair chance."

These students do not appear to orient their attention in this class primarily in terms of its "radical" content. They certainly do not use the course to recruit an academic social language with which to reflect on their own privileged circumstances. Rather, they appear to orient to the cultural capital the class offers them to construct themselves as "worldly people," despite their limited access to the realities of a diverse world (and they all acknowledge they have actually experienced very little cultural diversity). Ironically, the social studies teacher worried about losing his job because of how "radical" the content of his class was. He need not have worried—the content was largely irrelevant.

The upper middle-class teens, in our interviews, seem to speak out of a life world that has been deeply interpenetrated by the social languages and discourses of professional families, schools, and public sphere institutions. They already fashion themselves in terms of an (anxiety-filled) movement through achievement space wherein they accrue skills, attributes, attitudes, and achievements as capital that will make them worthy of success. We see here, I believe, children (after all, they have not yet even gone to high school) on their way to being shape-shifting portfolio people in the new capitalism.

The working-class teens, in our interviews, seem to speak out of a life world oriented toward dialogic interaction and much less interpenetrated by school-based and public sphere discourses. In other work, I have argued that this is so, in part, because they often view schools and other public sphere institutions, and sometimes the adults in their own families, as representing an "authority" that rarely seems to respond to them in affective, dialogic, or interactional ways, but mostly in terms of decontexualized facts, laws, and rules (and stand-alone literacy).

It is ironic, perhaps, that although current sociocritical efforts at school reform value an interactional, dialogic stance, often associated with the much cited Bakhtin, we find this stance primarily in our working-class teens who face a future without a stable working class. On the other hand, although current cutting-edge "thinking pedagogies" stemming from cognitive science value conceptually explicit social languages connected to academic discourses, we find such social languages used by our upper middle-class teens to distance themselves from the social, cultural, and political inequalities of our "new times" and to hold firm in their belief in their own essential merit and worth, despite their ready acknowledgment of their very privileged circumstances.

CONCLUSIONS

I have no definitive conclusions to offer. What I have attempted to do here is simply to look at two different examples through the lens of the new capitalism. I have been concerned with the ways in which the production of new kinds of people are at stake in the changing relationships among school, society, and the economy. We are living in a time of rapid change and transition. Schools are often caught in a contradiction wherein they are, on the one hand, held "accountable" for inculcating basic skills under the standards and testing regime and, on the other hand, are asked to give children the creative and adaptive critical thinking and learning-to-learn abilities suited for an age in which facts, skills, and information all go quickly out of date. Amidst these tensions and contradictions, we cannot so much draw firm conclusions as begin to think about the parameters and directions of change in progress.

A theme of this volume has been the multiple links between theory and practice. Indeed, in this chapter I have argued that there is a divide between our theories about how the world is changing and the practices in our schools. As the testing and accountability regime grows ever stronger—under the impetus of policies like the No Child Left Behind legislation—this divide becomes stronger and stronger. Families who can find spaces where the divide is mitigated—either inside elite school programs or in high status programs outside of schools—benefit their children. Families who cannot do not. We literacy researchers can begin to deconstruct this divide and the ways in which it systematically disadvantages some children only by paying a good deal more attention to the relationship between schools and our changing society.

James Paul Gee is the Tashia Morgridge Professor of Reading at the University of Wisconsin at Madison. He is the author of *Social Linguistics and Literacies* (Falmer Press, 1990/1996), *The Social Mind: Language, Ideology, and Social Practice* (Bergin & Garvey, 1992), and *An Introduction to Discourse Analysis* (Routledge, 1999), among other books.

REFERENCES

Coles, G. (2000). *Misreading reading: The bad science that hurts children.* Portsmouth, NH: Heinemann.

Drucker, P. F. (1993). *Post-capitalist society.* New York: Harper Business.

Drucker, P. F. (1999). *Management challenges for the 21st century.* New York: Harper Business.

Engelmann, S. (1980). *Direct instruction.* Englewood Cliffs, NJ: Prentice Hall.

Fountas, I. C., & Pinnell, G. S. (1996). *Guided reading: Good first teaching for all children.* Portsmouth, NH: Heinemann.

Gee, J. P. (1996). On mobots and classrooms: The converging languages of the new capitalism and schooling. *Organization, 3,* 385–407.

Gee, J. P. (1999a). *An introduction to discourse analysis: Theory and method.* London: Routledge.

Gee, J. P. (1999b). Reading and the new literacy studies: Reframing the National Academy of Sciences report on reading. *Journal of Literacy Research, 31,* 355–374.

Gee, J. P. (2000). Teenagers in new times: A new literacy studies perspective. *Journal of Adolescent and Adult Literacy, 43,* 412–420.

Gee, J. P., Allen, A., & Clinton, K. (2001). Language, class, and identity: Teenagers fashioning themselves through language. *Linguistics and Education, 12,* 175–194.

Gee, J. P., & Crawford, V. (1998). Two kinds of teenagers: Language, identity, and social class. In D. Alverman, K. Hinchman, D. Moore, S. Phelps, & D. Waff (Eds.), *Reconceptualizing the literacies in adolescents' lives* (pp. 225–245). Mahwah, NJ: Lawrence Erlbaum Associates.

Gee, J. P., Hull, G., & Lankshear, C. (1996). *The new work order: Behind the language of the new capitalism.* Boulder, CO: Westview.

Greider, W. (1997). *One world, ready or not: The manic logic of global capitalism.* New York: Simon & Schuster.

Hacking, I. (1986). Making up people. In T. C. Heller, M. Sosna, & D. E. Wellbery, with A. I. Davidson, A. Swidler, & I. Watt (Eds.), *Reconstructing individualism: Autonomy, individuality, and the self in Western thought* (pp. 222–236). Stanford, CA: Stanford University Press.

Reich, R. B. (1992). *The work of nations.* New York: Vintage.

Rifkin, J. (1995). *The end of work: The decline of the global labor force and the dawn of the post-market era.* New York: Putnam.

Rifkin, J. (2000). *The age of access: The new culture of hypercapitalism where all of life is a paid-for experience.* New York: Jeremy P. Tarcher/Putnam.

Thurow, L. C. (1999). *Building wealth: The new rules for individuals, companies, and nations in a knowledge-based economy.* New York: HarperCollins.

Globalization on the Border: Reimagining Economies, Identities, and Schooling in El Paso

Char Ullman
University of Arizona

El Paso, Texas, was once a hub of the booming U.S. garment industry. However, when the North American Free Trade Agreement (NAFTA) made worldwide cheap labor easily available, the low-cost labor of El Paso lost out to the slave wages of Indonesia and Guatemala. Now there are 26,000 displaced workers in this city of 700,000 who are hoping to become retrained for the global economy. Most of the laid-off workers are Mexican-American women in midlife. This study compares two educational venues for learning English and retraining, highlighting the reproduction of inequality at one school and the possibilities of a more liberatory approach at the other. Data were collected through interviewing, participant observation, and document analysis. Analyzing the data through a feminist postcolonial lens, I seek to clarify the position of education in the global economy, and contribute to the struggles of people who refuse to let globalization determine the course of their lives.

In 1910, a visiting reporter who observed El Paso's burgeoning industries and its strategic importance as a railroad hub commented that the Texas city was a "strong and hardy, pushing city bound to be the Chicago of the Southwest" (Luckingham, 1982, p. 35). El Paso is at a crossroads that cities like Chicago have come to: the reimagining of its economic base in light of globalization, specifically the loss of manufacturing jobs in an increasingly service-oriented economy. Along with economic revitalization, the two cities have something else in common: a long history of educational inequity that has circumscribed the economic options of minoritized peoples, benefited majority populations, and shaped the parameters of identity for everyone involved. However, the similarities probably stop there, because El Paso and its sister city Ciudad Juarez, Mexico, comprise the largest international community along the Mexico–U.S. border. It is a *frontera* between nations, cultures, languages, and economies, and it is its own border world, which is in many ways a microcosm of relations between Mexico and the United States.

This chapter explores the effects of globalization on Mexican-American women in El Paso. Data were gathered in the summer of 1998, but I was fortunate to have spent 9 months previous to this study conducting research on a related topic in El Paso via telephone interviews and archival research.[1] This confluence of interests deepened my knowledge of El Paso's economic and cultural context.

Situated in the traditions of Bowles and Gintis (1976) and Willis (1977), this study focuses on the reproduction of social class through education. It also owes much to Levinson, Foley, and Holland (1996), who explore resistance within the reproduction framework, and to Suárez-Orozco (2001) and Yon (2000), who expand cultural reproduction to include globalization. Like Suárez-Orozco (2001), I see globalization as a process of change resulting in "the deterritorialization of important economic, social, and cultural practices from their traditional moorings in the nation state" (p. 347).

In this case study, I explore how social identities are reproduced through schooling, along with the individual and collective acts of resistance that continue to make schools places of possibility and change. I interviewed 14 Spanish-speaking women (in Spanish), observed English as a Second Language (ESL) classes at two separate schools (one with multiple sites), and conducted interviews with program directors and teachers. I also collected program documents from each school, triangulating data to understand the multiple perspectives involved. I came to this work as an interpreter (Stake, 1995, p. 97), with the goal of understanding the complex dynamics in El Paso, and with a personal history in adult education as an ESL teacher.

THE EFFECTS OF NAFTA

In the early 1990s, with the enactment of the North American Free Trade Agreement (NAFTA), the garment industry began to leave El Paso. Many companies moved operations to Central and South America, while others went to China and

---

[1]This project was funded by the Southwest Institute for Research on Women (SIROW), Tucson, Arizona.

Southeast Asia. Still others moved 100 yards across the international bridge, into Ciudad Juárez, Chihuahua; this meant factories that had paid workers up to $10 an hour in El Paso could offer as little as $1 an hour on the other side of the bridge. Before NAFTA, El Paso had been home to garment manufacturers such as Farah, Sun Apparel, Aquatech, Stephanie Fashions, and Levi-Strauss, along with numerous small apparel companies. There also were legions of small businesses that supported the garment industry, such as laundries, presses, and thread and button companies. Today, virtually all of these companies have closed their doors. NAFTA's effects have extended beyond the garment industry, as well. Other plant closings in El Paso have included Hasbro, Johnson & Johnson, Alcoa, and the large copper company ASARCO. The list goes on and on. In this city of only 700,000 people, there are more than 26,000 displaced workers who have been certified as NAFTA-affected. El Paso is the most NAFTA-impacted location in the United States.

Statistics collected by the Texas Workforce Commission offer a perspective on what plant closings have meant for workers. El Paso's job loss rate in 1999 averaged 200 jobs per week. Fully 97% of the workers who lost their jobs were Latina or Latino, and two thirds were women. Of those women, one third were single heads of households.[2] Most of the women were 45 years of age or older, and had not attended school since the sixth grade in Mexico. The vast majority were monolingual Spanish speakers.

For people who have had little experience with formal education, the challenge of returning to school after many years can be great. Simply being in a classroom is often an anxiety-producing experience for those who have spent most of their lives outside this context. Because the skills people acquire to function in life are not the skills that tend to be valued in school, returning to school can be an intimidating experience, invalidating established identities (Wrigley & Guth, 1992). Many of the women told me that ageism as well as racism and sexism were palpable realities in their work lives. Once they meet their educational goals, which for many of them included learning English and earning a general education diploma (GED),[3] the promise of a job and the ability to again support themselves and their children is by no means assured.

---

[2]Unfortunately, the operational definition of "single head of household" makes invisible any intentionally nontraditional families, specifically those reconfigured because of economic need or queerness.

[3]A GED is an alternative to a high-school diploma, which is available to those who are not able to finish high school while still in their teens.

PERSPECTIVES ON WOMEN'S WORK

Mohanty (1997) points out that women's work in "third world" contexts is often consciously conceived by multinational corporations as "supplemental" (without benefits), because their real work is conceived as childrearing. The work that Mohanty describes—female lacemakers in Narsapur, India, and East Asian women who work in the electronics industry in the Silicon Valley—is full time, and most of the women who work these jobs are the main breadwinners in their families. However, patriarchal ideologies of heterosexual womanhood are incorporated into a capitalist agenda that allows corporations to label women's work as lesser. In this way, corporations can maximize profit by devaluing women's labor in ways that are supported by local cultural norms.

Because garment manufacturers in El Paso treated workers, both male and female, in a range of ways, it would be difficult to say, based on the data, that these particular ideologies were at play in El Paso as clearly as they were in the scenarios Mohanty (1997) highlights. However, I do argue that media inattention to the effects of NAFTA on the border as opposed to its effects on auto workers in the midwestern United States, for example, is evidence of a combination of hegemonic processes. The marginalization of Latina and Latino workers, many of whom are perceived to be undocumented (which is not the case for workers laid off from the garment industry), is evidence of nationalist ideologies that dismiss them as not being "real" Americans. Another factor is that hegemonic gender ideologies combine with nationalist projects to portray women's labor as less important than men's.

The auto industry, which has for years symbolized individual freedom and capitalist innovation in the United States, was portrayed nostalgically by the mainstream media. It was seen by many as a historic relic that had to be left behind to make way for progress—high-tech innovations. On the other hand, the experiences of Mexican-American women who sew jeans, a symbol of America's working class and industrial past, has been broadly ignored. This view of history moves from one technical innovation (the assembly line in Detroit) to another (Microsoft in Seattle). The reality is that women's work, along with the work of Latino men, is made mostly invisible. For Mexican-American women, this results in a doubly deepened obscurity. However, in spite of this marginalization, the work of Mexican-American women has been central to the development of capitalism in the United States.

LANGUAGE IDEOLOGIES ON THE BORDER

Although accurate descriptive statistics have been hard to come by in the area of language proficiency, the vast majority of women in El Paso who have been laid off from the garment industry are Spanish speakers who speak little English. Teachers and administrators have reported anecdotally that some students in the dislocated worker programs speak Spanish as a second language and come from Indigenous-language backgrounds, but no systematic study of language background has yet been conducted. The federal monies available for worker retraining have been used to combine English, job skills, and GED classes. Given the fact that these funds are available for 24 months and that most workers are not literate in Spanish, it could take years for them to learn enough English to study for the GED.

Educators and politicians alike stress the importance of learning English for the El Paso workforce. The President of the El Paso Chamber of Commerce has stated that for the city's economy to shift from manufacturing to a service base, as the rest of the country allegedly has, employees need to speak English (Victor Grado, personal communication, May 17, 1999). Although there is a certain amount of logic to this claim, I suggest that there are two more foundational motives beneath this view.

The first reason has to do with linguistic imperialism. Because El Paso has historically been a place where U.S. companies have sought cheap, Mexican, manual labor, the nationalist project, which involves Americanizing the populace through the teaching of English, has not been a priority here. Mexican Americans in El Paso have not needed to become assimilated Americans, because they were more useful to U.S. companies as Mexican laborers who happened to work in U.S. factories. This was true until NAFTA put El Paso into the larger global market. What was once cheap labor for U.S. industry is now in the midrange compared to wages throughout Latin America, China, and Southeast Asia.

The push to teach English is clearly correlated with globalization. Phillipson (1992) argues that English-speaking countries have specific policies to encourage the spread of English internationally. Phillipson notes that there are links between the development of English as an international language and the development of global markets; he also sees a connection between the development of those global markets and U.S. policies for teaching English to immigrant populations. Pennycook (1994) researches this ideology in the publications of the British Council, where imperial sentiments like the following are commonly expressed: "Teaching the world English may appear not unlike an extension of the task which America faced in establishing English as a common national language among its own immigrant population" (British Council Annual Report, cited in Pennycook, 1994, p. 22).

The recent emphasis on English language teaching in El Paso is temporally linked to the trade tariff changes of NAFTA, which led U.S. companies to move operations involving manual labor abroad. On the U.S. side of the border, this has meant higher job standards for manual laborers in El Paso. The ability to speak English, along with a GED, are now required, even though the new service industry has not yet made a dent in El Paso's unemployment rate, which vacillates between 9% and 14%. For people who need jobs immediately to survive, the prospect of spending 2 or 3 years learning English is not a particularly salient choice. However, government benefits do accompany this course of study. As minimal and precarious as they are, they are better than no income at all.

Why have government officials decided that learning English will "retool" this workforce? Given the fact that most of El Paso's laid-off workers are middle aged and have little experience with formal education, it is unlikely that they will be able to apply for jobs that require high levels of English anytime soon. Perhaps the real goal of federal funding for these women to attend school has to do with linguistic imperialism, which has made government officials recommend the study of English over other more quickly attainable skills for this populace (e.g., technical training).

A second reason is that the federally financed study of English in adult education keeps thousands and thousands of El Pasoans out of the job market. It puts their job-seeking on hold until local and federal officials can attract new businesses and develop a different economic base. As children see their parents and grandparents fall deeper and deeper into poverty, all the while being told that they cannot find work until they learn to speak English, the fear of not speaking English—or of speaking Spanish—is powerfully transmitted to the next generation. Educational policy is always connected to national economic plans, but El Pasoans are now feeling more than that. They live with the wildly unpredictable effects of the global economy on their everyday lives.

BORDER IDENTITIES

Soy *un amasamiento*, I am an act of kneading, of uniting and joining that not only has produced both a creature of darkness and a creature of light, but also a creature that questions the definitions of light and dark, and gives them new meanings. (Anzaldúa, 1987, p. 81)

Anzaldúa's (1987) powerful vision of living with many identities, between worlds and between languages on the U.S.–Mexico border, is at once physical, psychological, and deeply metaphoric. She reminds us that "the struggle has always been inner, and is played out in the outer terrains" (p. 87). Awareness of oppression must precede inner change, which for her, precedes social change. Because "nothing happens in the 'real' world unless it first happens in the images in our heads" (Anzaldúa, 1987, p. 87), Anzaldúa's task is to build yet another bridge: that between the intrapsychic and the social worlds.

The poetry of Anzaldúa's (1987) theory has much in common with Bhabha's vision of the *third space*. He defines the third space as a postcolonial place or a hybrid culture with the potential to "displace the histories that constitute it, and set up new structures of authority, new political initiatives, which are inadequately understood through received wisdom" (Rutherford, 1990, p. 211). Seen through the eyes of both theorists, El Paso is not the meeting ground of two distinct cultures, but a space of ambiguity and possibility that brings into question the common categories used to explain the world. It is a place where the struggles of global capitalism, racism, sexism, and ageism play out though external and internal processes.

If the transformative images of Anzaldúa's *masa* and Bhabha's third space are metaphoric representations of border identities, then it is useful to consider them in relation to theories of physical place and identity. Crow (1996) writes that "place can be seen among other constitutive representations of identity" (p. 3). He argues that identity cannot be reduced to social relations in general, and that " 'land' gives the notion of place a seemingly irreducible materiality" (p. 3). Remembering place and grounding metaphors of border identity in the physical border itself is essential. Although *borderlands* refers broadly to the dislocation of modernism, for El Pasoans, the border is both metaphorical and highly physical. Poverty is a reality on the border,[4] as is the increasing military presence on the U.S. side, which means, among other things, that Mexican Americans are typically mistaken for undocumented migrants by the border patrol. Dunn (1996) has documented the "low-intensity conflict doctrine" (p.

---

[4]Poverty among Mexican Americans in El Paso, the majority of the population, reached 43% throughout the 1980s (Dunn, 1996, p. 161), only to increase exponentially throughout the 1990s and into 2000. In 2001, more than 50% of El Paso's Spanish speakers were unemployed.

176) that has grown out of immigration and drug enforcement policies on the border. The result of these militarization efforts has been the social control of Mexican Americans on the border along with serious and repeated human rights abuses (Dunn, 1996).

Many of the women I interviewed expressed strong feelings about the land of the border and what it meant for them to continue living there. A number of them told me that they were advised by their NAFTA case workers to either return to Mexico and work for extremely low wages, or move further north in the United States. However, moving was not an option that any of the women I spoke with had entertained. Even though one employer, Levi-Strauss and Company, had offered relocation benefits after closing its plants, none of the interviewees said they had ever considered moving. Although kinship ties and social networks extend into Ciudad Juárez, their children are in El Paso. Even though work is hard to come by in El Paso, for these women whose families migrated from Mexico to find work, putting their feet down and refusing to move at the urgings of corporations or governments is a commitment to their identities, to their sense of place. In this postcolonial context, it constitutes an act of self-determination.

As NAFTA continues to threaten border identities in El Paso, how has it affected Mexican citizens in Ciudad Juárez? Even though the life has been drained from El Paso's economy, the *maquila* system in Juárez, as well as its population of some 3 million, has grown exponentially. That growth has brought with it a great increase in social, economic, and environmental problems that affect both sides of the border. Established by the Mexican government almost 30 years ago to bring foreign manufacturing plants to the area, the *maquiladoras* are assembly-line plants that dominate the border; the *Twin Plant News* reports that as of late 1998, there were 2,839 of them ("Maquila Scoreboard," 1998, p. 45). The maquiladoras once employed Mexican workers from the border region and southern Mexico, but since NAFTA they have begun to employ residents from both sides of the border as well, with an estimated 2,000 U.S. citizens working in maquilas in Juárez (Ortiz, 1999). Most of those workers are highly skilled—engineers, plant managers, and accountants. There are no job prospects for El Pasoans who want to return to Mexico to work in low-skilled jobs. That work is done by Juárez residents and migrants from southern Mexico. If one thing is certain, it is that the border is ambiguous and its multiple meanings are continually in flux. It is a place of change, as well as possibility.

A BRIEF HISTORY OF SCHOOLING INEQUITIES
IN EL PASO

Working-class Mexican-American women in El Paso have a long history of gendered employment that easily dates to the turn of the 20th century, if not before. Historically, most Mexican-American women who worked outside the home were domestics or washerwomen in White households. In the late 19th century, the garment industry began to employ Mexican women, but at significantly lower wages than White women were paid (García, 1981). By the 1970s, Mexican-American women came to dominate in this industry, with low wages still a defining characteristic.

The El Paso public school system has played an important role in the production of Mexican women and men to work as laborers in area corporations. From the start, public schools in El Paso refused to educate Spanish-speaking children. In 1892, an elderly Spaniard started a school for Mexican children, the Mexican Preparatory School, which prepared Spanish-speaking children to enter public school in English. Although this school was a great advance, as it meant the difference between nothing and something, its influence was limited. After the death of founder Olivas V. Aoy just 3 years after the school's inception, it was turned over to the public school system. By 1887, it had more than 200 students and only three teachers (García, 1981). García (1981) has written that "ironically, it graduated few Mexicans to other public schools ... because despite new knowledge of English, most Mexican children had to seek work after the early grades to augment the family income" (p. 111).

Although the 1954 *Brown v. Board of Education* decision has improved this intense level of school segregation, Mexican Americans are still more likely to attend overcrowded schools with poor resources than are their White counterparts (Arias, 1986; Rumberger, 1991). The public schools in El Paso, like those throughout the country that serve predominantly Latina and Latino, African-American, Native American, and other minoritized peoples, have focused on manual education and the production of servile workers. Historically, the curricula for Mexican Americans in El Paso centered on carpentry, sewing, laundering, and domestic science, as well as Americanization (García, 1981, p. 112).

On the border, the cultural production of the docile manual laborer has long taken precedence over the production of educated Americanized citizens. This reality has helped El Pasoans maintain linguistic identities, but continued their economic and cultural domination. In this place where "first" and "third" world economies meet, capitalism and nationalism are closely aligned. Gellner (1997) offers the reminder that nationalism can be a kind of "collective forgetting" and an "erasure of ethnic origins." (p. 45). This process toward national unity through collective forgetting has not been a priority in El Paso until now. Because El Pasoans are no longer among the lowest paid workers American businesses can find, they are available to be included in the national project. Auerbach (1993) notes that Americanization or the inculcation of immigrants into the culture of the nation-state is central to the history of language education in the United States and abroad. When and where Americanization is employed is closely aligned with the politics of globalization. Although childhood education for Mexican-American youth has been influenced by federal mandates removing the curricular focus on manual education, adult education has stepped in to fill that void. Adult education programs offer important learning environments for many people, while they also have continued the tradition of curricula that emphasizes the production of gendered, servile workers, but at a different point in the life span. For Mexican immigrants, many of whom have limited schooling in Mexico, entering this educational and economic environment is similar to growing up in El Paso before desegregation.

What are adult educators to do? Adult learners commonly go to school to get better jobs. Because their education in childhood was often limited or interrupted, there is foundational learning in literacy, language, and general education that needs to be resumed for them to develop the job skills they often desperately need. Time and money are constant constraints. In this chapter, I compare interviews with and observations of Mexican-American women in two adult education settings. They are El Paso Adult Learning (EPAL), a large, multisite publicly and privately funded adult education program, and Trabajadoras Unidas, a school at a small, grant-funded advocacy organization for Mexican and Mexican-American women in the garment industry (all names are pseudonyms).

EPAL offers courses in ESL, basic literacy in Spanish and English, and GED. It also offers workforce training and development for those who are unemployed or underemployed. With classes offered on five campuses and seven community locations, it is the largest adult school in El Paso. However, EPAL appears to be conflicted about serving the needs of workers it terms "precollege" students. Because El Paso has been certified as a NAFTA-affected city, federal and state funds are available to retrain dislocated workers, and EPAL has developed courses accordingly. Each student is supposed to receive educational funding for 18 to 24 months, although red tape has made that untrue for many. Given that a high percentage of women laid off from the garment industry have limited schooling, the funding for their retraining is minimal, and the employment outlook for El Paso is grim, attending EPAL does not offer much social or human capital.[5] Women typically use their NAFTA retraining funds for workplace ESL, in courses such as "Bilingual Basic Care Attendant" and "Bilingual Childcare Worker." Men tend to take "Bilingual Plastic Injection Molding Operator" and "Bilingual Basic Electricity."

Although politicians discuss the learning of English as an educational prerequisite for the new kinds of jobs that El Paso hopes to attract, this idea is in sharp contrast with everyday reality. The Mexican-American women who have been laid off from factory jobs as a result of NAFTA are being retrained to perform a new incarnation of the same jobs they and their ancestors have done in El Paso for more than 100 years—domestic work. This work, which is lower paid and less secure than the factory work they had been doing, has been transformed from private employment in the homes of the wealthy to the public arena of child care. An important difference, however, is that now the children who are being cared for are not only those from upper and middle-class White families, but also those from middle- and working-class Mexican-American families.

Even though child care has a history of servitude in El Paso, the reality is that El Paso has the second youngest population in the United States, and child care is a much-needed service that is used mostly by working-class, Spanish-speaking families. Ironically, English is now a requirement for women who want to work in child care, even if they are caring for Spanish-speaking children in their own neighborhood. The state has stepped into this once private sphere and made it a site of Americanization.

As the women enrolled in workplace ESL classes at EPAL make clear, there are institutional barriers that make learning English profoundly challenging there. El Paso is a city in economic transition, so it is difficult to know what kinds of jobs will be available in the future. It is also difficult for EPAL, as an

---

[5]Social capital is "the aggregate of the actual or potential resources which are linked to possession of a durable network of more or less institutionalized relationships of mutual acquaintance or recognition" (Bourdieu, 1986, p. 248). It is the relationships that lead to increased wealth or status. Human capital (Coleman, 1988) is the marketable skills one possesses. In the El Paso economy, gaining human capital is a long-term endeavor for dislocated workers.

institution, to know just how to educate people for work. Because the educational and economic realms of this city are in such flux, it is not surprising that students have expressed feelings of tension and anxiety as they talk about schooling, work, and their future.

When NAFTA made it possible for corporations to look outside the United States in their quest for cheap labor, the goals of nationalism, specifically the teaching and learning of English, replaced the need to produce manual laborers through schooling. However, the promise that learning English would lead to employment in a service industry that was just around the corner appears difficult to fulfill. Reproductive educational forces have shaped El Paso's educational system for hundreds of years. If schools like EPAL do nothing but continue to educate learners the way they always have, no matter how many moments of exemplary teaching happen, social inequality is necessarily reproduced.

This is how it works: EPAL is inundated with laid-off workers looking to retrain, and there are insufficient numbers of qualified teachers available. This means that less-than-qualified-teachers are hired, and they use curricula that does not fit students' developmental or workplace needs, because they do not have the time or funding to mold programs specifically for these students and their employment needs, which may change from day to day. In this situation, student success is unlikely. Educational funds provided for NAFTA-affected workers emphasize student achievement (attainment of high levels of English proficiency or a GED) without funding the educational infrastructure. This means students' failure is reinscribed, and as Bourdieu says, "history turns into nature" (cited in Luykx, 1999, p. 103).

The result is that workers are kept out of the job market for a longer period of time, and when they attempt to reenter the workforce, their inability to find jobs can be attributed to their lack of school success as individuals alone, not taking systemic barriers into account. Inadequately funded adult education programs then become a way for the city or the nation-state to dispose of people, specifically Mexican-American women in midlife, who do not fit its vision of the prosperous service industry that El Paso hopes to attract.

STORIES FROM EPAL

The 12 women I interviewed at two sites of EPAL had been laid off from the garment industry and were receiving federal dollars for retraining through a $45-million economic development grant that the city of El Paso received from the U.S. Department of Labor. All had been unemployed for more than 1 year, and had been surviving on a combination of NAFTA and unemployment benefits—usually $140 a week. Most had never before received government assistance, and were unhappy about doing so. Everyone had problems receiving checks and getting the correct amount they were due.

Amparo was 44 at the time we talked, and she was born in Juárez. After working at Sun Apparel for 18 years, eventually bringing home $9.10 an hour with benefits, she found herself in a 9-month program to earn a certificate that would allow her to work in child care. As a child care provider, the most she could expect to earn was $5.15 an hour without benefits. Without health insurance, she had been unable to afford hormone replacement therapy, and she explained that without this treatment, she had trouble sleeping, headaches, and memory loss. "El entranimiento," she said, "es mucho estress. No puedo recordar nada [The training is a lot of stress. I can't remember anything]." There was no time for studying, she explained, because "el tiempo para estudiar es despues de cocinar, cuidar los ninos, limpiar ropa, casa ... no *hay* tiempo [the time for studying comes after cooking, taking care of the children, washing the clothes, cleaning the house ... there *is* no time]." Although the life responsibilities of all adult learners make their study in adult education programs an arduous journey, it is especially difficult for people like Amparo, for whom there is no illusion that this great sacrifice will yield even a fraction of the economic security she once enjoyed.

Another woman, Irma, worked at Tony Lamas, a boot manufacturer, for 8 years, and had been unemployed for a little over 2 years. A native El Pasoan, she was 36, and the single mother of a 4-year-old son. Then in a Level 3 (of four) ESL class, Irma's recounting of her classroom experiences at EPAL was especially graphic. In one course, she explained that the teacher brought a large rubber ball to class, and "Jugamos con una pelota, cada clase, sin *una* palabra de inglés [We played ball during each and every class, without speaking a word of English]." In another class, she noted that "El maestro ecribió por el pizarrón en ingles. Puro ingles. Y salió sin decir nada." She explained that this teacher would write on the board in English, and then leave without a word, leaving the class to their own devices for 3 hours. "Fue difícile, pero me aguantó." It was difficult, she said, but "I endured it." At the time of this study, she was enrolled in her third ESL class, explaining in Spanish that she still spoke no English. In this course, she noted that the students were at very different levels, and the teacher seemed unable to teach a multilevel class. Her feeling was that she had not learned what she needed to learn and again, her English instruction had not been useful to her.

Compared to what other women reported to me, Irma's experiences were not uncommon. What is uncommon, however, was Irma's conclusion that her failure to learn English was the fault of her teachers. Most of the other women I interviewed, all of whom were older than Irma, said their teachers were good, but that their study of English was very stressful. They talked about their inability to remember words and to stay awake in class. Irma saw that her classes did not give her what she needed, and said that she complained to the coordinator. She told me the coordinator urged her to "give the teachers a chance" and that certain teachers were "going through hard times." I should mention that of three ESL classes I was scheduled to observe, only one was "observable." By that I mean that when I arrived at the other two, despite my protests, the teachers turned the classes over to me for interviews, and promptly left the premises for the duration of the class, some 3 hours. When I asked Irma why she was studying English, she said "para defenderme en inglés [to defend myself in English]." Perhaps there is a sad irony in the fact that her efforts to learn English at EPAL have allowed her to exercise her skills in self-defense, but they have not led to her learning English.

Bourdieu and Passeron (1990) discuss the need to let go of "the illusion of the neutrality and independence of the school system with respect to the structure of class relations" (p. 141), and the data presented here seem to offer a fairly salient example of their interrelatedness. However, Bourdieu's framework offers little possibility of variations within class, or along the lines of race, gender, or ethnicity. If anything, these data highlight the interplay between these various aspects of identity and the ways in which they shape everyday practice. I would argue, along with Mohanty (1997), that our naturalized assumptions about work and the worker are essential to understanding the sexual and ethnic politics of global capitalism. She notes that global assembly lines are as much about the production of people as they are about providing jobs or even making profit. It would follow then, that school systems interact with the economic and social needs of capitalism, and that this very much involves distinctions along the lines of gender, race, ethnicity, age, and sexuality, as well as more situated locations of class.

It would seem that the history of education for many working-class Mexican-American people in El Paso has centered on the ways in which educational systems have constructed them as menial laborers, from childhood through middle age. Because cheap Mexican labor has historically been the reason most companies moved to this border town, those same companies were invested in their workers not acquiring the cultural and linguistic capital of the middle class.[6] Even though these companies have left the area, these ideologies remain salient. Politicians, businesses, and schools such as EPAL continue to be a part of the reinscription of these ideologies. EPAL is not unlike many underfunded, understaffed adult education programs across the country. When many teachers work part time and do not have opportunities for meaningful professional development, and when the courses reproduce the stereotypes of the Mexican as menial worker, social roles are inevitably replicated. At the same time, there are always dedicated teachers and administrators who do their best within these constraints, and EPAL is no exception. The administrators there have a strong commitment to social justice. However, because the problem is systemic, their best efforts do little to alter this endless reproduction. Teaching practices and social conditions that maintain the status quo are institutionalized, and students' lack of achievement is blamed on their essential unteachability (Mehan, 1996). The political, economic, educational, and social structures that have co-constructed these "failures" remain invisible.

The continued nonachievement of these students is then used to naturalize racist stereotypes, a process of colonial discourse that Bhabha (1994) calls *fixity*, fixing the colonized subject in time, leaving the colonizer free to change and grow. EPAL can be understood to have responded adeptly to El Paso's changing economy with courses tailored for their students' new needs. However, given the economic, cultural, and social climate, it does not matter. Students are seen as unable and unwilling to learn English, just as they have been for more than 100 years.

STORIES FROM TRAJABADORAS UNIDAS

Fortunately, this kind of structured inequality is continually contested by people in El Paso, both individually and collectively. An advocacy organization, Trabajadoras Unidas (Women Workers United), has established a school based on Freirian (1970; Freire & Macedo, 1987) and cooperative learning principles (Kagan, 1992) that seems to be successfully breaking some of these ideological and practical barriers through its courses on English and entrepreneurship. Trabajadoras Unidas was founded in 1981 in response to two brands of oppression within organized labor. The first focused on the xenophobia of the American Federation of Labor local, which rallied against companies hir-

---

[6]Cultural capital is the cultural background and preferences handed down from one generation to another (Bourdieu & Passeron, 1990, p. 30). Linguistic capital is the language, accent, and register passed down the same way (Bourdieu, 1977, p. 651).

ing foreign laborers, and the second was the sexism within the Union of Needletrades, Industrial and Textile Employees (UNITE), which ignored the specific problems of woman workers. Trabajadoras Unidas is an organization that embodies the kind of border identity that Anzaldúa (1987) describes. Although it is not technically a labor union, it is a nonprofit organization dedicated to the empowerment of women in the garment industry. It is also a major player in the local political scene. The activism of Trabajadoras Unidas brought national attention to the crisis on the border in 1997 when organization members occupied the offices of the Texas Workforce Commission and blocked traffic on the international bridge for a day. These actions eventually led to the city of El Paso receiving a $45-million grant for economic development from the U.S. Department of Labor.

Trabajadoras Unidas works from a Spanish-speaking immigrant base, organized through a workers' center. It focuses on seven areas in the creation of sustainable communities: employment, health care, peace, education, nutrition, housing, and political participation. With the help of local and national grant funding, the organization has advocated for women working in and dislocated from the garment industry since its inception in 1981. Led by Chicana and White women,[7] Trabajadoras Unidas recently opened a school to allow dislocated women workers (and some men), to use their federal educational benefits in an environment in which they are constructed as powerful and capable people. Trabajadoras Unidas classes are part of a mission to create sustainable communities. The all-day class session I observed was conducted bilingually, by two female facilitators, one Latina and one White. It was a window into one module of an integrated curricula that is a situated reworking of a microenterprise ESL program for adults. This particular module dealt with the skills needed to plan and present a conference on microenterprise. There were three groups, and one worked on planning a binational conference, another on a national conference, and the last, on a local conference. All of the modules deal with skills for starting a small business and community-based organizing and development. By the end of this intensive 12- to 18-month course, students created a business plan that allowed them to apply for small-business loans. Although each student wants her or his business to be successful, an equally important goal to the teachers and members of Trabajadoras Unidas is for students to develop a sense of how they can work cooperatively as small business

---

[7]Knowing that these terms (along with others I use, such as Mexican American) have contingent and ambigious borders, like all aspects of identity, I use them to situate rather than define the participants.

people. For Trabajadoras Unidas, having a thriving business is just as important as creating livable communities. The tension between these individual and collective goals in the classroom is what one teacher described as "a meeting of the contradictions of the organization: resistance versus self-sufficiency."

In the first activity I observed, students used computers to write letters to local, state, and national representatives about their needs as dislocated workers, urging them to increase funding for NAFTA benefits. Each of the 16 students sat in front of a computer, with teachers circulating and offering suggestions. Students consulted with and advised each other, mostly in Spanish and sometimes in English, about the content and language of their letters. I asked one woman why she was studying English, and she responded, "Para hacer negocios" [to have a business]. This response offers a stark contrast to Irma's need for self-defense in English at EPAL.

Later, students divided into three previously established groups based loosely on the kinds of businesses they were planning to start. One group was for people starting child care centers, and another was for merchants. One person in the merchant group planned to have a Mexican imports store, another was preparing to run a candy shop, and another was a cabinetmaker. They all planned to sell their wares in a collective center that they were planning to create that would be oriented toward tourists and the local community, called *El Mercado del Pueblo*. The third group was comprised of people whose future businesses had no particular logical connection—the categories included home health care, restaurants, and bakeries—but because of the class size, three groups were needed.

The first group, with the aid of a facilitator, assumed cooperative learning roles to read and discuss an article about marketing a small business. All of the groups chose the articles they read, and alternated in their cooperative learning roles. This group's conference was local, focusing on the specific needs of border workers and the businesses they are creating. The second group, also working with a facilitator, discussed an article about colonialism and multinational corporations in the Philippines. The mission of this group's conference was to build coalitions between border workers and people of many racial and ethnic backgrounds who are struggling for economic self-sufficiency throughout the United States. The third group worked with an aide who was hired on a part-time basis to help with the class. She was a former garment worker who then owned a small business. This group worked on an international conference, focusing on who to invite to the conference and why, and how to get in touch with them. There were diverse opinions about the conference among group members. Some wanted it to focus on the needs of small business people on the border and to include local politicians such as the mayor and the director of the Chamber of Commerce. Other group members wanted to concentrate on the ways in which their struggles were connected to those of the Zapatistas in Mexico, and they hoped to invite Zapatista representatives to speak. One facilitator explained to me that although the idea of planning a conference was a way to contextualize and integrate skills, the facilitators did want the conference to actually occur. The module posited working with organization staff people to get funding for the event, and to have the three groups come to some kind of an agreement about the scope of the conference.

This third group spent a significant amount of class time discussing whom to invite to the conference. Using cooperative learning roles, and speaking mostly in English, with some code-switching, their ability to negotiate with each other in English, and to make sure that everyone was a part of each decision was, in my estimation, exceptional. The facilitator explained that the last time they had worked on this project, they had decided to invite representatives of the Zapatista movement to their conference. A man in the group snorted in response, and the facilitator said, without emotion, "Do you disagree with the Zapatistas being on the program?" The man did not respond, and a conversation ensued about the significance of the Zapatista struggle for workers along the border. After that conversation wrapped up, another woman responded to the man who had apparently been displeased about inviting the Zapatistas to speak at the conference. In an example of great facilitation she said, "Maybe you can think about why you object to the Zapatistas coming to our conference, and we can talk about it tomorrow." The group then went on to determine who the other speakers would be, and each one volunteered to call someone on the list. Not only did I observe examples of engaged learning, autonomy, collaboration, and the plan to negotiate ideological diversity, but I also saw women assume leadership roles in the classroom, with each other, men, and their teachers.

The kind of learning I observed in the classroom of Trabajadoras Unidas offers a counterdiscourse to the reproductive model and that predominates in El Paso's adult education. However, political pressures threaten not only this school's curriculum, but its very existence, as well. When El Paso received $45 million to retrain NAFTA-affected workers, a government agency was set up to distribute benefits to dislocated workers. Some employees of this agency disagree with the politics of Trabajadoras Unidas and have made it difficult for women workers to use their benefits there.

The school at Trabajadoras Unidas seems to be a place where women and men co-construct their individual and collective identities, as people striving to create sustainable communities, and interestingly, as entrepreneurs. Through the educational experiences they have in this school, they appear to be gaining both personal and political power by globalizing their collective identities to include Indigenous people in Mexico, and to envision themselves as entrepreneurs.

This school seems to represent a powerful break from the reproduction of inequality through education in El Paso. Although it is not perfect and faces significant challenges, it is a place where what Levinson and Holland (1996) call "the paradoxical potentialities of schooling" (p. 22) are at least partially in the hands of the students. Certainly students at Trabajadoras Unidas are not always cooperative and concerned with "the common good." There are conflicts and people do not always listen respectfully to each other's opinions. However, the competitive model of relationships that predominated in the factories is slowly giving way to a more cooperative approach. The school is a space where relationships among learners and between teachers and learners can be continually renegotiated. The ideological perspectives that are part of Trabajadoras Unidas make it an important new learning environment. It allows learners to construct their identities within new relations of power.

It is my hope that this initial study will inspire educational anthropologists and others to consider the contrasts between more traditional educational institutions and those that challenge received notions of schooling. The study of teaching and learning in this and other alternative settings contributes not only to a general understanding of educational processes, but to the political struggles of people who have refused to let globalization determine the course of their lives.

Char Ullman received her doctorate in the Department of Language, Reading, and Culture at the University of Arizona. Her research focuses on issues of identity, language, and education, with a special interest in immigration.

REFERENCES

Anzaldúa, G. (1987). *Borderlands/la frontera: The new mestiza*. San Francisco: Spinster's/ Aunt Lute.

Arias, B. (1986). The context of education for Hispanic students: An overview. *American Journal of Education, 95,* 26–57.

Auerbach, E. (1993). Re-examining English Only in the ESL classroom. *TESOL Quarterly, 27,* 9–32.

Bhabha, H. K. (1994). *The location of culture.* New York: Routledge.

Bourdieu, P. (1977). The economics of linguistic exchanges. *Social Science Information, 16,* 645–668.

Bourdieu, P. (1986). "The forms of capital." In J. Richardson (Ed.), *Handbook of theory and research for the sociology of education* (pp. 241–258). New York: Greenwood.

Bourdieu, P., & Passeron, J. C. (1990). *Reproduction in education, society, and culture* (R. Nice, Trans.). Newbury Park, CA: Sage.

Bowles, S., & Gintis, H. (1976). *Schooling in capitalist America: Educational reform and the contradictions of economic life.* New York: Basic Books.

Coleman, J. S. (1988). Social capital in the creation of human capital. *American Journal of Sociology, 94,* 95–120.

Crow, D. (Ed.). (1996). *Geography and identity: Living and exploring geopolitics of identity.* Washington, DC: Maisonneuve.

Dunn, T. J. (1996). *The militarization of the U.S.–Mexico border, 1978–1992: Low-intensity conflict doctrine comes home.* Austin, TX: The Center for Mexican American Studies.

Freire, P. (1970). *Pedagogy of the oppressed.* New York: Continuum.

Freire, P., & Macedo, D. (1987). *Literacy: Reading the word and the world.* Westport, CT: Bergin & Garvey.

García, M. T. (1981). *Desert immigrants: The Mexicans of El Paso, 1880–1920.* New Haven, CT: Yale University Press.

Gellner, E. (1997). *Nationalism.* London: Weidenfeld & Nicolson.

Kagan, S. (1992). *Cooperative learning.* San Clemente, CA: Kagan Publishing.

Levinson, B. A., Foley, D. E., & Holland, D. C. (1996). *The cultural production of the educated person: Critical ethnographies of schooling and local practice.* Albany: State University of New York Press.

Levinson, B. A., & Holland, D. C. (1996). The cultural production of the educated person: An introduction. In B. A. Levinson, D. E. Foley, & D. C. Holland (Eds.), *The cultural production of the educated person: Critical ethnographies of schooling and local practice* (pp. 1–54). Albany: State University of New York Press.

Luckingham, B. (1982). *The urban Southwest: A profile history of Albuquerque, El Paso, Phoenix, and Tucson.* El Paso: The University of Texas at El Paso Press.

Luykx, A. (1999). *The citizen factory: Schooling and cultural production in Bolivia.* Albany: State University of New York Press.

Maquila Scoreboard. (1998). *Twin Plant News, 13,* pp. 10, 45.

Mehan, H. (1996). The construction of an LD student: A case study in the politics of representation. In M. Silverstein & G. Urban (Eds.), *Natural histories of discourse* (pp. 253–276). Chicago: University of Chicago Press.

Mohanty, C. T. (1997). Women workers and capitalist scripts. In M. J. Alexander & C. T. Mohanty (Eds.), *Feminist genealogies, colonial legacies, and democratic futures* (pp. 1–29). New York: Routledge.

Ortiz, V. M. (1999). Only time can tell if geography is still destiny: Time, space, and NAFTA in a U.S.–Mexican border city. *Human Organization, 58,* 173–181.

Pennycook, A. (1994). *The cultural politics of English as an international language.* New York: Longman.

Phillipson, R. (1992). *Linguistic imperialism.* Oxford, UK: Oxford University Press.

Rumberger, R. (1991). Chicano dropouts: A review of research and policy issues. In R. R. Valencia (Ed.), *Chicano school failure and success: Research and policy agendas for the 1990s* (pp. 64–89). London: Falmer.

Rutherford, J. (Ed.). (1990). The third space: Interview with Homi Bhabha. In J. Rutherford (Ed.), *Identity: Community, culture, and difference* (pp. 207–221). London: Lawrence & Wishart.

Stake, R. E. (1995). *The art of the case study*. Thousand Oaks, CA: Sage.

Suárez-Orozco, M. M. (2001). Globalization, immigration, and education: The research agenda. *Harvard Educational Review, 71,* 345–365.

Willis, P. (1977). *Learning to labor: How working class kids get working class jobs.* New York: Columbia University Press.

Wrigley, H. S., & Guth, G. J. A. (1992). *Bringing literacy to life: Issues and options in adult ESL literacy.* San Mateo, CA: Aguirre International.

Yon, D. A. (2000). *Elusive culture: Schooling, race, and identity in global times.* Albany: State University of New York Press.

(Re)writing Inequality: Language of Crisis Implications in California Education Reform

Christine L. Cain
Loyola Marymount University

The 1998–2000 Los Angeles Times *project, "Reading by 9," created news via adaptation and extension of a socially stratifying and divisive literacy crisis proposition. Interviews among educators and with* Los Angeles Times *journalists suggested diversity in literacy ideologies that nevertheless found consensus in iconic binding of English to social success. Crisis served as a discursive attention-diverting strategy, through stereotyping those with a language "handicap," reifying the relationship of English to education success, and distorting the processes of teaching and learning to read.*

> Failure to teach our children to read is a catastrophe of epic proportions. But it is not inevitable. Unless we dramatically increase the number of children who learn to read well, we will in the next five years consign nearly one million to lives of poverty and distress.   —"We All Need to Help" (1998, p. 3)

Literacy reform language in the recent *Los Angeles Times* "Reading by 9" series was strident and apocalyptic. A problematized language–literacy linkage is ideologically significant. Such "explanations" justify poverty and distress by recursively signifying particular sets of social relations (Gal, 1998; Woolard, 1998). In editorial policy reminiscent of "status politics" and statist language-as-a-problem agendas, the *Los Angeles Times* "ritually degrades" (poor, primarily Mexican-Latino) students and their cultures, implicating an unmarked alternative of standard English-speaking, Eurocentric, middle-class family mores as a reading education ideal (Gusfield, 1986, cited in Woolard, 1989, p. 269). Signifiers of social identity and status related to reading by age 9, in English, were also centerpieces of recent political platforms, political initiatives, and revised education standards.

The *Los Angeles Times'* coverage of education, especially in "Reading by 9," continues a tradition of literacy as in crisis or as a conditional solution to crisis since Nebrija's *Grammatica Castellana* in 15th-century Spain. Crisis serves as a discursive attention-diverting strategy that in this example negatively stereotypes those with a language "handicap," reifies the relationship of English to education success, and distorts the processes of teaching and learning to read (Illich, 1983; Irvine & Gal, 1996; Macedo, 2000). Practices of building on students' cognitive and experiential diversity, providing access to books, and critical literacy approaches—considered by many educators and policymakers to have the greatest influence over education outcomes—were minimized or erased from view (Cazden, 2001; Krashen, 1999b; McQuillan, 1998; Moll, Amanti, Neff, & González, 1992; Rand Institute, 2000).

"Reading by 9" is a significant ideological event. As conceived and implemented, it revived socially stratifying and divisive public discourses through exaggerated, dichotomous imagery, certain assumptions of cause and effect, and erasure of the authentic attributes of some non-English speakers (Irvine & Gal, 1996; Macedo, 2000; Ruíz, 1984). "Reading by 9" was not merely coverage of education reform news, but in one of the great news organizations in the country, the series created news via an adaptation and extension of a dominant discourse (Blommaert & Verschueren, 1998; Schudson, 1996). "Reading by 9" was a vehicle for a neoconservative literacy ideology that makes claims of caring about the interests of the non-English-speaking poor, ministering instead to publishers', advertisers', and other corporate interests (Donald, 1991; Woolard, 1989, 1998). Elements of the ideology include English-only in schools, and the primacy of language correctness over language and cognitive richness, recursively implicated through the *Times'* acceptance of the "failed" bilingual education premise and strict phonics reading instruction methods, to ensure minimal competence at the lowest cost among those who, because they do not speak English (or standard English), have purportedly created a burden on the system. This ideology circles the wagons around those who are not a "burden," remythologizing language as central to crisis, and effectively overshadowing examination of the root causes of more politically volatile reforms (Bourdieu, 1991, 1997; Irvine & Gal, 1996; Mehan, 1997; Woolard, 1989).

This chapter focuses on the apparent language-as-a-problem orientation that generated my initial interest in southern California education reform discourses (Gramsci, 1997; Ruiz, 1984). I subsequently conducted semistructured interviews among 6 education journalists and 12 educators (6 teachers and 6 principals) from late 1999 through the spring of 2000 (Cain, 2002). I reviewed 1998–2000 *Los Angeles Times* education writing, recent California political initiatives, State of California Department of Education materials, and political platforms (California Reading Initiative, 1999; California Republican Party Platform, 2000; Democratic National Platform, 2000; Democratic Platform, 1996; Hakuta, 1998b; Reading Language Arts Framework, 1999; Republican Platform, 1996, 2000). The background material is dealt with briefly, and I have limited the use of participants' comments while attempting to show how complex and textured narratives may connect to the public uses of language.

Language ideology among individuals and in institutional viewpoints is historically contingent and responsive to social structures and experiences of a particular social position (Woolard & Schieffelin, 1994). I assumed that interviewees' language is purposive through choices of language strategies (e.g., explanations), and in the cultural content carried in language conventions and devices, expressing and reformulating language ideologies to achieve particular ends (Bourdieu, 1991, 1997; Linde, 1993). I sought patterns in explanations, images, choices of grammatical forms, topics, and cause-and-effect propositions in "Reading by 9" and other recent political and education writing, and interviewees' words (Woolard & Schieffelin, 1994). Gee's (1991) definitions of literacy provided context for the ways in which explanation and image conventions about language may form or reformulate literacy ideology. Gee suggests that literacy is the "control of secondary uses of language," or the habituated routines of language outside family or other intimate domains (p. 8). Literacy as control of the secondary uses of language explicates connection of "discourses that lead to social goods in society" with "dominant literacy" that is a materially and symbolically effective social resource (pp. 8–9). Dominant discourse, acquired at home by some students and reinforced in the language routines of schooling, usually results in dominant literacy. Students not exposed to dominant discourse in the home will not necessarily acquire dominant literacy, or more important, "powerful literacy." This has significant implications for education and social life (Gee, 1991).

It is important to state that as much as discourses may serve to structure and maintain the status quo, the emergent quality of social life also arises from discourse dialectic. Discourses are not static, and multiple discourses may be present in homes and communities of varying social strata. However, the meta-level awareness required for critique (or "powerful literacy") is made problematic by the social structures and experiences of particular social positions, and must therefore be explicitly taught (Bourdieu, 1997; Gee, 1991). In recognition of the effects and processes of dominant discourses and dominant literacy followed here, I asked in what ways the idea of crisis and language-as-a-problem might be related to nonmainstream students' access to dominant, but especially to powerful literacies. First I sketch the recent political landscape as context for "Reading by 9," as well as certain historic sociopolitical connections among language and literacy.

THE SOCIOHISTORICAL AND POLITICAL LANDSCAPE

Is there a literacy crisis? Among many prominent educator-observers of the southern California scene, the answer is "no" (Berliner & Biddle, 1995; Hakuta, 1998b; Krashen, 1999a, 1999b; McQuillan, 1998). Public confidence in education may be problematic, especially among students, parents, and teachers who experience second-class education environments, but the terms of the education reform debate are seldom developed by such individuals. Pinpointing root causes of second-class education conditions, such as quality of political leadership, voter attitudes about diversity, and cherished ideas about school funding, requires seemingly difficult self-examination and apparently painful viewpoint changes among those who do control the debate (Kozol, 1992). Other root causes, such as 1970s changes in California school bond issue mechanisms, economic cycles, and population shifts, are of such incremental yet complex influence on education that they may be hard to "see." Many who understand education reform to be complex also view reform as manageable without repressive language and culture ideology (Berliner & Biddle, 1995; Hakuta, 1998b; Krashen, 1999a; McQuillan, 1998; Moll et al., 1992). Why then is crisis invoked at all, and why is the "other" so frequently the target?

The convention of crisis, linked with language or literacy in public discourse, has deep historical roots. Nebrija created the 15th-century *Grammatica Castellana* for Queen Isabella as a means to control the grassroots development of literacy and support her consolidation of power and authority (Illich, 1983). Following Britain's defeat in the colonies, urbanization, industrialization, and increasing poverty, along with "seditious" materials such as

Thomas Paine's *The Rights of Man*, converged in social unrest (Donald, 1991, p. 213). In mid-1790s Britain, and at the Hampton Industrial School for southern "Negroes" and Native Americans after the U.S. Civil War, public education was to engender "industry and piety" among the lower classes (Anderson, 1978; Simon, 1960, cited in Donald, 1991, p. 213). Britain's 1790s status politics demonstrated, with "often lurid statistics" the link between illiteracy and criminality, discursively implicating "strategies of surveillance, regulation and training" to ensure that the poor stayed in "the rank they are destined to fill in society" (Colquhoun, 1806, cited in Donald, 1991, p. 215). The "added advantage" to the state was to pay teachers "the lowest rate ever paid for instruction" (Donald, 1991, p. 215).

The correct usage of English came to be linked with intelligence (i.e., logic), character, and patriotism (Heath & Mandabach, 1983). These ideas transformed into opposition to languages other than English in any public forum (Heath & Mandabach, 1983; Szasz, 1988). As the United States grew and consolidated, there was not just a perceived need for norms of behavior, variety restriction, uniformity, and conformity, but a need for a "sophisticated ideological response to produce new forms of consciousness" (Donald, 1991, pp. 213–214; Heath & Mandabach, 1983). The hegemony of standard language literacy, accompanied by an "actual stratification of literacy" is driven by "the association of language with national unification; the association of literacy with mobility; and the indexical fixing of an authoritative literate tradition"—or "schooled literacy" (Collins, 1991, pp. 232, 235, 247).

Heath and Mandabach's (1983) review of the history of English language dominance in England suggests that implicit policy, connected to ideology regarding what it means to speak English and speak it correctly, was crucial to literacy stratification in education and in society. These connections, in the form of viewpoints, cultural models, or schematics for how the world (should) work are still present in U.S. and California public discourse(s).

Recent examples of dominant discourse linking language with crisis and with "particular sets of social relations" include ubiquitous official English initiatives—for example, California Official English Initiative Proposition 63 in 1986 (Draper & Jiménez, 1996). Also, Proposition 227, the "English for the Children" initiative to eliminate "failed" bilingual instruction, was passed by a majority of White voters despite opposition from a majority of Latino voters. The initiative was ostensibly to ensure that all children obtained the language of success, at the expense of developing academic proficiency in two languages.

The proponents of 227 contended that the failure of bilingual education was evidenced by high Latino dropout rates and California students' low reading scores on national tests in 1992 and 1994—myths dispelled in McQuillan's (1998) analysis. Krashen (1999a) reports that one-third of California's Latino dropout statistics included young immigrant laborers who never enrolled in school. Fewer than half the Latino school population were actually limited English proficient (Macias, 1997, cited in Krashen, 1999a). Far less than half of the Latino dropout rate may have been composed of students with some level of bilingual education, and contrary to the claims of the English for the Children Initiative, effective bilingual education may actually reduce dropping out (Rumbaut, 1995, cited in Krashen, 1999a, p. 6; Tse, 2001).

Hakuta (1998b) was the 1997 National Research Council (NRC) committee chair for a report concerning the needs of English-language learners and native language programs in schools. This report was cited extensively by proponents of Proposition 227, English for the Children. Hakuta responded to a court in northern California for a preliminary injunction against Proposition 227, noting that those who cited the report as favoring Proposition 227 did so by ignoring some research, emphasizing inconclusive research, and simplifying outcomes of studies with multiple variables. Hakuta allowed that some of this may have resulted from misunderstanding, but detailed the multiple misrepresentations by those he characterized as otherwise reputable researchers, who, in their eagerness "to bend the truth" propounded "egregious" misuses of research analyzed in the NRC report (Hakuta, 1998b, pp. 44–49).

Before Proposition 227, crisis invocation in California public discourse had not recently been more pronounced than in Proposition 187 (the "Save Our State" Initiative) passed in 1994. The thrust of this initiative was to identify and turn back "illegal" people of color with limited English. Such targeting may be inferred from the Proposition 187 mandate for police, educators, and social service providers to identify and report suspected illegal immigrants— that is, how does one know whom to suspect? Language and ethnicity became markers of "illegality" in schooling, generating "hate" language and otherwise having a chilling effect on the learning environment, despite the ultimate determination that all provisions of the Save Our State initiative (except production of false documents) were unconstitutional (Mehan, 1997). Two Proposition 187 positions borrowed from historical models grew large in later Proposition 227 arguments and in the *Times'* "Public Education: California's Perilous Slide" and "Reading by 9" series. One position was that immigrants are a burden on the system, destined to re-create cultures of poverty. The corollary, significant to Proposition 227's focus on language of instruction, comprised poverty as not merely a function of economic structures and policies, but language as handicap, and poverty as choice.

WHAT WAS "READING BY 9"?

"Reading by 9" was the *Los Angeles Times'* answer to the problems delineated in its special report, "Public Education: California's Perilous Slide" (1998). The "Reading" page, subtitled "The ABCs of helping youngsters achieve literacy—The first skill," appeared in the Sunday Metro section, often accompanied by logo-embossed reading-related editorials, and front page and Metro section page one articles each week. "Reading by 9" was initiated by then-publisher Mark Willes, a former business executive without media industry experience. The following example is from an early editorial; it illustrates in a manner similar to the crisis rhetoric examples noted earlier, exaggerated, emotion-laden language (e.g., "tragically," and the likelihood of "going on drugs," "welfare," and "to prison") with the strategy of employing correlations ("research shows") as causes. The use of unqualified, decontextualized statistics and correlations as cause begs several questions never answered by the *Times*: Who are the students in the "two thirds" category? What is the nature of the "research [that] shows"? Are there alternative interpretations?

> Tragically, almost two-thirds of young children in the Los Angeles area are not able to read adequately. Yet reading is the basis on which virtually all other learning depends. And if children do not learn to read by the third grade, they almost never catch up. Research shows that children who do not learn to read are much more likely to go on drugs, ... welfare, and ... to prison and far less likely to get a good job. ("We All Need to Help," 1998, p. 3)

In "Reading by 9" editorials and articles, "literacy crisis" was used interchangeably with failure, illiteracy, and catastrophe. This writing also constructed literacy crisis through dichotomy, prototype, and feature cluster conventions, image schemas from which invocation of one feature in the cluster comes to denote all others (Blommaert & Verschueren, 1998; Woolard & Schieffelin, 1994). Three apparently taken for granted ideas were typical:

1. Some languages and cultures (primarily Mexican-Latino) actually contribute to school and lifetime failure, and other languages and cultures

(White and Asian) ensure school and lifetime success (introduced in a May 1998 *Public Education: California's Perilous Slide* special report).

2. Learning to read in English by age 9 was equated with literacy.
3. Rigidly scripted phonics reading instruction indexed a primary solution to the poverty–illiteracy equation.

CULTURE OF FAILURE

The *Los Angeles Times* special report "Public Education: California's Perilous Slide" was presented as a three-part insert (six to eight pages each) on three subsequent days in May 1998. The first-page headline on the second day, "Language, Culture: How Schools Cope," was subtitled "Influences Outside the Classroom Can Determine Success or Failure." On each of the pages of each insert, print was overlarge, full-color photos filled the top half the first pages and were prominent on other pages, and each first page contained a blue box entitled "Key Findings."

One example of a key finding in the May 18, 1998 "Language, Culture" article read: "Culture is important: Cultural influences have a big impact on success or failure. The success of Asian American students contrasts sharply with other ethnic groups." This section contained uncontextualized statistics and "expert" analyses in articles that contrasted the success of Asian and White students with the failure of Latino and African-American students. These themes were revived in "Reading by 9"-logo embossed introductory writing to the "Reading by 9" series in the fall of 1998. In one article, "Facing the Poverty Factor" (Sahagun, 1998a), and in an editorial "Bars of the Mind" (1998), the *Times* established culture of failure elements as a foundation for "Reading by 9."

"Facing the Poverty Factor" (Sahagun, 1998a) profiled a 9-year-old Mexican-American boy, Arturo, and his family (names are my pseudonyms). The writer positioned emotionally and experientially evocative ideas to support the premise that the family's language and personal habits caused Arturo's school failure (Cobarrubias, 1983; Ruiz, 1984). The chain of reasoning was subtle, yet apparent in the unrelenting focus on everything that was wrong with the family. The following descriptors and paraphrases of other information are in the order provided in the article.

Arturo's family lives in a converted garage. Arturo "sits slumped on a lumpy blue couch" with three brothers (there are seven children in all), watching television instead of doing homework. Arturo's father is "depressed after failing to land a job on a nearby street corner." Arturo tries to do his homework, but is unsupervised and distracted by the television. "[T]he one hundred worst performing schools [are] ... clustered in the poorest neighborhoods." Arturo's school was "successful" with middle-class students in the past, but schools "fail" with poor students. The writer states all parents want their children to succeed, followed by a seemingly unrelated comment about Arturo's parents who "even went to a yearlong domestic violence class last year," which helped them focus on the needs of their children. Arturo's proficiency in English is "first and foremost;" and his "parents need to be involved" (Sahagun, 1998a, pp. A1–A3). However:

> [Arturo's parents], who ... immigrated to the United States from Mexico City in the mid-1980s, say they are anxious to try new strategies. But they haven't learned to speak English, which would dramatically increase their ability to support their children's education and boost their earning power. (Sahagun, 1998a, pp. A1–A3)

The November 8, 1998 "Bars of the Mind" editorial began with the words "[p]risons are filled with men and women who cannot read," followed by the caveat "inability to read of course does not condemn one to a life of crime ... but the correlation cannot be ignored." The remainder of the editorial made good on the advice to not ignore the correlation, propositionally supplementing the image of (illiterate) criminals with "lurid" statistics: "[n]early two out of three Southern California third-graders fail to read at grade level;" "[r]eading failure is one likely cause for the frustration and anger that result in delinquent behavior;" and "68% of inmates can't read well enough to hold a job." Illiteracy conflated with school failure and crime in words such as *cripple, at-risk, long-term consequences, handicapped, failure, delinquent,* and *recidivism.*

The following journalist was one of four (of six *Times* journalists interviewed) who indexed the literacy crisis with references to language. My questions are in brackets.

> [There is some scholarship that says that if you teach children in their first language they can build on cognitive connections they've already made and then transfer those ...]

> I think that it's a great benefit to any student to learn a second language, or a third language. And I think that that should be pretty standard. But that's a little different than bilingual education, in which, the goal of bilingual education is

to kind of wean students into English. And uh I think the connection isn't so much, I don't know whether bilingual education is a good thing or a bad thing ... I voted for abolishing it for a couple of reasons. One, I just didn't think it's the job of the state to guarantee all immigrants that they're going to get a first-rate education. I mean, that the state is going to go overboard to make up for the handicap that they bring with them by arriving here without speaking English. So I just don't think that's the job of the state really. And the other reason was that, that the proof of that was that the resources that it would take to accomplish that were so great that the state really wasn't doing the job ... it was a failure. So they weren't really learning one language or the other formally and properly as they should have been. (Journalist interview, 1999)

[And what about the literacy crisis?]

I've seen it. I've spent some time in classrooms. I've listened to children speak. I've seen their writing. I've seen a lot of kids in junior high school who couldn't read and write. And I think it's a real crisis. I think that in Los Angeles, we have at least two languages. Two forms of English .... I think that we're almost at the point of having a high dialect and a low dialect of English. I think that would be ... not positive shift in the direction of American society. (Journalist interview, 1999)

Two other journalists commented about the literacy crisis in terms of the perceived inadequacy of bilingual education, and a fourth spoke of children with primary languages other than English as making education "harder to do." In contrast, only 1 of 12 educators explicated the literacy crisis as "caused by" students having a primary language other than English. Educators tended to address language with examples about learning English themselves, or learning Spanish to teach effectively. One teacher, however, spoke of language as a problem in terms of the shortcomings of bilingual education and of students' language experiences, reminiscent of the images of "handicap" discussed earlier.

I don't know if you've heard of LAP and Pre-LAP [language assessment program] that you give children ... to find out if how much they know of their native language and their second language? And I would have these 4-year-olds and 5-year-olds come in and they would be nonfluent in their primary language, and nonfluent in English. But what do we do? We reteach them their primary language so that we can teach them English. And that to me made no sense. If they didn't know the color red or the number six in their primary language why teach it to them and then teach them in English? It was very frustrating. I thought it was a real disservice to the students. (Teacher interview, 2000)

Journalist discourses penalized students for language handicap and dialects in ways otherwise unthinkable. In contrast, three of six principals (who spoke Spanish as a second language, none of whom were Latino) and four of six teachers (one Latino and one Filipino) suggested that well-constructed bilingual education is a useful and important instructional tool. Yet among educators and journalists alike, cultural competence linked to English fluency was the implicit alternative to the culture of failure proposition. Cultural competence indexed a language component similar to Gee's (1991) ideas about dominant literacy. A typical formulation was the significance of a "language-rich" environment, as in the teacher's earlier contention that some of her students were "nonfluent" in English or in their primary language (this assessment is questionable; the teacher is only fluent in English, and the LAP test is highly simplistic). Even the import of a language-rich environment is contested (e.g., Whose language? Whose definition of richness?), and more complex in its relationship to academic achievement than was known or acknowledged by most interviewees or in "Reading by 9" (Heath, 1982; Krashen, 1999a; Moll & Dworin, 1997).

After the "Reading by 9" introductory editorials and articles in late 1998, direct references to problematic language and culture virtually disappeared in the series and related articles and editorials. Negative language and culture stereotypes (i.e., culture of failure), as in "Facing the Poverty Factor," were replaced by an implicit model connecting education reform elements advanced by the *Times* with a culture of success schema introduced in "Public Education: California's Perilous Slide" (see Fig. 12.1). Doctrines of language correctness have long been conflated with class and race or ethnicity in the English-speaking world, especially related to power (e.g., status politics) and nation building. The culture of success model illustrates such an interpenetration.

The *Times'* dominant discourse included particular parenting habits, skills, and values as a solution to the literacy crisis, advanced in four Reading Page columns and some articles. The following are some of many possible examples. The "Head of the Class—Reading Tips and Notes" column ran from fall 1998 to fall 1999. "Reading Partners—People Making a Difference" ran for about the same time period. "Discovering Books" (intermittent) was retitled "Treasured Books," and "Check It Out" (books recommended for young read-

TABLE 12.1.

"Reading by 9" education reform and a culture of success.

Education reform model	Culture of success attributes
English-only instruction.	Must learn English at home, or be taught English at early age.
"Systematic, research-based" reading instruction (explicit letter and phoneme mastered before content and literature introduction).	Read to children in home; parents read at home and volunteer at school; children "reading-ready" for academic development.
Standardized testing in English.	Parents model question/response discourse.
Accountability: rewards, punishments, control, winners and losers.	Assimilated, middle/upper class, employed, tax-paying, law-abiding citizens.

ers) was carried until the Reading Page was discontinued. Few Reading Page columns or articles acknowledged the wide diversity of students' backgrounds and languages in Los Angeles public schools (1.3 million students in California have primary languages other than English; of these, more than one-half million are in Los Angeles County; of these, about 80% are Spanish speakers). No columns or articles recognized bureaucratic or resource limitations for parents' access to bookstores or libraries, e.g., a driver's license is required to obtain a library card (1997 Language Census, California Department of Education, cited in Hakuta, 1998a).

"Head of the Class" columns were written by publishing executives, principals, teachers, and academics. Column content was implicitly directed to English-speaking, middle-class parents. Topics included (a) how to evaluate early reading programs, standards, and principal and teacher practices; (b) preparing children prior to schooling through phonological/phonemic awareness, reading daily, decoding, and books in the home; (c) homework strategies, books in the home, and reading out loud to older students; and (d) literacy development through writing, spelling, critical reading, and comprehension discussions.

Only two "Head of the Class" columns (from 47 Reading Pages sampled) were about children who came to school speaking a language other than English. In one column entitled "2 Languages, 1 Set of Skills," Gutiérrez (1999), a UCLA associate professor, addressed the main idea that children who read in another language, and whose parents read with them at home, can transfer the skills to English reading and writing. As if to counterbalance Gutiérrez's biliteracy stance, the (only) other explicit language-oriented "Head of the

Class" column by Chu (1999), assistant professor of Library and Information Science at UCLA, began with an anecdote about her childhood embarrassment with a mother who never learned English.

The "Reading Partners" columns profiled volunteers and famous writers and actors as role models, and bookstore owners, publishers of children's books, and library services as examples of "where to go" and "what to look for." Not addressed were children learning to read in more than one language, resource limitations of time and infrastructure (e.g., transportation), or bureaucratic hurdles (e.g., obtaining a library card).

In 47 "Check It Out" columns sampled, among about 330 books recommended to parents and young readers, only one book, *From the Bellybutton of the Moon*, by Francisco X. Alarcon, contained "short bilingual poems that capture family fun in Mexico" ("Check It Out," 1999c). Three of 47 "Check It Out" columns contained clusters of "Latino-oriented" books. On September 26, 1999, in addition to the Alarcon book, six books in English by authors with Latino last names were "to celebrate Hispanic Heritage Month." On August 8, 1999 five books "introduce[d] the Mexican muralist [Diego Rivera]," and on May 12, 1999, five books were proposed "to commemorate Cinco de Mayo" (Check It Out, 1999a, 1999b, 1999c).

LITERACY AS READING BY AGE 9 IN ENGLISH

Another "Reading by 9" taken-for-granted idea was that learning to read, in English, by age 9, as determined by the Stanford Achievement Test (9th ed.; SAT 9), is the same as literacy; with the reverse implication that not learning to read in English by age 9 equals illiteracy. As Gee (1991) defines it, literacy is control of secondary uses of language (e.g., how to talk to your teacher or fill out a job application), but these minimal manifestations do not necessarily implicate dominant or powerful literacies. Dominant discourse may not be learned at home, limiting access to social resources. Powerful literacy, or the metaknowledge to critique other discourses, is learned by "exposure to models in natural, meaningful, or functional settings" such as (initially) in the home and in intellectually challenging academic settings (Gee, 1991, p. 8). Proposition 227's elimination of bilingual education provided for one first-language-supported year to learn English, seldom carried out in practice. Language experts agree that 5 to 7 years of support are required for mastery of academic English (Wong Fillmore, 1991, cited in Cummins, 1997; Krashen, 1981). Without first language support, or exposure to dominant or powerful literacy models in the home, to what extent is academic literacy possible, versus lower level (stratified) mastery of "basic" reading and writing? Crisis language that negatively essentializes the attributes of some students, ignoring or trivializing indecent conditions, including lack of comprehensible language of instruction, makes remote the possibility of powerful literacy for most second language learners.

"BASIC EDUCATION" (PHONICS) CURES POVERTY

The third taken-for-granted idea was the *Times'* "reform" support for recent California State Standards directed to the purported two thirds of students who do not read adequately, or four out of five who do not read at grade level. Despite the contradictions inherent in the *Times'* rhetoric linking non-English speakers with the literacy crisis, the phonics-cures-poverty trope is accomplished through the convention that all students benefit from the same scripted phonics curricula. The rigid scripting, for up to 2.5 hours per day, "achieves" literacy that often does not include social studies, science, art, and music (California Reading Initiative, 1999).

From late 1998 through 1999, the *Times* advanced phonics as the solution to "dismal" reading scores at least 28 times. In a sampling of 47 Reading Pages, seven articles mentioned phonics in the headline, in the subtitle, or in lead paragraphs to index what was most important or most interesting (e.g., Helfand, 1998, 1999b; Yates, 1999). In a sampling of reading-related articles and editorials other than on the Reading Page but imprinted with the "Reading by 9" logo, 10 mentioned phonics in the headline, in the subtitle, or to index what was important or interesting (e.g., Helfand, 1999c; Sahagun, 1998b).

In a sampling of other *Times* reading and education-related articles without the "Reading by 9" logo, phonics was the main topic or was referred to in 11 articles (e.g., Helfand, 1999a; O'Connor, 1998; "Phonics Foot Draggers" 1999). Phonics was a salient example when the word *basics* was used, as in "teaching the basics" or "education basics." *Methods, literacy, tools,* and even *standards* were also used interchangeably with, or as examples of phonics instruction. Phrases indexing phonics instruction included "education plans that work," "weak spots" (vs. the strength of phonics), "education reform," and "read fluently" (in English).

Many instructional approaches to beginning reading since the 1500s have proposed some emphasis on explicit letter–sound recognition. Although it is true that the State of California has mandated a strict interpretation and application of phonics instruction in all public schools, this controversial mandate has not been questioned or problematized in the *Times'* coverage. As Krashen (1999b) and McQuillan (1998) point out, phonics was already an important element of the instructional approach (whole language) it replaces, and reading test results were "remarkably stable" during the time preceding and during the application of whole language methods. Educator interviewees proposed that phonics should be only one part of well-constructed early reading instruction, that individual student needs dictated its use and emphasis, and phonics drills in English do not help second language learners acquire the language quickly and effectively.

Yet phonics was nearly a mantra in "Reading by 9." Given the controversy among educators and scholars of the one-size-fits-all position, it seems that a skeptical stance, a metacritique, would have occurred among at least some of those writing about education for one of the premier newspapers in the country. What was it about phonics that gained such a level of support with so little critique?

There is, it appears, a misguided understanding of phonics instructional value on two levels. Phonics drills in English do not support reading acquisition among second language students. Some facility with pronunciation and spelling may accrue to semifluent or fluent speakers of English, but even for these students, such facility is at the expense of comprehending challenging content. In my recent observations in first-, second- and third-grade California classrooms (and from teacher feedback), a substantial portion of the 2.5 hours of reading instruction time is spent in whole-group activities in which students "all together now" speak letter sounds and blended sounds from writing on the blackboard. Non- or minimally fluent English language learners mimic without comprehension and are held back in grade. On another level, the overwhelming emphasis on learning to read through phonics diverts the education reform debate from authentic learning for every student. The shameful tactic promotes a factory model for producing robotic teachers and readers, preparing students for minimum-wage or other low-end jobs (Thompson, 1984, cited in Woolard, 1998, p. 7). The business model for education has been further extended, providing a windfall for publishers of phonics-related curricular materials, by limiting expenses for "unnecessary" science, social studies, and first-language support—in a state where immigrant students (whose parents pay taxes) are becoming the public school majority (Hakuta, 1998a; Mehan, 1997).

Emphasis on English phonics and standardized testing distorts the education reform debate. Concerted attention to equity in teacher salaries, numbers of librarians, guidance counselors, principals, and teachers per student, and very low per pupil-expenditures is subsequently devitalized (Berliner & Biddle, 1995; Gee, 1991; Gilmore, Goldman, McDermott, & Smith, 1993; "How California Compares," 2000; Wells, 1995). There is some economic room to be "like us" for the few students who manage to learn dominant literacy under an English-only, phonics regime. For the many without the opportunity to connect their language(s) and cultural and cognitive experiences to intellectually challenging new contexts, the distribution of social and intellectual resources will remain deeply stratified (Moll & Dworin, 1997; Moll, Tapia, & Whitmore, 1993).

CONCLUSION

Cultural models may go without saying, yet may also have directive force through invocations of authority or expertise, powerful images, or familiar propositions, such as those used in the language-as-a-problem thesis of "Reading by 9." Four journalists concurred that it was unlikely people who most needed "Reading by 9" information were actually readers of the *Times*. If the people (presumably those like the family profiled in "Facing the Poverty Factor") who needed the information most were not being reached, then who was the audience? From explicit statements in their narratives, in culture and language schemas, and in "Reading by 9" content, it was possible to glimpse the imagined readers to whom journalists wrote—they wrote to people like themselves, in contrast to those who "face a lifetime of failure." They wrote to sell papers, and to satisfy other attendant interests of the publisher.

Making sense through interest and power-laden ideas and language constructions is the essence of most language usage. For this study of "Reading by 9," or for any understanding of the goal-oriented nature of language, the issue is not whether this occurs, but what kind of meaning is being made, by whom, directed to whom, and to what ends. It was important to ask how the attributes and interests of some were "envisioned as morally and socially superior" through unexpressed assumptions or causal relationships in "Reading by 9" and other reading-related writing (Woolard, 1989, p. 269). It was also important to ask how it was that the authentic attributes and interests of others were erased, and replaced with "coded and transformed" linkages of a language to a social image (culture) of illiteracy, poverty, and crime (Irvine & Gal, 1996; Ruiz, 1984).

In a country of immigrants such as the United States, idea clusters featuring immigrants, language differences, and poverty in stories of illiteracy or education difficulties are familiar, but contested. Deep cultural and experiential complexities underlying so-called achievement differentials are illuminated and placed in perspective in education reform approaches that consider language at minimum a resource, and maximally, a right. "Ways of talking about the 'Other' are necessarily ways of talking about ourselves" (Woolard, 1989, p. 276). If public language has constitutive power, shaping the ways we think and talk about public institutions such as education, it is no small matter that a newspaper's editorial policy forms its arguments in favor of dominant interests while trivializing the interests of those with less power and resources. The self-doubt apparent in constructions of crisis and reifications of "our" attributes continue to obscure clear apprehensions of mutual, long-term, maximized interests in pluralistic education, and in the wider social, economic, and political spheres we occupy together.

Christine L. Cain received an MA (1997) in social and cultural anthropology from Arizona State University, and a PhD (2002) in Language, Reading, and Culture from the University of Arizona. She is interested in practice implications of language ideologies in education. She teaches at Loyola Marymount Graduate School of Education in Los Angeles.

REFERENCES

Anderson, J. (1978). The Hampton model of normal school industrial education, 1878–1900. In V. Franklin & J. Anderson (Eds.), *New perspectives on Black educational history* (pp. 61–96). Boston: G. K. Hall.

Bars of the mind. (1998, November 8). *The Los Angeles Times*, p. M4.

Berliner, D. C., & Biddle, B. J. (1995). *The manufactured crisis. Myths, fraud, and the attack on America's public schools*. Reading, MA: Perseus.

Blommaert, J., & Verschueren, J. (1998). The role of language in European nationalist ideologies. In B. B. Schieffelin, K. A. Woolard, & P. V. Kroskrity (Eds.), *Language ideologies: Practice and theory* (pp. 189–210). New York: Oxford University Press.

Bourdieu, P. (1997). *Outline of a theory of practice*. New York: Cambridge University Press.

Bourdieu, P. (1991). The production and reproduction of legitimate language. In P. Bourdieu (Ed.), *Language and symbolic power* (pp. 43–65). Cambridge, MA: Harvard University Press.

Cain, C. L. (2002). *Literacy, politics and power in California classrooms*. Unpublished doctoral dissertation, Department of Language, Reading and Culture, University of Arizona, Tucson.

California Initiative Statute Proposition 187. (1994). West California Legislative Service #6, 1994, pp. A78–A81.

California Initiative Statute Proposition 227. (1998). West California Legislative Service #3, 1998, pp. A6–A9.

California Reading Initiative and Special Education in California. (1999). Sacramento: California Special Education Reading Task Force, California Department of Education.

California Republican Party Platform. (2000). *CaGOP.org*. Retrieved October 8, 2000, from www.cagop.org/resources/platform.html

Cazden, C. (2001). *Classroom discourse: The language of teaching and learning* (2nd ed.). Portsmouth, NH: Heinemann.

Check it out. (1999a, May 2). *The Los Angeles Times*, p. B2.

Check it out. (1999b, August 8). *The Los Angeles Times*, p. B2.

Check it out. (1999c, September 26). *The Los Angeles Times*, p. B2.

Chu, C. M. (1999, June 20). Expert advice. *The Los Angeles Times*, p. B2.

Cobarrubias, J. (1983). Ethical issues in status planning. In J. Cobarrubias & J. A. Fishman (Eds.), *Progress in language planning: International perspectives* (pp. 41–85). New York: Mouton.

Collins, J. (1991). Hegemonic practice: Literacy and standard language in public education. In C. Mitchell & K. Weiler (Eds.), *Rewriting literacy: Culture and the discourse of the other* (pp. 229–254). New York: Bergin & Garvey.

Cummins, J. (1997). Knowledge, power, and identity in teaching English as a second language. In F. Genesee (Ed.), *Educating second language children* (pp. 33–58). New York: Cambridge University Press.

Democratic National Platform. (2000). *Prosperity, progress, peace*. Retrieved October 8, 2000, from www.democrats.org/about/2000Platform.html

Democratic Platform. (1996). Building with broad planks and unaccustomed harmony. 104th Congress, Second Session. J. Austen (Ed.). Congressional Quarterly Almanac LII, p. D-60. Washington, DC: Congressional Quarterly, Inc.

Donald, J. (1991). How illiteracy became a problem (and literacy stopped being one). In C. Mitchell & K. Weiler (Eds.), *Rewriting literacy: Culture and the discourse of the other* (pp. 212–227). New York: Bergin & Garvey.

Draper, J. B., & Jiménez, J. (1996). *A chronology of the official English movement*. Retrieved February 26, 2004, from the University of California Center for Multilingual, Multicultural Research Web site: http://ww-rcf.usc.edu/~cmmr/Policy.html

Gal, S. (1998). Multiplicity and contention among language ideologies: A commentary. In B. B. Schieffelin, K. A. Woolard, & P. V. Kroskrity (Eds.), *Language ideologies: Practice and theory* (pp. 317–331). New York: Oxford University Press.

Gee, J. P. (1991). What is literacy? In C. Mitchell & K. Weiler (Eds.), *Rewriting literacy: Culture and the discourse of the other* (pp. 3–11). New York: Bergin & Garvey.

Gilmore, P., Goldman, S., McDermott, R., & Smith, D. (1993). Failure's failure. In E. Jacob & C. Jordan (Eds.), *Minority education: Anthropological perspectives* (pp. 209–234). Norwood, NJ: Ablex.

Gramsci, A. (1997). *Selections from the prison notebooks*. New York: International.

Gutiérrez, K. D. (1999, January 3). 2 languages, 1 set of skills. *The Los Angeles Times*, p. B2.

Hakuta, K. (1998a). *General information on limited English proficient (LEP) students in California public schools*. Retrieved January 10, 2001, from http://www.Stanford.edu/~hakuta/lepstats.html

Hakuta, K. (1998b). *Supplemental declaration of Kenji Hakuta*. [Prepared motion for preliminary injunction for Proposition 227 (*Valeria, G., et al. v. Pete Wilson et al.*, U.S. District Court of Northern California No. C-98-2252-CAL)]. Retrieved February 26, 2004, from http://www.Stanford.edu/%Ehakuta/unzSupplementalDeclaration.html.(links)

http://faculty.ucmerced.edu/khakuta/archives.html."OldStanfordSite"; MyOldSite; BilingualEducation; FullListof Papers

Heath, S. B. (1982). Questioning at home and at school: A comparative study. In G. D. Spindler (Ed.), *Doing the ethnography of schooling* (pp. 103–131). New York: Holt, Rinehart & Winston.

Heath, S. B., & Mandabach, F. (1983). Language status decisions and the law in the United States. In J. Cobarrubias & J. Fishman (Eds.), *Progress in language planning: International perspectives* (pp. 87–105). New York: Mouton.

Helfand, D. (1998, October 25). Some professors resist state's reform formula. Law mandates phonics. *The Los Angeles Times,* p. B2.

Helfand, D. (1999a, January 27). L.A. schools unveil plan to strengthen reading ... A minimum of two hours a day. *The Los Angeles Times,* p. B1.

Helfand, D. (1999b, July 25). A renaissance read on phonics. Huntington Library ... helped pave way for mass literacy in England. Parallels persist 400 years later. *The Los Angeles Times,* p. B1.

Helfand, D. (1999c, February 11). Teaching the basics, finally .... A Sacramento middle school trains 13-year-olds in phonics. *The Los Angeles Times,* p. A1.

How California compares. (2000, October 27). *The Los Angeles Times,* p. B2.

Illich, I. (1983). Vernacular values and education. In B. Bain (Ed.), *The sociogenesis of language and human conduct.* New York: Plenum.

Irvine, J. T., & Gal, S. (1996). Language ideology and linguistic differentiation. Revised paper prepared originally for the Seminar on Language Ideologies, School of American Research, Santa Fe, NM.

Kozol, J. (1992). *Savage inequalities.* New York: HarperCollins.

Krashen, S. D. (1981). Bilingual education and second language acquisition theory. In California State Department of Education (Ed.), *Schooling and language minority students: A theoretical framework* (pp. 51–79). Los Angeles: California State Department of Education.

Krashen, S. D. (1999a). *Condemned without a trial: Bogus arguments against bilingual education.* Portsmouth, NH: Heinemann.

Krashen, S. D. (1999b). *Three arguments against whole language and why they are wrong.* Portsmouth, NH: Heinemann.

Linde, C. (1993). Explanatory systems in oral life stories. In D. Holland & N. Quinn (Eds.), *Cultural models in language and thought* (pp. 343–368). New York: Cambridge University Press.

Macedo, D. (2000). The colonialism of the English only movement. *Education Researcher, 29,* 15–24.

McQuillan, J. (1998). *The literacy crisis: False claims, real solutions.* Portsmouth, NH: Heinemann.

Mehan, H. (1997). The discourse of the illegal immigration debate: A case study in the politics of representation. *Discourse and Society, 8,* 249–270.

Moll, L. C., Amanti, C., Neff, D., & González, N. (1992). Funds of knowledge for teaching: Using a qualitative approach to connect homes and classrooms. *Theory Into Practice, 21,* 132–140.

Moll, L. C., & Dworin, J. E. (1997). Biliteracy development in classrooms: Social dynamics and cultural possibilities. In D. Hicks (Ed.), *Discourse, learning and schooling* (pp. 221–246). New York: Cambridge University Press.

Moll, L. C., Tapia, J., & Whitmore, K. (1993). Living knowledge: The social distribution of cultural resources for thinking. In G. Salomon (Ed.), *Distributed cognitions: Psychological and educational considerations* (pp. 139–163). Cambridge, UK: Cambridge University Press.

O'Connor, A.-M. (1998, October 11). Conference urges balanced program for young readers ... including those learning English, to read fluently by the third grade. *The Los Angeles Times,* p. B3.

Phonics foot draggers. (1999, March 15). *The Los Angeles Times,* p. M4.

Public education: California's perilous slide. Special Report. Why our schools are failing. (1998, May). *The Los Angeles Times.*

Rand Institute. (2000). *Improving student achievement: What NAEP state test scores tell us.* (Rand Education Rep. No. MR924). Santa Monica, CA: Author.

Reading Language Arts Framework for California Public Schools, Kindergarten through Grade Twelve. (1999). Sacramento: California State Board of Education.

Republican Platform. (1996). Prosperity, self-government and moral clarity (104th Congress, Second Session). In J. Austen (Ed.), *Congressional Quarterly Almanac, LII* (p. D32). Washington, DC: Congressional Quarterly.

Republican Platform. (2000). *Renewing America's purpose: Together.* Retrieved October 8, 2000, from www.rnc.org/2000/2000platformcontents

Ruiz, R. (1984). Orientations in language planning. In S. L. McKay & S. C. Wong (Eds.), *Language diversity: Problem or resource?* (pp. 3–25). Boston: Heinle & Heinle.

Sahagun, L. (1998a, November 1). Facing the poverty factor. *The Los Angeles Times,* pp. A1–A3.

Sahagun, L. (1998b, November 11). L.A. Schools chief orders phonics lessons. *The Los Angeles Times,* p. A1.

Schudson, M. (1996). *The power of news.* Cambridge, MA: Harvard University Press.

Szasz, M. C. (1988). *Indian education in the American colonies, 1607–1675.* Albuquerque: University of New Mexico Press.

Tse, L. (2001). *"Why don't they learn English?" Separating fact from fallacy in the U.S. language debate.* New York: Teachers College Press.

We all need to help teach our children. (1998, October 18). *The Los Angeles Times,* Special reprint section, p. 3.

Woolard, K. A. (1989). Sentences in a language prison: The rhetorical structuring of an American language debate. *American Ethnologist, 16,* 268–278.

Woolard, K. A. (1998). Introduction: Language ideology as a field of inquiry. In B. B. Schieffelin, K. A. Woolard, & P. V. Kroskrity (Eds.), *Language ideologies: Practice and theory* (pp. 3–47). New York: Oxford University Press.

Woolard, K. A., & Schieffelin, B. B. (1994). Language ideology. *Annual Review of Anthropology, 23,* 55–82.

Yates, N. (1999, September 12). It's child's play. Teachers supplementing with ... phonics and other skills. *The Los Angeles Times,* p. B2.

Commentary on Part III
Can Schools Effectively Challenge Coercive Power Relations in the Wider Society?

Jim Cummins
University of Toronto

The papers by James Paul Gee, Char Ullman, and Christine Cain all examine in a lucid and powerful way the relationship of schools to society. They show clearly how coercive power relations in the wider society penetrate into the role definitions of educators (e.g., their mindset, expectations, and attitudes) and the organizational structures of schooling (e.g., curriculum, assessment, and language of instruction). The resulting interactions between educators and students promote the production of certain kinds of student identities that, in turn, serve to reproduce existing patterns of social stratification. Ullman describes how adult educators and displaced workers in El Paso, Texas, created a counterdiscourse (based on Freirian principles) and implemented educational structures and relationships that challenged rather than reinforced coercive power relations in the wider society. Similar examples of empowering educational programs for school-age students have been described in this volume (see, e.g., chapters by Candela, Hornberger, McCarty, and Remillard & Cahnman) and elsewhere in the literature (Cummins, 2000, 2001).

Unfortunately, however, these examples of programs that challenge coercive relations of power tend to be small-scale, isolated, and difficult to sustain over the long term. The question I was left with after reading the three chapters in this part was, "Is academic analysis powerless to change coercive educational structures that systematically reproduce patterns of social inequality?" Expressed in a potentially more optimistic way, the issue becomes this: Can we articulate the research and theory regarding how inequality is created in schools such that educators and communities are enabled to resist these coercive processes and institute educational structures and relationships that affirm students' identities and academic achievement? I analyze each of the chapters in more detail to explore how their analyses of the societal and instructional roots of underachievement can be applied to implementing sustained change in coercive educational structures.

Cain's analysis of the discourse surrounding the teaching of reading in California highlights how processes of indoctrination work to frame the "literacy crisis" as a phenomenon with a particular set of causes that lead naturally to a particular set of solutions. The causes are located in attributes of low-income culturally diverse children, families, and communities together with the failure of schools to compensate adequately for the "deficiencies" that children bring to school. These deficiencies include students' inability to speak English and their lack of exposure to a print-rich environment supplied by parents who read to them and explicitly develop their phonemic awareness.

This discourse acknowledges that academic underachievement is concentrated in schools that serve low-income students; therefore, these are the schools that must improve if their students are not to become "a burden on the system." The discourse goes on to invoke "scientific proof" that the twin causes of underachievement among these students are:

- Ineffective teaching of reading as a result of the educational system's failure to implement rigorous phonics instruction; the alleged neglect of phonics for many years is attributed to the prevalence of "whole-language" instructional methods in the schools.
- Failure to teach English effectively as a result of the fact that "limited English proficient" students have been "trapped" in bilingual education programs that expose them only minimally to English.

Once the phenomenon and its causes have been framed in this way, the solutions are clear:

- Require all schools to teach phonics in a systematic direct way (preferably through prescribed "teacherproof" reading programs such as Open Court).

- Require schools to immerse all English learners in English-only instructional programs that will enable them to overcome the disadvantage of speaking a language other than English at home.

Cain documents clearly how the *Los Angeles Times*, in numerous articles and editorials, locates "the problem" in the language and culture of students and their families. The articles also link the language and culture of the community to a "social image (culture) of illiteracy, poverty, and crime" that creates a significant financial burden for the taxpayer. The impact of the "culture of poverty" is acknowledged ("[T]he one hundred worst performing schools [are] ... clustered in the poorest neighborhoods"); however, families are implicitly blamed for their failure to emerge from their impoverished status due to their failure to learn English and adopt middle-class parenting habits.

The solution, therefore, does not entail addressing the conditions that create poverty. Instead, the primary solutions require the schools to compensate for the linguistic and cultural deficiencies of parents and children. Schools are now required to teach children English as rapidly as possible, ideally at the expense of their first language, and impose scripted phonics-oriented curricula. Cain notes that in the articles she analyzed "phonics is repeatedly invoked, becoming almost a mantra in 'Reading by 9'." She also notes that in her observations in California classrooms, a substantial portion of reading instruction time is spent in activities in which students "all together now" speak letter sounds from writing on the blackboard.

Clearly there are empirical issues that need to be addressed in all of this. For example, to what extent is there research to support the pillars of the new reforms? Is it true that:

- Bilingual education failed to teach children English and raise academic achievement?
- Whole-language approaches were actually implemented in schools and failed to teach children phonics and decoding skills?
- English-only immersion is backed by considerable "scientific" research, as Rossell and Baker (1996) claim?
- Teaching phonemic awareness and phonics effectively will solve the literacy crisis?
- State-mandated high-stakes standardized tests will increase accountability and student learning?

Space does not permit a detailed analysis of all of these issues. Suffice it to say that, as Cain suggests, there is little evidence, "scientific" or otherwise, to support these claims (see Cummins, 2001, for a detailed analysis).

Gee's article adds an additional dimension to this analysis. Specifically, he asks what kinds of people are envisaged and constructed by different forms of pedagogy. In the new capitalism of the 21st century that is rapidly replacing the old industrial capitalism, the successful "symbolic analysts" (in Reich's terms) are at the top of the economic "hourglass," separated from the service workers at the bottom by a shrinking middle class. Gee suggests that students are "selected" at a very early age for certain kinds of pedagogy that will direct them toward their preassigned niche in this new economic order. Social class, ethnicity, and language all serve as markers that influence teachers' expectations of, and interactions with, particular students. This is seldom an intentional discriminatory process on the part of teachers or administrators; it is simply seen as necessary to meet the needs of individual students.

The result, as Gee points out, is that low-income students are much more likely to experience skills-driven, prescripted, direct instruction than their more affluent peers who are seen as capable of advanced independent work that requires and invokes higher order thinking. In Gee's terms, "We are getting better and better (in a technical sense) at simultaneous skilling and deskilling poor children (i.e., they pass basic reading tests and still go on to fail in school and end up at the bottom of the society)." They do not get the opportunity to learn the "skills" required to become "symbolic analysts" or to adopt identities that would orient them in this direction.

As in Cain's analysis, Gee highlights the consequences of a standards-driven, teacher-proof, direct instruction pedagogy on students' academic achievement and identities. This pedagogy is largely directed at poor and minority students and evaded by children in private schools, magnet schools, charter schools, schools in affluent suburbs, and those students identified as "gifted," a category into which minority and poor students are seldom placed. In both analyses, we see a societal discourse, backed up by "the hegemony of a certain narrow body of largely psychologically driven 'scientific' research" that operates in coercive ways to the detriment of subordinated group students (see also Cummins, 2001; Gee, 1999).

The claim that this discourse is coercive needs to be evaluated in relation to the empirical research that has provided the "scientific" backing for implementing scripted, teacher-proof reading programs for low-income children.

Contrary to the way in which much of the empirical research has been interpreted, the data are unequivocal in showing that a focus on immersing students
in literacy, involving extensive reading and writing for authentic purposes, is a
crucial component of successful reading comprehension development. Immersion in literacy is at least as important as instruction in phonics and phonemic awareness. The following conclusions regarding what the research on
reading is saying emerge from a detailed analysis of this literature (Cummins,
2001, chap. 4):

1. Decoding skills are a necessary but not sufficient condition for reading comprehension development; many low-income students who appear
to perform well on standardized tests in the early grades experience a
"Grade 4 slump" when reading comprehension rather than decoding becomes the primary focus of standardized tests of reading.

2. The most effective approaches to developing initial reading skills
(decoding) are those that combine extensive and varied exposure to meaningful print with explicit and systematic instruction in phonemic awareness
and letter–sound correspondences.

3. Systematic phonics instruction can enable second language learners
to acquire word recognition and decoding skills in their second language to
a relatively high level, despite the fact that their knowledge of the second
language is still limited. These decoding skills, however, do not automatically generalize to reading comprehension or other aspects of second-lan-
guage proficiency.

4. After the initial grades, reading comprehension is predicted primarily
by the amount that students actually read; extensive reading provides access to a wide range of vocabulary that has consistently been shown to be
the strongest predictor of reading difficulty; psychometrically, measures of
vocabulary knowledge are virtually indistinguishable from measures of
reading comprehension.

In light of this research, the problems with the "phonics as panacea" mantra
are immediately obvious: The predominant instructional focus on transmitting
phonics rules in isolation that has come to be the norm in many classrooms, as
described by Cain and also by Gándara and her colleagues (Gándara, 1999),
fails to develop the foundations for strong reading comprehension that requires students to read and write extensively and to invest their identities in literacy. The Grade 4 slump, documented repeatedly among low-income

students exposed to teacher-proof direct instruction (e.g., Becker, 1977; Snow, Burns, & Griffin, 1998), simply illustrates this process.

Neither Cain nor Gee (in these chapters) discuss in detail how educators might resist this coercive process and establish alternative directions for promoting critical literacy and educational achievement among low-income and culturally diverse students. This challenge is taken up by Ullman, who describes the "structured inequality" and social reproduction that working-class Latinas and Latinos in El Paso have experienced in schools and society over generations. She also describes how community groups have contested the educational and social discourses and processes that have constructed them as menial laborers incapable of being educated. The adult learning programs organized by Trabajadoras Unidas permitted "learners to construct their identities within new relations of power." In a context where use of both Spanish and English was encouraged and technology was integrated as a tool to enable students to use language to achieve their goals, Ullman reports engaged learning, autonomy, and collaboration. Women and men in the program co-constructed their individual and collective identities as members of an international struggle for justice, identifying with other colonized people. They were also enabled to envision themselves as entrepreneurs capable of using English within their small businesses.

Inspiring examples of educational programs that challenge coercive relations of power can also be found in the literature on schooling low-income and culturally diverse students (see, e.g., Cummins, 2000; Frederickson, 1995; Peterson, 1994). However, the overwhelming trend is in the opposite direction. Schools succumb to the prevalent societal discourse and focus on direct instruction of the skills to be assessed by ubiquitous high-stakes standardized tests.

So why is this a problem? The overt rationale for the current trend is encapsulated in George W. Bush's presidential slogan (and now policy) of "No Child Left Behind," a sentiment with which very few educators could disagree. The problem with the current discourse and its impact on schools is twofold:

- Despite its apparent "scientific" pedigree, this discourse largely ignores the research on reading comprehension development; as a result, it fails to provide the instructional conditions for sustained growth in reading scores beyond the later grades of elementary school, as illustrated in the Grade 4 slump phenomenon.
- The dominant discourse adopts a naive and simplistic analysis of the causes of underachievement among low-income and culturally diverse

students; consequently, the solutions or remedies have little prospect of success in reversing underachievement.

Each of these points is discussed next.

WHAT CONDITIONS ARE NECESSARY FOR READING COMPREHENSION DEVELOPMENT?

After the initial grades, reading comprehension is predicted primarily by the amount that students actually read (e.g., Postlethwaite & Ross, 1992). Extensive reading gives students access to the vocabulary required to comprehend the increasingly complex language of textbooks and other instructional materials (e.g., literature). Commenting on the relationship between vocabulary and reading, Nation and Coady (1988) point out that "vocabulary difficulty has consistently been found to be the most significant predictor of overall readability" (p. 108). Once the effect of vocabulary difficulty (usually estimated by word frequency or familiarity and word length) is taken into account, other linguistic variables, such as sentence structure, account for little incremental variance in the readability of a text. They summarize their review as follows: "In general the research leaves us in little doubt about the importance of vocabulary knowledge for reading, and the value of reading as a means of increasing vocabulary" (p. 108).

Thus, decoding skills are a necessary but not sufficient condition for the development of reading comprehension. Gee (1999, p. 364) has expressed a similar point in discussing Snow et al.'s (1998) National Academy report, *Preventing Reading Difficulties in Young Children*:

> Interventions based on stressing phonological awareness and phonics do not enhance comprehension, though, of course, comprehension is the basis of learning, and reading is rather pointless without it. Furthermore, although a stress on phonological awareness and overt phonics instruction does initially help at-risk students, it does not bring them up to par with more advantaged students, and they tend to eventually fall back, fueling a fourth-grade or later "slump" (this fact is amply documented in the report; see pp. 216, 228, 232, 248–249, 251, 257).

The Grade 4 slump simply reflects the fact that students whose reading instruction has focused primarily on skills development, narrowly defined, often have not been reading extensively enough to encounter, let alone master, the kind of vocabulary that is increasingly reflected in the curriculum as students progress through the grades.

In short, by discarding the "whole-language" emphasis on extensive reading in favor of intensive phonics, the current reading dogma ignores the bulk of scientific research on the instructional conditions that promote strong reading comprehension. Under the current regime of truth, low-income culturally diverse students are unlikely to be any better off at the end of elementary school than they have been in previous years.

WHAT ARE THE CAUSES OF MINORITY GROUP UNDERACHIEVEMENT AND HOW CAN SCHOOLS REVERSE UNDERACHIEVEMENT?

As Cain, Gee, and Ullman point out, the causes of underachievement are rooted in a societal structure within which schools have systematically reproduced social inequality (see Cummins, 2000, 2001; Ogbu, 1992). Inequitable funding of schools in low-income areas in comparison to schools in high-income areas is just one indicator of this coercive social structure. The framework presented in Fig. CIII.1 presents a causal model of the ways in which coercive power relations in the wider society impact the interactions between educators and students, constricting the interpersonal space within which learning occurs and identities are negotiated.

The framework proposes that relations of power in the wider society (macrointeractions), ranging from coercive to collaborative in varying degrees, influence both the ways in which educators define their role and the types of structures that are established in the educational system. Role definitions refer to the mindset of expectations, assumptions, and goals that educators bring to the task of educating culturally diverse students. Educational structures refer to the organization of schooling in a broad sense that includes policies, programs, curriculum, and assessment. This organization is established to achieve the goals of education as defined primarily by the dominant group in the society.

Educational structures, together with educator role definitions, determine the microinteractions among educators, students, and communities. These microinteractions form an interpersonal or an interactional space within which the acquisition of knowledge and formation of identity are negotiated. Power is created and shared within this interpersonal space where minds and identi-

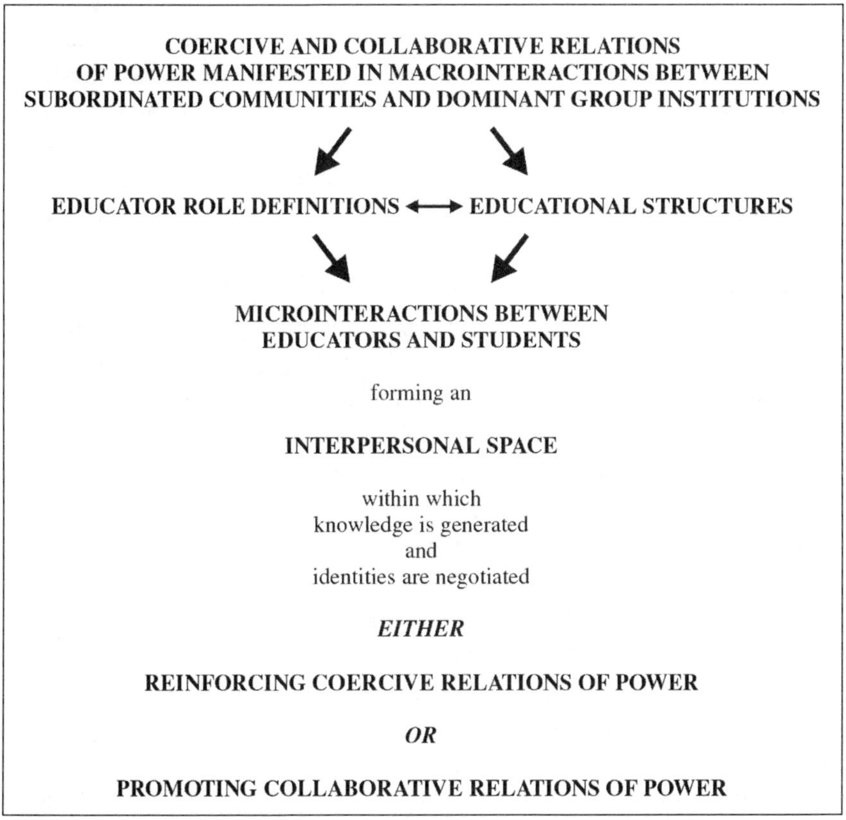

**COERCIVE AND COLLABORATIVE RELATIONS
OF POWER MANIFESTED IN MACROINTERACTIONS BETWEEN
SUBORDINATED COMMUNITIES AND DOMINANT GROUP INSTITUTIONS**

EDUCATOR ROLE DEFINITIONS ←——→ EDUCATIONAL STRUCTURES

**MICROINTERACTIONS BETWEEN
EDUCATORS AND STUDENTS**

forming an

INTERPERSONAL SPACE

within which
knowledge is generated
and
identities are negotiated

EITHER

REINFORCING COERCIVE RELATIONS OF POWER

OR

PROMOTING COLLABORATIVE RELATIONS OF POWER

FIG. CIII.1.   Coercive and collaborative relations of power manifested in macro- and micro-interactions. From Cummins (2001). Reprinted by permission.

ties meet. As such, the microinteractions constitute the most immediate determinant of student academic success or failure.

These microinteractions among educators, students, and communities are never neutral; in varying degrees, they either reinforce coercive relations of power or promote collaborative relations of power. In the former case, they contribute to the disempowerment of culturally diverse students and communities; in the latter case, the microinteractions constitute a process of empowerment that enables educators, students, and communities to challenge the operation of coercive power structures.

In short, to reverse patterns of underachievement, the microinteractions between educators and students must challenge historical and current patterns of coercive power relations in the wider society. Ullman's example of the adult English as a Second Language program instituted by Trabajadoras Unidas illustrates this process as do many other examples involving school-age students.

The ways in which the dominant discourse frames the issues (as documented by Cain) eschews any acknowledgment that societal power relations are at all relevant. Instead, a new set of slogans (e.g., "No Child Left Behind") and superficial panaceas (teaching phonemic awareness and phonics will enable all children to succeed) obscure the operation of coercive power relations. In fact, this discourse not only obscures power relations, it constitutes these relations. The result is that the current social structure will reproduce itself, and communities and culturally diverse students will again be blamed for their own failure.

How can we establish and promote an effective counterdiscourse to challenge this process? First, we need to document the patterns of academic development that emerge from the current "back-to-basics" accountability-oriented curricula and programs. If the analysis of the reading process briefly sketched here is accurate, mean achievement rankings in reading should drop progressively in the later grades of elementary school and beyond.

Second, we need to document more fully the pattern that has emerged in programs that combine more adequate pedagogy (e.g., in reading) for bilingual and culturally diverse students with an active challenge to coercive power relations in the wider society (see Beykont, 1994; Ramírez, 1992; Thomas & Collier, 1997). Typically, in these programs, students' English reading achievement accelerates toward grade levels in the later grades of elementary school.

Third, we need to explain, in clear and credible ways, why and how these patterns of achievement occur under different pedagogical conditions. In particular, in our preservice and inservice teacher education programs we need to communicate to teachers and administrators that they do have choices, despite the fact that their instruction is policed by standardized tests. If the analysis offered here is accurate, then teachers do not have to choose between the cause of social justice and their students' performance on standardized achievement tests. Instruction that challenges coercive power relations is the best way, perhaps the only way, to boost students' academic achievement over the long term. Succumbing to the anemic instructional vision of the dominant discourse will not provide the conditions for long-term academic growth among bilingual and culturally diverse students. In short, we need to engage educators in critical discussion that identifies contradictions and inconsistencies in the dominant discourse and exposes its likely consequences for low-income students.

Jim Cummins teaches in the Department of Curriculum, Teaching, and Learning at the University of Toronto. His research focuses on the challenges educators face in adjusting to classrooms where cultural and linguistic diversity is the norm. He has published widely in the areas of language learning, bilingual education, educational reform, and the implications of technological innovation for education. His 1986 article, "Empowering Minority Students: A Framework for Intervention," was reprinted by *Harvard Educational Review* in 2000 as part of its Classics Series. His recent publications include *Language, Power, and Pedagogy: Bilingual Children in the Crossfire* (Multilingual Matters, 2000).

REFERENCES

Becker, W. (1977). Teaching reading and language to the disadvantaged: What we have learned from field research. *Harvard Educational Review, 47,* 518–543.

Beykont, Z. F. (1994). *Academic progress of a nondominant group: A longitudinal study of Puerto Ricans in New York City's late-exit bilingual programs.* Unpublished doctoral dissertation, Graduate School of Education, Harvard University, Cambridge, MA.

Cummins, J. (2000). *Language, power and pedagogy: Bilingual children in the crossfire.* Clevedon, UK: Multilingual Matters.

Cummins, J. (2001). *Negotiating identities: Education for empowerment in a diverse society* (2nd ed.). Los Angeles: California Association for Bilingual Education.

Frederickson, J. (Ed.). (1995). *Reclaiming our voices: Bilingual education, critical pedagogy and praxis.* Ontario: California Association for Bilingual Education.

Gándara, P. (1999). *Review of research on instruction of limited English proficient students: A report to the California legislature.* Santa Barbara: University of California, Linguistic Minority Research Institute.

Gee, J. P. (1999). Critical issues: Reading and the new literacy studies: Reframing the National Academy of Sciences report on reading. *Journal of Literacy Research, 31,* 355–374.

Nation, P., & Coady, J. (1988). Vocabulary and reading. In R. Carter & M. McCarthy (Eds.), *Vocabulary and language teaching* (pp. 97–110). London: Longman.

Ogbu, J. (1992). Understanding cultural diversity and learning. *Educational Researcher, 21,* 5–14, 24.

Peterson, B. (1994). Teaching for social justice: One teacher's journey. In B. Bigelow, L. Christensen, S. Karp, B. Miner, & B. Peterson (Eds.), *Rethinking our classrooms: Teaching for equity and justice* (pp. 30–38). Milwaukee, WI: Rethinking Schools.

Postlethwaite, T. N., & Ross, K. N. (1992). *Effective schools in reading: Implications for educational planners. An exploratory study.* The Hague, Netherlands: The International Association for the Evaluation of Educational Achievement.

Ramírez, J. D. (1992). Executive summary. *Bilingual Research Journal, 16,* 1–62.

Rossell, C. H., & Baker, K. (1996). The effectiveness of bilingual education. *Research in the Teaching of English, 30,* 7–74.

Snow, C. E., Burns, M. S., & Griffin, P. (Eds.). (1998). *Preventing reading difficulties in young children.* Washington, DC: National Academy Press.

Thomas, W. P., & Collier, V. (1997). *School effectiveness for language minority students.* Washington, DC: National Clearinghouse for Bilingual Education.

Afterword
Reclaiming Critical Literacies

Teresa L. McCarty
Arizona State University

> If education could do all or if it could do nothing, there would be no reason to speak about its limits. We speak about them, precisely because, in not being able to do everything, education can do something. As educators ... it behooves us to see what we can do so we can competently realize our goals.
> —Paulo Freire, *Pedagogy of the City* (1993, p. 25)

The chapters in this volume have taken us from the micro to the macro to the spaces in between—from everyday, minute-by-minute literacy practices to their larger manifestations and consequences in a globalized economy. We have been reminded, as Elsie Rockwell so aptly puts it, of the need to "recover a historical perspective," and to situate our inquiry within the social, economic, and political contexts in which literacy practices are shaped and expressed. We have been led to new understandings of the profound and continuing inequities in schooling for linguistically and culturally diverse learners, and, at the same time, of the possibilities for critical multiculturalism and social change.

If a single theme rings throughout this volume, it is of the richness and promise of multiple literacies and the pedagogies that nurture them. Yet we need not look far to observe a very different reality, as unitary, monolingualist, and monoculturalist perspectives dominate the educational and political landscape. As Knobel (1999) writes in *Everyday Literacies*, despite theoretically grounded innovations in language education, "very little has actually changed in most classrooms" (p. 6). Much more disturbing is the fact that reductionist views of literacy and the regulatory regimes that attend them are overwhelmingly imposed on students of color and the poor. In his evocative autobiographical memoir, *Lives on the Boundary*, Rose (1989) warns that these pedagogies breed "attitudes and beliefs about written language that, more than anything, *keep* students from becoming fully, richly literate":

> The curriculum teaches students that when it comes to written language use, ... they can only perform the most constrained and ordered of tasks .... It teaches them that the most important thing about [literacy] ... is grammatical correctness, not the communication of something meaningful, or the generative struggle with ideas .... It's a curriculum that rarely raises students' heads from the workbook page to consider the many uses of written language that surround them in their schools, jobs, and neighborhoods. Finally, by its tedium, the curriculum teaches them that [reading and writing are] a crushing bore. (p. 211)

Although *Lives on the Boundary* was published in 1989, Rose could have been describing state-prescribed curricula in classrooms and schools today.

IN SEARCH OF "REAL" TEACHING AND LEARNING

In 1980, I began my own inquiry into these issues at the Rough Rock (Navajo) Community School. As described in chapter 3, the school at Rough Rock, founded in 1966, was the first U.S. school to have an all-Indian governing board and to offer instruction in the Native language and culture. By the early 1980s, however, responding to a resurgent national conservatism emphasizing "back to basics," Rough Rock had adopted a prepackaged basic skills curriculum. Presentations on the program instructed teachers to first demonstrate an isolated reading skill, after which students were to practice it in small steps with teacher prompting; finally, students were to independently practice the skill. If "students ... show too many errors," the program presentation cautioned, "the teacher goes back through the previous three steps once again, making sure that students demonstrate high accuracy" (McCarty, 2002, p. 134).

I recall observing elementary classrooms and listening to Navajo students call out English sounds and words. Years later, when I asked my Navajo colleagues about this program, they agreed that students had acquired perfect English diction in those classrooms, but little comprehension of text (McCarty, 2002, pp. 134–135).

Putting aside for the moment the impact of these pedagogies on the development of critical or powerful literacies, we can ask another question at the heart of the present fervor for direct, phonics-based reading instruction: Did Rough Rock students' achievement, as measured by their test scores, improve as a result of their participation in basic skills? An outside evaluation at the time showed some pre/posttest gains on the Comprehensive Test of Basic Skills, although students' scores, on the whole, remained well below national norms. Further, some of the highest gains were made by students whose teachers were identified as "low implementors" of basic skills (Educational Evaluation Systems, 1982). Indeed, from the time I began working at Rough Rock in 1980 until the present moment, the most significant increases in standardized test scores occurred during the 10-year implementation of the Rough Rock English–Navajo Language Arts Program (RRENLAP; see chap. 3), which used an explicitly whole language, literature-based, bilingual and bicultural approach.

More than 20 years have passed since my initial work at Rough Rock. In some fundamental ways, little has changed. The school is still underfinanced and hyperregulated by the federal government. The 1965 Elementary and Secondary Education Act, which underwrote the basic skills program, has been replaced with the No Child Left Behind Act of 2001. Under this legislation, Rough Rock has acquired a new stigmatizing label—underperforming—a designation based largely on standardized tests. This label subscribes the school to Reading First, a central component of No Child Left Behind, which mandates scripted, phonics-based reading programs identical with those used 20 years ago in basic skills.

At a school board meeting in late 2003, the education director described the "corrective reading program" being introduced to respond to these new–old pressures: "We need to do remediation," he said. "Once we get students up to level, we can go with real literature as the core program," another administrator added hopefully. During a visit to the school later that school year, under intense pressure to raise test scores, teachers repeated the same rationale: "We're just doing direct reading instruction for the time being, until we can get the kids' scores up, ..." "It's not *real* teaching ... but when I look around the table, I can see kids doing things. They're on task." One teacher described a new practice called curriculum mapping: "It means you have a lesson plan for every day of the year, so that anyone can come in and teach your class."

In an allegedly democratic society, what does it mean that some students are the beneficiaries of "real teaching," and others are not? That some students engage with "real literature," whereas others decode stultifying drills? That "on task" for some students (and teachers) means docile compliance with curricula that "anyone can come in and teach?" If teaching and learning are not "real," what are they?

The absence of "real" teaching and learning is the epitome of a colonizing education system devoid of the critical intellectual dimensions of language use. The effect is to deskill both teachers and students, reducing them to technicians and facilitating the manufacture of consent (Macedo, 1994, p. 36).

Multiply the situation at Rough Rock by the thousands of so-called underperforming schools in the United States—nearly all of which serve poor and working-class students, English-language learners, and students of color—and the separate and unequal state of education in the United States comes into stark relief. What kinds of student identities are being constructed through these dividing practices? Who is being empowered—and who is being disabled and left behind?

POSITIONING CRITICAL LITERACY RESEARCH "IN THE FRAY"

In their analysis of the politics of literacy teaching, Allington and Woodside-Jiron (1999) document the ways in which educational "research" (their quotation marks) shapes the nature of curriculum reform. Critiquing a 1997 consensus document on "30 years of research [on] … how children learn to read," Allington and Woodside-Jiron show how the report's flawed (autonomous) view of literacy research, with its emphasis on phonemic awareness and the separation of comprehension and decoding, became a policy lever in several key U.S. states. One of those states was Texas, home of then-Governor George W. Bush. With Bush's ascendancy to the presidency in 2000, this view of literacy became the template for one of the most restrictive federal education policies to date.

The reigning extreme autonomous view of literacy cannot be decoupled from larger social, economic, and demographic shifts. As Edelsky puts it, "Whenever people start talking about a literacy crisis, you have to ask …, why this now?" (cited in Teale, 1992, p. 328; see also McQuillan, 1998). In the context of growing numbers of English-language learners and students of color in

U.S. schools, current state-prescribed pedagogies can be seen as a regulatory strategy aimed at stifling "dangerous" diversity—difference based on race or ethnicity, language, and social class deemed to be threatening to national unity and the interests of the power elite (Lomawaima & McCarty, 2002; McCarty, 2004; see also Macedo, 1994; Macedo, Dendrinos, & Gounari, 2003). These literacy practices, Gutiérrez (2001) observes, have become a panacea for "dismal test scores, high student mobility, and the growing demographic of English language learners" (p. 565). The fact that affluent and middle-class White students elude these pedagogies (see Gee, chap. 10, this volume) heightens the disparities between the privileged and those already marginalized within these systems of control.

To rephrase the words of Freire that preface this section, recognizing education's systemic limits, it nonetheless behooves us to see what we can do to confront and reverse these systemic inequities. Critical ethnography is a powerful ally in this struggle, providing valuable insights into the complex conditions that promote or disable literacy learning for linguistically and culturally diverse learners. Equally important, critical ethnography offers penetrating understandings of the politics of literacy education reform (see, e.g., Hamann, 2003, pp. 440–441). Yet the intersection of our work with state and national policymaking is often neglected; literacy research, Willis and Harris (2003) note, is often positioned "above the fray" (p. 295). Ironically—and to the detriment of those with and for whom we work—this tendency abets extreme autonomous views in seizing control of education practice and policy.

The commitment to social justice demands that we (re)position critical literacy research "in the fray," moving our work from the margins to the center of political and social action. Put another way, our work challenges us to struggle even more valiantly against the theory–practice divide. The relationships among research, theory, practice, and policy are mutually necessary and reciprocally implicating: "Theory–practice, popular knowledge–scientific knowledge, ... reading the word–reading the world are some of the 'undichotomizables'" (Freire, 1993, p. 101).

The chapters in this volume speak to the potency of theory–practice complementarity—from the activist research of cultural insiders (e.g., Nicholas), to collaborations between school- and university-based researchers (e.g., Gilmore & Smith, McCarty, Remillard, & Cahnmann), to critical interrogations of classroom interaction (e.g., Candela, Gee, Hornberger, Ladson-Billings) and discourse (e.g., Cain, Ullman, Whitman). Even as these studies add to the scientific research on literacy learning, they summon us to apply scholarly knowledge toward social justice ends. Our work must be more than "just research," González (2001, p. 392) reminds us; it should constitute "a kind of policy activism." This implies new forms of *engaged scholarship* in which we document in "clear and credible ways" (Cummins, commentary, this volume) the value of pluralistic literacy practices, identify more publicly accessible outlets for our work, and participate dialogically and actively with our publics.

Finally, we should not surrender achievement analysis to currently ascendant experimental designs. Ethnography is singularly positioned to provide rich, robust data on how student learning can be enhanced under particular conditions. Critical ethnographers must speak more directly to the "language of power," including the language of achievement scores and tests (Sleeter, 2004, p. 135; see also Moll, 2004).

This volume represents a further effort to expose and dismantle the multitude of disabling divisions that cripple the liberating potential of critical literacy research. We invite readers to join us in this effort, and to see what we can do to reclaim critical literacy practices and policies for the students and communities with whom we work.

REFERENCES

Allington, R. L., & Woodside-Jiron, H. (1999). The politics of literacy teaching: How "research" shaped educational policy. *Educational Researcher, 28,* 4–13.

Educational Evaluation Systems. (1982). *1981–82 evaluation of the Rough Rock Basic Skills program.* Rough Rock, AZ: Rough Rock Community School.

Freire, P. (1993). *Pedagogy of the city.* New York: Continuum.

González, N. (2001). Finding the theory in practice: Comment on the Hammond-Spindler and Watkins exchange. *Anthropology & Education Quarterly, 32,* 388–392.

Gutiérrez, K. D. (2001). What's new in the English language arts: Challenging policies and practices, *¿y qué? Language Arts, 78,* 564–569.

Hamann, E. T. (2003). Imagining the future of the anthropology of education if we take Laura Nader seriously. *Anthropology & Education Quarterly, 34,* 438–449.

Knobel, M. (1999). *Everyday literacies: Students, discourse, and social practice.* New York: Peter Lang.

Lomawaima, K. T., & McCarty, T. L. (2002). When tribal sovereignty challenges democracy: American Indian education and the democratic ideal. *American Educational Research Journal, 39,* 279–305.

Macedo, D. (1994). *Literacies of power: What Americans are not allowed to know.* Boulder, CO: Westview.

Macedo, D., Dendrinos, B., & Gounari, P. (2003). *The hegemony of English.* Boulder, CO: Paradigm.

McCarty, T. L. (2002). *A place to be Navajo—Rough Rock and the struggle for self-determination in Indigenous schooling.* Mahwah, NJ: Lawrence Erlbaum Associates.

McCarty, T. L. (2004). Dangerous difference: A critical-historical analysis of language education policies in the United States. In J. F. Tollefson & A. B. M. Tsui (Eds.), *Medium of instruction policies: Which agenda? Whose agenda?* (pp. 71–93). Mahwah, NJ: Lawrence Erlbaum Associates.

McQuillan, J. (1998). *The literacy crisis: False claims, real solutions.* Portsmouth, NH: Heinemann.

Moll, L. C. (2004). Rethinking resistance. *Anthropology & Education Quarterly, 35,* 126–131.

Rose, M. (1989). *Lives on the boundary.* New York: Penguin.

Sleeter, C. E. (2004). Context-conscious portraits and context-blind policy. *Anthropology & Education Quarterly, 35,* 132–136.

Teale, W. T. (1992). A talk with Carole Edelsky about politics and literacy. *Language Arts, 69,* 324–329.

Willis, A. I., & Harris, V. (2003). Afterword. In A. I. Willis, G. E. García, R. B. Barrera, & V. J. Harris (Eds.), *Multicultural issues in literacy research and practice* (pp. 289–296). Mahwah, NJ: Lawrence Erlbaum Associates.

Author Index

Subject Index